TOMB OF
SAND

TRANSLATED BY

TOMB OF SAND

GEETANJALI SHREE

DAISY ROCKWELL

TILTED AXIS PRESS

2.

Before all this there'd already been one death. That of a man, whose wife refused to lift herself up with his cane. This man was the husband of this same mother and the father of this same daughter. His presence was still felt, even in death. But regardless of whether or not he had died, it seemed his widow certainly had. At least that's how she looked as she lay in her room.

Their room. In a corner of the house. *Their* bed. In winter. Thick quilt. Hot-water bottle. Woollen cap. The cane still hanging from its hook. The cup still sitting on the teapoy by the bed, with no water in it. When he was alive, this was where he placed his teeth at night. In the morning, he'd reach first for the teeth, then for the cane.

Outside, tooth-chattering cold; inside, Ma, teeth a-chatter.

She was a bundle, shrinking ever more from moment to moment, sending out a scrambled signal from within her vast quilt that she was still in there somewhere. The bundle scrunched-up on one side, then slid up a bit, then down, then over there. Was she testing to see how far she could spread herself? Or was she just turning her face away, turning her back on her children and grandchildren, and in the process dragging herself towards the wall to press against it with all her few-years-shy-of-eighty might to see if she could slip into it entirely?

The wall plays a special role in our story. (As do the doors, since you use them to get from one side to another, from here to there, on and on through the centuries, from forever to forever).

It's not an unusual wall. No special artistic features. Not a Thar desert wall studded with tiny mirrors, or a wall covered with a collaged design of rocky peaks or some such, with different shapes and colours, or spangled with tinsel garlands and printed with designs for a wedding; nor was it seized with a duplicitous desire in the sweep of modernity to appear old while being new, nor eager to trick our eyes into seeing a plastic wall as mud-plastered, bristling with fake grasses, or set with a mosaic pattern in smooth marble; nor still was it an awesome, colourful, tall, shiny orange-blue-green wall made by multinationals that would never fade or scratch or peel, imperishable, immortal, enduring.

It was just a simple brick-and-cement wall—a yellowing, whitewashed, middle-class wall, holding the ceiling, floor, window, and door together, with a network of pipes, wires, and cables arrayed within, enfolding the entire home in its wallfulness.

This was the sort of wall towards which Ma, now just this side of eighty, was sliding, gradually. A cold wall, during those winter days, and riddled with cracks, the way ordinary walls can be.

What can never be known for certain was whether the wall was playing the greater role in pulling Ma towards it, or whether it was her own desire to show her back to her family that drew her in. Ma just kept getting closer and closer to the wall, and her back became a wall itself, keeping at bay those who came to coax and cajole: Get up, Ma, Get up!

★

3.

No, I won't get up, no getting up, not now, the bundle wrapped in the quilt mumbled. No, no, not now, not getting up.

These words alarmed them, and her children grew more insistent. They were afraid. Oh! Our dear mother! Papa's gone and he's taken her with him!

Stop sleeping so much, please get up.

She keeps sleeping. She just lies there. Eyes closed. Back to them. They whisper.

When Papa was alive, she had put her all into looking after him. She was alert, at the ready, no matter how tired. Busy getting ground to a pulp; very much alive. Irritable, upset, coping, faltering, breathing breath after breath after breath.

Everyone's breath flowed through her, and she breathed everyone's breath.

And now she's saying she won't get up. As though Papa was her only reason for living. Now he's gone, has her reason too?

No, Ma, no, the children insisted, look outside, the sun is shining, get up, pick up the cane, it's hanging right here, try some roasted rice, it has peas in it. Maybe she has loose motions, give her a digestive powder!

No, I will noooot. No, nyo, nyooo, Ma mewls.

She's tired, poor thing, alone and defeated, lift her up, get her involved; entertain her! Sympathy flows from them immeasurable as the waters of the Ganga, washing over Ma's back.

Noooot nooooow, Ma tries to scream. But her voice comes out a whimper.

Did Ma think that her children's efforts to make her live were pushing her into the wall? Was that it? When footsteps neared the room, she'd turn her back, she'd stick to the wall. She'd play dead, eyes and nose closed, ears shut, mouth sewn, mind numb, desires extinct; her bird had flown.

But the children were also stubborn. They dug in. How to make eyes nose ears grow on that back?

It was all the same old, same old to her. Same squabbling and squalling. Same fire, fuel, and flour. Same wash the diapers. Nyoooo, nyoooooo, she repeated.

Here was no machination: her words—machinelike. A machine winding down. A worn-out mechanism. In the languor of conserving energy, she mumbled weakly, no, nnnnno, nnnoooo.

Nooooo not gettting up anymooooore.

Just a few words, but they alarmed the children. Ma is dying!

Words. But what are words, really, hmmm? They're mere sounds with meanings dangling from them. That have no logic. They find their own way. Arising from the squabble between a sinking body and a drowning mind, they grab hold of antonyms. The seed planted was a date tree; what blossomed was hibiscus. They wrestle with themselves—wrapped up in their own game.

No, now I won't get up: who was playing with the fear and death of that phrase? These mechanical words became magical, and Ma kept repeating them, but they were becoming something else, or already had.

An expression of true desire or the result of aimless play?

No, no, I won't get up. Noooooo, I won't rise nowwww. Nooo rising nyooww. Nyooo riiise nyoooo. Now rise new. Now, I'll rise anew.

★

4.

A sapling of a word. Creating a ripple all its own. Full of hidden desires. The noes of the dying hold their own secrets. Their own dreams.

Like this. A tree grew, took root. But: tired of the circling shadows of familiar faces, of the embrace of leaves of familiar fragrances, of the chirping on the branches, of the same old vibrations. And so it came to be that the tree felt stifled and murmured, *no, no!*

But there is wind and rain, and the puff of no that flies up between them and takes the form of a snippet. A scrap, that flutters and flaps and flit-flit-flitters and swirls about the branch into a ribbon of desire that wind and rain unite to bind there. Each time they tie another knot. One more knot. A no, not. A know knot. A knew knot. A new knot. A new desire. New. Nyoo. Becoming. The new refusal of no. Flutter, flitter, flap flap flap.

So it's the same old tree. The one you see right in front of you. A plume of smoke—*no no no*—on its trunk and low-hanging branches, trailing and dangling from above—*no no nyo*—and then the branches and shoots—hands and fingers—leap towards the moon in the sky—*no nyoo*—new new.

Or from the ceiling. Leaping dragging. Or from the wall.

Where it has found a hole, or made one, from where a tiny being, a jagged breath, crawls out. Breaking down the wall, puff by puff.

★

5.

Who can really hate their own? But certainly they can exasperate.

Get up.

No.
Sunshine.
No.
Soup.
No.

Back. Silent. Wall.

As soon as Sid arrives, he's rushed to her. Sid, her favourite grandson. Siddharth, now Sid. The one and only person she can't completely turn her back on.

She's been lying here since morning.

She even went to the bathroom later than usual, then came back and stayed in bed.

No eating, no drinking, not even touching tea to mouth.

Flowers blooming, but she doesn't care.

Chrysanthemums, but she doesn't see.

Sid has his own ways. Comes and goes with no one the wiser. Out jogging, or at the gym, a cricket match, a tennis tournament, swaggering around with his guitar, teasing, joking, parents scolding, he quick-witted and clowning with all. Slips inside with bat or racket, throws something on the floor, sprinkles water on his hands, face, tosses aside a t-shirt, sprinkles talc, grabs an apple and starts to chomp, and straight to Daadi's room.

Granny, naughty girl, get up, up and about!

Daadi's *no no no* won't fly here. What should the back do now? At this breath of fresh air?

She whimpers, but fondly. T'so cold. Whisperwhisper muttermutter. She melts a little.

An excuse. But a true one. Once uttered, truer. Really truly. Trembling within the quilt, trembles tumbling loose like a mouse running through the dark, Ma tenses and hides, but Siddharth is Sid. Must give it a try. So she whispers her mother's old rhyme of winter: *chilla jaara din chaalees, poos ke pandrah, maagh pachees— bitter cold winter for forty days, fifteen for the month of Poos, twenty-five for the month of Magh.*

Speaks, after silence, and quotes a melodious proverb. The voice sings. A wavy wave. *That bbbitter cccold for ffforty days fffifff-teeen for Poos, twenty-fffffive fffor Mmmmagh.*

Awesome, Daadi! You and me should enter the Grammies, we'll win for sure!

Sid ran to fetch his guitar. He slung it around his neck and jumped onto Daadi's bed. He began to strum and sing at the top of his lungs in his own style—*just chill, chill … just chilly cold, the cold forty days forty forty…fifteen for Pus, on Pus and twenty-five for Magh, for Magh, yo yo yo…same old*

One couldn't help laughing. Ma smiled slightly. She simply couldn't turn her back on this child. She couldn't stay dead, dying, around his zesting, zing-zanging pizzazz.

If it were anyone else, she'd turn her back, close her eyes, a half-dead bundle. Indifferent to every role: mother wife widow, mother-style wife-style widow-style, or wrap them all into one: family-style role (roll?), and fed up with all of them.

And so, at the slightest sound at the door to the house, she'd curl up and die, huddled against the wall, lifeless back turned towards the world.

But the door stayed open—metaphorically, that is. Someone passing by. They make a sound. Ma's well-trained ear recognises instantly, from a lifetime attuned to the sounds of others, that someone has just entered through the door.

The door...

★

6

The door. Not many knew that this was no ordinary door. Generations had dwelled within the walls it upheld.

The door to the home of her eldest son. Where the walls take on different forms over time, but in reality exist within the shelter of that open door; where that same home stays standing, generation after generation.

Such is the fate of the homes of eldest sons.

This particular eldest son—let's call him Bade—had long been employed at the sort of government job that involves many transfers, so his homes and walls kept changing cities, and his door remained open in all districts.

Shifting walls. Do the walls in Bade's home glide? Do they dance? Is the door an ox that pulls the walls of the home like a cart? This is the same home in which the father (and grandfather) of the family had always scolded his servants and his offspring. Once, this home had been on the banks of the Ganga, near fields of roses, in the eastern soil of Uttar Pradesh. Then, leaving some denizens of the household amongst the fragrance of flowers, the rest had gone to live near the perfume factories of nearby cities. Some, one hears, branched out from roses and attar to opium fields. Among these, a few became opium-eaters themselves, and called themselves zamindars.

Finally the day arrived when the eldest son of the home, father of the eldest son of the present household, and husband of the present living-dead mother, split off from those decadent and debased relations. Taking nine thousand rupees as his share of the walls, he became a government servant and set out on an expedition around the nation, multiplying his tribe as they moved from one bungalow to another, unaware that despite taking his share of the money and leaving, he'd brought the rose-fragrant home with him, simply pouring it into different structures of bricks and mortar.

However, he hadn't done anything dishonest on purpose, so it wouldn't be fair to call his actions deceitful. He was unaware of the tenacity of walls, this proclivity of theirs, and how when the next son takes the reins, they will travel with him as well. Vehicles change, hearths change, times, cities, heights, widths, everything from here to there, Lords of Inconstancy all, but from the beginning of time until forever, that same home, walls and door will live on.

But why badmouth the father here? Our great social scientists have been barking up the wrong tree. They've maintained that the joint family is breaking up, the ancestral homes are collapsing; Indian style is becoming selfish style. But the joint family is an invisible home—they didn't think of that —and homes are made of gliding walls—they never imagined that either. Dancing gliding flouncing sweet-smelling walls, and holding them all together, a quiet door. Open. Upright. Through which anyone can come or go. Go and come. And keep coming, keep going.

When you go through something you tear through it. So what if it's a door? By walking in and out, you tear its heart wide open.

That which is torn develops an increased capacity for insight and forbearance. A capacity to experience sensations that escape the notice of others. That's what it's like, see, the door to an eldest son's home through which generations ooze.

The door to Bade's home knows it must remain open no matter what, and there are no constraints on those who enter —in terms of time of arrival, advance notice or knocking before entry. Always free to be and free of charge. You might have just come out of the bath wrapped in a towel, and some relation from the village who has dropped by with wife and kids is standing there, and all you can do is smile and yell for tea and snacks, drape some clothing over your body, and never stop to wonder how long these guests plan to stay. The son needs a job, the daughter's getting engaged, someone needs to gain admission somewhere—they could be glad or sad or greedy or needy, who knows what's brought them to the door. You might've just applied a skin-toning face mask, or be colouring your hair with mehndi, when suddenly, your sister-in-law appears, to introduce some friend to Ma who might make her feel better, and it's meal time too, so everyone *must* eat after all, and you must go about face mask still smeared on, looking like a ghost. Or the grandson could be sharing juicy gossip with girlfriends or boyfriends, and saying things like *fuck you screw you*, and then someone suddenly appears at the door. Seeing, hearing, smiling, adding comments and critiques, chiming in with personal perspectives. The word *privacy* isn't even in the dictionary here, and if anyone lays claim to such a right, she is eyed with suspicion. What's she hiding, after all? Seems fishy.

And what does CCTV comprehend of the all-knowing secrets of a door? It has blind faith in its own technological perfection, so how could it understand there's such a thing as a door that sees all, hears all, records all, and has been doing so long before *it* came into being? Everyone has been going back and forth through it since forever.

Nonetheless, sometimes someone comes along: one or two or even three who are just about to come through it when they stop—*hmmm*—was that a breath? A foot, lifted to enter, pauses, hovers in the air. A drama unfolds in that moment. Arrested in midair, dramatically balancing, a foot upraised as though startled, and now can't decide whether to forge ahead or return whence it came. As though in a quandary as to where the world lies: ahead or behind? Which is reality and which is make-believe?

The raised foot becomes a hovering question—*am I on this side or that?*

Every time Bade's sister pauses in this pose at his door, the thought flashes through her mind—*have I been acting until now, or am I just about to start?*

★

7.

Bade's sister disliked airports because she found herself in them all the time. She felt like a tiny bug among many, trapped in a laboratory. Fake lights, fake passions, fake pushing and shoving. Bugs like her, crammed into every crevice, all terribly busy and awfully foolish, running in every direction, looking for their gates. Everyone's been dressed in clean and crisp attire, and everyone's had identical wheeled suitcases attached to them that pull them along. In this glittering fluorescence, their every movement is observed, their every particularity captured by the cameras. That bug just stroked the collar of its Louis Vuitton blouse with its tiny hand, and that one has stuck its finger up its nose!

What sort of procreative sport is taking place in this vast arena? Did the scientists gather us together when we still nestled inside our eggs under controlled heat and light—our incubator—to see us hatching, foolishly waving our arms and legs in the air, rolling upside down, then fleeing in old age? From confusion to Confucian. The bugs stand in line, the bugs break the line, the bugs scatter. Alert eyes follow them. Suspicious, interrogating.

The egg cracks, rocks, is x-rayed.

It's okay for bugs to be bugs, but for humans to be bugs, *ack*, the infamy!

Keep a stern eye on them. Watch. Assess.

But really, this watching, this assessing—it's an experience that travels across lifetimes for sisters and daughters. Just when they want to flee their families and they've lifted a foot to step away and they're lost in self-doubt, wondering whether they should go inside or come out—they arrive at the airport. Fleeing one type of surveillance, they fall under the eye of another. They chafe at the environment in a familiar fashion and develop an understandable loathing for airports.

★

8

Something must be said about the daughter. We'll call her Beti. After all, she's one of the two main women in this tale, and will make her presence felt throughout. Both women are integral to the family and so are bound by a love that both fattens and starves. Whatever fattening and starving hasn't already happened will surely occur in due course.

Let's not bring up all the past moments and stories here, since we have no need for them at present. They're over now, and we don't need to remember everything all the time. Like when Beti was growing up and Ma had not yet grown old, and the household was constantly roiled with controversies over social codes, traditions, culture, protection, and Ma would grow short of breath as she tried to calm everyone else's breathing.

But the funny thing was, amidst all the to-do, Ma managed to forge a path towards the forbidden.

Like the window opening out into the guava orchard. It was Ma who had cleared this hidden path for Beti's comings and goings. Inside, there was a constant uproar of *No, absolutely not, she won't go out!* And in the meantime, Beti leapt through the open window and fluttered off like a bird. Only Ma knew. For the rest of them, by the time they heard she wasn't in her room, Beti was busy playing antakshari, singing at the top of her lungs on the train *chug chug chug* with her posse. She would climb a mountain, or plunge into the sea, or break off shards from the stars and swing from brittle bits of straw, fall apart, break down, and through it all, Ma still had confidence in her, and when those stars and straws evolved into the forms of friends and lovers, Ma would still open the window wide for her to leap out and go to them.

The window had become so useful that Ma had also learned how to hoist herself up, pivot and jump out. She came out in the silence of night with snacks—shakkarpara, mathri, bati chokha, tied up in bundles—and she'd meet up with Beti, banished from home, hidden away in the dense karonda bushes along the boundary wall, where they'd giggle like little girls.

And let's not forget the day Ma handed a bright green Banarsi sari over the bushes to her banished or runaway daughter for the wedding of one of her girlfriends, and measured her while getting pricked by thorns all the while, so she could alter the matching blouse for the occasion. And the way those two women hid at such times, frightened, chatting, glancing about anxiously, bursting with laughter: it was like the forbidden romance of the century—enough to bring tears to the eyes.

But we shall not allow our tale to stray through bygone days.

The present context is this: Beti, who lived alone, had come to uplift Ma, lying alone. But there was no open window yet. It was winter.

★

9.

Beti. Daughters are made of wind and air. Invisible even in moments of stillness, when only the very sensitive perceive them. But if not still, then stirring…and oh, how they stir… and the sky bows down so low you could reach out and touch it with your hand. Dry earth cracks nightingales rise gurgling springs surface. Hillocks peek out. The unique expanse of nature unfurls on all sides and suddenly you realise your perceptions of distance and depth have got mixed up. A breath falls on hair like a soft petal, feels like a boulder in the roaring sea. That which you had imagined from a distance to be a snow-covered peak, is, up close, her finger, and will not melt. The wick of your wits dissolves and the overshadowing darkness remains a mere shadow. As when night falls and it keeps on being night, or if it's daytime, and day stretches ceaselessly on. And the wind blows as the soul sighs, whipping everywhere tossing and turning into a witch, and flinging itself on everyone, everything.

Daughter. You love her. You fear her. Now you see her. Now you don't.

All women, don't forget, are daughters.

★

Once upon a time there was a childhood. A clear white light filled the air and earth seemed to join the sky. You swayed in the sky, your tiny arms upraised, and you took your first steps.

The egg…cracked…rocked…fled…

Then the wind began to blow and the clouds began to sway. Silver dust rained through the air. A distant mountain was concealed by a cloud, lending it the appearance of an enormous lounging elephant. A tree peered in at the window and rustled in the breeze and every leaf showered down like rain.

Beti's lower lip trembled with weeping and Ma picked her up. What happened next was that Ma became the trembling lip. She rested Beti's head on her shoulder and began to hum to soothe her. She told her that the large elephant was waiting for Beti to come and ride it, and the two of them would sway together, and the leaves gossiped: *listen, listen, they're telling stories.*

And Beti smiled. And this made Ma smile too.

Beti's weeping gradually stilled and turned to sighing, and Ma too switched from sobbing to sighing.

Beti fell asleep and Ma draped her imagination in gorgeous dreams.

And at that moment, love took the form of a body. Ma's breathing calmed, Beti's turned to gurgling, and the elephant's back shouted for joy.

Because…

The leaves said love is not good for the health.

Either it's unselfish and you would gladly give your breath to another, or it's egotistical and you will devour another's breath.

In love's struggle
one withers, as the other blossoms
one is shaded, the other illuminated
one's a sheep, the other a shepherd
one's the feet, the other a towering head
one's a glutton as the other starves
one rides the winds as the other is trampled underfoot
one blossoms, the other fades

This was the custom in the time of this tale, and this was the room where one arrived by walking through the door, and this was where Ma lay, back to the world, as though dead.

She had grown tired of breathing for them, feeling their feelings, bearing their desires, carrying their animosities. She was tired of all of them, and she wanted to glide into the wall with a tremor; if a bug slipped into a crevice would the crevice itself start breathing?

*

One can speak of love at any time because love is lovely. It is natural. Also tempestuous. When love is boundless it breaks out into the cosmos. Its essence reaches a pinnacle and the drive to overpower one another flames out. The difference between thrum and flame is erased and it neither stops for anyone, nor hesitates at any boundary. Its gleam spreads in every direction, casting the world in magic. So magical that the air shimmers. A palace of mirrors. A mirage.

Now who is real, and who is the reflection?

So beautiful.

So powerful.

That God hustles out of the way.

The love between a parent and a child can make God fade into the background, and effusive love makes the breath run from here to there, so one might collapse for loss of breath, and the other puff up with the breaths of both. One completely disappears, while the other grows so bloated it could burst, discharging a filthy, foul-smelling essence.

★

For example, once there was a mother. Like all mothers. Who had said to her son, You are my God, and the son said to her, You are the Great Sacrificing Goddess laying waste to everyone's sorrows. Both began to map their selves onto one another, and one became a boa constrictor and the other the object of love. One of them huffed and puffed, the other gasped for breath. One grew fatter, the other shrank. So much love that their two lives became one.

Conventional wisdom had it that this was perfectly fine for the mother, because what was left of her life was moth-eaten and bare. What she'd got were bonus years. The son had given her rebirth. But another opinion held that it didn't exactly work out so well for son, did it? It was still the start of his life, but now his time and youth got bound to his mother, right? His back had doubled over from lifting her up and helping her fly, and this was a very sad thing.

There was also a daughter. Like all daughters. So mad with her father's love that no man could be his equal, and neither was the father prepared to hitch his princess to some lesser being. So it was the father who became the cure for any ailment, the topaz for any ring, and then that girl's youth and life, if not entirely, but more than half, evaporated.

★

10.

Enough. Let's get back.

Although the tale has no need for a single stream. It is free to run, flow into rivers and lakes, into fresh new waters. But for now, we must insist on not straying, so for the time being we simply won't. Let's return to where we began this story, to the land of the two women.

★

11.

What can be said about life? It knows how to spin a narrow orbit, a path so short it's finished the moment it starts. But it also knows the vast expanse of time, as when we step from a small lane out onto an open street, which in turn joins a historic highway like the Grand Trunk Road. It brings new twists to the story by merging with the path after a long distance; the path trembles from the growling of trucks and tractors; it's wrapped in the softness of Silk Route; it is amazed, wondering where these streets have come from, from what eras, via caravans, via frontiers. And where have I come from, and where am I now, after traversing so many lifetimes? Am I still the same path, or an even smaller one from long before?

But who will ask these questions, and when, and who has come up with the answers?

For now, there's a room, there's silence, and Beti is coming to Ma.

She's the younger sister of Bade, and he shouts out loud when he sees her.

Shouting is a tradition, an ancient custom upheld by eldest sons. In a masterful style. The practice only superficial; it doesn't matter if eldest sons truly feel such ferocity in their hearts, but whatever their feelings, they must be cloaked in this guise. It is said that Bade's father shouted from the heart, whereas Bade's real mood never reached boiling point. The father had shouted until his retirement; then he'd handed the yelling over to his son and grown relatively peaceful himself. Bade had wrapped himself in the majesty of even louder yelling, and he'd begun to glitter and glow. Now, in just a few months, he too would retire to ample leisure, and the yelling would fall to Sid. But for now, he still raged.

Yet Bade was not shouting at his sister. He wasn't even speaking to her. He shouted because his pyjama had got wet. He hadn't wet them himself, it was the chrysanthemums; they'd jumped out at him. On seeing a bowl of mattar paneer in the hands of the maid. Bade saw it, that is, not the chrysanthemums. No, no, not that! What happened was, he jerked his head so the hose he was using to water the chrysanthemums wiggled, then the chrysanthemums jumped, and the stream of water hit his pyjama. At this, he jumped, and yelled at top volume, *not that!* And he went inside shouting, leaving the hose still flowing.

Must she kill us by feeding us leftover vegetable dishes!

Mem Sahib said to serve it, replied the maid absently. Bored of these real or feigned set-tos between husband and wife.

Also: his sister had arrived.

Make something fresh. You can't serve them rotten food. Don't even give it to a beggar, he'd die and you'd get sued!

Well, you are the limit. Mem Sahib, a.k.a. his wife, a.k.a. the sister-in-law, a.k.a. the daughter-in-law, so we'll call her Bahu, confronted him angrily. Bhaiya is coming this evening. You were saying last night, there's just a little left, serve it to him for dinner. Now it's turned to poison? And she flared up in English: Stop undermining me in front of the servants. That's why they don't listen to me, and it does you no credit either!

Throw it away. Bade glared at the maid, who stood with the bowl by the fridge, still as a statue.

I've tasted it. It's first class. She's also brought friends, there are two of them. I'm putting it with the rest of the food, so we don't fall short. The wife glowered at the husband, either to make peace in front of everyone, or to indirectly inform her sister-in-law.

Serve whatever's fresh, whether it's too little or too much, if you can't make anything else, Bade snapped at the maid. Get rid of this.

Put it back, spluttered his wife, I'll eat it.

Put it back for her. No one else is going to eat it.

If I die, you can say he killed me.

When was this shouting and glowering mere banter, when childish wrangling, when joking, when irritation, and when was it simply something to do? The maid was never sure.

Of course Beti had heard, the ears on one's back are rarely blocked. And indeed, her friend may or may not have been aware of the household's quirks. Whether or not the chrysanthemums heard, it made no difference to them. It was their season, they were enjoying leaping up at the slightest thing, and so continued on with this pastime. They weren't even worried that Bade would soon retire, that he would leave the garden, and that there was no knowing what the next tenant's proclivities might be. What if they paved over the lawn and flowerbeds like people do nowadays to avoid dust and mites? Or planted wheat or corn or some such, instead of flowers, to save a bit of money? But the chrysanthemums weren't thinking ahead, they weren't about to stop leaping, and they bounced about as though they had springs coiled inside them.

★

Several times larger than the enormous mansions of civil servants in small cities are their enormous lawns, flower gardens, orchards, and fields. Sometimes they even have pools, ponds, fountains, and follies. At one point, during the reign of Victoria, large marble—they absolutely could not be fakes—statues of the Queen welcomed visitors to the gardens. Now that there was no longer any fear of being called a traitor for every little thing, they stood forgotten, but not disrespected.

In large cities, the houses began to grow smaller. But there too, where the buildings were now the trees, and dry mounds of earth were flowers, the homes of officers were oases in the desert.

Heaps and heaps of chrysanthemums.

As soon as you entered Bade's home, you saw them through the sliding glass doors at the end of the long hallway: bordering the lawn, chrysanthemums of every colour and size.

Beti saw Bade watering the flowers. The sun shone and a golden stream glistened beyond the tree in back, as though the Almighty had rubbed his hands with sunshine, scattering the glistening droplets.

Beti's back had heard the entire paneer conflagration. Only Ma knew what her own back had heard.

When Beti went off to Ma's room to gaze at the back, Bade said to the maid, Tell Amma that the sun is shining and the chrysanthemums are in bloom. Set chairs out on the lawn. Why doesn't everyone come and sit outside?

He then turned his attention to the future of the chrysanthemums. That is, what would happen when he retired and moved into a flat like everyone else in the city? How many could he pot and take with him? If you fill those tiny balconies with pots, there's no room for your clothing, your self, or anything else.

The chairs were set out on the lawn, but Bade sat alone. Just like his late father, who used to sit out there in the winter sun, half turned toward the chrysanthemums, and half toward the section of the house that could be seen through the glass door and the large door opening into the hallway. Father and son both had the ability to roll the pupil of the left eye into the left corner and the right into the right, so that both halves of the world might come into view at once, thus ensuring they knew everything that went on. They must be made of different stuff, eyes like that, that can observe the sights in both directions. Or maybe they weren't actually observing at all, and their eyes just rolled about?

He could hear his sister speaking.

Chrysanthemums everywhere.

A *no* from Ma.

But Ma, all colours and sizes. Football, spider, flat, clustered, all bouncing.

But why would she agree?

Purple, white, yellow, pink, even green.

Waving towards the sky above the lawn.

I'll take you, okay, why don't you bring your cane.

No. Please. Dizzy. Cane. Nyoo. Sunshine. Nyooo. Flowers. No no no no no nyoooo…

Bade got up. Went into Ma's room. Stood next to Beti.

The two met without making eye contact. Smiled unsmilingly. They hadn't spoken in years. The bitterness was gone, but the habit remained. They couldn't even remember their old sibling banter.

Are you getting up? he challenged Ma's back. How long has she been here, do feed her! Have something fresh prepared, otherwise they'll just feed her rotten leftovers from the kitchen.

★

Step inside and darkness shadows the room for a moment. The sunlight you've left behind turns to memory and disappears. Then a faint shade of warmth ripples across the closed eyelids. Then, slowly, the eyes grow accustomed to the darkness.

The eyes which have also grown on the unwilling back. Which see the fingers of Beti reaching towards it. Which insist: *we will lift you up*. Which smugly declare: *we know how*. Which touch the back, rub it, caress it, as though their insistence will descend into the veins of the back and finally the back will have to acquiesce, how could it not?

The daughter trusts the dexterity of her hands. That when they touch, all opposition will dissolve.

But the back makes a ripping sound and contracts. *No, no*, it mewls.

But this is Beti's word. Her birthright. Saying *no* to absolutely everything and everyone chirping at her and trying to calm her down. Say yes, sweetie, take this, darling, *bitiya rani bari siyani*, Chanda Mama has brought lovely snacks from far away, delicious, come on and try them on your plate, no, give it to her in a small cup, here you go, my little dolly-wolly.

Bade, who was ten years older than she, sometimes egged her on. No, say no, shake your head, and say no! Enough! She's saying no, isn't she!

Everyone adored the little girl's *no*. As a child she was made of *no*. To the point that anyone trying to get her to do anything would tell her to do the opposite and she'd immediately cry, No! and do exactly what they wanted. Eat the rice, not the paratha. No, I'll eat the paratha. Take tea, not milk. No, milk! Milk! Throw out the blue, not the red. Red, red, not the blue, no, no! You're awake, right, don't go to sleep, keep your eyes open. Noooo, I'm closing my eyes!

No, no, get it out of here, sometimes Ma would say when the cook would come in with the green chili coriander mint chutney, it will sting her mouth. But Beti heard her beloved word *no*, and she'd scream and growl and kick up a fuss: *no, give! No, want!*

Everyone laughing happily with her *no* somehow disappeared with childhood, but her *no* grew up with her. No, I won't sew, no, I won't wear a dupatta, no, I won't be locked up, no, I'm not you. There was so much no, no, that even when she was going to say yes, her lips would first say no. Drink tea. No, I'll drink tea. It's very cold. No, it's very cold.

A path opens with *no*. Freedom is made of *no*. *No* is fun. *No* is nonsensical. Nonsensical, but also mystical.

But Bade had to change tactics as she grew up. It was fine when she was younger: go ahead and don't listen to anyone then, but as she got older, she had to be told what to do and what not to do. There's no question that an elder brother must signal his disapproval to his sister, joining forces with the parental tone. When his sister's lovers entered the fray, objections piled up, and Bade despaired. Today Baldy Patel, tomorrow Glasses Guy, the next day Bearded Dude—and when all three qualities were rolled into one and the daughter of the household, that is, Bade's sister, became the subject of the town's gossip, the full gravitas of Bade's ancestors came to rest upon his shoulders, and the time came for more severe measures. Forbid the whole household from communicating with her, do not prepare her special coconut barfi, no watching TV with her, no making eye contact, no smiling at her even by mistake. Then she will rue the error of her ways, and the era of misery will be over.

But it wouldn't do to throw her out for misbehaving, to bar the door of the home to her, and so he hadn't liked it one bit when his sister had moved out herself and set up home elsewhere. When you live here, he thundered to Ma, why would she run off elsewhere?

But the feet of girls who say *no* are made of some other stuff, and while later they will hesitate at the door, they take off boldly in their early years.

That he, Bade, had to have the door and hallway scrubbed with phenol was another matter. The baldbeardglasses guy, Beti's godknowswhat, who'd come in on the pretext of carrying in or out some heavy baggage, had polluted the premises. One had to scrub thoroughly after that, driving the ghosts and ghouls out with a broom.

And so what if you swept them out with a broom? Thereby hangs another tale. But for now, consider the matter lost in the mists of time. Right now, Bade is standing in his mother's room, a little behind his sister, a little beside her. The two are separate, but staring at the back together. Baldy, a.k.a. Beardo, a.k.a. Four-eyes, is beyond the scope of this story, and the brother pities his sister's lonely life. She might be all set in terms of home, money, work, but when all said and done, she is still alone.

How had the *no, no,* stopped coming from this side and started coming from that? There must have been some confusion. Not for Bade, but for his sister. From Ma, not from me? The word—once so useful in my life—must have been dislodged from the dust where it lay, but it's not that special anymore, because one must have someone to say it to, and I'm my own master now...but it belonged to me and only me, so how did Ma get her hands on it?

What need was there for Beti to ponder all this? All that happened was that *no* continued to emanate from Ma's back.

★

Twitching and snapping, the back becomes flat like a wall. But a living back can't become a wall, can it? It can if it wants to. What it wants to say is, *I won't hear, won't see those voices trying to make this dying old woman live.*

Old habits are addictive—like booze and bidis. The back has already become a sieve. Everyone's dishonour, rage, comprehension, have already poked it full of holes. Where to stick the stopper? Now she sniffs things out before hearing, seeing. The familiar *knock knock clap clap.*

Beti is busy trying to stir up her enthusiasm for chrysanthemums—their size: *football!* Their colour: *purple!* She prides herself on being able to forge trails through difficult terrains. That's how she managed to create her own home outside the family home.

Gardener, ask Ma where to put the bouquets, says Bahu, wanting to play a role as well.

Don't make them with besan. It sticks in the belly. With moong dal, ask Ma how we should make them? Bade pipes in.

All plotting to look the most sympathetic.

Rudeness and taunts have also slipped through the cracks. Hey, move aside…I'm going to be late…look you didn't set the phone down properly again, you must stop your government freeloading…Phatoo will come in the evening, make fresh kheer, don't bring out the cashew barfi, it's been sitting around all month…the washerman burned this expensive kameez, now where will you get a new one, from your in-laws, an American kameez…tell the driver to fill up on petrol in the meantime, and to give the receipt to me, not to you…you spilled water, do you want Ma to slip? If she gets up she'll slip…that's why you want to get her up…oh, so that's what I said….if you're making a joke it should at least be funny…how was that a joke, even if she wants to get up she won't, knowing there's a plot afoot to make her slip and fall or finish her off with poison, he'd get up only to find someone else prepared to knock him over or poison him….what, really sir, you'll say anything! … okay enough, you're just spewing nonsense…I'm telling Ma right now…brilliant, then she'll jump right up…she simply doesn't want to get up, she knows everyone's upset, but…

Hmph huh shush bicker bicker and nag and nag and on and on and on.

Now the back is turning its back. How can it turn its back even more? It's slipping into the wall. How can it immure itself further?

There's a mark on the wall. Is the wind causing it or is it doing it by itself? Maybe it's a bug. Or is it the wind? Or breath?

★

If only I were a bug.

The wall is cold to the touch. A tiny being glides across it. A tiny breath. Make a crack somewhere, slip into the wall. With a minute movement the soft clay splits…unwittingly my feet bore in.

A sweet fragrance quivers in the air—of clay jugs and pitchers, of cool entombment in cool earth.

Stay lying down. Wordless, free from company, like breath, paused, just a little, that's all, a scrap effervescing in the air. If the bug puffs she'll fly away; find the embrace of the earth.

Let this be my tomb.

A coolness descends into her heart which is pleasant, calm, not the kind of numbing chill from outside. The peace of the wall, not the carrying-on occurring behind her back. That panting behind her that makes her wonder how the breathing of the whole world has caused her own to collapse.

Ma closes her eyes, finesses her silence, stops her breathing so that no one will know there's one breath left: one tiny life form. Let it slip into the wall, let it slowly glide forward, let nothing get in its way to ruin its rhythm, let nothing break its stride, suppress it, make it fall off the edge.

And if the mud wall is hollow, what then?

The mud wall is hollow. The being that emerged from her heart invented itself as it went along, forging a path through the mud. Let it invent its own breathing pattern. Let it flow in paths of its own creation. Let it course into its own veins, its own puffing, its own effervescence. Was Ma boring into herself as she slipped into the wall? Carving forth her own routes. Gliding into her own arteries and aerosols.

A tiny being in the dark; the edge of a breath. Motes of dust flying up as it glides. A faint flame of desire falls across her closed eyes. From air. Into air.

The tomb of sand has shifted.

★

Every tale has its haphazard elements, but such features aren't necessarily hazardous. The mark—or spot—which could be a bug, has appeared on the wall, and its legs—whisper-thin shadows—are digging a tunnel through the brick and mortar. Heat shines from its eyes and emanates faintly from the tunnel, and the meaning of *emanates* here is the way steam rises gently, and just the faintest trace of a lost breath can hang suspended from it.

In order to see this buggish spot, you must lie silently for a long time pressed against the wall, transforming into a bundle in the quilt, turning your back to the world.

Behind the back is everyone else's breathing. A throng of worry and sympathy.

Open the window, it must be stuffy for Amma.

Pull the curtain back, I'm sure she dislikes the darkness.

Why is she in that pose, facing the wall?

Why is she lying there awake, but with her eyes closed?

There are children playing outside, Ma.

The Mahabharata is coming on TV, Ma.

Bring the newspaper, play music, make spinach and onion pakoras, ask *who what why*. Through memory, through conversation, reheat the life she has lived, and serve it to her anew. So she will breathe again. So her soul will snap out of it. She will be reminded of what she used to do. But now, as they remind her of that life, it feels like she's not living it herself, the living is being done *to* her. She's being turned into pakoras. Moistened, ground, grated, cut into pieces, reclining in boiling oil *eek eek* flip flop sliding into bellies and disintegrating.

Throw it out, a voice flaps weakly. Is the bug's voice the type that burrows into the ear? Flap flap *It's all rubbish in there. Fling it out the open window. Cheela, football-sized chrysanthemums, water, button, chaat masala, doormat, toothpaste, cumin, kalonji. Keys, poppy seeds, needle, cough, mucus, snot, bile, breathing, entanglements. Throw them all away.*

Could the wall be moving back and forth behind Ma's back, encircling her so that nothing she doesn't want can get to her?

Only that faint flapping.

★

15

It's like they say: no use crying over a bug when an elephant's reaped the harvest. You might well wonder how such a thing happened, and can an elephant really harvest a crop? Well, if you insist on getting hung up on details, fine, we have here neither elephant nor crop. Here we have only a home, a family, and its members, entering and exiting through the open door. They don't harvest anything, only belch up bucketloads of compassion.

The ability to show compassion is the primary goal of all family members; it is the means to fraternity love peace happiness. If you can bestow a *poor thing* look on someone else, you become their Sorrow Destroyer: godlike! and begin to relish the sight of your own reflection. And thus the family will support you through thick and thin. Some become deities, the rest, paupers.

Like Beti. Poor, poor thing. Scolding, lecturing, sweeping under the carpet, it was all necessary to get her back on the path. But she *was* a poor thing. Very, very. Silly girl, raised with the vanities and wilfulness of a pampered princess. Ignorant of the pitfalls around her. Unknowing. And those taking advantage of her, the worthless folk leading her astray, whom she categorised as lovers. Over and over, she ended up alone.

When she couldn't bring her respectable officer brother and father to heel, she packed her bags and left home. Alone, poor impoverished little thing, once she'd left. She didn't even settle down anywhere and get a job. She wrote for this place one day, gave a talk at that one the next. Bade had arranged for the purchase of a couple of her totally-incomprehensible-to-everyone books at the Secretariat library. Beyond that, she just wandered about willy-nilly, her clothing and hair done up like some kind of peasant, clad in crudely- fashioned attire: a burlap kurta, a tattered pyjama, or an absurd ghaghra she got for thirty or forty rupees from a village in Rajasthan or Gujarat. Penury radiated from her person, and her family wept tears of sympathy when they beheld her.

In fact one wonders if, who knows, maybe those meetings in the bushes were not so secret after all. That compassion *had* played a role—Bade was allowing Ma to make some sort of arrangements to nourish her, clothe her, for as long as she remained on the street. When she came back, all would be well: she has a home, after all, a family. What else does she have? Who knew if anyone even socialised with her or invited the poor thing over, but if she moved in with any of those good-for-nothing folks, the family would be dishonoured. The way she was going, she could end up in exile.

Oh, oh, such compassion it could burst the floodgates and drown them all!

The compassion did not vanish altogether, but they certainly were surprised when newspapers and journals began printing photos of her, and television stations began airing interviews with her as well, where her views were discussed. About women's consciousness, sexuality, the female orgasm, what gibberish, good God.

The compassion entered even more troubled waters when the poor thing bought a fancy flat in a fancy neighbourhood, and a TV, microwave, and a car too. They learned she was always on her way to or back from the airport—traveling all over the world. There were irritable whispers in the house about how things are done with sleight of hand nowadays, whether right or wrong, just to earn money and a name, if you're good at networking, and if you're a woman, and young, then, then…well. The whispers would break off because such sentences could not be completed or because this was as much as could be said openly. Even then, Bade cautioned Ma against talking to Beti too much on the phone and so on, and you're not to go there under any circumstances; we cannot legitimate her lifestyle.

But when Beti began to get invitations to parties at Rashtrapati Bhavan, it was no longer clear who should be avoiding eye contact with whom. It seemed odd that the whole world would be talking to her, the President even! but that the family alone refused to communicate.

Tell her to come over, Bade told Ma one day. She has no one, and here she can have some home cooking. Bahu also gave her some of her essays, asking her to take a look—few people write on these topics, after all. And this was also an angle that would give her a sense of being included so she wouldn't continue feeling scorned.

And now, the moment we've arrived at, brother and sister stand side by side, staring at Ma's back and thinking, *Poor thing, Ma. What wouldn't I do to revive her?* Such were their leaps of compassion.

★

16

All of these are characters in this story: the bug, the elephant, the compassion, the door, Ma, the cane, the bundle, Bade, Beti, the Reeboks that Bahu wore, and the rest of the gang, who will come up in due course.

But wait, Reeboks? Why are you bringing up footwear?

There are those who say that long ago, the Reebok was a poisonous snake that went slithering about the southern portion of the continent known as *America*. It underwent a transformation when someone wrapped it around his feet in order to jump about with greater agility, and it is said that all the snake's bravado entered the person who wrapped his feet in its skin. But now Reeboks are only known for their current incarnation, and the company brings forth new types of shoes, not snakes, generation after generation. All types of shoes. One has spikes on the bottom, another has holes on top, a third has cushioned soles that bounce like rubber balls. That is, the Reebok species and subspecies have grown stronger with time: they hug the earth with their tentacles and breathe fire, and who now remembers that it originated with a snake?

The Reebok clan has grown so large it has beaten the Sikhs, the Gujaratis, and the Chinese, all of whom like to boast that they have reached all corners of the world. The Sikhs used to be proud that one of their number had even reached the shores of Iceland, complete with turban, kara, and kirpan. But Reeboks have defeated all three, taking the form of not only shoes, but socks, gloves, hats, bags, and bras: is there any form in which they have not manifested their brilliance?

Indeed, they've attained the highest pinnacle of achievement in all of the following fields: walking, running, yoga, and dance.

But why make these assertions, one might ask? There's no straight answer to that, but there is a walking talking quivering example of the power of Reeboks in the home in which this tale is set, namely, in the person of the one and only daughter-in-law residing there, Bahu. Everyone knows that from the day she first donned a pair of Reeboks she spontaneously began to take long, long walks all by herself, started taking an interest in jogging with her girlfriends, and began learning yoga under the tutelage of the gurus in the neighbourhood park. Started taking an interest? Just like that? Or did she run towards it? And during holidays when the neighbourhood moms had time off from the demands of their children's schools, this same Bahu became a guru herself, and taught popular yoga classes in summer and winter.

And lately it's been heard that she's enrolled in salsa dancing classes, and who knows how often the door is startled into wondering, *What is this*? *Ousted Beti entering; reigning Bahu departing; how are the Reeboks engineering this topsy-turvy situation?*

It also might have seemed like the daughter felt guilty she hadn't done her duty and thus had turned about and walked back in; and the daughter-in-law, reassured that she had fulfilled hers perfectly, walked out.

But there is no indication that the door or anyone else felt this way. Not yet, anyway.

★

17.

Everyone agrees that brides do not wear Reeboks to their weddings. Nor do they pack Reeboks in their dowries. Even if they're marrying into the home of a respected government officer. The Bahu in this tale is not alone in this.

Nor in this: that her fair complexion and lovely figure were pleasing to her in-laws. Nor in this: that due to these factors the prognosis for the coming generations looked fine to everyone. Nor in this: that Ma would share with her all sorts of beauty secrets and child-rearing techniques, and that Beti, her modern sister-in-law, would teach her as well. Nor in this: that she departed for her marital home to make her dreams come true, feeling utterly, utterly alone in this world. An unfamiliar home, unfamiliar folk, unknown customs.

Like most new brides, the new daughter-in-law of this home sat down to weep on the very first day. She'd gone to use the toilet and it had got blocked. An uproar broke out in the wedding home: there were so many guests, even one out-of-order bathroom was the End of the World. After much pandemonium, a sweeper had come running to help, and a home-made cotton pad wrapped in cloth and soaked in blood was extracted from the toilet. Beti brought Bahu a sanitary pad,

instructing her to kindly wrap it in old newspapers and throw
it away in the wastebasket.

The humiliation of having what one might call her dirty
laundry aired in public instantly taught Bahu that she must
learn what to throw away and how. When she went on her
honeymoon she wore the kind of sparkly tikli bindis you find
at fairs and such on the banks of the Ganga, and her braid
swung with parandas of red and gold. She discarded the bindi
for a defiant kumkum, a full moon rising in the middle of her
forehead, which expanded as the years passed, eventually
changing hues to match her sari or suit. And she jettisoned the
braid as well, and let her hair down, so it flipped and flapped
like a whip as she walked.

Now who could stop the rise of Reeboks in the world?
And so it came to pass. Reeboks began showing up in stores
and advertisements, and one day her son said, Ma, you should
get some Reeboks, and he bought her a pair.

Not Sid, but his younger brother, who was due to be
mentioned, and now he has. And who, since he departed for
Abroad, crossing the seven seas, is sometimes not mentioned at
all, which is why he hadn't yet come up. But he too plays a
role in keeping traditions alive, he's been mentioned now, and
will be again on occasion. Every mother has the sort of son
who tells her, Ma, you have been sacrificed on the family altar.
Women of every race and creed meet this criterion. To what
has already occurred the son adds imagined oppressions and
exhorts her to put on her Reeboks and stamp out of the door.

★

18

One wonders: did the youngest son have trouble laughing because life was getting tough? Or had he lost the ability to laugh? Or had he never had it?

Oh, tell me, what makes a character important? In the tale of a poor home, wealth is an important character, whereas it's beauty in the lives of the ugly, for India, it is Pakistan and America that play the characters of villain and hero, respectively; the most important character in the tale of a blind man is an eye, it's a leg for the lame, a home for the homeless, employment for the unemployed, sleep for the sleepless, and if you've had enough of this, look: the most important character in every person's life is the thing that they lack. Thus, for this son, laughter played a key role.

He was the youngest son in the household and not much need be said about him, because this story is really about the elders, even if they'd prefer it wasn't. He's not even present in the story right now, but we're not going to dwell on that, because for the moment, the operative truth is that that which is lacking plays a critical role. Anyway, he was present earlier, the way his grandfather had been, that is, the husband of his bedridden grandmother. In the end, his grandfather passed over to the next world and the son himself passed over the ocean to Australia and became known as Overseas Son. By virtue of which an invisible thread of the joint family travelled to a distant shore.

This son was as serious as Sid was rowdy. He was as industrious and composed as Sid was rambunctious and loquacious. This was the promising son, and to him, the brawling of Sid's set seemed a waste of time: the uncouth and fickle culture of the middle-class. Sometimes he even found their behaviour obscene. That's why he stuck to his own business, only spoke as much as was absolutely necessary, and if he did have to speak, but didn't feel like it, he didn't make idle chitchat and only broached timely topics. He ate a balanced diet, got plenty of sleep and never sat about idly. There was always a book in his hands to which he gave his full attention, whether on the toilet in the morning, or standing in a queue somewhere, or on a train, bus, or car ride. He was always expanding his knowledge base, and that's why he knew a great deal about history, geography, religion, philosophy, science, psychology, geology, economics, political science, urban studies, and how many things have been ruined and are being ruined in all of these aspects of life, thanks to which he was always an emotional wreck. But his health had not yet been ruined.

Personal qualities—characteristics—can become characters in our life dramas too. That there was a character that overshadowed his entire life by virtue of its absence—Serious Son, which is what we will call him until his travels transform him into Overseas Son—would not have been discovered had he not gone to another city on company business. They say unforeseen events play important roles in our lives, whether for good or ill. Just as love blossoms in our lives and death shows us the exit, laughter can enter our hearts and exit from them too.

There's no need here to get into the question of whether laughter entered or exited the heart of Serious Son, or when it came and when it went. The important thing to understand is that a sudden conflagration at the seashore alerted him to the importance of laughter. And that led to him feeling exceedingly glum.

He'd had a bit of free time after a meeting, so he'd walked out of his hotel and gone to sit on the beach, where he felt happy, more or less. More or less, because there wasn't much left in the world to make one feel truly happy. Wherever you look, the same hideousness, the same consumerist greed, the same fake culture, and the same flittering flimsy frivolous ineffectual people who only know how to imitate and ape, so they belong neither here nor there nor anywhere. He steered clear of them all as much as possible, and stayed focused on his work. But here he encountered the singing leaping ocean, whose leaping and singing were genuine, and therefore highly agreeable, so he first ordered himself a beer; and second, went and sat at the most remote table and chair at the edge of the coconut-thatched café shack with his book open before him, and turned his face towards the sea. Whenever the tumescent tumult of tacky tourists encroached, he'd drag his table and chair closer to the sea and sit contentedly, more or less. He even dozed.

If anyone had seen him from afar, it would have made for a charming painting—the vast sky, the immense sea, and wedged into the corner, a tiny fragment of a scene in which a young man was seated in a chair with a beer by his side and a book in his lap. The waves lapped at the edges of the scene, retreated, then returned, as though they might at any time carry the scene off altogether. The scene itself seemed mysteriously drawn into the waves.

But no one actually saw this scene from far off. The one person who did see it saw it up close. Specifically, this witness was a plump, giggling little boy.

Serious Son loathed children. And also their parents, who plastered their offspring's adorable exploits all over the internet. And if there was anything he hated more than tiny foolish milk-puking babies with googly eyes and wobbly heads, it was fat fresh lurching prattling spittle-oozing gurgling gleeful toddlers. Like the one that saw him.

The child was making the rounds from one table to the next—a baby bull on the loose, tipping one person's glass, trying to knock over another's chair, and when no one was watching, the baby bull would suddenly jump forward and give someone a smack.

And way over there sits one individual, utterly unaware of this toddler's presence: how could this be acceptable to the spoiled little prince? Here was a challenge! His goals changed. Donald Duck waddled over to Serious Son dozing by the ocean. The sea swirled about the legs of the table and chair and all was peaceful in the ocean's din, when little Fattikins raised a hand and planted a baby smack on Serious Son. Serious Son was startled. But he would not allow anyone to spoil his alone time. And yet here was the child again! With another slap, followed by a demand that he laugh! Serious Son opened his eyes and made a horrible face when he was slapped for the third time. Then all the futility of the world was brought home to him, and he turned and grabbed the pup by the neck and waved him in the air. If you ever come back here, I'll throw you in the water! he cried. The child howled at the ocean and his freshly minted parents came running and set about battling Serious Son: how could anyone behave this way towards a child? Everyone else adores him, and here you are, incensed by a child's game? Oh, is slapping a child's game? asked Serious Son, nettled. You're the ones spoiling him, and kids like this stay spoiled even after they grow up. What do you mean? asked the parents. All he was asking was for you to laugh. Are you unable to laugh?

Serious Son got up and left. The world, wrecked by destructive humans, rematerialised all about him. The sand, defiled with beer cans and plastic bags, the earth, colonised by white people, the flabby Indian bandar log, the cacophony that fancies itself music and makes nature weep, the laughing screaming stupid people, *laugh*, they told him; what's there to laugh about—look at all you've done to this nation! Fume fume fume. Serious Son went back to his room, fuming. And fell asleep.

And dreamt that he sat peacefully by the seashore beneath the vast sky, the waves softly lapping at his feet, slowly deepening their affectionate caresses, and now his chair bobs up lightly at every love-shove, and now the ocean brims with affection and he is lifted high atop the waves, and now he's seated on a throne in the sea, and all the tourists on the beach have gathered to watch him, along with their plump fresh children, and he is explaining to them, *Idiots, imbeciles, look at how you breathe, think about how you ape foreigners as you breathe; that's why your lungs are full of pollution not oxygen, that's why you're sputtering stuttering not breathing. Dude, do your own breathing for a change, and teach your children to do the same.* At which a small football-shaped child comes lumbering to the front of the group and screams, *The king is naked! Laugh!* And the roaring of the crowd on the beach swells—*He can't laugh!* and a massive wave breaks over him and suffocates him, and a furore breaks out and his heart palpitates horribly and suddenly his eyes pop open.

His heart is beating fit to burst. And the sentence bounces towards him like a football. Growing continuously smaller, it turns into a marble, crossing the boundary of wakefulness and sleep to leer at him in the darkness: *Can't you laugh?*

The moment of waking is full of innocence. As we wake, we are unarmed and vulnerable. The dreamer wonders what he should forget and what he should remember. The heart of the awakened one pounds and the sentence stares at him mutely: *Can't you laugh?*

The question sticks to him all the way home. And Serious Son's quiet disquiet now becomes disquieted disquiet, and this new absent presence becomes his difficult life partner, this omni-absent laugh, which jeers at him: *Dude, can't you laugh?*

Serious Son was well-versed in interpreting such ills as imperialism, colonialism, feudalism, commercialism, and he knew that it was these that had put him in this state, so there was nothing left for him to imagine that would gladden his heart and make him laugh—but it was one thing to be unable to laugh for some particular reason, and another to be unable to laugh at all. Once such doubts take root in one's mind, laughter disappears for even the best of us. The thought that one hasn't even the tiniest bit of a smile can make a person feel helpless.

That can't be, thought Serious Son with agitation. *Hmph, I can't laugh—what kind of bullshit is that?* and he chuckled at his own understanding of the situation, which was noted by Julius Caesar.

Julius's eyes opened early each morning, after which he'd go out for his walk. The home of the irritable-faced neighbour, i.e., Serious Son, was on the way, and Julius had got in the habit of seeing the irritable face grow more irritable the moment their eyes met. First and foremost, Serious Son was annoyed at his name: that it wasn't just *Julius*, but also *Caesar* on top of that; and after that, Julius's very British performances would start up whenever he bumped into anyone, and then Serious Son's annoyance would know no bounds. This annoyance could be heard in the rustling of the breeze, which Julius Caesar detected as well, because his hearing was particularly sharp. Besides, he too enjoyed annoying the annoyed one, the way most others did. They would either change their route upon seeing him, or take pleasure in the encounter, out of sheer pig-headedness.

Today, as well, he was just about to make a show of his British manners when a new expression on the irritable face ruined his plans. So instead of the usual *sit shake hands dance*, he began to *bark bark bark*. The irritable neighbour had a weird sort of wrinkly mug. His lips looked like a cloth viciously ripped in two, with a scrap hanging down. His eyes were sunken into his flesh like two burrowing worms. Shoulders seized by earth shaking jerks and small shrieks burst through the cracks in the torn face.

Upon hearing the barking, Julius's master also looked that way and shivered. He wondered if the irritable neighbour was having a fit. But Julius understood completely: *Oh, he's trying to laugh. He's trying so hard.* Elated with his new discovery, he barked some more; but as he barked he also began to feel sympathy. His master, however, dragged him away by the leash, without commanding him to waltz, shake hands, etc.

This incident only served to increase Serious Son's unease. *What did I just do, was I laughing? Or not?*

He stretched his lips wide again and forced a chortling from his jaws, and swift as an arrow, turned toward the veranda window to take a look before the laughter disappeared. That same torn face, outstretched lips, protruding teeth, squinting eyes. *There! Who says I can't laugh? Isn't that a laugh? It is, isn't it?*

But the situation only grew more grave. *Can't laugh, doesn't feel like laughing because doesn't laugh, or simply doesn't know how to laugh, really how can it be, doesn't everybody laugh? Who doesn't know how to laugh? So have I forgotten how to laugh, or was I just born this way?* His heart began to pound, his face puckered up, and his forehead broke into a sweat.

The fear that he didn't know how to laugh became Serious Son's constant companion, and to laugh became his most fervent wish. He began to practice whenever he could: sometimes alone, sometimes when there was someone else around.

Sometimes he'd even search someone out on purpose.

It would be morning. Around six. Newspaper delivery time. When he heard the paper drop, Serious Son would get up; he'd hear the pounding of his own heart, jump in front of the mirror and stretch his lips out long and pointed at the corners, like a moustache. He'd bare his teeth and freeze his facial expression and the newspaper boy wouldn't have made it to the door before he leapt out. He'd take the paper from his hand, show his face, and not understand why the boy gaped back before hightailing it out of there. Serious Son would come back inside, the expression sealed on his face, and look in the mirror, but his laughter could not be kept alive in its glass. He continued to practice. As he read the paper, he'd work on emitting bubbles of laughter. His face would twitch in a *ho ho hu hu ha ha*, but his eyes sagged sadly.

That is, as in the Bihari pop song, *Aara hile Chhapra hile De-variya hile*—everything wiggled and everything jiggled—except for his laughter.

Only Julius Caesar stood witness to his laughterless pain. He did try to help. He barked whenever he saw him, and wagged his tail as if to say, *Look at me! We laugh like this!* But who had time to appreciate this sensitivity? He even barked to draw attention to the earsplitting guffaws of the elderly men gathered in the park, as if to say, *Learn from them!* But he was the one whose throat got sore. Nothing else came of it.

That is, the laughter continued to go missing.

On top of that, when Serious Son infiltrated Sid's rowdy gang and stood around for a while, witnessing their enthrallment with Pepsi, beer, chips, wild songs and dances, and didn't instantly turn away in disgust and leave, Sid chalked up the new contorted face to yet another entry in his brother's roster of irritable expressions.

Of course, there were those who did notice Serious Son's ripping face, that the stitching of his sullen visage was beginning to show and that he was breaking out in hives, and that the hives began to shake and twist and he began to make a *thunk thunk* noise in anguish, but since these people were not in regular contact with this son, they'd move away from him after a momentary shock. And anyway, everyone was in a hurry, taking care of their own business.

Serious Son also had business to attend to. His inner turmoil had its place, but so did his work. Yet these days the search for his missing laughter had infiltrated even that. This was a big problem, because where was he going to find something worth laughing about at work? He tried the joy of laughter in the company car, but the driver's jaw dropped and his eyes popped out in astonishment, and Serious Son's laughter was nipped in the bud. The driver's Michael Jackson uniform, and his *Wow, oh shit*, the consumerist culture of the street, the sun sobbing quietly amid the pollution, the ill-mannered city that lay beneath, discoloured by dust, rust, and bird shit, the obscene malls, everything for sale, even water, the little girl tapping on his window was selling it, she's doing this instead of studying and she's dressed in rags, performing a filmi number between the cars; educated girls crossing the street, their clothing shrunk smaller than their minds, and any random guy you address, in whatever Indian language, answers in English, and in bad English at that, even the Hindi spelling on the signboards is wrong, and as for spellings of English words, the less said the better. By the time he's got to the office, Serious Son's mood has soured but his face still longs to laugh.

His face tries at every opportunity, while his heart attempts to suppress his irritation. The things he used to say with disgust, he's dying to say with a smile. For example, when his colleagues were missing during the guest of honour's speech but one hundred percent present at cocktail time, or when the secretary brought Gujarati pizza, that is, sugar-sprinkled, or when someone proudly named a new flavour of their famous ice cream brand *Jack the Ripper* and the canteen worker dubbed his son *Laloo Hitler*. These people aren't even illiterate, but they do such things nonetheless. If you say *Gandhi*, the other person will say *Sanjay*. If you say *Ustad Amir Khan*, then everyone thinks *Aamir Khan from QSQT*. What with these daily occurrences that usually wipe a smile off his face, Serious Son peels away his serious face and plasters it with laughter instead. But why would no one comfort him by recognizing his bared teeth, outstretched jaw, and the hissing popping bubbles of laughter? Some gazed in horror, others looked away. So his lips continued to strive but the sadness in his eyes only deepened.

Bahu, whom Serious Son had started to call *Ma*, because what is all this shortening of Siddharth to *Sid* and Pushpesh to *Push* and Shatrunjay to *Shat* and Ma to *Mom*? Bahu, his mom, sensed her little one was besieged by worries. *He's worried about me.* She just knew it. The household's male chauvinist ways had bothered him since childhood. As he emerged to go to the office, she would come running and pop a fresh laddu —sesame, amaranth, besan, boondi, or some such—into his mouth to cheer him up, and she would say, *Rest a little, don't be hard on yourself for the mistakes of others,* and, *I am fine thanks to you, my darling, no one can be too hard on me.* As he departed, Serious Son would rest his head on his mother's shoulder for a moment, and his eyes looked sad and the laughter would not come.

He had grown even more serious than before, and fretted like a worried mother, but Bahu had not thought beyond this yet. She hadn't seen it all: how her baby was getting up at night in terror, scrubbing at the washbasin in the morning as he stared at himself in the mirror trying to laugh *hoo hoo hee hee,* flecks of foam flying everywhere and unable to laugh when face to face with anyone, his flesh and muscles contorted in a hiccuppy dance, his bones a-chatter.

But how long could she remain ignorant of his state? She saw that instead of giving a scowling scolding to the colony's children for raising a racket at cricket, *What is all this crude language you're using, you don't know English just because you pick up a few English words, learn your own language first, then go learn as many others as you wish, because that's the only way to breathe evenly, otherwise you'll run out of breath, and you jokers will huff and puff, go somewhere else and play, stop making noise,* he instead picked up the canvas ball rolling towards him and threw it back and guffawed strangely, and cried, *Good shot!* and made a peculiar crumpled face. Bahu was next to him, she'd pulled a muscle in yoga, was leaving the house to go to physiotherapy with Serious Son. The cricketers were in their own little world, but Bahu was shocked at her son's odd expression, and started keeping an eye on him from that time.

So the story went on from there. Bahu saw that he wasn't sleeping, his appetite had gone the way of his sleep, and his face was blotchy. Horlicks, Bournvita, Chyawanprash, Rooh Afza, fruit—she started following him around with all of these things, worrying he might be growing thin. But her son's laughter was trapped and the attempt to unearth it was sapping his strength. At night he'd awake, heart pounding, liver aquiver, guffaws foaming from his mouth, his stomach churning with anxiety, and the deepening chasm echoed horribly with emptiness, with not even finding an H of a HAHA—forget the next three letters.

So the story was stuck right at that point.

★

If a story is stuck somewhere, it becomes evident that there's more of it to be told. We can't sweep it out of the way just yet. It's merely stopped for a breather, we have to wait and pick it up as it will, go along with its speed when it will.

Think of a story as a living being. There are countless beings and countless types of beings. Physiques, lifestyles, screams, conversations, breaths, tremblings, horns, mutenesses, ways of living and dying, all different. So running off in the middle of a story in a huff is simply not acceptable. Let it live its life, find its own denouement. A butterfly's tale is a few days aflutter, a bee gets four weeks abuzz, a mouse drools over a handful of crumbs; if a dog lives twenty years, good for him, and yes, if you're a parrot, turtle, or elephant, you get a full century. The wretched cockroach won't even die when fired from a cannon. If you want to talk about snakes, you could tell a tale of serpentine wonder: the head can go, a bit of leg too, a bit off the top a bit of the toe, but the tail keeps dancing.

Here's the thing: a story can fly, stop, go, turn, be whatever it wants to be. That's why our wise author Intizar Hussain once remarked that a story is like a nomad.

And you may well fall speechless. Because if a story wants, it can stand in one place, refusing to budge. Take root and become a tree, which is another life form. An immortal witness of everything from the gods until now. Planting the twists and turns of the story in curling stems. Laying it to sleep among leaves, perfuming the breezes with it.

Marvellous beings, stories. Preserved in death and in stone. In endless trances that evolved into tombs, surviving from one lifetime to another. The tombs turn to stone, then liquefy, then evaporate into steam and shimmer up, rendering you idolatrous with their silence. And that steam, too, can raise an entire story.

The tale of laughter will continue on. It will stop where it will. At a full or unfull stop. Laughing or keeping lost laughter unlaughed. Fully spontaneous.

The gardener has no permission here: to artificially shape the garden, forming a boundary hedge, measuring here, pruning there, perfectly precise, standing like a scrap of an army under a flag of false pride: We've got this garden surrounded! This is a story garden, here, a different light and sunlight rain lover murderer beast bird pigeon fly look sky.

★

An ailment to beat all ailments. A life growing increasingly difficult. The problem was stuck right where it was, but that in itself moved it forward. Exhaustion hunger face contorted moment by moment in the laughter-struggle so why wouldn't the eyes look fatigued sinking into black sockets? Why wouldn't food and drink bring about a state of indigestion, a round of constipation or diarrhoea? Why would the joints not ache and the brow not burn? That is, one symptom after another and after that, a third, and the illness becomes laughter cramps. The son fell ill.

In a city where numerous diseases are in a state of constant outbreak, whether from mosquitoes or water or air or food— why not a laughter germ? Who would have thought it? Certainly not the mother of this son. But she fretted over him, and though her child said no, the doctor finally came. The remedies went from wet compress to painkillers to multivitamins, and then moved on to tests. No end of maladies to be checked for, for all symptoms mimic one another. It's always this way with medical jargon and diagnoses. Check for flu, typhoid, dengue. Gastroenteritis. Malaria. Chikungunya, influenza, pneumonia. Or…good God…It couldn't be ss-ss-ssomething else, could it? She was so anxious she could barely breathe. But all the reports came out clean. Broad-spectrum antibiotics were prescribed. But he didn't get any better. He was talked into cortisone injections. They were useless. Bahu cooked his food with her own hands, but still his health deteriorated. Even though her younger son used up all his remaining vacation days, the illness simply would not go away. *I'm fine*, he kept saying, and the tests,too, showed he hadn't caught anything.

What was Bahu to do? She began to massage his forehead with balm to help him sleep, and she sent for the servant Ratilal's nephew Fitroo so he could massage his feet after school, even if he was sleeping, because my little darling must get better, and he started getting up at night to look in on him, and every task that someone else could do for her younger son, Fitroo began to do.

One vacation day she noticed that Ratilal was sitting and massaging Serious Son's feet himself. Oh, I see, so your nephew has put you to work here because you're on leave? Bahu asked, thinking this must be what had happened. The next day she saw that Tillan sat at the foot of her son's bed, massaging his legs. On another day it was Ghanti on duty. Bahu was startled, *What's going on! First this one, then that one coming into the house, where on earth is Fitroo?*

Then it turned out that Fitroo had refused to do it. *Why did he refuse?* He says Serious Son is not well. *But that's why I asked him to massage his legs*. No Ma'am, no Mem Sahib, he says, Serious Son makes faces, and sounds come from his belly.

Once it all came out, it was easier to talk about.

Chimpoo, the newspaper boy, is also scared. You ask him please.

Then she was told that as soon as Serious Son saw Fitroo his face begins to crack and his mouth made a kind of sobby sound. Fitroo couldn't figure out what he was trying to say. Once he said Serious Son was surely crying, that's why he couldn't talk. Then Serious Son got tired and fell back on the pillow.

I was massaging his legs but he wasn't paying attention. He kept his eyes closed and it was like something was stuck in his mouth, but he wasn't managing to get it out. Just then Chimpoo came to the door with the paper. Serious Son jumped up and made that strange face at him. Chimpoo threw the newspaper at him, Ooh, lord! and ran. He says he does the same thing every day. Something's happened to him.

Bahu gave them all a tongue-lashing but now her heart began to pound, and she broke into a sweat. She increased her surveillance so that one night she also saw—her son was sitting up in the semi-darkness, *ha-ha hu-hu* sounds pouring from his lips. Was this laughter? But it was as though laughter had been cut from a piece of paper and pasted to his lips. His eyes, cheeks, nose, forehead, all unlaughing. The mouth bursting with these sounds. Mismatched.

But why would someone sit alone in bed and laugh?

How could she broach the subject with her son? When her two sons had been small, she'd admonished them at times: Don't make faces, the wind will change direction and then your face will get stuck that way. But now, when he was taller than she?

And now she began to notice it was happening all the time. As though her son were pasting a laughter-shaped sticker on his face, sometimes a large one, sometimes extra small, but none matched with the rest of his face. The sound that erupted was also wrong for the size of the mouth. His mouth opened in a small *ooh*, the voice stretched out in *ha ha*. The mouth opened with a long *hahaha aah*, the voice said *hee hee*.

Something was wrong. Very wrong. Her heart broke for her son. Such a brilliant son, his school record had been so good, such a wonderful job at such a young age, when had he come down with this *ho-ha-hee* illness?

Finally Ramdei took control of the situation. She took Bahu and Serious Son to the tomb of Bahke Fakir. There, Pir Nabina, more than 100 years old, worshipped with flowers at the tomb of his saint. His complexion was blue-black and his eyes a brilliant saffron. He was tall and wore a black cape and a necklace of large round orange stones. He didn't look one bit blind, but Ramdei said his eyes don't see this world, they see everything beyond it. Pir Nabina held Serious Son's hand and took his pulse. He pressed his hand. He peered inside him. This made his eyes roll backwards in his head.

There are blue marks on his feet.

Yes, Ramdei pressed her palms together.

He gets a fever at night, in the morning it's gone.

Yes, Pir Baba.

His complexion is sallow; his mouth hangs open.

Yes, yes.

He shakes his face about violently.

Yes, said Bahu.

The mouth and voice refuse to follow the dictates of one another.

Huh?

When the jaws crack open, a faint *hee hee* emerges; when the lips part slightly to emit a drawn-out *ha ha*.

Yes, yes.

Air bubbles burst from the mouth.

Yes, Pir Huzoor, they rise from his belly.

From his heart.

Ffffrom his hhhheart?

Pir Nabina let go of Serious Son's hand. His pupils rolled back into place. He sat down silently and began waving his tongs about in the air. His eyes gleamed.

His illness? both the women asked fearfully. What is it?
His illness is that he cannot laugh.
Pir Nabina had spoken.

★

_____

19

Wind blows ferociously. Or arrives on tiptoe. Things move at their own pace. Things change, and that's also why they move ahead. Keep moving.

The laughter departed, stayed away, returned—who knows what happened to it in all the twists and turns—but one thing's for certain: the cane arrived.

We'll never know unless we question and counter-question Serious Son and Bahu, reading between the lines and behind them too, what Pir Nabina's precise role was. Directly after the illness was identified, Serious Son's company gave him a promotion and sent him abroad, making him the CEO of the overseas office. Overseas does not mean Nepal or Bangladesh, it means Germany, Australia, America, and so Serious Son travelled to Australia, and became Overseas Son. Not evident from the pictures he sent once there was whether he was still _hahaha_ without a smile, and whether his jaws were still stretched out laughterless and the bubbles in his belly still popped from his mouth imagining themselves to be something else, and whether the environment still inspired his disgust, or if, once there, he now deemed malls, merchandise, and materialism praiseworthy.

So basically, the laughter departed across the ocean, and the cane arrived from overseas. It arrived bringing Overseas Son with it, who had come home for a few days to share the joy of admirable employment with his mother-father country. He arrived bearing gifts. Shirts, cotton wool, flowery plastic commode cover, t-shirts, nonstick pan, chewing gum, kangaroo key chain, koala paperweight, socks, fridge storage containers and bottles, and *Ma*—a.k.a. Bahu—*Whenever you want, please come visit, and this is from an early bird sale, and this is from a closing sale and the cane was half price but still cost one thousand rupees*, and he didn't have to say that it was *Oh, what a cane!* No one had ever seen or heard the like before, what to say!

It cost a thousand rupees, said Bade proudly, it has every single colour, enthused Beti, If you want, you can unfold it and walk around with it at full length, suggested the people who saw it, or you can fold it up and put it in your purse, and Overseas Son said, The cane is for Daadi, and Bahu said, Go on, go give it to her then.

The cane entered Ma's room and stood propped against the head of her bed. It was lightweight, shiny, thin; it made you want to fly, dance, make a splash, tap it, rest on it for support, send butterflies into flight. Golden in colour. Covered with butterflies of every hue. Blood red, grey, turmeric yellow, dark grey, rice-paddy green, turquoise, purple, black, parrot green, white, all the wings aflutter. Floral. Striped. The wings. The cane's handle a beak. It contained smiles, flying, chatter.

Who had ever seen such a cane? Could it be made of gold? Its original sale price was stickered on the neck. Everyone's eyes popped in surprise when they saw it. And if you jerked it, the butterflies flew up. And the cane could do somersaults *clack clack clack*, and if it felt like it, it folded up small, like Alice in

Wonderland. A mere hand-span of a stick that you could press beneath your arm and no one would even notice. Are these butterflies, or magical fairies? If you jerk them, they start flying out *fft fft fft* and the cane grows long. Alice-as-cane.

Overseas Son returned to Australia and the cane rested by Ma's bedside as though it were a member of the household. All who came greeted it, looked at it, touched it, extolled it. Made it shrink from large to small, expand from small to large. When they flung it into the air, it clicked to attention. Fling it up again, and it takes a bow with its head, torso, every part of its body as though it has just finished performing its role, then collapses into itself. Everyone gazed on in astonishment.

Everyone, that is, except for Ma, who was still pressed against the wall, unimpressed by the array of colours in the room.

Colours have a theatricality all their own. They don't come into being just because they exist. They can lie in place, buried. When the breath rises softly, glides around here and there, only then do colours shift. They blink, look about, giggle crack up cry out. Act childish, or prance romantically. Lie down dead, rise again. Then they swing into action, as though they hadn't been there before, even though they had indeed existed.

Everyone opens Ma's window, but she won't look out. A kite has got caught on the branch outside. Did it have ground glass on the string that sliced the other lines? Was the kite made of silk or paper? Was it sewn onto bamboo sticks? Did it get cut down? Was it heading for a fall and got stuck in a tree? It is also multicoloured: orange, purple, pink. Colourful yet discoloured. These tatters: did they flutter or flit?

We'll find out when Sid comes. When the cane flaps its wings, something will happen. When the butterflies fly, Ma's eyes will fly open.

★

20

Sid came. Looking neither to the right nor the left, he snatched up the cane as if to fly away, then came shooting over to perch on Ma's bed.

Wow, Granny, look at this. Fly it around in the air *woosh swoosh fwoosh*. *Clickclickclick* he opened and closed it, then extended it full length, then closed it all the way up. When it's small, it's a flute, here, play it. Open it all the way, slap the scoundrels once or twice on the shin, *smack thwack attack*, Granny, my own. And take this, stretch it out, it's our airplane, Granny, yours and mine, the cane that flies the skies, let down your hair, Granny, stupid! You sit in front, me behind, let's tour the world!

Oh, oh, careful, Bade cried, it cost one thousand rupees!

Says who? thundered Bahu, Why are you telling the half price?

I bought it for Daadi, Overseas Son reminded from the phone. I was the one to suggest she keep it beside her, Bahu informed everyone. There's not a single colour missing, I told Ma, try to find one, boasted Beti. I was the one who explained its potential to her, Bade said in his eldest son tone. That is, everyone claiming the idea came from them, as is the way with all families.

But the rainbow? That was where the real idea came from.

★

Oh, the rainbow! Time for my entrance. Because I was the one who saw it. If anyone's going to mention the rainbow it'd have to be me. I won't mention it, of course. But I know. Because I notice more than the others, and I realise more than them, too. I watch, silently, noting who came, who spoke, whose face lit up with what expression, and where the rainbow appeared. Of course that occurs when I happen to be there by some stroke of chance, then for sure, I was present at that very moment and it happened right in front of me.

I enter at the rainbow. Now's my chance. I'll tell you all about the rainbow and come leaping across these pages just as it does, to shine for a moment.

The rainbow glistened. In the beer I held for my buddy, during that party to which I, too, was invited, when I followed Sid to see his Granny in her room, and Sid picked up the cane and started monkeying around.

Sid, my buddy, opened the cane and shut it—*snap crack pop* —and all the butterflies began to flutter about at once. Butterflies, butterflies, everywhere, wow! Every colour swarmed through the air. Sid's Granny was feeling ill from, you guessed it, old age. His grandfather had passed away. The same old story: What will Granny do now? Just lie there. Whenever I saw her, she was taking bed rest.

But my friend's funny. His laughter's infectious. The kind of guy who'd make a corpse look up from the funeral pyre to see who'd laughed so uproariously. I'm not like that! I'm…

But I'm not here to talk about myself. This isn't my story, there's no need for me here; I'm not even a character. And yet —the page is a stage! Even if someone doesn't belong here, they'll gleefully embrace their moment when handed the tiniest opportunity. Like when an actor says *rain* in a scene on the stage, and someone like me comes on to demonstrate a stream of rain *fsssh* with a squirt gun. He's supposed to go away after that, but now he's onstage, it takes real discipline to exit again. He stretches the moment out, pulls the trigger on that *fsssh* as long as he can and waves his arms around a bit to attract the audience's attention, and have them stare at him for one glorious moment.

Like the old schoolteacher who was made the Private Secretary to the Chief Minister who belonged to the same caste. For three years, his destiny glowed as though the full moon shone upon him daily. The Private Secretary immediately threw himself into every scam in the book: usury bribery lechery Mercedes Benz foreign travel, every single type of corruption. He redecorated his home, got his daughter married, got jobs for his son and nephew, and then, when his term was up, he returned, docile as a cow, to the bonds of honesty poverty treachery. But as long as he had the opportunity, he played his part on the stage to the hilt, over and over.

I'm in the same situation. Why should I let this opportunity pass me by? And so I shall come again to play my part. If you missed the first shot, then take a look at this!

But it doesn't suit my ego to come barging in. I'll be ignominiously pushed aside; no one will let me stay for long. It'd be better for me to say my few lines before I get kicked out and head into retreat mode. My time onstage will last only a few moments. Enough for me to say this: *A rainbow shone. It sparkled*. I was the very first to see it. I can't say whether anyone else saw it or not. But I did.

We'd just entered the room. Glasses of beer in hand. *So stuffy*, I thought. Sid picked up the cane and rushed ahead. But his beer didn't spill. May I? I asked, opening the window. A broken kite hung from the tree outside. The butterflies flew up from the cane. Perhaps the kite wriggled. Sid's Granny turned over. She was forced to open her eyes.

Get up, Granny, you lazybones, are you going to sleep all winter, or what? *Chill, winter, chill…* Sid propped up her pillow, sat down next to her, and began to sing a song about taking a trip on a cane into the sky, *enough zzzz zzzz,* the chorus an imitation of her snoring. He hugged her. Struck a pose with the cane.

If there's a pose, well then, time for a photo. Who will take it? Yours truly! So I took out the mobile. Who should I give the beer glass to? I gave it to Sid. So Sid put his own glass in Granny's hand. Naughty girl, drinking beer. Quick, take the photo.

Nooo noooo, Sid's Granny made some *nu nu*–type noises and sort of smiled and up it jumped—the rainbow, that is. I saw it myself. Colours leapt from the kite—or from the butterflies—the rainbow jumped up and dove into Granny's glass, where it rippled. And from there it twinkled in Granny's eyes. Rainbow here, rainbow there, rainbows, rainbows, everywhere! And the one reflected in the eyes the most sparkly of all. It's all captured in the photo. Here, the rainbow; there, the reflection. Believe, don't believe: come and see the photo yourself, what more can I say?

I can't say more because I can't become a character in this story. But I was also at the party. Well, it wasn't just any party, more like A Feast to Remember. Everyone came—myself included—and I was the witness to the rainbow. That's why

I've said so much. But now my time's up. I take a bow and leave these pages. Whatever comes next won't be said by me.

*

21

Breath is like a tiny bug. When it begins to disappear, it's a tiny wisp of a gasp that wriggles free between the gusts of air and the fierce winter chills and all the powerful ins and outs of the breaths of everyone around, and escapes—like a bug. The little bug burrows into elderly Ma, who lies perfectly still in her bed, trying to squeeze into the hole, to escape all the huffing puffing breaths coming behind her. Just like in holes—the deeper you go, the wider they open. The bug-like breath a chisel, chipping away at its own suffocation, thus creating the hole, so that it can pierce the darkness, and let there be light, and it will get a puff of air.

Air and light. And if it finds water anywhere, a colourful arc will form.

A colourful arc? What's that? A bow of rain. A rainbow?

★

22.

It wasn't the Last Supper, but it was the Last Lunch. An affair to remember. The Sun had received a special invite that day to appear in All His Splendour. These were the final days of winter and the last days before Bade's retirement. This moment would surely add Lustre to the Golden-Hued Radiance of the Sun. After this luncheon, only His Slenderest Rays would be so blessed. After leaving this house, He would hang suspended in the dusty sky, while the blackened air, heavy as iron, would dash about like a putt-putting scooter scattering His Rays hither and thither amongst the city's building jams and traffic jams. And only a handful of stragglers would notice these rays and guess at His Full Splendour, and their hearts would be gladdened. But there were still a few days left on this lawn, amongst these chrysanthemums, so pretty please, do come, O Sun King, O Surya Maharaj.

The Sun rarely spurns invitations from outgoing civil servants. He must know that the officers will go to great lengths to ensure that this will be a party the likes of which no previous officer could ever have dreamed. Such fragrances will waft, such laughter will burble, such adornment of bodies there will be; there will be gardens, tables, and chairs and servants attired in Mughal-style garb. My Brilliance will burst forth with such force upon witnessing all this; the earth dwellers can hardly imagine what I shall do, I shall pick up some tasty morsels in My Fingers, soften them in My Heat, envelope them in My Warm Breath, and thus I too will enjoy some of the delicacies. In My Sunfire Style. I need neither bite, nor chew; I merely inhale.

So the Sun dropped everything He was doing, leaving God knows how much of the world in darkness, and came to enthrone Himself with His orchestra. Fireworks. All sorts of marvels on display: cascading from the branches like waterfalls, burbling down the walls like a river, flaring up between the leaves like torches, blazing like lamps along the branches. Flaring and sparking. And gyrating across the neem leaves like Catherine wheels. And up to His Mischief in the Sky too: now giving the curly locks of the clouds a golden cast, now causing them to ripple. Or dressing them in spinning skirts sewn together with yellow luminescence, then grabbing hold of their hands and swiftly twirling them about until they burst out with golden cries of delight, and if the people below couldn't hear, it was only because the soft green grass they wandered over was itself undulating in golden waves, causing a couple of ladies in high heels and gents in designer shoes to lurch about and perhaps the rest did not stumble but were toddling along under the influence of something altogether different.

The chrysanthemums bounced about like footballs, heedless of where they went, whether they'd live or die: would they be crammed into flowerpots in a flat or remain showy princes in the garden of the next officer? Supremely unconcerned about anything else, they focus solely on this splendid occasion, as they bend over the passing trays, and wink and flirt as though a few bites, a few sips, are just for them.

And even on this day, efforts are underway to get Ma up:

Oh, tell Ma the sun is out!

And what a party it was! The date was immortalised in government files for evermore. What a last lunch Bade gave! Everyone who was anyone was there. Government employees new and old, bigwigs from the princely states, such as the Nawab Bahadur of Mamdot, or the Maharaja of Dhrangdhra, and also mill owners, such as Baghelu Ram and Petrolpumpwallah, and film personalities such as Nadia Asharfi and Panchu Kumar, and writer-newspaper types such as Tutu Goldy and Barbara Chhatri, and scores of other Very Important People as well. They say it was such a memorable party, every year new folks add themselves to the list of attendees. Those who missed it suffer from an inferiority complex, and in order to save face, are forced to lie about their attendance. True, there were some about whom it was publicly known they couldn't attend, such as a Senior Retired Officer in the Customs Department who at the time of the party had gone to take possession of her new Bali home. She already had homes all over the world—one in Goa, one in Calangute, one in Godaud village in Gazipur, one in Peru, Massachusetts, in the jungle, where if there's a knock on the door and you open it, you'll find a bear standing before you, palms pressed together, head bowed, begging you to invite him in and feed him honey; a home in the French Alps, in Gorbio, one somewhere by the sea in Denmark, one in Hungary, one in Edmonton, Canada, one in the south, by a temple, one in South America, near a lost but not extinct tribe, and perhaps a handful more in various other places, but the call from Bali just had to come at that particular moment, and on an international matter, and so what if you are from Customs, you simply must comply. But everyone else was present, and happiness was at its peak because where there's clout there's a queue, but if you lose the first, the second is quick to follow.

At that time everyone was swaying about Bade's lawn, the whole atmosphere was asway. The flowers winked, the clouds dallied, the leaves waltzed. The grass grooved, the people rocked. The Sun tinted the clouds.

Tell Ma the flowers are in bloom.

Things got a bit out of hand when the crockery and pottery, that is the pots and pans, began to wink. And to fall, too. The servants were scolded—Are you sneaking sips of the beer as you serve?

In the wake of dancing leaves grooving grass prancing sunlight, the leaping breezes barrel in like a band of small girls, playing all about Bade's home, snapping and scolding and lurching about, stopping here and there, but resting on no one in particular.

Aha, aha, what fun! Dancing singing conversation!

Open Amma's window.

And what aromas. A row of stalls lined one side of the lawn. Chinese, chaat, burgers, pasta. Barbeque, mushroom, potato, capsicum, seekh kabob, onions, reshmi kabob, pineapple. Puri, kachauri: filled with tomatoes, peas, dal. Pulau, palak paneer, mutton, chicken, fish. Jackfruit, aloo dum, parval, stuffed bitter gourd. Dosa, idli, uttappam: made of rawa, rice and suji. Pizza corner, pau bhaji corner, salad and fruit separate, food of every type. In such a heady atmosphere, what need for the sort of buzz that comes in bottles? But this is the age of excess, and the home of a Very Important Officer too, so in this arena too there is plenty—chilled beer, gin, sprite, fruit juice, vodka, white wine, rosé, red wine—pomegranate red, bright red, even topaz-red—cola, Pepsi, lassi, shikanji, jal jeera, twinkle-winkle sparkle-farkle.

And the jalebis, imaratis, balushahis sizzle and dance in the karahi. Ice cream, crème brûlée, kulfi, tiramisu, gulab jamun, soufflé, water lily seed kheer, sweet potato kheer, rice kheer. Halwa: moong dal and carrot, shahi tukde, cake, malpue, pastry. Papad, pakora, chutney, sauce, dips, pickle. How much should one enumerate? Have you come here to eat, or make lists?

But nothing compares to the topic of food from that-a-way —from where they used to grow roses. Such amusing battles cropped up between Bade and Bahu, everyone had to laugh… it's just that the spousal joshing could turn to anger at any moment. Bade was from the east, his wife from the west. If he asked for bharbhara, makuni, tikkar, guramma, she would make jhordoi, phajita, matha ghuinya, and on one occasion it came to such a head when the wife modernised the recipes of her in-laws' home and came up with a sattu—barley flour— milkshake. Sacrilege! Unthinkable!

Turn Amma's feet towards the sunlight.

Thankfully, no one attacked anyone at the Last Luncheon, and Bade did his home region proud by smugly flying the flag of his beloved regional dish, baati chokha. Around this station gathered the most well-heeled crowd of all, and how could it not attract a throng of rootless urbanites? How many of them had ever seen mango trees in mango country, let alone clusters of green mangoes hanging on branches? They didn't even know how to pronounce *baati chokha*.

Behind the house, where the lawn petered out on its way to the vegetable garden, a bit of brush had been cleared, and it was here that embers of cow dung cakes were burning in a metal container with baatis baking on top. On a large plate nearby sat the baati stuffing: the coarse grain flour and unique eastern UP-Bihar-style pickle made from large red chillies, crushed and mixed with garlic and salt. The crowd watches as Yadav ji forms the dough into balls. He fills them with the pickle mixture and places them on the dung patties to bake. As he shapes the dough, he stops to flip the baking baatis with the tongs. Everyone's watching Yadav ji as he bakes the baatis, fans the flame, and flips them. Everyone watches as the magic unfolds. Once the baatis are cooked, Yadav ji plucks them up with the tongs and brushes off the dusting of ash that's settled on them. He dips them into the fragrant cow-milk ghee in a nearby pot. The Sun recognises His own Hues in the shimmering ghee. Yadav ji places the ghee-rich baatis on a tray. As he cooks, everyone *oohs* and *aahs* and *vahs* as though offering cries of praise at a poetry recitation. As Yadav ji serves the ghee-dipped baatis in leaf bowls with baingan bharta, all the women reach out their hands. *I'm eating this even if it turns me into a football!* Bursts of laughter erupt on all sides. Yadav ji smiles and hands a bowl of fresh, hot baati to the next one. Yadav ji has travelled all the way from a far-off village to give the lunch party baatis extra pizzazz at the feast of his eldest son's boss, that is, Bade. Bade had got Yadav ji's eldest son a job in the railways, and now he too goes to visit him on occasion and stays in government quarters with his son.

Everyone longs for government employment. Chaprasi, constable, typist babu, driver, gardener, anything, so long as it's in a government office. Then you can breathe a sigh of relief for the rest of your life. You'll get training, education, take out a loan to reach your goal.

So there was Yadav ji, but there were also generations of the faithful here, whose parents—or their parents—or whose children—or their children—or they themselves, Bade—or his forebears—had helped secure the lucky charm of government work.

Like Vilas Ram and his wife, Rupa. He'd been ten years old when he came fleeing from the mountains. Having failed time and again to gain employment at Bade's place, he finally passed class ten, a necessary requirement for a government job, and after snivelling for years under Bade's patronage, slipping into his home respectfully wearing a cap, all the while getting older, he was given a permanent position in the CAG office after a few years on temporary status. He went back to his village at one point and got married. The next time he went, he returned with Rupa, and after that he produced two or three sons without needing to go to the village, and they would arrive at Bade's home at all hours of need, that is, both their need and Bade's, and when it came time for the Last Lunch, they simply had to be there. Then there was also Paltoo, Genda's husband, who had gone to the Atomic Energy Guest House where Bade had had him hired as the gardener. Every week he'd bring them bouquets: gladioli, tuberoses, sweet peas, carnations, you name it, which were arranged in the vases of the house, as per Madam's, that is Bahu's, wishes. And Kanthe Ram, who was Vilas Ram's uncle, and had come to the city to search for the runaway boy, and then never returned, because he saw his own future was here too. Bade, due to being a government official even after losing village, Ganga, roses, opium, attar, was everyone's Zill-e-Subhani, their Shadow of God, their Great Provider. A crowd would queue up in his durbar, their requests and paper slips writ large on their faces: *Please set this one up somewhere, get this one enrolled at such and such, have this one's illness looked into, this one's promotion is stalled, get it moving again, and this one had a false report entered at his police station, please, save him. If you just put in a word, Sahib ji, to the chief engineers…that Pendse Sir in the what-and-what municipal department, if you just give him a call …the medical superintendent knows you, they need a guard there.* Rati Lal came running back twice; once from the DG's place, where he was hired on the recommendation of Bade, who said go anyway and do as they say and soon as they can they'll admit you into the police, but for now he'd been placed as a sweeper at the police lines which he found intolerable, and the second time he came back because he'd been put to work in the private publishing house of the police officer's son as an odd jobber ferrying paper and books, etc., just do this for the time being. Bade explained that the whole province was under the DG, one of these days he would have him admitted into the police, but Rati Lal was not sure. He slept comfortably alongside all the other policemen on a bed with a quilt spread over him, got buttery roti, mutton, chicken to eat, but this is private, I want a government job and only that, please make it governmental, even if the salary is less than this, it must happen, otherwise what's wrong with Bade's home—he's from our village after all, he belongs to our caste. When Rati Lal's daughter came to the bungalow holding her mother's hand on holidays, she called Bade 'Papa' and Bahu 'Mummy' and they didn't mind at all. He will get him hired somewhere. Until then he can just do odd jobs. He can help look after the grandparents. He'll do everything, inside outside the house, running all about. Go ask about this at the electrical house, take this to the telephone office, go get milk and eggs, tie this up with twine, cook the vermicelli, put the keys in the locks, sell the newspapers to the rubbish collector, roast the corn, wrap it up and bring it nice and hot, take down the trunks, put the heater up, could you massage my toes, here, would you mind oiling my hair, make wicks for the clay lamps, scrub the puja dishes with ash and bring them here…I will do everything, and whatever is left, I'll do that too, and one day for sure they'll get me a government roost, for you Bade Sir, are the Protector of All. So many, oh how many, you have settled well in their lives and careers.

And there were also all those who addressed Bade with sundry kinship terms: Oh uncle, brother, nephew, son, brother-in-law, child, I am your brother, father, nephew, brother-in-law, beseeching his help, you must do this for me, you have to do this for me. Now if we get started on these too this topic will never come to an end.

This was what motivated all who were there, who had come with love from wherever they had been installed, they came to bow and scrape. Atomic and Water Boards, BSF AG Offices, the Collectorate, Health, Water, Disability Departments, Finance, Commerce, Popular Administration, and on and on and so on and so forth and their bosses too who were making double use of their own servants, with a *Move this out of the way, boy,* here, and a *Garbar Singh, bring me a beer* there.

It should thus be understood that a single strand connected all the guests and helpers taking part in the party, which resonated with every single demand, command, reprimand.

There were as many helpers as there were guests; Bade's home was a Raunak Mahal, a Palace of Merriment. And the door stood open for all who wished to enter, be it air, aroma, folks, serving dishes; and inside, they would find Kali Charan roasting Kashmiri spices, or Nandan Singh removing ice, dahi bada, and all sorts of other chilled things from the fridge; or Susheela, Kanthe Ram's daughter-in-law, washing and drying the fine glassware, along with Leelavati, her mother-in-law. Even Kanthe Ram's wife has arrived today, despite the crippling pain in her leg, but when you see her she is seated, leg propped up, bossing everyone around. Kripa Shankar is arranging crystal mugs on a tray, and Laltoo will fill them with beer. What to say? And if one starts, where to stop? Because no one is in a hurry, but late in the afternoon, heading in towards evening, people will begin to consider getting up to go and then they'll have to stop by the paan stall where Benarsi or Magahi or sweet leaves are washed in mineral water, then dried, then…if we described this entire process now, then what to leave out, such as the slaked lime, Gulkand, supari, cardamom, cloves, peppermint, liquorice, kimam, chewing tobacco—really, there's no end.

Absolutely everything was available, but today's round, it bears repeating, was won by Yadav ji's baatis. So much laughter bubbles up around him that the women who usually keep their lips pursed so they won't develop wrinkles now grin from ear to ear, laughing openly, their smile lines deepening and here to stay. Which means: all mouths were open wide, wrinkles outstretched.

Shift Amma's head towards the window.

Even the foreigner has been defeated by the baatis: his country, his culture, everything about him.

Foreigners have been purposefully overlooked so far. They are white people. The West. If you have them around it becomes all about them, because the world is their oyster. They are the ones who are creating it, and destroying it, but everyone sees them as the Creators; the Rest are perceived as the Destroyers, because they, the West, are the Centre, and the origin story is set by the Centre. The Rest are the rest. The kite, the decimal point, tea, the zero, typing, gunpowder, all come from over here, but only when they reached the West did they made their debut in the world. All the hues come from the Rest—black, brown, yellow—but the uncoloured, not the coloured, came to be considered the One True Colour. the West and the Rest: the former are reality, the latter, dull, drab, worthless. Memory comes from them, forgetting from them too. They had forgotten ancient Greece, which they consider the origin of their thinking, for centuries and centuries. It was the Arabs who enshrined that memory in their own treasury of knowledge, otherwise, how else would the West have experienced the Renaissance? But it happened and it took place in the West, so the Arabs ended up becoming the Rest as well.

But why drag animosity and hostility into this Last Lunch? It was the good fortune of the foreigners that the Sun fell upon their locks, so all that came were warmly welcomed. And after all, there will always be foreigners at such parties.

Go ahead and be enchanted by the sight of them, but at least don't let them become The Best right now. Why bother to list their names? Allow them to buzz about in the sunlight amongst the tents of snacks, sweets, and other delicacies. Let their eyes pop out like the baatis they goggle at, as they wonder at this marvel, crying, *Amazing! What is this miracle!* and let them feel the spice and excitement on their tongues.

One such white person, that is, a colourless, colour-free individual, had arrived with Beti. Name of Arild. But since the absence of colour is considered the most desirable colour, he drew the winning score. Everyone greeted him warmly. The Sun entwined with his golden hair, and as he wasn't wearing any glasses, his blue eyes glittered. Wow, how lovely, wow, how amazing, wow, how yummy, he kept saying, and the people who greeted him kept hold of his hand extra long and laughed loudly.

Come see Ma.

Where are you from, bhai, someone asked at the beginning of the party. No, not like that—like this: Where do you hail from, brother? And then other people started asking: Where is Iceland anyway? Is that Eskimoland? But where?

No, no. Not Eskimoland. But also, actually, Eskimos are Inuits. And live in Greenland, some of them.

Then who is from your land?

Nature.

And you?

We are the useless grasses and weeds that have grown up amidst it. Water, volcano, rocks: those are the citizens. Understand? Rocks. That's what we have in our country.

We have everything in our country: Bade took up the baton of hostliness. Anything you can think of: any religion, any animal, any fruit or vegetable, any natural creation, any misfortune, be it McDonald's or an illness, any dishonesty:

manifold, multifaceted, abundant. Even an abundance of deprivation. Of timelessness, of starvation, of floods, of joy, of fun.

Beti also laughed. She began to take part in the game as well. Name anything in any corner of the world, we've got it here: Ice, sea, kiwi, strawberry, blue eyes, mangoes...

Mangoes? Bade's wife took up the thread at mangoes. This was everyone's hobby horse. All things in the world on one side, mangoes by themselves on the other. The mango contains multitudes. Any long list of things could be substituted with a list of mango types just as long.

Ah yes, the mango! All foreigners present bow their heads in respect.

Oh, mangoes, how we love thee. Shall we count the ways? A chorus of voices rose at the party like the cries of bettors in a gambling den.

Dashehri.

Chausa.

Ask Ma for some other names.

Totapari.

Langda.

Rataul.

Badami, ratnagiri, amrapali, sindoori, fazli, neelam, deshi, kishanbhog, and that most pale and white of all the mangoes, the safeda...

Like me. Ha ha ha. The foreigner must have known that every country has its openness, be it regarding attire, or witticisms. So he thought, *before anyone else does it, I'll just make fun of myself.*

Yes, like you, said Beti with a chuckle. Today no one needed to avoid anyone else's gaze. On the contrary, today even her baggy, saggy clothing had its place. She was an odd duck for the folk of such gatherings, but at the same time she was a world traveller and someone who appeared at swanky dinners. Today she wore a beige and turmeric batik lungi, a blue-and-black floral Rajasthani kurta and a purple-and-red striped dupatta slung sloppily over the whole thing in an inelegant manner, tied at the waist at one end, flung over her shoulder on the other. It was neither Eastern attire, nor Punjabi, nor a sari, nor anything else recognizable. No matching colours, no interesting mismatch. But she had with her a white friend, who wore an expensive suit-boot-tie, and that boosted her status. His acceptance of her made her world-accepted. The two of them had just returned from Bhogaon, where they'd been researching something about the education of girls in traditional families that they planned to write about. What exactly, no one understood, but they did learn that the market for the education of girls these days was hot.

Everyone went on with hilarity about Bhogaon as they had about Iceland: what godforsaken place is that and where on the globe, across what oceans, and why on earth are you going there, and who on earth goes to Bhogaon, and there was much merriment at the unfamiliar and funny name of the place: Bhogaon, hahahaha, so ridiculous—it sounds like a curse word!

Now please do tell me, said someone handing Arild some baati on a leaf plate, do you have a Bhogaon where you're from? Ah, but we have one here. And do you have baati? Because we do.

No—Arild admitted defeat, a wonderful sport. He rolled his trousers to the knee and squatted down, garnering much praise that he was able to sit like us. He squatted down next to Yadav ji and soon he too was making and serving baatis and the laughter at the foreign chef enthroned in the garden echoed all the way to the street.

But Ma just lay there, her back utterly disenchanted with all the blasted merriment.

★

The door does not dance. Everything passes through it: people air colour laughter sunlight flies aroma gnats dust motes bits of intoxication snatches of conversation flotsam jetsam. Door wide open. Standing perfectly quiet. Still. Placidly cool for centuries. It sees all, hears all, understands the heads and tails of things with no head or tail at all. Those who hear for only a moment don't understand the context, and in this atmosphere they don't even care to, and in this age, what's hard to understand is not worth struggling with, but the door does not see with superficial narrowed vision; it recognises the unpresent. It is experienced, sagacious, solid, learned.

Ravi Shankar had been playing inside. Someone's wife found him depressing. So now it was Shammi Kapoor—*Aai Aai Ya Suku Suku*. And then at some point that turned into Sufi qawwali. But when Sid and his gang changed the music again and put on earth-shattering dance music everyone gets up and starts to dance. It all started with Never-Repeat Saloni Sunder, the young-at-heart ex-wife of the ex-governor. She always wears saris and everyone always says they could swear they'd never seen her wear the same one more than once.

Such mentions are a code understood by those in the know, while everyone else wonders what they're whispering and giggling about. For example, the moment they encounter Brigadier Tota Ram Jhapota, or just at the mere mention of his name, they immediately start the usual conversation: That even when asleep, he's dressed in crisply pressed trousers and shirt, a belt cinched around the waist of the one and a tie round the collar of the other, and anyone who's arrived suddenly at his home in the dead of night has confirmed this. But there's a disagreement as to whether or not he takes off his polished lace-up shoes to go to bed. Then someone will say that he even wears pressed underwear and doesn't take that off either. And as always, someone must interject *But look he does have four kids*, at which someone else will chortle, *Stop it there are children present,hush hush,* and the children wandering nearby feign complete innocence, deafness at the insinuations, etc.

Thus passed the afternoon, ready to go on until evening melted into night, and still ready for more, as if the lamps must burn in every colour until dawn—*shama har rang mein jalti hai sahar hone tak.* There is nothing but love and affection, camaraderie, amiability, affability between everyone. No complaints or accusations, the host, the guests, gentlefolk, bathing in fountains of sunlight, jostling together, but no one crying, *Get out of my way!* No one higher than any other, or lower, no *this is yours this is mine*, shabby fashion too is fashion these days, New York and Paris styles are glamorous as ever, and everyone said, *Wow, what a lunch party! So exciting.* And thrilling conversations, and endless eagerness, about Ma, about getting her up.

Get Amma up.

Ooh, where are you getting the mustard oil from?

It's in Amma's room, ask her.

Put sugar cane juice in my gin.

Give some to Amma.

Will she drink gin?
Ha ha hee hee. I only drink such a mixture if it's organic.

Amma will say yes.

Give us the chrysanthemums when you leave.

He'll get an Australian passport. But it's not as though he's forgotten us. He calls every day.

That one (meaning Overseas Son) looks after his Mom. This one (meaning Bade) after his Ma.

Ma is snoring softly. Real or fake? No one knows for sure these days. Finding her sleeping when they enter the room, they tiptoe away again.

She's sleeping.
Let her sleep.
But she sleeps all the time!
She doesn't want to do anything.

Bade is worried about the chequebook. Every time they need her to sign something they have to get her up. He should tell Sid to get her signature on several cheques at once. Invest money judiciously, otherwise it will just rot in the bank. Ma doesn't bother with all this, she's not into it at all. But she's not into anything. That's the problem.

Poor thing.

Ever since Papa.

Introduce her to the blue-eyed fellow.

No, no, let her be.

Tell her Maksoo's here; then she'll get up.

Oh, come now, she won't sit up for anybody's name.

She's in a deep sleep. Listen to her snoring.

Like she's whistling.

Urgent announcement. Everyone please take an aloe vera plant before leaving.

Give me chrysanthemums, they'll be better for my health.

Pour whiskey into your ear, all the dirt will rise to the top. Drunk.

Did you put in Amma's eardrops?

You take care of everything. Men think they're doing it. Could he have done any of it without you?

I'll dance on one condition: that I get a turn with each of the ladies.

Are we planning to stay here till dawn, or what?

Tell her Madhusudan wants to see her, then she'll get up.

She won't get up, she just lies there.

Bhai, your jalebis are amazing, but your sandals are even better.

It's herbal, it won't do any damage.

Sandals? Herbal?

They live in an old folk's home. Those days are coming here too.

There was a monkey lying dead in the water tank. Since then we've been getting Bisleri.

He's Pakistani. Which is very non-herbal.

It'll be good if they come, our children are not going to take care of us like this. Even if they want to, their partners will put up a fight.

You really take good care of your mother, bhai.

What floor is the flat on?

They're laughing, the dancing couples.

Second? Where will you put the chrysanthemums? Tiny little balcony.

There isn't a lift.

So where will Aunty go? (meaning Bade's mother, a.k.a. Ma)

She'll climb up, slowly, but the chrysanthemums…

Where else will she go but with us? There's only us to take charge of her. Who else will take the responsibility? (meaning Bade's mother)

Not all the servants will go.

We'll end up being the servants, what else?

But anyway, your family members keep coming, that helps.

To gobble up all our food. They bring their friends as well. They conveniently feel like family when they come for a visit, but otherwise they're modern and alone.

She never gets out of bed. Why would she need to go down the stairs? (Bade's mother)

My son gave her such a lovely cane but she won't get up. (Bade's mother)

The door is silent. Resolute. Watching, listening to everyone. The back has its back to all.

The cane lies still; Sid has shown off its trick today as well. What he hasn't shown is that it can be lifted up and held straight, outstretched in the air, like a tree, but who knows where ideas come from, and when.

★

23

There was a time, they say, when all was fixed, and there was no zig, no zag. At least that's what they say; it's up to you and me to decide whether or not to believe it. That each human was safely ensconced in his or her own role in society and knew how to behave with whom. For example, a Japanese person knew at which angle to bow in greeting, and for how long to continue to bow, even after so-and-so had disappeared round the bend. An elder knew that one need only raise one's eyes before speaking to get a young person to jump up and carry out one's wishes. A tree knew that as soon as the first drop fell, the rains had come, and it was time to ripen the fruit and let it drop. Et cetera.

But now all of nature is plagued with confusion. The time when the raindrop will fall is no longer fixed; will it forget to come, will it stay, or will it come and close its eyes and doze and then forget to blink? We don't know. The tree will feel cheated and wonder where it's supposed to grow its fruit, the birds will hang suspended in the air, feeling cheated, wondering if the snow will melt over here or if it will already be dry over there, so where to fly, and many will die off in such moments of confusion, and neither snow nor rain will fall, instead it will be the birds that rain dead from the sky. The aubergine will forget it's an aubergine, and if you stick it with a needle, it will scream and turn into a pumpkin. The aubergine lacked the right genes, but now all the fruit and vegetables have lost their taste, and bananas taste like flour, spinach like acid. Even vegetables like lauki will shrivel up and have a dusty rusty taste like something from a dunghill. That is, nothing is clearly recognisable and everything has become a topsy-turvy mishmash; all the other things will also turn into a topsy-turvy mishmashes, and then they won't know what came first, the chicken or the egg. Did the egg have any link to the chicken at all? Or the chicken to the rooster? Even that much is a blessing, but when a machine which prides itself on its precise mechanical qualities, and thinks, We don't have that waywardness that humans have where it's sometimes this, sometimes that, what we know, we know, and we don't suffer from the disease of creativity, that makes people say this today, that tomorrow, if even its mechanical precision gets flawed, then what trick of fate might it be? The cell phone will tell you one minute, this number is out of service, then the next *this number does not exist,* and then, whaddya know, the number works! So then naturally, what has happened will happen: the jacking and hijacking of roles; the back-to-front of related relationships. How does mankind soldier on, or animalkind, or lock, stock, and barrelkind? It's all gone missing from democracy nowadays.

So that's it, then? But no, it's not over yet. Leaf leads from leaf to leaf—as in a banana clump—and belief to belief. As mentioned above, the cells have got messed up in all the push-shove. The millions and billions of cells which bind the material world. Their placement was fixed. If this lot joins together, they make this shape and this unit and this entity. But the cells have been jostled too and the accounting for the cells of the aubergine pumpkin lauki poison have got all discombobulated. What will they turn into if they get stuck together? They don't remember anymore. And there are chaotic never-before odd couplings. This with this and that with that. Speak of this then this is the story, blend these cells with those then another story. This story belongs to these cells, and if you join some of these cells with those ones, you'll get a different story. Join a belly with a back and get one story, a belly to a wall and get another, and peel the back away from the rest, and you get another and another and another.

At the Last Lunch, the cells of the collective were all gathered in one place and the resulting unit was tasked with eat, drink, and be merry. Only the back was turned. Alone and separate from all the partying parts and apart from the entire family growing fat as from a swelling injection. The thought of throwing one's self into eat, drink, be merry recalls the back to a life which no, no, no more please. An attack on the turned away back. A bedlam for the torn and worn.

This isn't just hee hee ha ha it's hoo ha, it's brouhaha. It sandpapers the back, creating sand. She sinks into the sand, and the sand spreads further. One can walk on it. She can walk. She walks along. Barefoot, wind blowing. Sand swirling. Immersed. Years of dreck turn to sand and begin to fall away. Let her slip, tumble; she will be freed, she will keep shrinking, growing lighter. So light, she'll start to rise from the sand. As from a tomb. As from a trance. As from a tomb-like trance. She will begin to fly with the particles of sand. A whistling sound will emerge from her mouth; it will tremble in an unfamiliar world, binding air to air.

★

People never tired of chatting about the Last Lunch, for years to come. Everything and anything had happened there, supposedly, and in every account something was still left out, so the accounts never came to an end. Everyone had come, everyone had taken part in the festivities. The heap of discarded clay cups and leaf plates grew so mountainous, it seemed to boast, *Who can top me?* And the Municipal Committee paid its respects by refraining from removing said mountain for several days. Grass, leaves, straw rustled about as though fragments of dance and song had lodged in them and still shimmied away inside.

But after the party new goings-on got going. The party had been like a wedding. That is, an end-of-being-an-officer party —so a wedding to top all weddings. One could say that now that the officer party was over, things were like they are after a wedding, when the bride and groom have gone on their honeymoon. Brooms sweep, tents and canopies are dismantled, the pavilion is removed, the chairs, decorations and durrees are loaded onto trucks, everything rented or leased is returned, and now a new commotion breaks out, accompanied by the melody of the post-wedding lament. That is, the rituals have been carried out, and the time has come to depart from the wedding home where the marvellous party was held, to set out for a simpler dwelling.

And thus, after the lunch party, Bade's home began to empty out and was filled instead with the shifting and shuttling of labour. Clouds of dust flew about as all belongings were packed in boxes, sewn up in sacks.

A reliable old battalion: Vilas Ram, Kanthe Ram, Rupa, Susheela, their children, etc., all were present because one should keep an eye on workers coming from the outside: make sure nothing gets a scratch or crack or is whisked off midway. Everyone was coated in dust and sawdust and overseen by Sahib and Mem Sahib—Bade and Bahu.

This was not a party, but there were rounds of tea and refreshments, things chugged along, hot snacks and lukewarm hospitality for the workers, and through it all, the pandemonium of the wind returned.

It isn't easy to squeeze everything out of one home and into another. What to take, what to leave behind? What had to happen happened, because no matter how much we believe in our own uniqueness, we're just like everybody else. Husband and wife clash and clang. Whether meaningful, meaningless, or meaning-neutral, there is no lane or nook where their clanging does not resound. A painting and a framed photo, a leather seat called a pouf and a carved vase—if one of them got these packed, the other would remind them that Sid and Serious Son, when they were small, kept demanding water at night, but you never woke up. The other says that the trash cans buckets floor mat shoe cupboard must all be taken along, then the ledger of marital complaint opens—the diamond jewellery set that had been given to Bahu by Bade's family and was much flaunted is brought up and faulted as not half what it was claimed to be, taunted as second-hand, and she had got it checked at the jeweller's, and had felt so embarrassed.

Throw out the files, they're of no use.

I bought all these things, I have the right to decide.

There's no room there, you're just in the habit of filling every available space.

Look over here, all my things fit into this tiny corner, that's what it will be like there too.

The whole house is full of your rubbish.

Whose is this? And this? Susheela whose nonsense is filling every box and every cabinet? And this is Amma's, which she doesn't even look at…

Don't speak of Amma. She takes up no space, she doesn't use anything.

But her stuff is here. All around. And she'll go there to live too, with all her possessions, used or unused.

And we'll store the flowerpots on our heads or what? The plants might die but you still don't think we should give them away…

By the time Sid entered swinging a tennis racket, the heat was at its pinnacle. Now what? What happened, he asked Susheela. Who said, suppressing a laugh, Mem Sahib is saying to make khichadi; Sahib says to make parathas.

Ai, don't lie. I said make whatever you need to, just tea for me, snarled Bahu, putting the phone aside for one moment, and then returning across the seven seas to complain about her ghastly situation.

Rubbish! Bade leapt up in the next room. What I said was, parathas are more sensible. Khichadi will go cold.

There's so much dust everywhere, parathas are made out in the open, Bahu again, holding the phone away from her face. Amma also eats light.

Amma will only get up if she smells the fragrance of parathas.

But she won't get up.

What do you mean? Bade was enraged, as if there was a hidden meaning to Bahu's words.

Did you hear, did you hear? Bahu told her younger son across the seven seas. This is how he picks on me.

Mom, why are you ruining his party. He wants to enjoy himself there, you're bothering him with the problems here, interrupted Sid. He tried to cheer everyone up. Just think, he's probably sitting around with his white girlfriend drinking beer. And here you are gritting things up with the taste of dust and khichadi.

Would any mother act this way? Because of her, he can't even have a girlfriend. She keeps him stewing in her worries. Every time you look, she's picking up the phone to register a complaint with Overseas Son.

Parathas, Susheela suggested softly.

See? Now even the servants are stubborn and don't respect me, Bahu's voice echoed across the world.

Maybe, suggested Sid, trying out another joke, my little brother has got himself a black girlfriend. Or Chinese!

Never. He tells me everything.

Or a boyfriend, Sid teased further.

Both parents looked startled.

Did you clean the idols? rebuked Bade. Change of subject.

Only the one in Mata ji's room is left.

We'll pack her room last. We'll move them all then. Go make tea.

Man worships the idols he himself creates. But not those that God has made. This thought rose from someone's mind and swirled away in the dust.

Sahib, we're out of tea.

What are you mumbling, Kanthe Ram? Have you taken down the curtains? Count the curtain rings and pack them up.

Then get tea from the store, Bade glared motioning towards Bahu.

Bahu turned her face away, still holding the phone.

Sid took out his wallet.

That's why there's no respect. She won't even get the tea.

I'm the one who gives money every day for everything. After lunch I was the one who gave the tips.

And the one who's quietly filling her own kitty.

I have my own account, I have no need to steal from you.

You don't take one paisa from your own account. You just spend on yourself, and guard all the rest.

I buy the gifts for the children; the shirt Sid is wearing, that seat cover of Ma's…

That came from Australia, why are you telling lie after lie?

See how he talks! The thing I brought from the hospital to make the commode seat higher, that's what I'm talking about.

Hospital stuff is all freebies.

You two are like a pair of schoolboys.

Hospital stuff is free, so what would you have spent on that?

So will he give free things?

No, he won't, I'm the one who gives free things.

You menfolk think just because you spend on some of the big ostentatious necessities, that everything is your doing. All the unscheduled expenses fall on my head.

Such as?

Such as on your relatives who always show up at mealtimes …

Ah, so yours don't?

And their daily changing friends.

Hide your stinginess, Madame, at least for the sake of your reputation.

Honey for Ma…

Don't bring up Ma.

Why not? I buy the honey.

Because it's from your cousin's farm.

So what, Amma…

And Amma, who contributes everything here? Bade growled.

You would know that. You're the one who makes her sign everything so you can invest her pension all over.

Oho, the two of you.

Mem Sahib, please take your tea.

Dirty mind! Would Amma want her money to be wasted? She signs willingly. Her money has been put to good use—that land in Ghaziabad, the NOIDA flat…

Oh, wonderful, does she even have any idea where her money is going?

It's all hers, all in her name.

Like she'll use it! Well, come on, let's stay in her cottage in Sahupuri. It'll be better than the pint-sized flat you're taking her to.

If she wants to, that's where we'll go. And if she won't go, she'll give it to her grandchildren. I have nothing to do with it. And I don't get saris and jewellery purchased either by Amma or by my sons.

Arre, arre, the two of you, Sid scolded.

What do you mean? Say it openly.

Forget it, don't say anything. Don't bother, don't do anything, intervened Overseas Son on the phone.

He's saying don't do anything, said Bahu, to indicate that she was not alone.

It's easy to sit all the way over there and be the director.

Plan a visit here and just come, suggested Overseas Son.

He's saying, leave everything and come to me, crowed Bahu victoriously.

Well go then. Then you'll see.

Okay, behave. Everyone fell silent at Sid's voice.

One of the labourers was conversing nearby. His words echoed in the silence: Lord Ram ram-bles into our hearts—that's why we call him Ram.

He started on hearing his voice alone in the quiet and fell silent.

And thus, the journey towards retired life now underway, the couple raised such a ruckus that all other din faded to silence.

★

25

Where do customs come from? someone must have asked. From a sparrow, came the terse reply. Upon which, an orator gave an entire speech on the subject.

A synopsis is presented here:

In the medieval period, there was once a country with medieval jungles. The jungles covered the mountain slopes and the fruiting and flowering vegetation bore such names as: oak beech poplar pine chestnut lime. Birds nested in the trees and jested with sparrows morning to evening. The forest echoed with cheerful cheepings and fond bondings and greetings of Ram Salaam, Ram Salaam.

Among these, one sparrow came to be especially beloved and adored by all. The Sun was so delighted by her that He would drop down a garland of flowers for her to swing on, sometimes bathing her in a fountain of golden rays, and sometimes He would just shine and twinkle and make merry with her. He felt so merry with her, and so delighted, that she became a fairy with red-tinted wings. Because the colours of those who embrace melt into one another. Now the sparrow flounced about even more, and the towering trees shadowed her with affection, and when she boldly hopped about on their branches, waves of redness infused their leaves, and in some weather the trees were so dense with red foliage, it seemed they were covered not with leaves but with cascades of scarlet flowers.

And everything as far as the eye could see glowed red.

Then a horseman rode in from far away. He beheld the scarlet hues. His muscles pulsed. This excited his horse who ran and tried to leap into the redness of the Sun. The intoxication of the red forest thrilled them both. There was no limit to the horseman's ambitions because he had money and a gun. First, he made his home on the hill. He planted potatoes and lit a fire where potatoes roasted in their jackets and men gathered round to sing and dance about the blaze.

The red fairy of the red forest stared on wide-eyed. She who had only known goodness and plenty of love, what did she know of fear and hate? She went hopping towards the festivities. Her eyes had grown larger than her entire body. What is a sparrow anyway, besides two large eager eyes and a heap of feathers? What is that music playing, and that dancing? She shrugged off the warnings of her elders, the trees and the fragrant earth. The Sun wished to warn her, but she retorted, You, Sir, are just red with envy.

The horseman saw something flap up that looked like a butterfly. He saw that the flames of the fire had reddened from the fluttering of her wings. He realised this was the redness that had spread throughout the surrounding forest. It was his nature to get excited by the latest craze and she was utterly delightful. The horseman was smitten. Such a lovely sparrow fairy! He got up and began to dance. The red fairy, considering this a summoning, began to dance on his head with cries of glee. Then on his shoulder, then on his nose, then on his chest. The fire too began to dance and romp and pepper itself with the redness of the red fairy, leaping higher and higher to touch her. The festivities had reached their peak.

She'll burn, someone laughed. She'll be tasty, joked another. The gun had also fallen in love. The horseman understood the gun's state of mind. He picked it up in his excitement and held it near the sparrow so they too could dance and sing together. Small as a robin but pride sky-high. At the touch of the gun, the sparrow's hips swivelled all the more. Oh, how well we make it dance, thought the gun, bursting with triumph. The group rollicked with such revelry that the gun made the fairy prance in the air dance atop the bullet and the whole forest was dumbfounded.

We all know that sparrows wander about and boldly go where they will, all the world over. They build nests in people's homes, skip hop jump on human shoulders and near their feet. They chat with themselves in mirrors and sometimes when the conversation gets heated they beat their own heads thinking if I beat myself then you'll be beaten, at which the mirror too gets soaked in blood trying to settle the matter amicably between bird and reflection.

And this now is the gist of the speech:

In the red forest the custom changed in broad daylight or in the dead of night—the sparrow became synonymous with fear. Customs fit to memory. So that no one remembers what had happened, they may not even know, but the heart feels fear thereafter, century after century. Just as the Urdu poet Firaq Gorakhpuri has written:

> *Ek muddat se teri yaad bhi aayi na hamen,*
> *aur ham bhul gae hon tujhe aisa bhi nahin*
> *I have not thought of you for ages,*
> *but it's not as though I've forgotten you either.*

This is the nature of customs. From then on, at every noise, the sparrows of the Red Forest began to behave as though the hunter approached and that the purpose of every gun was a display of machismo. They'd quickly hide their faces in the brush. Centuries passed, the hunters died or were killed, hunting was declared illegal, guns became binoculars or cameras, horsemen became bird-watchers, but the sparrows turned into bundles of fear. The custom carries on, even after the rationale has ended. The ornithologist Salim Ali is astonished and thinks these cannot be sparrows that have turned pale on seeing me; they grasp a straw tightly. But they were and are sparrows even though this behaviour is not innate to the species. That sparrow was born the Red Fairy over whom the Sun was besotted and because of whom the forest filled with gaiety. Now the Sun only visits the forest upon much coaxing, sulking and threats, and when He does, His light filters through the foliage old, weak, faded.

So customs are not the invention of the Almighty, are they? In short, declared the orator, The Almighty crafted them one way, The Sun warmed them in another, and machismo then exploited them. Machismo is hidden in the layers of nearly every custom, and its repulsiveness makes it no less macho, explained the orator. Joyousness grew fearful, the dance collapsed, happiness faded, and from this mixture the next generation was born, which does not know the reason for the mixture but has already acquired its nature.

So nature became habit.

Habit is custom.

Thus ended the speech.

Only the first time is there a spontaneous reaction. After that, it's all habit. Habit is just another word for repetition.

Repetition becomes empty and meaningless, but it is also routine. If you hear a sound, then what do you do? You duck in fear. The Sparrow of the Red Forest still continues this custom. For this is now her culture. These are the rules for her behaviour.

And truly, we are all of us like the sparrow. Our bowing rising fighting loving performing of rites and rituals are all born of habit and repetition. So whatever we do and however we do it, we are just enacting what has come down to us as custom ritual habit: friendships, marriage, sarcasm, manners and bearing, speech, love life, rising, sitting, anxiety, sister-in-law, aunt, daughter-in-law, mother, elder son, his son.

Today's program postponed as of now. Tomorrow we'll reconvene at the same time, when you will be presented with the next speech.

Hey, shut up, speaker! Take away his mic!

★

26

The truth of the matter is this: that not all its facets are revealed at once. Some will never be known. The handover of the home and the resettling and dislocation of those who had gathered there proceeds apace. The faucet begins an obstinate drip as if to gloat, *You won't call the plumber right away! So I'll take it easy for a few days.* The TV and hot-water geyser throw in the towel as though they've divined they'll be forced to move, so why slog on anymore, we'd really rather not bother. It's a new season, a change in the weather, but same as it was this time last year, it just went out to take the air in the intervening days and now it's back. The spiders wander about fretting that the objects around which they'd spun their webs for all eternity are being pulled out from under them, and they rush about on their many feet pitter patter pitter patter for fear of being dashed to the ground. This just proves it! they grumble to one another, No one has time for Gandhi nowadays! And no one even gives them a moment to complete this perceptive observation, and instead they too are taken out and flung roughly onto trucks.

In other words, not even the spiders have any idea what's going on.

Or else you must be like Sid, who's not interested in gathering together meagre shards of comprehension and pounding them into medals of valour and parading about with them pinned to his chest. Do what you must, do it simply, but don't flaunt it. Be your emotions, don't just perform them. Everyone has seen those sad sacks who weep in anguish, then secretly glance in the mirror to make sure they look properly anguished, pricking up their ears to ascertain if their weeping sounds miserable enough, and then their noggins start nodding with excitement over their own behaviour, so they must raise an unseen hand to restrain the old bean to ensure it doesn't exhibit the wrong emotion.

So does that mean beauty is beauty only when it's unaware of its own charms? Because if it begins to gaze upon itself, the dense eyebrows lose their allure, the delicate bones lose their finesse? Thus the poets and fakirs have said that beauty lies not in traditional head-to-toe outer manifestations, nor does feeling reside in the desire to experience a sensation, nor aesthetics in art that is merely technically proficient. Rather it lies in the spark, even if misshapen, that resides in the soul which is innocent and not preening; like Sid's, but even more gaily unassuming. So our Sid would arrive, singing, *Granny, chill chill*, and seeing so many years of everyone's lives packed into lorries and tempos, takes out his wallet at his parents' bickering and covers unexpected expenses, saying what must be said whether grand or bland, and does none of this in a way that draws attention to himself.

As the house is emptied, what dances happily is dust. Sneaks in wherever it wishes, collects in thick layers wherever it wants, so thick you could write in it. Rains down upon faces, where it reigns in glory. But still being swept from Ma's room, and kept far from the gods.

Aside from these two parties, Ma and the gods, all else is unsettled these days. Eating drinking standing sitting. The khichadi vs. paratha battle swiftly tilts from custom to habit to tradition. On this day there's a cricket match under the auspices of the American Centre. First of all, they were getting Americans to play cricket. Second, America is America, where Lakshmi has run off to, casting aside all the prayers and worship of her home country. So Sid and his team were flying high.

Breakfast! Make it snappy!

He bathed and rushed into the kitchen like a whirlwind. *Gotta jet!*

But here was Susheela praying to Mother Kali, head bowed, offering hibiscus flowers. Sid paused two seconds, then whirled like a spinning wheel towards the open door to call for Kanthe Ram. He'd only just opened his mouth when Kanthe's prayerful voice wafted towards him from the servants' quarters, intoning a Sanskrit prayer:

jvālā karāl mṛtyu gramsheṣāsur sudanam triśūlam pātu no dhīre bhadrakālī namostute.

Dammit he's probably standing on one foot right now, and by the time he finishes his puja, he'll be standing on his head in the sheershasan pose. And if I ask Leelawati to give me a quick snack, she'll show me her swollen feet, and say, Bhayya ji, look how painful it is, I can't walk even one step, I'm tied to this bed.

So?

So. *Mom!* howled Sid, at which Bade emerged freshly bathed, with a large copper dish full of Ganga water, a towel wrapped around his waist, and ran into him on his way to the Tulsi altar. He'd come outside to pour the water on the Tulsi and the Surya. He gestured to his eldest son, *Over there*. Bahu stood in the corner of the lawn under the Pipal tree bowing before the red threads tied about the trunk. *Mom...* Sid began, but swallowed his words with the swiftness of a sportsman when he saw that his mom's eyes were closed, and that she was chanting. She'd come outside after completing her early morning puja at the inside shrine. She wore a brocade-bordered silk shawl from Vaishno Devi over her head, and held up the copper puja tray adorned with flowers, peras, a clay lamp, water and incense. Sid came to a standstill. Then he began to walk along beside her. Mom would stop to salute every god in the house and circle the tray to perform the aarti, spreading the fragrance of the incense. *Once she's done, I'll speak*, Sid reasoned to himself. But the aarti must be performed before every single statue and image, except for the idol Bade said was worth lakhs and he would sell it to a museum if it weren't a memento of his father's from his District Judge days; which he'd got on a dig. So he couldn't sell it, but since it was cracked, they couldn't keep it out on display, and it was in Granny's room behind the clothing in her almirah. But the absence of one idol made no difference —the puja flame twinkled in every picture frame and there was no wall in the house on which some form of a goddess or god was not installed.

(Wrong. None in the bathrooms.)

And so the light of the clay lamp flickered over the walls, niches, tables, and the scent wafting from the incense hung in the air, and mother and son were making the rounds of the whole house, Mom chanting, son waiting. Togetherness, in a new sort of intimacy. Both walking, then stopping. One silent, one muttering to the flame of the burning lamp on the tray, first with a wave of the hand towards the deity, then towards the lamp, so that in the end, afterwards, at aarti-taking time, everyone's blessing would exist in the flame, and holding up the incense, circling it round and round two or three times, so that it would waft over all the deities, and their blessings would reach everyone in the house. And the gods were infinite: Durga, Kanha, Shiv Ling, Shreenathji, Kali, Nandi, Shirdi ke Sai, Narasimha, Saraswati, Radha, Krishna, Rama, Sita, Sai Baba of Puttaparthi, Hanuman, Lakshmi, Parvati, Vaishno Devi, Santoshi Mata. Gods on the walls, gods in every corner, even gods behind the doors, gods in the shadows of flowerpots: can any place be concealed from the gods? Their reach is infinite. And then the pictures of the grandparents and the great grandparents, because the gods also dwell in our forebears.

And Sid, a picture of patience.

But when they reached the glass shelf in the TV room, he gave up hope. For here dwelt the Ganesha collection amassed by Bade and Bahu. Ganeshas of glass, metal, wood. One of rexine they'd got from the Saturday Bazaar. One printed on a betel nut. And then the artistic Ganesha of stone and wood, with the nearly shapeless trunk and belly, and here we go, on to the contemporary Ganesha, lounging on a deck chair, wearing goggles, sitting cross-legged, book face down, chest resting on his belly, and the one that was five-faced and Ravana-esque, but not actually Ravana, and the one performing the tandav dance—and then another absorbed in dance, and the one holding up an umbrella, and the one giving a speech on a mic, perhaps in a shirt and trousers. Each and every day His forms multiply. It would come as no surprise if, as we speak and Bahu prays, Bade, or someone else, were to reach out from behind and add yet another Ganesha to sit amongst his many existing selves. The tray would simply turn in that direction, and the flame and the incense would circle and swirl toward that one.

It would take longer in here than all the circumambulations around the house put together. *Oh lord!* Sid struck his brow in consternation. He forged ahead and peered into the fridge to see what was in there, but nowadays provisions were scarce.

He dashed over to the garage to see if he could ask Vilas Ram's wife, Rupa, or Vilas Ram himself, to cook him up a quick rumble tumble or a paratha at their place, *gotta run*! but before he'd even made it there, both appeared before him, ringing the bells for their prayer group *om jay jagdish hare swami jay jagdish hare bhakt janon ke sankat pal mei dur kare* all praying for help to put an end to their problems. *But my problem is not ending, proof that I am no devotee*, Sid must have thought with annoyance. *Time to put an end to all this and do some stomach puja instead, find a place protected from the incense smoke of religious rituals and lay my head in the lap of my beloved Granny and then get out onto the field of play!*

So he picked up an apple, went in, not to ask for rumble tumble, but to say *Oh, chill, Granny, let's boogie woogie,* and was caught off guard at what confronted him: *Uh oh, what if the whole gods and goddesses thing is going down in here too?*

Granny had—as of when?—picked up the new cane, and lay flat on her back, holding it in the air at a ninety degree angle, eyes closed, still as a statue, looking every inch an other-worldly idol.

Cane, straight in the air. But before Sid could laugh, make a joke, a voice emanated from her direction:

I am the Wishing Tree. I am the Kalpataru.

Whether she had been inspired by all the other deities inhabiting the house, or by something else, no one knew, because, after all, there's quite a lot that no one knows.

★

27.

Worry lines formed on Leelavati's forehead when she heard. This was the same Leelavati who was Kanthe Ram's wife, and Susheela's mother-in-law, and the mother of Hero, whose real name was Champak, and whom Bade had helped get training as a driver, and a government job, but then he was thrown out of the Circuit House because he'd driven the car of the MLA Babu Mijaji Lal under the influence, although he'd been chewing fragrant supari paan to cover the booze smell, but then he kept opening the car door again and again and spitting out streams of red juice, which bore a stench of paan mixed with cheap country liquor, and that was what Mijaji Lal's daughter smelled, since she was sitting directly behind the driver's seat, so when the front door opened a boozy whiff wafted towards her, and possibly a few spittle drops as well, which she, luckily or unluckily, couldn't see in the dark, and the luckiest thing of all was that Babu Mijaji Lal ji himself had once been an ikka driver and was at that time only Mijaji, but after becoming an MLA added on the *Babu* as well as the *ji*, and wore brilliant white homespun round the clock which even a hint of paan spit could besmirch, because as a legislator even the slightest hint of such a droplet could ruin his name, but who can draw the veil of darkness over smells, so it was his daughter's nose that sank Champak's ship, since her complaint was heard and the driver was thrown out, and since then Bade had dubbed him Hero, and whenever Kanthe Ram or Leelavati entreated him, Oh, Bade, please find him work somewhere, then Bade would have to remind them, Look, I did get him a job, that's how the guy avoided getting thrown in jail, otherwise he did pretty much everything wrong, so where should I recommend him now, but nonetheless he did anyway, and Hero wound up with an opportunity as a labourer for a building contractor in some other city, and Bade explained to him that if he would learn the work, he, too, would become a contractor, and he'd make more money than he could imagine, but, he added, after I retire, you will have to build our home for free, and Sid Baba's home too, and everyone laughed, and take Phussa, for example, he was merely a plumber in some society, his job was to set the tiles when they were making the bathrooms and change the sink and shower, and then he became such an expert, starting out with toilet seats and washbasins, then moving on to windows, floors, walls, Italian mosaic, and double glazing and sliding screen and shower units, and he began building modular kitchens, and then he started getting contracts for entire homes, and look how grandly he dismounts from his scooter, commanding a vast battalion of labourers that stands waiting for him at the gate puffing bidis hoping for contracting work from Phussa Boss today, just let him come, wait and see, and so despite a name like *Phussa,* he's become a *Boss* as well, and you too will become Hero Boss, but here, too, Hero made it through three months somehow or other, then became a truck driver, and after that a taxi driver, and after that, for a long time there was no word from him, but one day the wind changed, flinging him back to his parents with a horribly messed-up kidney, and Bade handed over the money for his medical treatment accompanied by a stern tongue-lashing, and overnight, Kanthe Ram and Leelavati had taken leave and rushed him off to the village, whence, after quite a long time, they returned, bringing with them Hero and his newly-wedded bride, Susheela, and the boy seemed to have straightened out and began to earn his keep, although rumour had it that now and then he still reverted to form, and one recalls at least one night when Susheela refused to open the door and Hero began to caterwaul tunelessly outside, *gulaabi aankhen jo teri dekhin / sharabi yeh dil ho gaya—when I beheld your intoxicating eyes / drunk became this heart of mine*—at which Susheela banged the door open and gave him such a slap it echoed long through the night, but the song stopped, and Bade's snores as well, because he woke up, but by then there was only the moaning of the wind, into which he shouted, Keep it down, there are important officers all around here, and now Hero hangs curtains in the officers' homes, from rings, too, and fashionable chicks and blinds, as well, and he has a son and a daughter, Prince and Gudiya, who come in from playing or when they come home from school, whenever they wish, they knock on the kitchen window, calling out, Hey Amma, give us some ice water or something to eat, and sometimes they're allowed inside and told, Okay, help your mother clear the dishes and dry them, or go pick some coriander from the garden, but don't pull up the whole plant, but if they're not allowed in, they avoid eye contact and sneak in anyway, and if anyone sees them, they hurriedly turn their backs, at which Bahu gets very stern, and tells them to turn around and say namaste, and what do you have in your mouth, why are you hiding it, if you want something just ask, don't take it, to which they reply to the mistress, No, Sir, nothing in my mouth, Sir, and they hurriedly turn to leave, and in the process of speaking and swallowing everything in one gulp, they begin to cough, and at this, too, Bahu will start in about how a mother should pay attention to the children's habits so they don't get spoiled, otherwise they will come to a bad end, and groans and moans on and on, but that day none of this happened except that Prince's Daadi, Leelavati, who was elderly, but not as elderly as the Daadi lying in bed inside, wrinkled her forehead and said in a serious tone that that other Daadi was *the Wishing Tree*, at which her grandson, Prince, snuck into the house on the pretext of saying something to Susheela, and looking neither to the left nor the right, so no one would see him, thinking if he didn't see them, they wouldn't see him, but he found no one to stop him, strode fearlessly into the elderly Daadi's room and tiptoed up to her bedside to see if she would repeat what he'd heard she'd said early that morning when she'd been lying there holding her cane straight up in the air.

She was silent.

What's that, Mata ji, Prince asked, trying to get her to stir, and he glanced all around surreptitiously. But there was no one there to scold him—Bade had gone to the office to take care of various leftover tasks with the files, and Mem Sahib had gone to the new house to do some arranging and unpacking, and Sid Bhaiya had a cricket match. So Prince was the emperor now.

What do you hear if you're sleeping? Or does a question asked by a child remind you of a promise once made? There was a movement in the bed and the cane which had gone from *no* to *new*, having slipped somewhat with the vicissitudes of sleep, now awoke and stood upright and alert as before, or shall we say it was held at a right angle, as though it had risen on its own, and it lightly roused the elderly Daadi, who held the handle in one hand, and rested the other across her chest, and spake thus:

I am the Wishing Tree.

The boy chortled with joy and rushed to spread the news to all the servants' quarters and the entire neighbourhood, setting off the rumour from one home to another like a chain of firecrackers.

★

28

You can become anything if the time is right. It's also helpful to be in the right place. We can talk ourselves hoarse discussing the failure of Muhammad bin Tughlaq's ahead-of-his-time ideas, versus the success of Mahatma Gandhi's right-on-time revolution. Wrong time for one, right time for the other. The same can be said for writers—like G.V. Desani vs. Salman Rushdie. Or film stars! Consider Dilip Kumar vs. Amitabh Bachchan. But this much is indisputable, that if the woman in this story hadn't used her new cane in a new manner, i.e., at a ninety degree angle, at that very moment, or had done it somewhere else at some other time, then what happened next wouldn't have happened, perhaps, and what occurred after the thing that happened, that wouldn't have happened either. For example, had Bade or Bahu been home when Ma had become the Wishing Tree, then they'd never have allowed this whole tree-nightmare to come to fruition. *It's just a cane; doesn't matter if it's new or old, everyone go home now and us too.* The other thing is that if they'd been home, it wouldn't have been the time for all the other neighbourhood bureaucrats to be away, and the servant community would have been hard at work inside under the watchful eyes of their masters, not at the gate, or at the bend in the road, or at various favourite spots, or busy chatting intensely, or reclining in the style of their masters, taking sips of tea, and a couple of them sipping coffee and gossiping freely.

So when Prince came rushing out like a whirlwind, snapping and popping all about like a bunch of Diwali crackers, the rest of the children and their mothers and fathers heard him, and the right place and the right time arrived simultaneously, and presented itself to all. Then everyone got excited and clustered and clumped about, brows furrowed, and asked Leelavati, what is this tree thingy that's happening?

You've never heard of the Wishing Tree?

What's that?

It's a Wishing Tree.

Prince lay down full length right there and holding a stick high in the air, he intoned:

It's this.

Sparks of laughter shot up like flower-pot fireworks, and the whole crowd was about to dissolve into mirth when suddenly Leelavati's face turned red with rage.

This is no laughing matter, she spluttered. This is a matter of great religious significance, do you hear? She dusted the flour off her hands into the bowl, covered the kneaded dough with another bowl, washed her hands, and wiped them on the border of her sari. Then she slapped down a seat between the flowerpots and the private vehicles—the officers had driven away to the office in government cars—and sat down and began to expound deeply on the topic. To whit:

The Wishing Tree stands where I come from in Chamoli—Joshimati. It's always green—not a single leaf dries up or falls to the ground. People come from every corner of the world to worship it, great holy men have observed their austerities in its shade, and the sage Durvasa embarked on his meditation beneath the Wishing Tree.

So is Mata ji the sage Durvasa? Prince had stopped laughing by now.

The passersby who had paused their walking or cycling to listen waxed serious as well.

Wouldn't she get angry at everyone's giggles? She wasted her life on everyone. Look at her age! And there they are snorting and bickering.

Look, one elder reasoned. Make sure not to wish for anything bad, because she's going to give everyone whatever they wish for. And he told the tale of a man who had got tired and unknowingly fallen asleep beneath the Wishing Tree. When he awoke, he was beside himself with hunger and thirst. And so, yes, a wish arose in him to receive something to eat and drink.

And lo, food and drink were laid out before him. What's this! He felt dizzy but delighted, and ate and drank his fill. After this, he was overpowered by the urge to sleep. If only I had an old string bed to stretch out on. An old string bed immediately popped up before him. The man lay down, but now he felt a bit fearful. What's going on? He looked up at the tree overshadowing him and shrank back. I hope a demon isn't hidden in there, he'll fatten me up, then leap down and open up his maw and swallow me whole. And so it came to pass! A demon hopped down from the branches and gobbled him up.

A little girl began to cry.

There's a demon inside and he'll eat me up, *gulp gulp*!

No, sweetie, no, nothing like that will happen.

People began to whisper.

Along with calming the little girl, many more stories were told about the Wishing Tree. Everyone learned it had been born of the Great Churning of the Ocean, and the children looked up and down and peered inside the house. A tree whose roots are spread out in heaven, and those who stand beneath it will have all their wishes fulfilled! And listen, Mata ji has become the Wishing Tree!

She has enormous power. You must touch her feet.

★

People formed a queue. They stood with their palms pressed together and went inside one at a time to bow before Mata ji's feet. She remained lying down, cane held high, though now it had drooped to a thirty-five degree angle, more like a branch.

Mata ji, please arrange her marriage. Her complexion isn't that fair, but no one's her equal when it comes to housework, and if the in-laws agree, she can visit the homes of rich ladies and dye their hair with henna and massage their faces and wax their legs, and all those sorts of things. No harm done if a bit of money comes in!

Mata ji, please give him blessings. He's slow at computers, so he wasn't hired, but now he's taking a course for nine thousand rupees. Anything is possible if you give blessings: it will definitely help his hands move more quickly.

My uncle has got his hands on the shop. Please kick him out.

Please bring electricity to our village.

Please give Dhanno a son.

Please let me jump into the Jamuna, right where the new bridge is, Mata ji, and make it so that I learn how to swim the moment I jump in, just like dogs do, so I can swim from one side to the other, and everyone will be amazed. Just once.

Please install a tube well at Laltoo's house.

Mata ji, would you be able to bring us the kind of TV that looks like a wall, at some point before we die?

Please make him speak amazing English. We're having him tutored. Please turn his luck around.

May your blessings continue. May I continue to have the opportunity to serve you.

Great Grandmother, my Sirri Chacha, no Acche Chacha, no, no, it was Sirri Chacha, he brought me such a pretty parrot from the village. Pramod told me to put it on my shoulder and go up to the roof. The parrot flew away, Great Grandmother. I can't find it anywhere. I looked on the roofs of all the other houses. How will I find it? It flew so high, right in front of me! High as a plane! Can you please just call out to it once? Its name is Ram Lal.

May peace and happiness prevail, Mata ji, please give a blessing.

Make the rains come at the right time in the village, Mata ji. Last year the whole crop got washed away when it stood ripe in the field. Our home also collapsed in the flood. We're still paying the interest.

Okay, so, I've never seen snow fall. Only on TV. Please make it so I wake up one morning and see the snow falling outside my window.

Please just bless me so I'll live a long prosperous life, I have no other wish.

Mata ji, I'm secretly whispering this into your ear; this isn't anything to say to anyone else, but I'm very upset, Mata ji. You see, my mister, right, whose missus I am, Mata ji, this wart that's above my lip, he doesn't like it at all, and I don't either, and we have a love marriage, so he says, I'll lick it and make it dissolve, and sometimes he kind of bites it, but I don't like it, so, Mata ji, if you'll get rid of my wart, please, I'll be so grateful and we'll be an adoring mister and missus, thank you very much.

May greed disappear, may all be well and good.

Mujtaba wants me to come to Sharjah, but I want to go to America.

May I continue to fear the Almighty in my heart, may I be satisfied with what I get, may I remain happy, may your hand always rest upon my head, and nothing else, Mata ji, that's it.

It was a very holy atmosphere, everything was extremely genuine, when Prince, impressed by the prayers, said, Daadi, can I have a toffee? and right at that very second, his eye fell upon a silver bowl, where three toffees lay among a collection of buttons, bindis, and safety pins. His request had been heard.

Daadi? Now he turned towards Leelavati. Peace had spread about this room that had been touched by a miracle.

Then Gudiya requested the nail cutter set which lay beneath the engraved brass dish from Muradabad, the one that Papa had had retouched with fresh paint, and when she'd come to put away once in that same drawer of the dressing table, she'd seen it had every size of nail cutter in it and a flat little stick with a rough surface you could use to file your nails into a rounded shape. The cane waved in agreement. Gudiya reached out and took the set, gazed gratefully at the Wishing Tree, and pressed it to her forehead as she bowed respectfully.

By late afternoon, quite a few pieces of clothing, old shawls, sweaters, saris, blouses, petticoats, and other sundry items, including a somewhat lumpy but still very warm sleeping bag filled with goose down, and an iron wok and chapati pan that nonstick versions had shoved aside and had been stowed on the top shelf in Ma's room, and various other things that had Ma's name on them, which truth be told was the case for every single other thing, because they weren't needed anymore; but who throws out a new thing that's grown old, or something from long ago that one has held on to, like the spiky stem holder for sticking in flowers and leaves and twigs in an Ikebana flower arrangement, or something brought for her, like a crescent-shaped inflatable airplane neck pillow, or two thick photo albums which are no longer necessary for arranging pictures in nowadays but who throws out a new thing just because it's getting old, and all the things packed away in Ma ji's room in special spots because they might come in handy some day, but not right now. The cane agreed to all requests, and the people picked up their boons with grateful hands.

And so it was that when sky had turned to twilight, and Beti entered the house, Leelavati told her with deep reverence, Beti, the Wishing Tree even gave the boon of a daughter to whom? To none other than the Goddess Parvati, who in her loneliness found much joy with such an auspicious companion.

It's not clear what Beti understood from this conversation, or if she thought the whole thing was just idle banter, but as she walked swiftly over to her mother, she glanced at the wardrobe, and something occurred to her. She opened it and leaned over, muttering, My Buddha…

Listening all day to everyone's prayers and supplications would make anyone tired, and thus, the tree, or the branch, a.k.a. the cane, fell down upon the floor. With a clatter.

Then Kanthe Ram cried out, No, no, Bibi ji! as though stopping Beti from picking up the Buddha. As though the Wishing Tree had expressed this with its clatter.

No, no!

Just then, Bade entered the room. He'd heard everything. He'd also seen his sister standing before the Buddha.

That cracked thing would go for millions if I sold it to a museum! It'll break, he added sternly. Not looking at anyone in particular.

In the absence of direct communication between brother and sister, who would inquire whether he spoke of the Buddha, the cane, or what? Now that the entire household was in a disarray as they prepared to move, the beat and the melody of every single interaction was inevitably scrambled.

★

29.

When Bade and Beti were children, the skeletal Buddha would appear before them whenever they went to take something out of the cabinet. They were always frightened when they saw that skull-like face with its sunken dark pits for eyes. But they got so used to seeing it, it was almost as if the Buddha had become someone they knew. Their friendly-elderly-holy-man-person in the cabinet, whose beard and body hair they kind of liked to think were growing along with his age inside the cupboard. Those hollow eyes seemed to close in meditation, as if they'd burst with brilliance if they suddenly opened. And those large Gandhian ears, they felt like running their hands over them softly, and they did, too. But what impressed them most of all was the Buddha's emaciated body, which, during his many years of meditation, had become a delicate network of ribs, nerves, and veins covered with a fine layer of skin, like a transparent covering. As though all impurity had fallen away, and all that was left was beautiful, smooth, motionless, genuine. Daily, the idol became more refined and more serene. Ma called it my *heart-of-stone* and the children called it *the Starving Buddha* and their father called it *her* heart-of-stone, and he'd gaze over at her warmly, and Ma would grab hold of his hand, and the children would burst out laughing at this affectionate display. The ancient meditating Buddha was cracked. A bit of the shoulder was missing, and now there was only one dangling Buddha ear. The other had broken off somewhere. In the sand.

The children did not know the tale of the Bodhisattva, in which Gautam Budhha, having relinquished all wishes and desires, began to practice austerities on the sandy banks of a river in order to attain release from the grievous cycle of death and rebirth. One sesame seed, one grain of rice, daily, just to keep breathing, that's it. The sand slowly covered him, and gradually he became buried in a tomb of sand. He was a skeleton, a cage of ribs. Once he went down to bathe in the river and the tomb of sand started transforming into a tomb of water, and it was then that Sujata saw him. She poured a distillation of the milk of one thousand cows into his mouth, for which reason the Buddha was able to return from his trance, and he announced that neither sand nor water was the highest good, but rather the Middle Path. But the mystical light-cluster of the tomb of water and the tomb of sand brought a glow to his face, a brilliant lustre to his every grace, every image, every memory.

As a meditator descends into her trance, her every limb is pressed down into the sand and water. The yogic austerities she practices are not weakened by this, so that man-eating forces come to gnaw and suck on her in the guise of fish and crocodiles and other suchlike creatures. If the body-in-meditation dips below the surface like a sailor at sea, you will find all different parts of it bobbing about separately in the water: the head and the arm and the kidney and the ear. Each of these are beings absorbed in meditation, and are comprised of brick, skull, bone, vessel, jewellery, idol, pearl, shell, sound, breath, feather, topaz, grain, heart, story, romance, pebble, bits and bobs, ears, eyes, and so on and so forth.

But digging holes is holy. Whether you are excavating or expiating. It gets out anything and everything. Be they from sand or earth, water or air, old bones and old tales take form through both digging and divinity.

This is why it's difficult to bring progress to places like Israel and Italy, because as soon as you take out a spade to build some fresh new invention, centuries past start peeping through—an ear or a nose, even the eye of Jesus, and the faith of the faithful is restored. This is what it's like in Sumer and Mesopotamia, as well: no sooner do they reach down below the earth than old tales begin to rise from the tombs. The solution to this has been to hit them hard and fell them from above. Before the deities sunken deep in the earth can blink, they've already been demolished.

Nonetheless it's rare for the existence of such a tomb, which is not really a tomb, but a deep meditative trance called a samadhi, to be erased. As in Bamiyan, when the arms of Satan arrived laden with dynamite, *Mogambo khush hua*, and super-villains everywhere chuckled evilly, but then the hills slid down to reveal more idols entombed in samadhi deep within the earth and these popped up in other places. Dynamite, perturbed.

Meaning, even if centuries erode them or beasts and birds nibble away at them—even if villainy is heaped upon villainy —these tales, these tombs, these samadhis, these idols, they just won't die, nor will they remain buried forever. They remain seated in an attitude of meditation and slowly the sand dunes cover them, and they stay covered as long as they are meant to be.

When the ancients and the village dwellers run across these tombs, they bow down to them in reverence. Sometimes they take an ancient stone and enshrine it in their home or stable—same thing, really, since the home is a temple, and cattle and sheep are divine beings…

The advent of the British brought the Anglo angle into the treatment of such samadhis. Entombed skulls, bones, tales became items for display in museums, libraries, sitting rooms, offices. Speculators also set their prices. After tugging and digging and digging and tugging out their stories—which activities they refer to as *research*—they go about calling themselves storytellers and historians. Egotism, that is to say, digging and deifying one's self, has wholly replaced the holey and the holy and set up shop.

But why waste the precious time of this story? The curious need merely scan the newspapers now and again, and they will quickly come upon reports of egotism mixing with business. This one is a recent item: a Buddha sat in yogic samadhi thousands of years ago, was then dug up by egotism, encased in a leather preservative, and plonked down in the marketplace, and now he swirls about Western museums and exhibitions in a state of wandering samadhi, undesiring, unthinking.

That's why Papa—the father of Bade and Beti—who's come into this story only in passing, always used to say that when English people rip such Buddhas in samadhi from the soil and lock them up in museums, it is simply theft. Also a huge racket. And if they couldn't find the whole Buddha, they'd make do with assorted body parts—a head, an arm, a leg—uproot it from the soil, and nail it to their walls. So we're not wrong to keep this idol in our home, he'd conclude. It belongs in our home, where it's respected. It's valuable but we mustn't try to make money off it.

But Papa, and after him, Bade, said they mustn't keep the cracked Buddha out. So it went into the cabinet behind the door. Amma would offer it flowers, and sometimes she draped the rudraksh rosary about its neck, or she applied red power and sandal paste and ceremonial rice grains to its forehead, or offered the ancient Buddha some rava.

Gradually the entire family grew to feel a special reverence for their Buddha. As though he were their household God, giving his blessing to all from his niche; protecting them. Everyone considered it good luck to open the cabinet door once in a while and gaze upon him with devotion. And later at some point, Beti had said: Please give him to me, I've not taken anything else, and I don't believe in not putting out cracked statues; it'll live out in the open at my place. Never, Bade replied via Ma, Papa brought it here, and its place is in this household. And even later, it happened that one of Bahu's early-morning-yoga-walking buddies told her a knowledgeable art expert could inform them how old it was and how much it might be worth, it seems quite genuine, after all, must be worth lakhs, at which Bade's wife asked, What's the harm in finding out, at which Bade thundered that Papa had got it on a dig, and only you would get the cheap idea of selling it, what do you understand of a paternal symbol?

Was it got by digging or divinity? None thought this was a story about digging, nor did they think that the idol would get lost, not even in their wildest dreams, or Ma, either, no one could ever have imagined that, even when they saw it had happened.

★

30

One can mourn, but what's gone is gone. Whether given away as a gift or a blessing, or even taken through theft. Let us flip through the pages of history: once the Kohinoor was gone, it was gone. When the grand bell at the President's Residence in Shimla departed, it too was gone. Once Tagore's Nobel prize was stolen, was it likely to return? Or Bhupen Khakkar's painting *The Celebration of Guru Jayanti*. Or youth. Or time. If you look on Google, you'll find whole languages that have gone for good: Ako-Bo from the Andamans, and Aka-Kora, A-Pucikwar; Vypin from Cochin, Bidjara from Australia, and many, many more than these, and they keep on disappearing, and maybe Hindi will too. And of course, if you spend too much time on Google, you too may be gone. The river Saraswati is gone; where does it flow now? The dinosaurs are gone, and we can even refer to those beings we never find to begin with, such as the Yeti, as gone. *Gaya bhi gaya—Gaya is also gone*—for where are the remains of that famous seat of learning, the city which was once Gaya? And what of Bodh Gaya? When the brains—the bodh—drained away, it too was gone—*voh bhi gaya*. And if people go, they are gone, and some have gone in such a way that they've disappeared even more than totally, the way the Papa has left the home in this story. He left, meaning he's gone, and whatever he left undone, was left for the rest of them to do, and they got caught up in that, and it was as though even the space in their memories for their poor father had disappeared, the space where memories of his goodness might be stored, as in the tradition of constructing memory houses after a person's death, unless you are Hitler or Bin Laden, of whom we have only bad memories, because they really were men of unmixed evil, whereas many others we think of as evil, such as Duryodhana, may also be remembered as good guys: Duryodhana becomes Suyodhana, and even Ravana has been praised deeply, and in our own time, Jinnah is recalled with both good and bad memories, but the sum total of the thing is this: life is life and death is death, and what is dead is dead, and gone is gone, and busy is busy. The gist being that if great beings and treasures and memories depart, never to return, what happens to ordinary everyday items? Nothing. Yes, not to be thrown out in the trash, certainly worth selling, but they—because now everything disposable is saleable, and the poor grasping meekly—they are also gone—because one woman was on her deathbed and it had seemed to everyone— this one's gone too—that she was about to meet her maker, but they did not suspect that there was a bit of a mix-up while God was calling his dear ones to him, and she had become instead the Wishing Tree which everyone came to her doorstep to behold, and to seek blessings from, morning to afternoon.

Most of the house had emptied out by the time the rest of the living had returned, and Google would not come in handy in this instance, at least, for opening with one click the list of what went, what all was gone. Eons lay thickly coated in clouds of dust here. That which was immediately spotted was gone and seemed for the time being useless—for instance, Susheela had always wanted that bundle of polythene bags that Amma regularly packed away, because one always needs bags to carry things about. The departure of that bundle made no difference to the price of tea in China so it was best to just keep quiet about it.

If something unprecedented occurs, one falls silent for a bit. At a loss for words. Yes, God resides in children, yes, in elders too, but this particular godly form, what to say, what to do, where had it come from? Would it not make one look cheap to kick up a fuss over a hodgepodge of plastic junk? And to inventory what has gone, and send a messenger off to go peeping in the servants' quarters of the officers' homes to see what new acquisitions are being shown off, so they could initiate *ghar wapasi—Mission Return Home*? Or send the police inspector with search warrants so he can go into homes and say what? Whatever you took, you may quietly return it. People would talk. They'd say, these fancy folk have no compassion, whereas we have so much. She is the mother, in the last stage of her life, elderly, alone, a fit of generosity got into her, so just accept that it did, and face the fact that some odds and ends are now gone. At least Ma got some peace and pleasure out of it, otherwise, she was just lying there, thinking, *I'm useless now, I'm of no use to anyone*. Realise that our happiness lies in her happiness and just keep quiet.

And when Rosie Bua came they fell silent indeed. Or were they glad? Who knows? Rosie was a hijra, she'd visited Ma for years, calling her sister: Behin ji, Behin ji, asking for baksheesh on Holi, eidi on Eid; she came for the children's birthdays and celebrations, sometimes she took something, sometimes she brought something, and everyone had seen her outside with Ma, on the lawn, seated on a low stool, chatting and snacking on dal moth with tea. And on Christmas…

But that sentence remains incomplete.

★

31

Some sentences remain incomplete thanks to the moment in which they began. Because when Rosie Bua, who had got wind of the Wishing Tree—because how could she not— slipped into the house, Bade and Bahu abandoned their squabble and stared at her, flabbergasted. Rosie Bua clasped her hands together in reverence, but not to them, to their mother, whom she called Behin ji, and who was now the Wishing Tree, and whom she was now facing, having scooted in behind the other devotees. Deep inside the house now, not just outside on the lawn.

Of course the sentence had to remain incomplete.

Behin ji, your copy of *Vinodini* and the sandals, she said, hands pressed together, and Bade and Bahu, who were staring from outside the door, feeling incomplete themselves, wriggled as though in imitation of the cane, and Rosie Bua understood. She removed the book from the shelf herself, and motioned to Leelavati for the sandals.

They were sandals from Singapore; Beti had brought them back for Ma from some trip—white, light as butterflies, meant for the beach or just kicking about in the sand. They had pink flowers and green leaves on them and Ma had told Leelavati in front of Rosie, I hardly ever wear them, I'll give them to her next time, after they've been cleaned. Rosie Bua had said, Leelavati, remember to set them aside. And Leelavati had got a trifle peeved, and thought, *Oh, now it's my job to look after Hijra fashions.* Then Papa had passed away, winter had come, and it wasn't sandal season anymore. But now it was.

He didn't want me to give them to my niece, he must regret it now, Bahu muttered to herself.

Rosie stuffed the items received in boon into the embroidered chenille handbag slung over her shoulder and unfastened her loose bun, letting her hair fall down her back. She took out a colourful clip decorated with a twist of beads, pursed it between her lips, then gathered up her hair in a feminine manner, both arms raised, and looped it around in the air, refastening the bun and stuffing the clip back in.

The rocking chair has been carried off, fretted Bahu, just to render complete the incomplete.

Rosie had already left.

Why are you bringing that up? That happened before all this. *Incomplete* moved forward, Bade now pushing it along. Anyhow, it was given to Neepa's gardener.

So he can do some rocking between the hoeing and weeding?

It wasn't yours to give to whomever you want.

It wasn't hers either. Bansi brought it for the entire household.

But of course, everything is hers, one of them said softly.

But that music system was mine. Another objection raised.

I paid for it, objection upon objection.

I can't find the thermos anywhere.

Arre, I bought it from the canteen with my uncle's canteen card.

But I paid for it.

The money is always yours, no matter whose it is.

Grumbling and bumbling the two reached an agreement that not everything had to be wedged into the new house anyway, it just had to be taken out of this one. Okay this way. A touch of humour in crisis mode.

They had to move, the couple agreed maturely, and took a deep breath.

★

32

They had to move, but these doors and walls must remain. Is the home offended? Will the walls and doors come along, quietly, invisibly? Like a soul which resides within? That which resides within is what turns a home into a castle, or a henhouse, as the case may be. It has nothing to do with the measurements of the perimeter—surely you've heard? But within a house reside its inhabitants, so are they the soul? Around and about them are crammed all the objects on which they lie sit swing, but Bade and Bahu hardly have it in them to ponder such things. And paying close attention to the specific qualities of the home at this time would mean diving into the sort of cogitation that causes carelessness.

The house had all but disappeared into cardboard boxes and it had grown difficult for living persons to squeeze in amongst them. It was impossible to reach one another amidst the boxes scattered all about and also to carve out a space alone for a moment of peace.

What was in these boxes, what was not? The answers to these and other questions would be discovered in the coming days if their recollection remained clear. All boxes are not opened at once upon arrival in a new home. You'll find one thing, another thing you'll keep searching for, and a fresh quarrel will break out about where the stupid thing has gone, and *you lost it* or *did I hide it* or *that one was given away too*. Bits of string, paper, boxes, all will be anxiously flung about willy-nilly, and then...

And then nothing. How can they retrace their steps? So that the thief, or the Wishing Tree, or someone else can tell them that this is how such-and-such thing went missing?

At some point in the coming days, they will definitely figure out that the Buddha was not even packed, that it had gone missing. As had the elderly Ma.

★

3 3.

So it's like this: let's expand upon the topic of the elderly missing mother. Or the vice can be tightened around her daughter, who's a free spirit of the new age, liberated from familial values, at least according to herself. Or we can expand upon both women in alternating accounts, but that would surely be misleading.

But here's the thing. Who knows where a path will lead. If there were only one angle, one path, then the whole thing would be finished as soon as it started. But no: paths tangle and new horizons unfold. And sometimes people set out on new paths to see where they may lead. Some consider it a blessing to live surrounded by clarity and cleanliness so they get the whole picture in just one glance and a shallow understanding from a shallow glance, which they mistakenly think is deep and full.

Understanding has become a much eroded, much abused word, to the point that its sense has come to mean *to establish meaning,* when its real sense is *to displace meaning.* To give you such a shock you see lightning. And that shock is so clear pointed wounding shiny sharp, and earth and sky get swept into that, and between them, the sea, flowing like conversation, to make sense of each other, to keep trying, without coming to an end.

Be it cloud be it wave be it smoke be it air

Be it hill be it beast be it stone be it shrub

The simple thing is this, that a finished product is something that sparkles and glitters. Ask yourself, silly, what shines brighter than a mirage, and is it really false that the ground beneath it isn't solid and the air above it has no substance? And when we look upon it, do not hope, desire and poetry spring up within us?

Such a small thing, so just and true, causing confusion by the whim, our desire to know what the first most basic and the original, true colour is and the source from whence it burst forth; but how to know the source, which cave, when at all times the shadows of sky and ground, mountain and wind, hop about like bouncing balls? Now black, now grass green, now red, now rough now shiny now shadowy now round now prickly. Who knows what it has been and what it has become?

So in every story legend fable myth there lies a dollop of the unfathomable and a dash of the riddle and every tale delights in its own existence even if it packs a wallop. And when a loved one is lost in a story's maze then all the heart's joy turns to a grief coloured with every hue, and still there's no fun to be had.

So these were the shades on their faces when they learned that Ma was missing.

But where is Ma ji? She was just here.

A feminist soul might say that she wasn't there before, either, hadn't been for years, taking care of the house and children she was a wandering shadow whose self was, in reality, missing. But an philosopher might get entangled in questions like who is real and who is the shadow, and has anyone ever known that? Can separate authentic life not exist in every shade?

Wittgenstein once said, I am happy to live at the foot of a mountain without ever aspiring to climb to the peak. But Ma's children were not Wittgenstein that they would sit about quietly and wait, nor were they the aforementioned feminists that they would say she was already missing before. Their belief was that Ma was physically here up till now, and since she's no longer to be found in her bed, she's gone missing.

She who did not rise, how could she have risen that she thus arose?

Their minds turned to curd: hue and cry occurred.

★

34

Susheela's memory turned somersaults as she tried to remember: when she'd placed the thermos of hot water and lemon wedge on the tray with the glass and plate and gone in, had Ma ji been there then, or was she already missing? She'd been rebuked, but this was unjust. A mouse in a mountain, that's what the old lady in the quilt was like. You could hardly tell which fold hid her shrunken body. And Susheela always came when everyone was still asleep, when the shadows of night still lingered, at the crack of dawn, her face hidden in her shawl like a lady bandit, steam rising from her mouth, her eyes shadowed by darkness. She'd tiptoe to Ma's bedside, noiselessly set out the things on the teapoy, then quietly slip away. One standing, one lying down. Both mice.

Bade's attention had been divided.

He'd bathed in a hurry to get to the office and was quickly doing his puja circumambulation, circling the diya flame all around the entire house in devotion, and he'd gone into Ma's room and waved it about. In the midst of this, he'd half-noticed the shape of the quilt and thought, as he glanced mid-prayer from the corner of his eye, look how she lies there, so lifeless, and now she doesn't even scold with that look of you're wandering about half-naked after bathing in boiling water, no wonder you keep coughing and sniffling. Perhaps it was due to his grief at this that Bade addressed himself, and sort of the bed, while openly displaying his semi-clad body. But then he really looked, and rushed at the quilt. They say he'd just sneezed, from the incense, which is so pungent these days, and the tray jiggled, and some little bell tinkled, which was not the regular puja bell, but the tiny copper one, next to the little pot of Ganga water, or was it the ringing in his heart, or...?

Amma! he must have, he definitely, cried out.

He cast a glance at the bell and another at the quilt, which was smoothed out wrinkled pressed down raised in parts folded here flung over there, as though something could be beneath it, or then again, maybe not. Then he looked towards the bathroom and touched the door. He opened it slowly, crying out, *Amma, Amma*, so if she was inside she could prepare herself. Then he picked up the quilt and pulled it as though searching for her in a game of hide-and-seek, and if Ma's braid appeared, or a leg or a toenail or a cheek, he'd cry, *I spy!*

By then everyone else had come in, and Susheela began to cry, and said, If I had noticed earlier, the tray would have fallen from my hand and the glass in the thermos would surely have shattered like what happened once before, and the other thermos Mata ji gave away as a gift, so this is the only one, and then Mem Sahib you would have to get a new one.

Then something occurred to Bade and what it was, was that it must be the size of that crack in the wall which grew and grew into a chasm and it must have swallowed his entire brain, as large as it might be, leaving him, at that moment, in a complete void, mouth agape, as though this were the sum total of his life and times.

★

There are umpteen methods for searching for a missing object in a quilt. One searches for a missing person in much the same way. One method is to tap the quilt, twist it like it's dough that's been kneaded, then pat it gently.

Here's another: you think, this isn't dough, it's a tent, and you raise and lower the corners furiously, and run your hand around inside trying to grab the missing object or person, and when you don't feel anything, you yourself race in behind your hand, squeezing yourself in this way, and sticking your head out that way, and you blink, wide-eyed, as though emerging from under water, panting, and your eyes flare and contract like a pair of nostrils.

A third: the quilt suddenly seems like a carpet, and you pick up all the bedding and fling it down again as though Ma might fall from it separately, as though she were a grasshopper, stuck inside.

Then you understand that the hidden item could take on any form, and could also change its size, at which point all places and things hold possibilities for you. As the search deepens, the senses grow intemperate.

So you imagine her taking the form of a silver toe ring, and you shake out the sheet like a delicate dupatta. You imagine her as a letter and feel beneath the pillow and under the mattress. A kitten! You poke at imaginary bundles here and there on the quilt so it won't slip from your hands and run away. If an elephant, you quickly fling the quilt in the air, then jump away so it won't go mad and attack you. If you imagine her as a firecracker, you light the matches and jump so they don't explode right above you.

The limits of the imagination have yet to be discovered. If you cross one limit, another will arise. Every shape takes form in the imagination, and Bade continued his search for Ma in ever new places. He even twisted the cup off the thermos, pulled off the top and peered inside; he also looked behind the photo of his father and inside the little box of cardamom pods. Under the bed, on the windowsill, inside the almirah; he opened the drawers, peeked in the toilet bowl; and each time Susheela's weeping broke out afresh: Where is Mata ji? She's not here!

But when Susheela picked up the mattress to peek beneath it, he scoffed: Are you mad?

No, I just thought, she wept quietly.

Thought what? he scolded.

That maybe Mata ji had wrapped herself up in the quilt by accident…somehow…

Or you could put it like this: that none among these was the shape of Mata ji, Amma, Ma ji, elderly Dadi, Granny chill, but rather the shapes of the senses taking leave like the flight of a dove, and it can also be said that whatever thing takes the form of a dove is the most imaginative of all, as is the dextrous magician who can twirl his wand and turn wood into a snake or something big into something small and bring the dead alive and bear the prone aloft and render the visible invisible.

In other words, everyone was thrown for a loop, and when they'd regained their balance somewhat, still slightly dizzy, they began to examine everything, utterly unaware of the distinction between believable and unbelievable. Someone even knocked on the wall, perhaps because they'd noticed the crack, which looked sort of like a wound, as though it had shrunk in the cold, then split open like a sore. It could have formed a hole, through which someone's breath could pass, as a thread through the eye of a needle, and come out on the other side.

Well, frankly, this was all pointless speculation. In a story you can make whatever you want happen, otherwise, how could you push a real woman through a crack in the wall like a pail and pick her up on the other side and splash her about?

Beti's eyes sought wood. Meaning Papa's cane. And then she began to search for Amma's brand new cane. But she wouldn't have had the nerve to imagine it as a snake that had set out at a poisonous clip with Ma wrapped around it.

And why would anyone even think about the Buddha, which had been sheltered, dignified, valuable, ancient; even if cracked, so what? It would bring in lakhs and crores if anyone sold it to a museum, so best to keep it inside, that way no one will see, know, think: it's all for the best.

So, as with many other questions, we'll get no answer as to why Bade stopped in the middle of the searching for the lost thing in myriad forms and myriad shapes, searching searching, and picking up the puja tray and clay lamp once more, he suddenly changed direction, so that the flame flickered and nearly went out, but didn't, and it sort of jumped, like him, and, after this, he opened with a bang the door of the almirah, where dwelt the Buddha, and whether he lifted his eye to look at it, or lifted the clay lamp to perform the aarti, a great wave of understanding rippled across his face when he realized that it was missing.

Actually, the truth was that he understood nothing at all.

★

35.

The state of families is rather like that of the city of Delhi, chock-a-block willy-nilly slapdash crammed scattered messy raptor-snatching nail-catching; old: Sikander Lodi; oldest: Indraprastha; glittering malls grime-blurred slums, and above and below the scraps of earth and sky, swinging betimes from the dusty bits of tinsel that hang from electricity and telephone wires, where occasionally the addle-brained stand too close: when they get a shock it cleans their clock. But neither does this make the city any cleaner, and nor does it shrink the population. Delhi and the family, ever-young, evergreen, resting on a bombshell bursting busting perpetually in motion.

Just as no one knows what's going on in Delhi, no one knows what's going on in a family. For example, the mother of this household: Where did she go, and why did she go? No one knows these things. There are as many words as heads, and how many heads on that day of torment? Because the people rushed to fuss and snoop, all of them, fast or sluggish according to age, excited or serious, and all very worried, *Oh dear, how did this happen, poor thing,* and an NGO worker came and asked threateningly, *What if this is a case of elder abuse?*

That day became a case study on class, where one could learn which classes have a certain flexibility, allowing their members to move this way and that; and which are built with the defences of a fortress, allowing for no movement, neither thither nor hither, keeping their members concentrated in one place. At some point a graduate student showed up, a sympathetic officer's son, who needed data on class classifications for his research project. He kept his laptop with him at all times, and swiftly pulled it out to take notes on this one's walk, that one's talk, and how each bore the markers of their class. His notes went something like this: One haughty lady slips in, head held sky high; a gentleman whispers *excuse me* as he crosses the hallway; and who is it that ignores everyone as they go banging by, and for whom does everyone make way, and who will ask a question the moment she arrives in the inner sanctum, and who will go into the servants' quarters and whisper, and who will just doze by the window, and who will sit down on the empty bed, and who will stand at the foot of the bed and rest his brow at the absent feet. This is not the place to go into details, but the young researcher took tons of meticulous notes, observing such particulars as which class was truly cultured and well-bred—the sign of a good family—and which displayed the crass egotism of the nouveau riche, and in which lower class there was a particular caste-specific indifference, and in which a selfish stubbornness. For now, it is enough to say that many of the types of classes spread out across Delhi had come together in this one place and that this had been a windfall for this particular student of class and caste.

The auto rickshaw drivers passing by stopped as well, engines still running, and asked what was happening, and some would continue on, and some would come to a full stop and join the crowd. Each to his own interest and preoccupation.

A little girl saw a gash on the wall outside of Mata ji's room. She often visited that wall to draw faces with a stick. She feared her mother would haul her up and say, *This is all your doing!* And then what would she say back? *Mmm hmmm,* she would say, *the wall shrank from the cold and snapped, maiyya, what do I know about this crack?* She didn't know that on the other side of the crack lay Mata ji's bed, from which she had disappeared. She just stacked three bricks, one upon the other, and stood teetering atop them. A crack can become a telescope, through this she attempted to peer, to slide her gaze within, as though cleverly threading a needle. She smiled secretly, less at what she eye-spied than at what she saw in her mind's eye. *Whaaa?* asked nobody, because everyone was stressed out for their own reasons. Inside, all was still.

Everything will be fine, said Bahu, not directly *to* her husband, but *for* him, which was their usual style of speaking with one another: half-turned-away. She will come, the way Papa used to go, without telling us, and return when he felt like it.

At that very moment Beti dashed the phone down and cried out in a rage that no one had cared until now, and now everyone was dying of sympathy.

To the servants it seemed that she had said this alluding to Mem Sahib, i.e., her sister-in-law. They began to speak among themselves, remarking that really it had to do with the difference between one's own blood and other people's blood —how can a non-blood relation feel anxious the way one's own children feel, that's why Mem Sahib is saying so easily, Mata ji won't go anywhere, she'll come home, and hasn't she been asking all along, where would she go? She'll just wander around and end up back here! Poor thing, she's become lifeless as a straw, she can't digest anything, just got down two grains with difficulty, one tiny phulka in the morning, a bit of soup in the evening, two bites of toast at everyone's insistence, and then went around complaining at the cost of everything.

Sahib doesn't keep his clothing in the almirah, locks up the fruity nutty sweets and chocolate there so Mem Sahib won't give them out to her friends and relations, shared someone with suppressed giggles.

Whispering, laughter, erupt.

Got on hot pink nail polish, does Mem Sahib, even today, breaks my heart. Sahib's face is all teary, it is.

She had that on before.

Couldn't she remove it? It's not like she has to do it herself —she just has to sit down and spread out her fingers and say, clean off my polish with remover.

In the meantime, Sid Baba isn't even here, and Overseas Baba spills all his worries into the phone. Listens to what his mother says from over there to make himself feel better. And his mother also registers every little complaint from here, with him. Today she told him she hadn't put honey in Sahib's tea, so he blew up. Poor thing is so disinterested in food and drink now, his face has become so thin, if he finds one type of tea to his liking, she even objects to that. She screamed at me that her green petticoat hadn't been laid out. Bhai, who can remember such things on a day like today, when everyone is upset, wondering where Mata ji is, and what could have happened?

That is, barbs are being thrown at the lady of the house in worried whispers, or anger is being vicariously vented on their own daughters-in-law, using this crisis as an excuse. Because it didn't seem to anyone that the wife felt pity when she saw her husband's face and that's why she would say, Take it easy, people don't just fly off.

Bahu's lips also began to quiver and large tears were ready to splash from her eyes, and like an arrow from a bow, she picked up her cell phone to dial Australia to say, Whether or not I open my mouth, I am the villainess, first your father, then your aunt, they're the only ones who worry, and now even the servants are after me!

And so it continued—Bahu dragging her heels on her way outside, and Beti dragging her sandals on her way inside. The two would stop in the doorway going in opposite directions, eyes meeting in a not-meeting sort of way, and if the door said anything, how could they hear it, that being merely one more occurrence among many.

Well, words are words, right or wrong, they just keep flowing, and who really knows how to keep their mouth shut, but the concern was Ma, who had just lain there for so long, back turned; then she'd become the Wishing Tree, then, poof, she'd disappeared into thin air.

★

36

She didn't come back.

But this sentence is misleading if you don't keep reading.

She didn't come back…

…to that house.

But no, if you put the two parts together, it's still misleading.

Being misled in this way is actually quite common. You hear just some of the words, don't hear the rest, take what you did hear and run with it, and the story twists and turns and flies off in another direction. For example, you're out buying vegetables, standing between pushcarts, and you hear someone say: I mean to say, where does one find his *sa* pitch? Which is quite an interesting question in itself, if it's about the note *sa*, and about where exactly in someone's singing range that note is located, since that's how it will be determined whether his or her singing is in the upper octave, the taar saptak, like that of Omkar Nath Thakur or Kumar Gandharva, or in the lower, like that of Amir Khan and Waheed Hussain Khan. But it could be that it's not about singers at all, but about the way some ordinary person talks, like where does that person's *sa* fall? Omkar Nath will always be Omkar Nath, same goes for Kumar Gandharva, even with thin voices, but if it's about someone's speaking voice then that note will make him whimper, or bleat. But yes, if they were speaking about a woman, then perhaps a thin tone, or *sur*, would not be so odd. But then why would a passerby raise such a question at all? If it were the sort of voice one didn't expect from a particular person, such as an effeminate male voice, or a masculine female voice, only then is there reason for such curiosity to arise. But we also don't know whether they meant the note *sa* that comes before the *re*, or the *sa* that comes after the note *ni*? Having purchased the vegetables needed for making sabzi bhaji, you might return home and lie down to rest your eyes a bit, or just because, and since things mostly happen just because, the question that person had asked as you were walking by might then start ringing in your ears, and you didn't have time then, but now you have the leisure to really sink deep into thought about what they could have meant, and you might hem and haw a bit, and wonder, what's it to me, but possibly you'll keep on trying to find an answer, or you might at the very least start asking yourself this question about the singing and speaking voices of all sorts of people, and wonder where does *his sa* fall, or *hers*? You'll never know the answer to the original question, about that particular person's question about someone's *sa* and where it falls, since you were worrying about buying the vegetables absolutely fresh, and you were obsessing about the pushcart vendors, not about tiptoeing behind like a shadow of the asker of this interesting question, to listen to the rest of the conversation, from which you would have learned more that would have made the context and individual clearer.

Or it might go like this—just because—you might be misled in a different direction in the process of trying to avoid straying in the first place. We're talking about returning home, but in this story, it's the home that's returning and the people who live there are changing location. So now are you saying that the home did not return? The same walls and door, but in new plaster? After leaving Bade's government home, did it travel with them? Did it climb up the two flights of stairs to the rented flat, or no?

That moment had not yet arrived, and why wouldn't it travel with them when up to now it has always done so? It isn't some elderly man who can't climb the stairs if there's no lift. If the home doesn't move as well, then that would be the first time something like that has ever happened in the cosmos. For that would mean that the door that has loyally accompanied them for generations has turned traitor. Truly, *that* would be the disappearance of the century.

Right, now let's talk of she who was missing, and so long as she stays that way, it can be said that she didn't return. To that government bungalow where a few days remained before the handover.

After thirteen hours, the elderly Mata ji was found, or so it is said. Or thirteen days, that too came to be said, and some even proclaimed it to have been thirteen weeks. In the end it's like this: days weeks months are like ribbons, which that trickster Time flings about as he watches for his own amusement, to see if anyone can measure them, but no one can, and whoever knows this ahead of time throws in the towel and blindfolds themselves with these same ribbons and says whatever they say is fine, and whatever you say is right too, but they did find her, didn't they? Those who go on and on debating the hours weeks and months are those who believe in one hundred percent exactness. How to explain to these guesswork experts that the moment is gone, and *when what how exactly* and *100 percent truth* are now lost in the rubbish heap.

Many details about the explosion on the Samjhauta Express were never found out, even though the highest grade of inquiry was undertaken and super-duper detectives were sniffing everything out, and by contrast, here there were only weeping blubbering family members carrying on and other people's wagging tongues, cunning attitudes, simplistic assumptions. Everyone spiced the story up, or consoled themselves, and the true visage of the original tale, poor thing, melted into the many other imagined faces.

Who could fit all the rumours into these pages? But trimmings and clippings and details will trickle in.

Bahu said resentfully that her son was calling constantly from far across the ocean, asking if this was any way to do things? And there were so many people in the house, and nearby, and I had gone for a while, for her sake, to get the other house cleaned for the rest of you, and back here all hell broke loose? He's very angry, he's asking how long we're going to wander about aimlessly, tell the police she's an old lady, tiny and weak, like a robin; who knows what state she was in when she set out, and where and how, and where she's lying now, in the dark, wounded, unconscious, it could be anything.

At which Bade trembled and scolded Vilas Ram, with a *Who told you to cover that up!* regarding the cloth thrown over Ma's heater.

Beti said tensely that she'd called the district police station, and she tried to mutter softly but her welling anger slipped out, it's all because of the new cane, if it hadn't come, then Ma wouldn't have picked it up, and she wouldn't have been able to lift herself up. But now she had got up, and someone had given her something to lean on, and the cane was missing too.

Look again carefully, the cane must be here, Bade's tone was stern and confused amidst the scolding, as if he thought that if the cane appeared somewhere Ma would be with it: under the bed, or behind the door. Ma didn't even know how to unfold it, he added hopefully.

No, no, it was already unfolded, sticking straight out, it was the trunk of the Wishing Tree, blurted out Kanthe Ram or Susheela or whoever, but when he or she saw everyone's faces the words immediately floated away.

And yes, there is proof but no need to waste space by supplying it here, Susheela wondered, what if the Wishing Tree had handed the cane to some cane seeker, and then Ma ji would have lost her support, but she immediately rejected this idea, because how can the tree be separated from its trunk, that would just be suicide. How could she have such a terrifying discussion with anyone? She asked only herself if anyone had asked the Wishing Tree for the Wishing Tree itself; should I ask my mother-in-law this, or not even her?

Wait, what sandals was she wearing? Or did she leave barefoot…? The thought occurred to Bahu.

Arre, what…! Bade thundered as though someone had questioned Amma's good taste and refinement.

Bahu glanced about, and murmured, because she was giving out all her sandals and such, that's why.

They must have realised with a shiver that Amma really was missing. Slowly, slowly, moment by moment, one by one, they would continue to discover what else was missing. And of course they worried about this too: that as the end grew nearer they would discover that though they felt robbed, the plunder was much greater than they had realised. The rest of their lives would be spent asking themselves what else they had lost.

★

37

It's nighttime if it's dark outside.

Pitch-black darkness. A few stray lights along the street and all the houses are wrapped in stillness. The world sleeps. One has to go up the hill to mourn. The path is rough. There are knotted ropes attached to nails along the cliffs. The ropes swing in the breeze. He has to cling to them to pull himself up. Every time he grabs the rope and it swings, it feels like it's breaking …and what if I fall? Like Sputnik. At one point, he grabs the rope, but it turns out to be a branch. He's petrified. His feet stumble into a rock in the evening breeze. It's inky dark so how could he know? But he has to go up, to mourn. He keeps climbing, grasping the rope so his body can hang on, and he climbs upwards, and suddenly a walking stick comes to hand. Now it makes a *click click click* sound and Bade begins falling through the air like a clod of earth. I'm finished! he screams as he tears at the air; then he takes off like a rocket. But in the opposite direction. Down. The scream stays up. Voiceless, he wraps himself around the stick as he descends rapidly. But it isn't a stick, it's the cane. Where had it been that it suddenly landed in his hands? *Click-click-click-click.* It unfolds. Amma is sitting in a bush; did she hand it to him? As he falls, Bade tries to see if it's the same cane? Butterflies fly up. By God, the very

one. Golden. Up. He reaches out his hands and kicks hard in
the air with his legs, trying to grab hold of something he could
use to pull himself up towards the bush. He falls into his bed
and it feels like an earthquake rising beneath him. His eyes
open. He is kicking his legs in the air like a child. Gas shoots
from his belly like a gun. He panics and looks next to him. His
wife is sleeping obliviously.

He has become Bade again. He gets up quietly and goes to
stand by the window.

Outside it is dark, because this happened at night. Lights
shine in some homes and on the street, carving up the
emptiness. Everyone is asleep.

How can this be, he wonders with a pang. When his wife's
hand touches his shoulder he turns. She is standing behind
him. She wasn't asleep after all.

His face wet with tears? Are the broken shards of his heart
scattered on his face? Who knows. Blackest night.

I'll be right back, he says, laying aside his wife's hand.

I'll come too, says his wife, pulling a dressing gown over
her nightie.

They walk out of the house, unsure whether on a mission
to lose or to find. Not out the front door, but the back, onto
the lawn, secretly, silently. Even the shrubbery stands quietly
because there isn't a hint of breeze. Before she became
bedridden, Amma had berated the gardener over how much to
water each plant. Amma would pick up the hose herself,
because those leaves must be bathed, but only water the roots
of these ones, if you pour water on top, the leaves will break;
they're just little babies.

Where's the hose? His wife looks around by the bushes. As
though it will appear in the dark.

The two of them open the gate and go out. Amma had once fallen at this gate and been found on the ground. Alone. Laughing. The gardener for the neighbourhood plot outside had helped her up and brought her gingerly back to the house. Mata ji had fallen over, he said, she was laughing, as though these two were the same thing. The doctor examined her to make sure there were no internal injuries. There were none. Afterwards, he told Bade that no one lets cataracts harden anymore. Nowadays they don't wait; they just do laser surgery to take the whole thing out. Her vision must have been hazy and she lost her footing on the step. It diminishes self confidence, please schedule the procedure. But why were you laughing? Bade had asked her. So she laughed again and said because I was hurting, son, at which Bade fixed her with a reproachful look. Arre, how foolishly I slipped, interjected Amma, at which the Bade's gaze grew even sterner, as if to ask, Really, is there any intelligent way to slip? And then Amma said, Arre, son, I was bleeding, and no one could hear, and the two of you were at a wedding, so I started to cry. But you weren't crying, you were laughing. That's right, I thought I was done for, or on my way out, so why should I cry on my way out, I'll just go laughing. Just then Nattu the gardener saw me, he was coming back from the mosque.

She'll probably be laughing when we find her, the thought occurred to him.

But she didn't forget her glasses, did she, one pair is here but there was also another pair. Let's look in the house and find out, thinks Bade, as he levels out the rocks and gravel so there will be no danger of tripping.

Nighttime. The air slumbers. The trees stand about forlornly. Two bodies emerge on the street for a walk.

Throughout the neighbourhood and beyond, they peer between the tree trunks, branches, roots, shrubs, into ditches, under culverts, down lanes, alleys, all of which they have already searched in the broad light of day with a veritable army. As though that which was invisible in the light of day will suddenly manifest clearly in the dark of night.

The night so dark it's cloaked in a sheet of black, and here and there small heaps of darkness seem to appear. Something could emerge from any one of these heaps, some fragment, some shard, might wink or sparkle.

★

38

Amma? Bahu blurted out. She looked quickly, to see if Bade had heard. Eyes opened or shut, neither sleeping nor waking, he lay beside her.

It's the clock, he said.

Tick tick tick tick.

Who knows why Bahu thought it wasn't the clock she'd heard, but the *tick tick tick tick* of Amma's heart. It was Amma's clock. Bade had brought it for her from abroad and it always hung opposite her bed. Stuffed into a nest. Constructed of plastic straw and twigs. There were two eggs crammed in with it, and a blue bird, wings outstretched to fly. The nest was fixed on the wall like a mirror. Just yesterday Bahu had taken it from Amma's room and hung it up in their room opposite their bed because the one in there had already been packed, and anyway, Amma…she found herself staring at it like a criminal. Could that be the sound of Amma scolding her? With a *tick tick tick tick*?

Bahu slipped into the bathroom. She'd been feeling strange ever since she'd put the phone down that night, when her son, after getting the update, had shifted topics, and said, Ma, what are you talking about? It's not like someone can just disappear into thin air: look carefully, she must be there. She wasn't getting up at all, and now she's run away, how absurd, where could she go even? Look carefully, maybe some alien shot her with rays and captured her and hauled her into outer space, or maybe a goddess made her invisible—he babbled all manner of improbable scenarios at her.

Hush, she shook her head, it's hardly possible for someone to be there one minute, gone the next. Unless you have enemies and some crook… She panicked. She couldn't allow Bade to hear the things coming into her head, otherwise…or abduction or ransom, oh my, why would anyone put Amma through such suffering? The poor thing's pushing eighty, there must be some decency left in this world.

Of course one always hears tales about people being there one minute, gone the next, and then who knew if they were alive, or…she felt fearful again—Bade was nearby, he'd kick up such a fuss at her for thinking such things, as if she actually wanted her to…

No one will believe me. No one ever does. She felt tearful. I set her room up so nicely, so everything would be easy for her—a thermos of hot water, a small player for her music, it's not my fault if she won't play it, a bouquet, I even had a TV installed and said, You could just watch the news. I was the one who thought of all the special touches, not him. These people installed a potty shower next to the potty on the left side, I switched it over to the right, so she could pick it up with her right hand and use it more comfortably. He always thinks big and he thinks that's what makes him biggest—Bade. His sister even put up that depressing dark abstract painting right across from the bed by Ram Kumar, or some other Kumar, who knows, that would horrify you the moment you looked at it— I was the one who shifted it over to the side, and put up a nature scene so she'd feel cheered by the view—jungle, bird, river—you'd feel like getting up when you saw that, but even that was interpreted as me trying to make my sister-in-law look bad. If it weren't for my son, I'd have run off long ago, it's for his sake I soldier on. I tend to her every need, I get up at night and peer in to make sure all is well, but the rest of them just show up and cry, Amma Amma, and that makes them feel like they're the ones doing everything. They've turned Amma into an excuse. My son is right to ask, is it a dharamshala you're running or a household?

My home has never been my own. He invited whomever he wished; when did anyone ever listen to me? Bas, enough is enough, my son says, now think about yourself for a change, and leave others to themselves.

But how? I'm so upset here, and even so, people keep asking me how she could have disappeared with you there? Does anyone actually disappear that way?

No one believed that her heart was pounding with fear too; sometimes Overseas Son fretted on the phone, and said, Ma, look after yourself, there are lots of people helping but ultimately you're the one taking care of things, if something happened to you, everything would go belly up.

Her husband is a lion on the outside, but timidity personified inside; his nickname was Mickey Mouse in school, Amma had told her.

She told Bahu that, and now she's gone off somewhere. But where?

Bahu relieved herself and began washing her hands, and as she scrubbed and scrubbed, her hands disappeared in soap bubbles. Was Amma washing her hands the same way right now? Her hands must be totally covered in soap and she must be starting to rub them together and maybe her hands were getting rinsed down the drain along with the soap? Had Amma started and looked down at her arms, and found they were fading away before her very eyes, as when a coloured photograph begins to fade away and vanishes completely? She must be frightened, she must have looked in the mirror and found no one there. At which Bahu grew fearful and looked in the mirror. But she was still there. She laughed lightly but the laugh felt more like a sob.

Perhaps a supernatural force has indeed arrived; had it made Ma invisible and run off with her? Or, maybe she's still sitting right here, laughing at me?

She must be right there somewhere, her son had said furiously on the phone. Bahu panicked and looked all around her. Is she? Amma, she called out softly, but then she came to her senses.

Or else some other planet had snatched her? After all, what do we know about the cosmos? We were all rushing about, this way and that, and she was lying asleep: it would have been easy to shoot rays at her and use them to imprison her and carry her to outer space.

The impossible things her son had suggested to her in his rage...they all seemed possible now. She progressed from laughter to weeping. Had such a thing ever happened before in the world? Had anyone just got up one day and never returned? Oh lord, where is Bade, if he even heard this... A writer went out for a walk one day and is still missing to this day, leaving his family suspended between hope and hopelessness. A child was playing with a ball, the ball got lost, he went behind a bush to get it back, and was never seen again. Neta ji also disappeared and was seen somewhere in the guise of a renunciant…or maybe not. And there was a husband who went out to get paan, never to return. Alam Sahib, remember him? His sister's husband went off to Pakistan saying he'd be back to get her, and ever since then she's become Intezar Begum – Our Lady of Perpetual Waiting…

Bahu came quickly out of the bathroom. She opened up the cabinet, picked out a sari, thought, *Why did I pick this*? the moment she picked it, *This was for Amma*. She'd said, this feels heavy to me, you wear it. But why was that the one I reached for? When she got it out , she noticed it still had the price tag stuck to it, that it was half-scraped off, the price missing, just the word *Paithni* remained. It seemed to her as though someone had half torn it off: *But why, I didn't do it, it's a mystery. Someone else did it,* and then she gazed all around again.

Amma, Bahu blurted out. The clock was *tick-tick-tick*ing. Amma's clock.

O, Lord, what are these things I'm imagining? She shook herself. For a moment she wanted to go back to Bade's side, lie against his back and close her eyes. But they'd spent so many years fretting and fuming at one another: that was now the most comfortable way to interact; if she did something affectionate they'd both be embarrassed. *Get yourself out of here*: she pulled on her Reeboks and picked up her handbag. What must be done must be done. On her way back, she'd get guavas; it makes all the difference if you pick them out yourself.

As she began walking slowly along, it seemed like everything was getting lighter, her mood was getting lighter with every step, lighter-lighter-lighter, she was becoming lighter, fading, now just outlined, and then…

Bahu was at the door. Beti was entering. The two of them sort of looked at each other. The door felt a tad bewildered:

the one who'd left was entering, and the housewife from inside was going out, and then they both continued forward, keeping their fear to themselves.

★

39

Beti began to want to be frightened. She was feeling sad, which was natural, because she'd woken up in the middle of the night. Is this any time to be awake, when there's still a shiver in the air, and the night is still dark?

How can it be so dark, she thought in a huff, when the moon is so close to full? Surrounded by shadows, it sparkles like a tiny sequin. Scattering a light that's not magical, but ghostly, a light in which everything shifts; nothing is solid anymore. As though a witch had plucked up the entire housing society and stuffed it into a net and placed it on her smoky billowing shoulders and walked through the night, as the houses shivered, the trees drooped, and the shrunken fragments of garden peered out anxiously. Badminton courts, flowerbeds, chowkidar cabins, too. The entirety suspended in the middle of her net, wriggling claws protruding, as if wondering, how will we land on the ground, will we be able to stand again?

Amma would have told her it was the eleventh day lunar moon, guessed Beti as she looked up, and was it the thought that was ghostly, or the moon, or was it she herself, as she walked along dejectedly outside in the society? Best to think of it like this: somehow everything had got messed up, and like the debate over thirteen hours or thirteen days or thirteen weeks, or months, no one could sort out the jumble, and no one could tackle the tangle of her memories.

Because now it had become like those childhood nights that just wouldn't end, and Bade and Beti were sitting up all night. The month of Chait will only come once Phagun is over. Rub your eyes, put on a sweater or jacket while still asleep, go outside. Outside there are preparations for the Holika bonfire, which drives the drowsiness from our eyes, and we run out hoping we might find twigs and branches in the bushes, or maybe one of the neighbours has left out a staff, a club, a cane, so we can grab it and throw it in the Holika, and we stare as hard as we can, looking in every direction, which makes our eyes sting and water. But Mantoori is a bit too alert: he had done all the sweeping while everyone was sleeping, and you won't even find a single straw now, forget a branch. How will we throw things in now? she worries, superimposing the Holika of her childhood on to the gathering and piling of sticks and branches for the bonfire in the badminton court of the current society, better think of running around in front or in back of the flats where you might find a staff, only it might not be a staff but a cane, a golden cane, swathed in colourful butterflies, and then pick it up and fling it hard into the fire for dahan, like it's a javelin and not a cane, and the butterflies will flutter fearfully, and body and soul, all will burn so bright this night will no longer feel ghostly. She started to wish the bonfire would ignite and make everyone's cane claims go up in flames; that cane that had needlessly disturbed their sleeping Ma. Scream to Bhaddari and he will come jumping out of the night, head and mouth hidden in his gamcha, at which the black dog sleeping beneath the streetlight will start barking. The dark has swallowed up Bhaddari's face and body, and a wrapped gamcha atop an empty garment walks towards you all by itself. He's the one who'll light the bonfire, but what's this mix-up she's started, her childhood Bhaddari hasn't even seen this badminton court, it was Mantoori who swept it, nor are the street light and dog here, and the cane has gone missing with Ma. She wished she could release an ear-splitting scream, a cry to bind together houses, shrubberies, pathways, the dark shapes of night, that would search out hidden things without any effort. Did she scream? That why we're sitting here with arms folded, the time has come to set the spark to ignite the wood on the bonfire, and then Amma will hand us green chana kernels so we can roast them in the fire, and then we'll come back, and we'll find the cots all set up out in the courtyard starting today, and we'll sleep for the rest of the night till morning, and what would they care about the cane as they lay there. And then we'll get up and play Holi, we'll splash the water yellow with the tesu flowers. Just then garlands of laburnum appeared to her swinging from the trees clad in the colours of night. And she felt angry—no Holi dyes can be made from these, they only swing down before you in order to mislead. Burn this too, rip it up by its outstretched roots, her beating heart burnt. The phone rang and a voice echoed across the oceans, a voice which sided against her, and she wasn't being spoken to, but she heard: Mom, no Mom, don't do anything to raise your blood pressure, think very carefully, let her children do something too, put an ad in the paper, isn't her daughter a writer or something, she always shows up with her posse, now let her show her power, and didn't they behave badly towards her, you never even raised your voice with her, but her son and daughter only speak in growls, remember how they even scolded Grandfather, one understands better from a distance, when you live close by you feel smugly convinced you're doing everything, I'm the one sitting far away, I'm the one who thinks of bringing her favourite things, anger boiled up in her; let their phones ring, go back in the house, let the holika burn when it will and let the witchy night fade away and I'll go in the dark of night to Bade's house, let's get cracking, how can we sleep now, let's get our act together and find her, and let's see, who knows, maybe Ma has crept back to sleep in her own bed. But there's no courtyard for Amma to have the beds made up outside, that's what she doesn't like about sleeping there, and so she keeps saying *nooo nyoooo nyewww*, poor thing, so tiny, just hold out your hand she'll climb into it, like that little bird that Bade captured in the dark when we were children. No, no, I won't hold it, I cried, and I ran, but Bade came rushing after me, and opened my hand and put the bird in. The bird fluttered, like my heart, which began to sink, and then it died right there, in my hand, and I couldn't let it drop, but I couldn't hold on to it either. It died, was killed, who killed it, will we ever be able to rise above the guilt? And how inconsiderate are our own people who scream about this one, scream about that one, don't worry about money, call anytime I'm here for you, and they're shouting close by, shouting far off and even shouting on the phone. Let the mobile ring, Beti grumbled in her thoughts, but why did Bade press the bird into my hand so it could die, or so it would die, and he could say I'd killed it? And she took the phone out of her waistcoat pocket and held on to it in just the same way she'd held the bird he'd handed her in childhood, so she wouldn't drop it, but she wouldn't hold onto it either, and the bird kept fluttering, ceaselessly fluttering. Her phone was ringing in vibration mode. It kept humming *bzzzzzz*.

Pick up. Say hello.
How does one say hello? For a moment she forgot.

★

40

Anything we say about the Mahabharata could also be said about families: they contain all that exists in the world, and whatever they don't contain doesn't exist. Not even in the imagination of a poet. That is, the gone-astray terrorist, the hot-headed leftist, the female and the feminist, the everythingist and the opti-pessimist, all in the family. Or in the Mahabharata; whichever you prefer.

The world is in the Mahabharata, the world is in the family, and thus the Mahabharata is in the family. The daily flare-ups —each one a Mahabharata.

For this reason, every member of the family knows that what exists in me exists in no one else, and what does not exist in me has no call to exist.

And that I have the brain; others have the money.

And that everyone has taken advantage of me, so from now on, I won't do anything—let the rest of them do it.

And that I'm the most tenderhearted despite living far away, while you are right here, yet so completely inconsiderate.

And I'm always the giver, and you are always the taker.

And wow, your wheeling-dealings are just because you're such a friendly soul, but if I do the same, I'm cold and calculating.

When you're quiet, you're polite; but when I'm quiet, I'm wily.

If you did it, it's good etiquette; if I do, it's fawning flattery.

If you say it, it's candid; if I do, it's just rude.

If I ask, it's obscene curiosity; when you do, it's sympathy.

If I do it, it's for my own convenience; if you do it, you're most beneficent.

If I do it, I'm being stingy; if you do it, you're being thrifty.

If I'm quiet, I'm acting proud; if you're quiet, you feel bashful.

I'm extremely secretive, but you're just reserved.

And my fashions are faux, whereas yours are cutting edge.

And if I lose something, what's the big deal, but if you do, you've been robbed, woe is me!

And if I do something it amounts to nothing, but your merest intention of doing something amounts to actually doing it.

That is, I am what I've done; you are what you've thought.

And what I said was scornful, but when you said it, it was just a joke.

When I said my piece, I was being a show-off, but when you had your say, it was the unvarnished truth.

And if I got it, I grabbed it, but if you got it, it was your right.

And if I said it, I was deluded, but if you said it, you were just right.

And when I get angry, I'm humourless, but when you do, it's self-respect.

And when I went and did it, it was my duty, but when you did, it was big of you.

And when I'm successful, I got help from you, but when you're unsuccessful, it was me who threw a spanner in the works.

And if I get stuck, I'm a slacker, but if you get stuck, you blew your chances.

And, oh, yes, if I don't get it, I'm a moron, but if you don't, you're innocent.

And, oh, yes, if you're enemies with me, I deserve it, but if I am with you, I'm jealous.

And, oh, yes, if I did it, I'm self-serving; if you did, you're self-effacing.

And if I don't do it, it's carelessness, but if you don't, it's helplessness.

And however much I've done is not enough, and whatever little you did is plenty.

And if my nose is crooked, it's ugly, and if your eye is crooked, it's artistic.

And, oh, yes, if I look good in a picture, the photographer was gifted, but if you look good, it's because you're beautiful.

And, oh, yes, if I'm fair, I look like a skinned quail, and if you're pale, you look like a foreigner.

If I'm dark, I'm Mr Eggplant Head, whereas when you are, black is beautiful.

If I'm fat, I'm Tubby Tubkins, if you're fat, you're pleasingly plump.

If I'm thin, I'm dry as a stick, if you're skinny, you're svelte and shapely.

And if I turn on the AC, I'm decadent, but if you do, you suffer from delicate health.

When I drink, I'm a drunk, when you drink, doctor's orders.

If speak in English, I'm giving myself airs, if you do, you're educated.

Oh, and if you need it, we're all one big family, but when I need it, you're separate and alone.

If I'm polite it's pretentious, if you are, it's pedigree.

If I live by the fruits of my labour, I'm a crude drudge, but when you cling like a leech, it's a cultural custom.

And yes, your work is the bee's knees, but mine's a hobby, if you please.

Family and my own decency have destroyed me. Otherwise I'd have been like you: director, professor, officer.

All right, then, you're not me, because you don't want to be me, but I'm not you since I could never be you.

I am responsible, dutiful.

My city has been highly cultured for centuries, whilst you choose to talk on and on about some recent goondas and give it a bad name.

Aji, once we've become a great civilization, we'll be forever free to go any which way.

And how can you carry on about the disrespect, rape and casting out of women, when this is the land where Gargi once beat Yagyavalk and Mandan Mishra's wife beat Shankaracharya?

Why do you see only cow dung and crap where Radha once danced, and Ganga descended from Shiva's locks?

Yes and no, no and yes, me and you, you and me, and you and I and Amma and we did so much and you were with her, but you didn't see and the poor thing grew older and she lay there and alone and didn't even know what she was doing and she's even forgotten and inventing some imaginary names and her memory's clearly affected and everyone went running.

★

41.

Those who came running were also in a state of confusion or were soon to be.

Take Beti, for instance. Night-day-childhood-now-sleeping-waking-Mantoori-Bhaddari, down-is-up and back-is-front—all these things had already taken place in her brain. Inside disorder: everything a mixed-up mishmash—the brain had slipped into the ankle and the foot had jumped up to where the head should be.

In the midst of this, new paranoia arose. What if Ma had run outside barefoot? Was she wearing both sandals? Were her socks matched? Had she changed her clothes, or was she still in her night suit? Eek, did she have a bra on? And did she bring the car keys? Oh, lord, did she lock the door? Should I tell the neighbour to check and fasten a lock on the door? Where did I put my phone? Did I pull the chain over or no? Is the gas off? The faucet? The balcony door? Did I even open it? Sunglasses? Money? Uff—money! There's going to be a horrible fish stench, I wasn't able to get the garbage out. She mentally inspected countless crimes: were her belly and back in the proper places and all knobs and locks properly turned. Usually they were, as happens even in stormy moments because moments are creatures of habit in their own ways—fingers turn on the gas, then even if the brain is all upside down, they'll start to itch and turn it off again automatically, without even registering it, and feet that have emerged from the house will not press forward until the lock has been secured, pulled on once just to make sure it's secured properly, yes, done.

Amongst these mental somersaults she reached the gate. She couldn't perform the real turn back because she had to fly. To the police station.

The chowkidar left off warming himself by the open fire and stood to open the gate. Beti drove the car out and thought about how this was the same time of day they used to drive out of the gate and turn right to go to school, and how there was a small bazaar there where they'd see Idiya warming herself by the fire and setting out large green bundles of greens from her fields—spinach, fenugreek, bathua, chaulai, dill, chana—in the darkness of dawn, and arranging them on her cart. When we got home from school we'd run over there to watch her weighing out the greens, the weighing pan with the weight so high and the one with the greens so low, and we were wearing long quilted coats, eating chilgoze Amma had stuffed into our pockets, which you don't see around anymore, nor such weighing or weights. Nor Amma. She drove on smartly, said something to the guard. And as she drove out, she cast a backwards glance as though looking back to see if everything still looked so ghostly. The holika had burnt, a pang arose, but that was a childhood time, a childhood home, a childhood bonfire. The now one would burn someday soon.

I'm mixing up this place that place, she jerked her head towards the road, as though saying, *Farewell, now you will no longer be you, nor I, I.* As if to say, *This ebbing night will rise now in such a day that will be new.*

Bade was also in a tailspin. First he pulled his trousers on over his pyjama, when he'd meant to wear pants with a kurta. Then he shrieked, the driver doesn't come this early! Because Susheela had handed him the key to the government vehicle. For a few moments, in which every instant seemed uncommonly long, the key to the private car played hide-and-seek, but here we go, found it. He didn't have the presence of mind to comb his hair, so he came out with the two knobby horns that grew from each side of his head early in the morning, screaming, Hurry up! Otherwise come with the driver! And he ran outside, then ran back in, to the puja room, and lit the lamp, bowed his head, and then went back out and turned the engine on.

His wife called after him, stop! I'm coming! But she was walking more sensibly. She'd washed her face, put on her sari, filled a thermos with hot tea, put biscuits, apples, bananas, a knife in a small bag, and had Amma's shawl on her arm. She gave instructions as she left for what to do in the kitchen, and to make Amma's bedroom and bathroom sparkle and change the sheets. Turn the geyser on. The small rug slips, so take it away and put down the jute carpet instead. And the flowerpots the gardener had set out yesterday, tell him to get the movers to pack them on it in front of him. Understand? Run and get Amma's comb, or any comb. Tell the gardener to put a nice bouquet in the blue vase and set it in her room, you understand, yes, the blue round one, there's a half moon carved along the top, it's glass, understand, not the terra-cotta one, the pitcher-shaped one, got it?

What were they saying on the phone?

That a small woman has been found.

Small or old?

They said she has a cane that unfolds *click-click-click*.
Oh goodness, Amma.
She's forgotten names.
Oh, Amma.
Where's the police station, it should be right here, how did they find it, we can't seem to.

*

42

What was that smile, could anybody say? No, nobody. Not even me. Had I been asked, which I won't be, because I've already had my scene and scooted out of the way.

It was…just…that type of smile.

The rest of what happened is all a matter of conjecture. There were only two holes in the wall, one going in, one going out. Threading a breath through, could she then be taken out of the other side and *click-click-click* unfolding the cane with a flutter and whoosh, out the gate? Why not?

There was some suspicion later that Ma had had some sort of goal, based on what Rosie Bua said. Having accomplished that goal, she'd turned back, and that's where the confusion had set in. She went past gate number fifty-two and walked along, the gate receding behind her with every step.

A woman, exhausted after years of subsuming her own rhythm to that of others, lying in bed for months, hanging on a breath which alone is hers, and after turning her back on everyone, she's started to recognise it somewhat, and, granted, a cane had also come her way, which could be turned into the Wishing Tree when extended, and anyway, even witches fly on canes, like brooms, so Ma was this Amma, who for so many years had remained immersed in her motherhood, who had now forgotten everyone and everything: is this not a birth, or a rebirth? And what newborn comes out a-toddling—don't they have to learn how to crawl and then to todtodtodtoddle—and the newborn gets lost, cries, smiles—does it not?

And ho, Ma smiled that smile.

Beyond gate fifty-two come civil servant's bungalows, one after another, some of which have visible numbers, others where the numbers are obscured by vines pillars pipes and after you pass 53 and 54, you can go on to 1053 and 1054, and after that, you really have no idea, and you think, what am I even doing, and what do I want from life, and the weather too is such that it makes you shiver, and the bed has slowly but surely made you forget how to walk. Let's just say that it was the cane that kept Ma upright, for everything inside her was steadily collapsing, one thing at a time, bit by bit, breath by breath, all understanding, all experience, all knowledge. She came out of a gate, and then there was the next one, and beyond that, the next, and so on.

Lurching, bent over, growing smaller, into the void, empty, lost, flying along, so that some children thought of Holi when they saw her, even though the season for that had already occurred, and they smeared her face with white varnish. But according to Sudhir Chandra, good people wander about full of hope in bad times—*bura waqt acche log*—so one passerby saw her, and thought, *Something is up with this old lady stumbling alone with her cane, wearing a bizarre baggy garment, and she's laughing like a madwoman who doesn't realise you can stop laughing after you start, or that it's more fitting to cry on certain occasions.* He scolded the young pranksters, What are you up to? What is this paint! and went up to the small woman and asked, what do you need, Mata ji?

Water, said Ma, her lips dry, and white.

What do you seek, Mata ji?

Gate, she said, but now how could she tell what she was saying and what she should say when he asked the number.

Who is at home, Mata ji?

Son, she said.

What does he do, Mata ji?

Officer, she said.

Your husband, Mata ji?

Anwar, she said.

Officer Anwar, who what why, this fellow hadn't a clue, especially when the Mata ji's speech was so crazed.

The passerby helped her to the nearby police station, which was not the one Beti had called, but, as we know: *Police: Hamesha aap ki, aap ke liye—The police: always for you, with you*—got in touch with their station, and everyone learned that a Mata ji of 80 or thereabouts was missing, and a marvellous golden cane had carried her away in a host of rainbow butterflies, and that this incident concerned house number fifty-two.

They all raced over and stormed into the police station at once.

Amma raised her eyes. All curled up like a foetus. A gaze that emanated from a great distance. As though rising from ancient births. Crossing over the hardship pain wandering sticking uprooting bumps on the journey. Arriving at this incarnation. In an ancient, aching body. Then a smile arose from the fatigue residing in every follicle, in every joint. That smile. When the lips tremble, part gently in a smile. In which faith happiness surprise recognition all flicker up in that very moment.

That smile. Amma's.

That single match which lights up the smiles of the entire family.

No, there's no use summoning me, I won't be able to describe that either.

The smile of a newborn who sees the world for the first time and for the first time looks at another.

★

43.

The heart breaks.

If a little girl looks at you and smiles, you are her world. If your mother looks at you like that, all is lost, you melt into a puddle. Such a simple emotion, so straightforward, not an ounce of artifice. Innocent, simple, trusting.

Dew. A far-off star. A single point on a rainbow. The caress of the breeze.

You just collapse in a heap right there.

Shall we go? Let's go.

As if she's been smoking, take that stinky-smoking-man-smelly blanket off Ma's shoulders, wrap her up in her own shawl. Come on, let's go.

How small Amma is. Just one hand-span above my waist. When did that happen? Was she pruning herself inside the quilt or something?

The white paint smeared on her face makes her look a withered old joker. Wiped with a wet hanky. The little girl whimpered, fidgeted. Still looked a joker.

Amma kept coughing. They stood amidst the swirling packing dust. The boxes had grown into a mountain. The door was open.

Amma's gaze foolish.

It's so dusty, Bahu apologised. Please come in here, Amma.

Back into the wall room? Amma reluctant. The bed is there.

Ma's eyes, devoid of connection. She sits on the edge of the bed as though about to rise.

How her feet have swollen. The veins seem ready to burst. The coughing fits won't let up.

Give her something warm to drink, something warm, Amma, you've caught cold, there's so much dust, why don't you put your head down here, let me massage her feet a bit, oh my, look how tangled her hair is, just like a sadhu's matted mane, don't worry I'll slowly comb it out for her. Everyone set about folding her up, smoothing her wrinkles as though she were a piece of fabric. Don't ask how she'd passed her days and nights, don't think about where she lay, where she went, how could you have left, Amma?

Amma lie down, sleep a bit. Straighten out your legs. Oh, see how tiny she is, she really has grown smaller. Close your eyes. Intently gazing. Close them, you'll feel more comfortable. They were still open. So lost.

Bade stood aside, watching. Ma is tired. She's forgotten. Was she telling them the wrong name? That she was Tara or Chanda? Husband's name too. The policeman said she said it was Anwar. Husband's name. No, that is not her husband's name. Her tongue is tired too. She must have used the Urdu word for husband: shauhar. Or maybe she said *officer*. She had the cane with her. It was the cane that got her recognised. Yes, an old lady, leaning on a cane.

Bahu stood by with a spoon—please take a drop, your mouth is dry. Beti moistened a cotton swab with cleanser and started removing the white paint. Perhaps even now everyone believed they were the one doing everything, while everyone else was just sitting around. They were preparing Ma for a new life.

Beti smoothed back Ma's hair, leant over and looked attentively to make sure there was no white near the roots. She swabbed with the soft cotton. Ma's eyes opened. Like a peaceful cow, she is being bathed. And then she said:

Let's go.

As if she were lowing.

Ma tried to straighten up, coughing, and a storm of sympathy arose within them all. Where had she been? What had she endured, and at this age?

Let her sleep. Bade kept watching. Amma needs rest, until then she won't be herself.

Right now, said Ma, straightening up amid coughing. Said to Beti.

Who knows if Beti even realised later that *right now* means *now,* the way *no* is *new.* At this moment, it was only Ma's meek smile and foolish gaze that struck her and she blurted out, yes, there's so much dust here, come to my house now.

From her point of view, she'd pulled off a marvellous feat —she'd managed to strike a blow at the people living here, she'd demonstrated the attraction of her own place, and she'd brought peace to an exhausted body-mind-beloved's soul. Sort of like Joginder Pal's character in *Sleepwalkers*, who insists he's in Lucknow when he's in Karachi, so don't upset him with the truth, show mature sympathy and just agree with everything he says.

Later, Bahu was definitely angry, and sad and huge tears certainly did come splashing down from her eyes, and she said, or didn't, but from her every pore radiated the accusation that we're the ones who have done for her our whole lives, shouldered the responsibility, put up with all manner of compromises, in good times and bad, without complaint, and now, in her final years, she's leaving us just to give us a bad name. Cane in hand.

Whose final years? This is yet to be known. A question like dry leaves, floating up in the sky. Like those other questions that learned and self-assured folk give flighty answers to, like she must have said *shauhar* or *officer*, why would anyone say *Anwar*?

★

44.

Some say this is a new age. Others say that when it comes to women, it's always a new age. New age. Meaning things have changed for women. (Things always change for women). Women are no longer in the roles they used to be in. (They're always in new roles). They've started coming out. (They've always done that). They go inside (always).

And always, at least once, every woman, whether this one or that one, whether small or big, finds herself at the door, one foot poised in the air, like a dancer striking a mudra, a pose, in order to reenter that home or that door which she has renounced and already left far behind, asking herself at that moment, *Is this my world in which I'm setting foot, or is it that which is receding behind me, where I had gone, or whence I've just come? I'd just come to peek in on my old familiars for a moment or two, that's it. Also, to rejoice that I no longer belong there; so what is this sudden disconcertedness? I wonder what I belong to: to what lies behind my back or what is before my belly? I'm in one place, my actions in another, ahead or behind, tell me, O Lord, where am I?* The foot falters a moment, floating in the air, like the hovering that occurs just a moment before dancing. At the open door, as though uncertain for one moment: should I go ahead, or should I turn back, and what is ahead, and what's been left behind, and what shall I do; what will happen?

This moment also increases the confusion, because daughters who believe they've gone outside, that they've left, at that very moment when they're going inside just to visit someone in there, someone from inside—Bahu, for instance—that very person brushes by the daughter on her way out, Reeboks asqueak. The daughter is entering, the daughter-in-law is exiting. From head to toe, her whole body is cast into a quandary: which limb to turn where? And she loses her equilibrium.

Because the new age is tangled with the old, it needs time to detangle its tresses and find a new way to style its bun. But we think the order of our life has become separate, we are different, we can't lean on the old walls, the knot of the old shoelace is gone, and there's a new horizon in our embrace. Then why are these walls closing in on me? The daughter assesses her wrists and fingers, she touches her forehead to make sure it's free, happy, no one has coloured it, there's no tikli, no bindi? Rather, sister-in-law has just brushed past, sindoor erupting like red lava from the volcano that is her brow. But she's outside, I'm in, topsy-turvy.

She stands here like this, baffled, time and again. Perhaps the cushions that lie ahead are a place where she can rest her exhausted hindquarters. The laces straps buckles which appear clear and separate in the pages of history and the slogans of feminists lie here in a jumble of odd shapes. Like you think you recognise Reeboks, but seeing them running races sometimes and beneath a sari at others, your brain blows a fuse. And for now it's the opinion of elders, and of Bade, that Beti has nothing to worry about—she's alone, free of the responsibilities of marriage, home, children, in fact she is a freelancer, so she is free of every responsibility, imagine such a fate where one is free, and a lancer to boot! Mistress of her own time, doesn't have to go to the office and slog from ten to five, or get stuck in traffic jams or marmalades; the money's good too, sleep all day if you want, stay up all night and sit anywhere tapping out articles on your computer. Not in the mood today? Try tomorrow! No one to dismiss you from your job. If Amma feels like going to her place, what's the harm, it'll be a break and Beti will also have family around. They'll have fun there a few days, the two of them, no problem for anyone. We'll fix up the flat and then bring Amma back. Yes, it'd be better if we had some cheques signed first, but Sid will go, I'll send him over; right now Amma is weary.

But weary or fit, prone or risen, there are still the same four cardinal directions: north, south, east, west. Shiva to the north, the head of a corpse must face south, the sunrise in the east, in the west, only the west, forbidden to the rest, all for the best. The air flows between all these four directions, but this is also the abode of suffocation. All romping, playing, diplomacy, politics here. And then vastu shastra and feng shui maintain that we must help energy flow properly. The desirous and the ambitious got busy working it out, so that you can know health, happiness, and why leave out wealth? But just as you don't need to be a music critic to name that tune, or read the Natya Shastra to be an art expert, so too, even without getting a bhumi poojan, or handing money to a vastu-shastra-feng-shui expert, you can create perfect harmony between air, light, food and water. Art lovers know this. Art specialists know this. That the heart is the true measure which can tell if the gait is amiss or the gradient atilt.

But enough about art. Ramanujan was a mathematician, yet unaware of how the detangling occurred. His answers were correct, but he was unaware of technique.

Of course, Beti is no Ramanujan, nor is she Amrita Sher Gill, but would it be wrong to say that without getting all involved in directional truths and directional auspiciousness, or even in indirectional inauspiciousness, she had come up with a lovely conflux of flow in her home and that she now went there with her mother?

Interval. Or another life? Or the life of another. The terminology requires clarification. But whether or not clarity arrives, Holi had come and gone. The streets had been scrubbed of colour. Powders and paints all wiped from faces now. But, yes, the white eyebrows of the old gardener were still pink.

★

PART TWO

SUNLIGHT

1.

The first thing you see when you open the door to Beti's flat is the green belt beyond the balcony at the end of the long open hallway, and above that, the blue canopy of sky. The sight brings peace to closed eyes, and might even inspire them to open.

This is not the door to Bade's house, where a slight vibration would stop Beti in mid-gesture as she stepped in or out, making her wonder, *Did someone say something?* Where she would be thrown into a quandary: *Is the me going inside really me, or am I back there? Where was I coming from?* Or where the Reeboks of her sister-in-law would cause directional confusion for her, raising questions as to which woman was the insider and which the outsider.

No, this is not that door. This is the door that opens to reveal a world created by Beti alone.

Of course, every door has its importance. It has its own personality, even in a ruin. Nowadays people only notice a door's imposing outer style, and use that to assess the financial worth of its owners. But a door can hint at so much more: the charm, caprice, awkwardness, romance, aversion, joy, uninhibited weeping, swaying, excitement, prickling sensation of the person crossing the threshold—when you pass from inside out, or outside in, take note. Doors have eyes: eyes that open, blink, stare, accuse, feel peace or boredom. Yes, yes, doors get bored—at the constant flow of the same people filing in and out each day. A door may avert its gaze, or even atrophy, like a limb falling into disuse. Sure, there's still blood in your veins, a covering of flesh, but you can end up with atrophied mind, eyes, soul, heart. And a turned back.

Did the bored door awake when Beti arrived supporting her collapsing mother? It peeked a bit from its hinges. The cane moved forward. Ma's eyes opened slightly. She was taking in the balcony across the hall, the green boundary wall of foliage beyond it, and beyond that, the domed medieval tomb. That first day, the soft sparks of the sun's last rays shone delicately through the thicket of trees. The sight of the Forestry Department's protected woodland was bound to please the eye and create a sense of peace. If Beti had said so, we might have doubted her, but there was no room for doubting the feeling that shone from Ma's eyes. In this version of Ma, at least: exhausted, limping, coughing, semiconscious.

That which is perceived in a state of semiconsciousness is true unvarnished reality. A somnambulant revelation. This is what causes deep meditative trances. Two colours have profound importance in art and beauty: blue and green. They signify the entirety of the sky; they comprehend all that exists in nature. From these flow oxygen; from these the knot unfastens.

And so, the colours blue and green saluted. Drowsy eyes travelled into the house, sliding down the open hall, beyond the books and pictures and furnishings, towards the clarion call of the balcony. Ahead, among the stand of trees, the green birds perching on the small medieval dome flew up in unison as if in a gun salute. Ma started and laughed.

Why did you laugh? asked Beti.

It just happened.

It just happened that you laughed. Beti laughed too.

Perhaps Ma felt her breath might return here. *I will indulge in some silence. I'll just be me, and no one else. I'll have my own rhythm, none other. No one else will make me fall, make me wobble.* And why shouldn't she think like this, here, away from boredom familiar and familial, away from the chaos, away from all the same old sounds, sights, objects?

Exhausted Ma could think all these things, because exhaustion is also a state of slumber, a trancelike state, where revelations are born.

But yes, an exhausted mind might not be thinking anything. This is also a possibility. Why couldn't it be that Beti simply understood the meaning of Ma's breathing, of her rhythm? Taking on the burden of all women, she'd been worrying about her mother's lamentable state. Today she was presenting Ma with a new life. She would make her live again. Inspired, she put her arm around Ma's shoulders.

Ma hesitated at the door, leaning on her cane. Assessing this virtually door-less, wall-less home. Beti smiled: *The gaze never gets stuck in my home; it's not obstructed in any way.* In the small hallway, umbrellas and sticks in a large porcelain stand. To one side, a shelf to place one's shoes, dusty from the world, and choose one of the pairs of colourful sandals arrayed there, if one wishes, while seated on the low carved wooden seat; next to that, a lightweight door decorated with peacock feathers, as though made of feathers itself, which is open, and leads into a guestroom decorated in lavender and green: here too, books, paintings, and idols; open the sliding door of the wardrobe there, and you will see long coats hanging, a folding ironing board and iron, a heater and so forth, and in the corner, beyond garlands of sandalwood flowers, a bathroom, and at a distance, another open door, though it's too far to see what's on the other side. The rest of the home a long, wide-open great room. Aside from the waist-high, lightweight walls or bookshelves, there are only playful partitions, like the ridges of earth that divide fields. Hmm, should one call these walls or what—the gaze leaps over them exuberantly, and slides into the study, where there's a table, chair, computer, bookshelf, and beyond these, the sitting room, where you can sit on the sofa, or on the old railway station waiting room armchair in front of the TV—but no need to turn on the TV like at Bade's house, where it plays all the time even when no one's around—and ahead, oh my, there hovers a swing on which to sway and gaze at the paintings hanging all around, or glance outside at the balcony, which at this time is on the other side of the open sliding-glass door, and to the right, the dining table and four chairs, and behind those, another low wall, and the kitchen, tomato-red and nut-brown, and on its wall, an open window, through which peers a neem tree, and in every direction, inside stumbles upon out, as though asking, *Are you more open, or are we*, and the gaze skips and plays in endless space.

Beti took Amma to the end of the colourful hall, to the door inlaid with stones of many hues. Here, she said. Inside is the main bedroom. An airy room. Here too are glass window and door, with neem, peepal and jhaad fanoos trees affectionately peeping in at you. Artistic objects on shelves. Walls like blue lakes in which one has the sensation of swimming like a fish.

Or of simply being exhausted. Ma lay down for a moment and began to snore softly.

Poor, bewildered Ma, thought Beti, becoming the mother now. Tears welled up in her eyes.

Whenever mothers see those they gave birth to in such a state, all their attention is pulled to a single point of focus. Then nothing can come between mother and child—no other person, no other desire, besides the desire to give one's child everything: *I'll make my child's stars twinkle.* All egotism and success on one side, mother-daughter on the other. There's no pride like a mother's pride.

Beti became the mother, and made Ma the daughter, and stroked her brow. *Now she's come home, I won't let her go away. How weak she's become, if it weren't for me she'd fall right over. She started panting just from walking such a short distance. She could have fallen down anywhere! So many people around to care for her, supposedly, but no one did look after her, poor helpless thing. She still has dust caked on her, here and there. How long must it have been since she bathed? Let her sleep. After that, I'll give her a sponge bath. You see if I don't bring her slowly back to life!*

Psychologists say that the aspect of our nature which comes to the fore the moment we enter a room or gathering has the strongest influence in shaping our future. As soon as she entered that room, Ma went to sleep, and the daughter became the mother. Now, when she wakes from sleep, there will be a new life. After that, it's every woman for herself, amen.

★

2.

Ma woke the next morning in a leisurely fashion. She stretched, eyes closed. Beti jumped out of bed.

A painting by SH Raza hung before Ma. Numerous orange dots flew into the picture from behind her eyelids and began to stir up Raza's dots, making them feel as though they didn't have to be locked up inside their boring metal frame. The name of the picture was *When the Wind was Wind*. Had Ma read it from behind her eyelids?

She opened her eyes and saw her daughter, and flashed a smile that made it clear that sleep had poured her exhaustion into its sack and dispatched it to a point of no return. Her gaze, darting about from here to there, was neither sleepy nor exhausted, neither erratic nor aggrieved, neither beaten nor bored. Neither apathetic nor thoughtless. No longer so tired, everything she saw and heard was the same old same old. Sure, it felt a bit dreamlike: *Am I awake or am I asleep?* A new gaze for a newborn, that cried, *Aha! Aha!* as the world unfurled before it for the very first time.

Ma lifted her hands in the air as if to embrace the light-soaked dots which caressed her face. She ran her tongue over her lips so she could taste their warmth. Babies are eager to stuff anything into their mouths.

(Once, as a child, Sid had stuffed an overturned cockroach into his mouth in this very spirit. It was removed, he was given a slap in exchange, and Susheela had consoled the sobbing Bahu, Don't cry, dear, we'd worry if it had been a snake, but it wasn't, was it?)

Ma stuck her legs out from under the quilt. Children turn their legs into all sorts of things when they're lying down: scissors, spears, tops, cycles, and who knows what. Ma did no such thing. But the gaze has no age, and in her gaze twirled a top that set off roaming through this new world.

Will you get up? Beti peered at her.

Of course she'll get up. How long has she been asleep? It's definitely time to get up now.

Beti seemed very tired. She hadn't slept well. She hadn't been able to sleep all night for worrying about Ma. If Ma moved just a little, she was on the alert—*What was that? What's happening? Does she need to go to the bathroom?* If Ma didn't get up, she felt even more alert. Was her breathing growing weaker and weaker still? She also found it difficult to sleep because of Ma's light, unfamiliar snoring, and then again, Beti was no longer in the habit of sleeping this close to another person. Ma shivered and wiggled as she slept, like a little girl dreaming, and periodically twitched as though shucking off her exhaustion. Then she'd snore even more deeply, but Beti would wake with a start and stare ahead unblinkingly, wide awake, as though seeing can only be done at night. What is it? she'd ask out loud, but Amma would be lying there sleeping happily. *Thank you, thank the lord*, Beti would think. Feeling deeply grateful and satisfied.

This was the first night. What was happening now would continue to happen. As the world sleeps, destiny shapes the future like a potter.

Ma did not say, *No, I won't get up*. She said, *Yes*. And began attempting to rise all by herself. Beti leapt up and held out Ma's cane, and held on to Ma herself, saying, Come, let's drink some tea on the balcony.

★

3.

So. The first moment. Which has already indicated the path forward. It will be morning, there will be tea on the balcony, there will be lots of jumping around. On the part of Beti. She began to leap up at Ma's every movement. She'd come running to help her at the slightest thing, like a fussing mother. During the day, of course, but also at night.

This will be the routine for the coming nights. Every time Ma gets up to go to the bathroom, which will be at least three or four times a night, once around eleven o'clock, once around two, once at four, then at six or six-thirty, Beti will jump out of bed, or at least she won't be asleep, but always at the ready. What little sleep she gets seems only to render her more alert. An ordinary movement and a leap and a question, or a switching on of the flashlight. Then Ma will snap, If you won't sleep, I'll stop getting up! But really, how was that feasible? One had no choice but to get up. And she was no longer that *I won't get up* bundle.

So Beti would keep quiet but wakeful. She'd silently watch Ma getting up: Ma would sit up, rest a few moments, then slip into her flip flops, shuffle her feet a bit, reach out for her cane, and get carefully to her feet; a dog would bark, a truck would pass, Ma would stumble, brace her hand against the wall, Beti poised to jump up but then dropping back. As Ma pushes open the bathroom door, the circle of light grows, and Beti quickly shuts her eyes. Ma is inside, there are some sounds: she's sitting down. All is quiet. For a long time. How long? Beti silently gets up, creeps to the door like a cat, presses her ear to it: Why is there no sound? Then, shuffling feet. Beti goes to the other bathroom; on her return, she hears nothing. What's going on? She peeks through the crack. Amma is sitting on the pot. She's peaceful, she's just sitting there, what to do? Beti goes into the kitchen, drinks some water, comes back...now what? Ma still hasn't emerged from the bathroom! Amma, Beti calls out from the bed. Go to sleep, snaps Amma sternly. Beti keeps quiet, then creeps out of bed again, presses her ear to the door and peers through the crack. What are you doing? Oh, do go to sleep! Ma says in a tone that's part angry, part pleading. Now the splashing of running water. Ma doesn't feel right unless she washes herself. Use the loo paper at night, Beti had said, then you won't need to go so often. You've forgotten how mothers make their children go, how they sprinkle water on them, and then the pee comes out. But Ma must clean herself with water. Then she has to wash her hands carefully, and she has to go again and again, and when she pushes open the door the light suddenly shrinks, and Beti instantly switches on the torch. Uff, you're not asleep, you'll be tired, Ma chides.

For this reason, sleep has abandoned Beti and gone into the next compartment, because she's used to sleeping in the dark. She's used to sleeping alone. She's used to sleeping without other sleepers wiggling nearby. She's used to sleeping with an untroubled mind.

Ma had rebuked her, but she felt such peace with her daughter close by, as her sleeping body demonstrated. At every slip and slide of Beti, Ma slid too, and each time nestled her head in the crook of Beti's arm. As though sleep depended on her body maintaining contact with Beti's, sensing Beti's presence, thus enabling her to let go of her worries and stretch out and fall asleep peacefully.

And so it happened, that at every movement of Ma, the already-awake Beti grew ever more so. She feared she might fall asleep and sprawl towards Ma; accidentally knock into her with a hand or foot, waking her up, so she kept sliding closer to the edge of the bed. And sleeping Ma kept seeking out Beti's presence, sliding right after her and sticking to her, as Beti lay holding her breath.

In the coming nights, Beti would lie scrunched up on the edge of the bed, teetering along the side slats, Ma's head on her arm, the rest of Ma's body taking up the entire bed. If Beti slid any further, her hands and feet would hang off the edge. By morning, Ma would be happily stretched out across the bed, and Beti shrunken, falling off the edge, feet hanging near the floor as though already preparing to stand.

Ma's eight-armed pose, her ashtbhuj mudra, was a sight worth seeing, but who was there to witness it? Only the sunlight. Which arrived each morning, kissing Ma's face, and then she would rise, and the two of them would sit and gaze affectionately at each other. Ma and the sun.

*

4

Ma began to rise with the sun and spread throughout the house, first with her eyes, then with her whole being.

When she saw Ma's eyes open amidst the dots of sunshine on her face, Beti would say, Let's go. She'd jump up and hand Ma the cane and support her as well. *She's suffered so, poor Amma, and she lay there so sadly at Bade's house; it made her legs steadily weaker, but I'm here now, we'll see if I don't make her nice and healthy. She teeters along right now, grabbing onto things, but she'll learn to walk. I'll teach her, just wait and see.*

The morning sun rose over the domed tomb in the woods across the way and winked at the balcony. Ma set out in that direction, then stopped. Beti grabbed onto her, and, Oh, oh, oh, I'm falling, I'm falling! Ma took a breath, then Beti took one, and their breathing became as one.

Early days. Ma had to find her balance, her own pace.

On the balcony, she lowered herself carefully into the easy chair and let her gaze roam about between sips of tea, sometimes straight ahead, sometimes behind twisting and turning with the sunlight. The sunlight began to roll about before Ma like a satisfied animal, and the entire balcony was tinted gold.

Beti believed that it was she who was leading Ma out to the balcony; she didn't know the sunlight cast a loop over the cane and tugged Ma insistently forwards.

As time went by, Ma was seen moving about the house with the sunlight: wherever the sun goes, there goes Ma, sitting or reclining. And sometimes standing, sunlight-smitten. In a home where the sky trees breeze come a-knocking at every window and door, sunlight flows in easily and plays with Ma affectionately, affectingly.

Yes, at first, Ma steadies herself from falling from the lap of sunshine *ah-ah-aha*; later she has seemingly grown up, and the two of them march about the house all day, arm in arm. On the balcony until breakfast, then when Ma's in the bathroom, then, who knows, the sunlight sneaks in there too because when she emerges, she's bathed in sunlight. (In the beginning the motherly daughter also slips into the bathroom with Ma because Ma is so weak. This detail may arise again in the future). Ma emerges, swaying along, leaning on sunlight and cane, shimmer shimmer, and seeing her gait, the sunlight is of course reminded of the swing. It smiles crookedly and leans down towards the swing to softly settle Ma in, and the two of them lounge there. (Beti thinks it's she who's settling Ma, but Beti is in the habit of thinking too much.) The sunlight is so fond of Ma's beaming on the swing that it shines and beams as well, even overdoing it a bit. The butterflies flutter in the warmth of the golden glow that coats the glittering cane resting by her side. The sunlight feels a bit too hot now, they seem to say, and squirm in its heat as Ma shifts a little. The sun understands this and snaps out of it—What am I doing! It begs forgiveness, lifts Ma up. The two of them go to the dining table, where the sunlight seats her nearer the shade, slides affectionately down to her feet and rests there.

Even after that, the two of them continue to move about together and, depending on Amma's wishes, the sunlight toasts her middle, warms her back, hums during her afternoon nap. *Ahh*: the sunlight descending into the body, the swinging of the breeze on the skin. As though for the first time the body is sensing itself, letting out a pleasurable sort of *ow ow* at the caresses of sunlight; Ma turns with the sunlight, throws back her head with happiness on the large bed, then pulls the pillow forward so it's crooked, scrunches it this way and that, as the sunlight plays with her.

Until evening, when it seats Ma on the sofa, turns vermillion and begins to melt away from the balcony window. It slowly recedes as though it really doesn't feel like leaving, but can't do injustice to the night; each must take its turn. It sprinkles a last bit of crimson on Ma as it finally departs. Ma wraps herself in her quilt, relaxed now. She knows full well, whether or not she admits it to herself, that the sun is sure to return tomorrow.

When Ma again has the strength to lift her arms, she will dip her cane into the sunshine and roam about all day colouring the walls of the house, such as they are, and everything else within those walls, as though with an uplifted brush. That is, she will take the sunshine on her rounds as though the two of them share a girlish bond: first my turn, then yours.

★

5.

But since everyone has their own self-delusions, why single Beti out for blame? The growing-bigger-daughter looks after the tiny mother so thoughtfully. Slowly slowly, day by day. And how carefully she cares for her, as though she's a glass doll. Amma too behaves as though she might break. Beti oils her hair. She parts her hair to make sure no white varnish or other such unpleasantness lingers. Ma still has trouble holding up her head, and she cries, *Eek ooow!* as she feels the fingers run through her hair.

Amma, Beti glares affectionately, turning into the mother figure.

But it hurts!

Ma cannot yet bend, nor turn. Just a little bit tires her. Beti will bathe her. She sends Mantoori to the bazaar to get holes drilled in the plastic chair, so the water will flow through and Ma can sit down comfortably. Ma sits wherever Beti seats her, however Beti wants, and Beti bathes and washes her. She objects weakly: Go away! Ick! I'm not about to take everything off in front of you.

Oh, come now, I'm behind you, it's not as if I'm looking anyway, and what does it matter, I'm your daughter, Beti scolds.

Eee oooh, when Beti rubs in the shampoo. Ma's body is revealed, as though it's emerging from ages of grime and weakness, and Ma is slowly getting to know it anew, and just now everything is extremely delicate, it hurts, *Eek owww*, wherever you touch it.

But there are chillblains on her feet. Ma got lost, didn't she? Blisters on her soles. Smooth the skin out slowly with the pumice stone.

Beti bends over Ma from behind and scrubs everywhere with the sponge. Ma whimpers as though feeling her body for the first time.

Beti splashes water and rinses her off. From beneath the lather emerges a shiny new body.

She sits her up and wipes her off. Then she wraps her in a large towel, helps her stand, and brings her to the outside room. Ma, soft and delicate and naked as a baby.

Look, Ma says. There are red and blue marks all over her arms.

Beti stunned. Did I rub too hard? Marks on Ma's back as well. These are marks of the missing-days story, which is also missing. Beti doesn't want to remind her by asking, *Where did you sleep? What did you eat?* Beti can't ask anything. Ma was wearing shoes when they found her, so did she leave the house on purpose? How? Alone? Leaning on her cane? Beti doesn't ask. She's busy getting rid of that nightmare, washing and wiping it away.

She pours baby oil onto her palms and rubs it into Ma's skin. Ma *ow eeeks* as though the pain is truly giving her pleasure and she's feeling it in every pore. She sees the orange juice, chirps with joy, and stretches her legs out languorously.

These are the early days. Beti does everything: the bathing, washing, feeding, walking. But she will not need to do this always. Ma will grow strong. She'll do everything herself. She'll bathe herself, wash, eat, walk. Beti will leave the room and Ma will cheerfully morph into an eight-armed being once again.

★

6.

A stem, a petal. Yes indeed, says Ma, drinking tea on the balcony. There should be plants out here. But when I have to go away on trips? Beti protests. Who will look after them then? Then who will look after them? Ma also says. They both laugh and decide on a gardener to help Ma sink her hands into the soil, and *Doesn't matter*, Beti thinks, *let her be happy, do whatever she wants, here there are none of those rules as at Bade's, none of his wife's demands, none of the foibles of the bureaucrats, wear as you want speak what you wish, we are free, let's make a garden on the balcony.*

Every day another plant walks in and climbs into another pot, then toddles about like Ma. Like baby Rama in Tulsidas: *Thumak chalat Ramchandra baajat paijaniyan—Ramchandra toddles along, anklets a-tinkling.* Ma walks along, stopping in bits of sunlight, resting her cane on a flowerpot, raising her hands in the air to stretch, resting them on her waist, swivelling right, swivelling left. The plants dance too, right and left.

What is happening, laughs Beti. She is enjoying Ma's slow awakening.

Feels good, waist feels sore, from sitting so long in the bathroom.

Amma speaks of pain, but in tones of joy.

You feel pain from everything, says Beti affectionately. If medicine goes in the ear the *owow* goes crackle snap inside. If I cut your nails, then *eek eek,* gritting the teeth.

It happens, Ma whimpers. Look, this has turned red.

It already was. Beti looks.

But it was a tiny dot. Look how it's grown. And look over here, this one's turning purple. And listen what happened yesterday: I was sleeping, and I wet the bed!

Ma says, Today I'll take isabgol and Gastromone too. Do you know how little came out? No more than the tip of a fingernail. Ma sharing her constipation pains. She clucks, cries out, unrestrained at the similes she chooses. These secret goings-on rage in her belly.

Wart mole pimple freckle: bursting and busting these was becoming Ma's daily ritual. Patting her arms and legs, glaring staring, pulling off clothing from here, extending limbs in the light and looking there. This one's itchy, too. It's spreading a bit, too. It's gotten darker. Last week it was just a pinprick, now it's more like a boil. What if something's wrong.

As if not just some boil, pimple, wart, but tiny tell-tale buds breaking out on the chest of an ignorant young girl.

Ma speaks of her body like an excited girl who says, Listen! Good news, my period's started, I won't go to school today, I'll take Dispirin and lie in the sun with a hot-water bottle.

Or secretly showing: look, hair has started to grow here.

She couldn't have any fun then, so now? Or whenever you feel the new shoots in your body, the budding, it's the time for the skin to ripple, to feel alive, ecstatic, start to feel the intensity of being born (again). Your body is your body, whether it's your sixteenth year, seventeenth, or seventy-eighth, you prance about strutting your burgeoning blossoming shape. An incandescent breeze may come, or the sunlight slap and makes you blossom and bloom like a tree or plant. She stoops over to examine and inspect herself, sniff at her armpits, her buds crackling open. When a new plant sways, it's not the wind that makes it dance, the ripples come from within, the neck seeks itself with exultation, it prances and struts.

No worries, Beti assures her, it happens with age.

Secrets. Notes between girls. My first day is like a gushing tap. Mine lasts a whole week. My third day is just drops, drip drip, then it's over. Dude, when I got up from my lesson, oh my god, there was a fresh spot on the sofa. I see it, my tutor sees it, both of us turn as red as the spot.

Amidst intimate conversations, girls burst out laughing. These joys of the body, they throw you off balance. Is a heavy flow more fun, or a light one? So hard to decide!

★

7.

All is peaceful. Nothing is happening. Just how Ma likes it.

Aah, says Ma.

Arre, softly, says Beti.

Ma is looking at her arm. What are you looking at, Amma? She is basking in the sun, Amma is. There's a mole on her arm. Look, says Amma. It wasn't there before. I don't like it. It doesn't hurt, does it? No, but it's yucky, it itches, Ma pouts.

Forget about it, Beti cajoles her.

Ma has forgotten. All that bickering behind her tired back.

D.V. Paluskar is singing Raga Shree, *Hari ke Charan Kamaal*. His voice circles softly above the mother-daughter conversation. The sun has bowed its head in an attitude of farewell. Beti turns a page. Sets the table with poppy-red plates. Pulls out her chair. Shuts the masala tin. Takes a bottle from the fridge. *Bzzzzz* goes the mixer. The hand on the clock goes *tick tick*. The redness of the sun will return tomorrow. The books all arranged on the shelf. Shadows laze about. The phulkari shawl flutters softly. A needle falls. The silent voice of night. Quiet does not mean soundless. It is quiet, nesting within sound. Silence gathers behind one's back. One hears the sound of one's own breathing.

★

8

And she begins to make music, that is, Ma begins to with her breathing. Long *looong* inhale *exhaaale*. Deepening. And other vibrations join in.

Aah aah ahahahaha aaahaho. Mouth stretching wide with yawning.

Oooooh oooo eeeeyamaa ooeeoommaa. Swaying side to side.

Hisssang ehhhheheech. Lifting the cane, spilling the sunlight and air over the wall.

Wheeee eeee eeee eeeeee. Finger in ear, itching hard.

She is digging inside and outside her body and expressing this with music.

A sigh for every position, arms raised: *oh*; leg out: *aiyaa*; bell ringing: *oh oh*; if someone visits, *whoosh*; eating roti: *kooot*. Nonsense words abound. Breathing ascends and descends in scales.

Body breath voice: a world of new possibilities.

This is exactly what a child does. It nibbles and kisses its body and experiments in all sorts of ways with its voice. This could be training for getting ahead in the world, or it could be echoes from a previous existence. Renounce some, adopt some, create others anew.

Mothers laugh and get annoyed. A child's beloved prattle.

Beti showers Ma with affection. What's this gibberish you're speaking. I'm going to record it. To play for all your kids. When you're alone, or mostly alone, eating drinking waking, even sleeping. Saying *aah ooh* as you turn over—deep satisfied grunts. When you eat, *uuumm umm chupp chuppp*, lips smacking together. When you drink, it's *slurp*. When you stretch, *eeenaaanunn*. Sounds even come from the bathroom: *aa aa aa hunhu hun*. Beti laughs.

But she doesn't laugh at night. She starts out of her slumber. Amma flings her arms and legs all about the bed as though rehearsing to repeat for the morrow, practising to step out into the world. Every attitude, every pose: *let me try and see*. And snores: *oooh aaahhhhooo zzzz*.

Among these new sounds, Ma sometimes throws in recognizable words. Oooh ooh oookay that part no *phuaarrai munhuie* ooh oh hood plaster ow. But they still don't make any sense. It's like she's making sounds just for the sake of it. She's got a new instrument and she's playing it; that's it, she's learning to play.

Beti doesn't understand this newly forming grammar. But she realises that these are all sounds of peace. Who ever said sounds have to be noisy?

★

9

Sounds of peace.

The *scritchscritch* of the broom on the street.

The newspaper man's sandals running. The *smack* of the newspaper dropping.

The outside door as it opens. A shaft of sunlight jumping in. A speck of grime flying with it.

The rustling of paper as headlines are read. The riffling of pages.

Branches brushing their leaves against the window.

One leaf sighing, floating down to earth.

The *meow meow* of peacocks in the thicket across the street. One can hear the fanning of their feathers, their feet circling in dance.

The sisterhood of Ma and the sunshine. Their whisperings. Their quiet voices.

The fine stream of water lapping the inside of the cup as it's poured from the kettle.

The sunshiney tea emerging from the see-through kettle is a sweet silence; all the same, Ma adds two spoonfuls of honey.

If you watch the champa flowers fall you will hear the sound they make.

A maid rattles a bucket in another flat.

Someone pounds fresh spices. The sweet scent sings.

Someone grinds cardamom in a mortar; the heart is gladdened.

Ma takes a long sip as though drinking in a bird's song.

A bird chirps in response outside.

The society gardener's trowel speaks in the earth: *scrape scrape*.

★

10

I'm not becoming a man, am I? I have a beard, look.

One hair, laughs Beti. Look, I have one in the same place. Yes, hair grows out of this place on my chin. Look, just one. It will keep getting longer.

Ma wants to pull hers out. Give me the scissors.

No, no, Beti gets nervous. I'll pull it out with tweezers. Amazing, I have a single hair in the very same place. We both have beards.

Hee hee hee.

Ma, like this with the foibles of her body, as though examining it for the first time. Or is this love, the way it is with love, the first time every time?

A love so full it envelopes from all sides. Through and through, all around. Inside and out. As though her body is a coat she used to wear right side out, but now wears inside out. The ripped lining now on the outside. The mildew will disappear with an airing. It looks upside downside ripped torn tangled flowing. Blue veins cysts blisters wounds patches. She seeks them out, caresses them, examines them, displays them.

★

11

Beti is having fun. Amma has begun to walk on her own, she circumambulates the house all aglow. What is this? A Hussain print. Was he looking for his mother? He never knew his mother, so he poured his imagination of her into his paintings. Wow, the wonder of art! And this? These are animals painted by the people of Bastar. Where they live, birdbeasthumannature, all are one, all protected, all respected, united. Wow.

The breathing of Beti within the now-returning breathing of Ma. The colour of Beti within the joyous colour of Ma.

Have you read all these books? Yes. Take some down for me, I'll start to read them. Right now, my eyes turn red if I try to read. They water.

Where were you that you got so weak? The question bubbles up inside Beti, unspoken. The heart melts.

Please lie down. Don't do everything all at once. Rest a bit in between.

★

12

The phone rang. It was KK. Beti quickly switched it to silent. What with Ma being a child that can't be woken. She'll talk to him later. He must have returned from Dar es Salaam. She'd forgotten. But even if she'd remembered, she couldn't allow him to come over yet. Certainly not to sleep. Amma is occupying the bed. For a few days, other relationships were to be postponed.

And besides, she didn't feel like seeing him. Beti knew, though perhaps only subconsciously, that a mother and a girlfriend cannot exist in the same body.

★

13.

Ma eats paratha and saag. Beti has arranged for the maid next door to cook for the two of them. She can't feed Ma her own usual: vegetables and grains all mixed up together—kichadi style—what KK calls *fodder*.

*

14

Beti enjoys introducing Ma to new experiences.

Watch it. It's an English film, very good. You'll understand everything. The pronunciation will get easier as you listen. It's about Nazi Germany. Based on a true story.

Mother and daughter watch films together. They laugh awkwardly at the Western kissing. *Chee chee*, Ma says in a completely un-*chee chee* tone—how can they mix their spit like that? They giggle like innocent girls. Is the redness on their cheeks from the sunlight without or the heat within?

★

15

She has told KK: let things settle first. Ma isn't well yet, come later. She couldn't say—not even to herself—that just as two swords cannot rest in the same sheath, mother and lover cannot inhabit the same skin. Or sleep in the same bed either.

Ma sleeps sprawled across the bed. She falls asleep the moment she lies down. As she sleeps, she reaches out and feels that Beti is there, isn't she, yes, she is, head, hand, knee, Ma sticks to her; she sleeps better that way. Beti on the other hand remains awake, but who cares, Ma is sleeping peacefully and this brings Beti comfort. By morning, Beti is practically off the bed; Amma stretched out across it. Beti sets her alarm, but turns it off, since she's already awake before it rings.

*

But there are other bells over which she has no control these days. Neither the phone, nor the door.

No one used to ring the bell here. No one ever dropped by unannounced. Those who came were expected at set times, and as soon as she heard them, Beti would open the door. KK had his own key. She would put out the trash, leave the milk bag outside. So those bells that usually ring daily in other homes were silent here. Beti did the vacuuming, the sweeping, the mopping too, and sometimes the company that did the cleaning at KK's office did a full professional cleaning here— webs, bugs, book dust, pipe rust. So everything was neat and tidy and there wasn't a cook because Beti looked after her health, yes, but she didn't fuss over food. Food for one person, sometimes two, and every now and then a party; what's so hard about that? It actually makes giving a party more fun: let's have a bit of excitement today! Italian, Chinese, Mexican, Gujarati, Bengali, Malabari—she'd give parties with all different flavours. And KK was skilled in the kitchen.

But now there was a bumper crop of bells. The cook's bell, the gardener, the sweeper-mopper, the fruit and vegetable sellers, the fresh coconut water guy, and the relatives. No one had a set time, and no one was the sort to call first before coming. Is it Amma's cell phone ringing? Is it the door? Beti is deceived every time; she isn't used to the sound of her own doorbell, nor to the ringtone on Ma's cell. She jumps out of her skin.

Family members near and far, and Bade and Bahu's friends and community, they all call. We've heard you're staying with your daughter a few days, that's nice, for her too, and how are you? Every day Bahu calls to ask, Should we come get you back, the new house is in pretty good shape now, your new room is full of sunshine. Bade phones to say, When are you coming back, shall we send over your bathing stool, are you getting anything to eat, shall we get some parathas sent over? Sid calls to say that he'll come see her when he gets back from Boston: I heard you snuck out to take a trip all by yourself, you should have waited for me, you should have told me, very bad grandmother. And the gardener calls to say Mata ji, the fish-flake fertilizer is available, they have bougainvillea, all different colours, even Mary Palmer, but they haven't got the Chinese Orange yet, I'll look in the other bazaar; oh, and I got the hose. The fruit seller calls to say the papaya is not the injected type, it's natural. The vegetable seller calls to say, Mata ji, I've brought bathua and dill. Mata ji says, bring black carrots too. She tells the maid to grate them, let's make some halwa.

When the doorbell rings suddenly, Beti picks up the phone and starts saying *Hello hello*. Then the front door opens, and she stares stupidly, wondering, *Who is this?* She doesn't recognise them, even though she knows everyone perfectly well, it's just her first time seeing them here. How can she get used to this new state of affairs?

One night the bell rang at one o'clock: Beti was flabbergasted. She rose with a start, pulled her shawl over her shoulders and ran to open the door, falling all over herself. There it was dark; all the same she thought she should call the guard and scold him, how had he sent someone without any warning? But the poor thing hadn't sent anyone, she realised as she woke up fully. It hadn't been the door but Ma's phone, and Ma had answered it. At this hour? Her anger shot up only to change to fear—at this hour? And she grew fearful as she heard talk of death. It was Bade who had called. Tinno Chachi living in far-off Edmonton had passed away. Sid had gone to see her only yesterday and she'd been quite cheerful, yes, she was over eighty, might even have been ninety, when we were with your Papa in Ranchi and we saw her then, that was more than twenty years ago, she must have been about seventy. There was a debate on age and Beti's fear increased with regard to the possible ages of death. For the rest of the night she kept peering anxiously at Ma. It wasn't as though she could sleep anyway.

She must find a way not to be disturbed by bells.

★

16

Amma has gone to sleep as though everything is and has been peaceful. And so it is. Since when does peace share a link with noise? Or noise with peace? When it's quiet, everything's quiet. There's peace all around, so you are calm, even if the outside world is engaged in a wild rumpus. If there's noise around then you too are noise-some, even in stillness.

★

17.

Ma begins to speak secretly. To herself, as though to say, I've talked to others, now I'll speak with myself. As though she's two beings, one looking at the other, and one tells the other, *Now go, bathe,* and the first one replies, *Yes, it's getting late, let me go bathe.*

Oh, but be careful, says the first.

Oof, that was a close one, laughs the second.

★

18.

She who can see with the mind's eye can close her eyes and see: Ma in her baggy clothes, with her slightly stumbling gait, with her hopping skipping cane, wandering about her daughter's home, almost hovering two inches above the ground, bobbing along within a delicate bubble of silence that contains droplets of rainbow-hued sunlight.

Silence is not broken by noise.

*

19.

Early in the morning, when Ma drinks her tea on the balcony, a blackbird whistles. A lilting tune.

*

20.

Slowly Ma pours herself into the crannies and crevices of the house. She feels as though she's flying. She likes it. *My feet don't touch the ground here.* She flies about silently. She listens to the comings and goings of her breathing. She hears the curling of a tendril. She hears the growing of the grass. She hears the undulation of the sunlight. She hears the descent of evening. She hears the unfurling of her own body. She hears the blossoming of the unfurling.

★

21

You pour yourself into the corners and hollows of your new home like air, observes Beti lovingly. Ma says, Air pours out of me as I move. Touch it, see how bloated my belly is. Wind comes out when I walk. If you release it, it flies up, and you float about in a balloon of air. *Ha ha ha ho ho ho*, both enjoy each other's coarse humour.

Lengthy conversations ensue over the belly, like: I eat so much here, but sometimes it comes out small as a lotus seed, or even tiny as a sesame. I feel like I have to go all the time, but I huff and puff and only pass air. My bowels have become so loose it always feels like something's on its way. My insides are all baggy and everything's backed up in there. It doesn't want to come out.

I'll bring you figs.

But you eat them all up!

Am I not getting older myself?

You also sit long on the pot; so let's both wander about breaking wind.

Oh my, Amma.

They laugh. Mother and daughter nest in intimacy. They egg each other on and address one another with the most informal forms of *you*.

★

22

See Ma digging in a flowerpot. Hear the lilting whistle of a bird's song. Beti has eaten some fried food and licks her fingers. All the butterflies watch. The sunlight grows aromatic.

Laughter: What are you doing!

More laughter: What are *we* doing?

The balcony and the whistle. The bird and the whistle. Amma and the bird. The flowerpots have arrived on the balcony. Ma's hands are always smeared with earth now. Green shoots pop up.

★

23

Every fruit has its season. In sawan and bhadon, the jamuns come plopping down from the trees, and in grisham the mangoes burst forth. In shishir, brilliant green parrots roost on the bright green guavas, and in a family, during the season of raunak, i.e., fun season, whistles begin to blow. And as they blow, they become more and more self-aware, and the attainment of such self-knowledge is not just for those who have reached nirvana but rather available to the bells too—ecstatic: *We exist! Oh, my! Oh, wow!* They begin to whistle fast and faster and near and nearer, so that every whistling thing catches the enchantment.

The whistle of the pressure cooker. Meaning, *it's done. Hurry, or it will burn.* But see Beti getting cooked herself, alongside the food, at the sounding of a whistle, while the rest of the bells and whistles now wish to test their impact. So they all start to buzz and ring and sing all the more. The phone, the doorbell, the leaves, the branches, the blackbird.

It wasn't Beti's fault. She just wasn't used to it. Every time she felt disconcerted, and every time she'd look from one device to another wondering, who is doing this? Then the carryings-on of the buzzing and whistling things became vengeful; she picked up the teacup, and the cooker shrieked, and the hot tea splashed. As soon as she sat down to edit her articles, the intercom buzzed to announce that so-and-so was coming to see Ma ji. Those whom the guard had already recognised would be announced by the doorbell screeching like a spoiled child, and Beti would again fall or knock something over. She could not yet tell whether it was Ma's phone ringing or a visitor's phone buzzing in a differently cacophonous manner. And anything and everything made her lose her balance or drop things.

Ring ring. Eh? Phone? Intercom? Bird chirping? Door? She'd jump up and stare at the door as though it were about to jump at her.

I'll open it, called the maid as she came from the kitchen wiping her hands.

Beti looked up dumbly as though seeing this sight for the first time. She would probably never get used to the Reeboks. As it is, if we see someone in a different place from where we're accustomed to seeing them, perhaps it's no surprise if we don't recognise them. The Reeboks slipped in through the door *thump thump.* She seemed to recall getting confused by this same *thump thump* earlier too and wondering, *am I an outsider or an insider, and what about her?*

But. She blinked and blinked. *But this is the door to my home, not to that one. I'm the one who's here, inside, and she's coming from the outside. This is not that house…*she turned to where Bahu had entered and was now touching the feet of her mother-in-law seated on the swing…*this is my house.*

Oh my, said Ma.

Bahu sat down on the swing giggling. So you've started to swing?

In my home, Ma swings. Beti could be allowed a touch of preening. But quicktothedraw requires quickwittedness, not the sort of dimwittedness that that goes about stumbling and losing balance at bells and whistles. The moment had passed, and by then the mother-in-law had started giving the daughter-in-law the tour.

Nothing is walled off here. Look, she swirls the cane about. Here's the whole hallway, and the study in one alcove, and in another, the TV room, and in another, the library, and in a nook, the tea room. Open the drawer, and inside is the tea kettle, the tea things, everything fits. Make the tea, shut it. You should set things up like this in your flat too. Ma was doing a PowerPoint presentation with her cane, showing off as though this was her own home she wanted Bahu to learn from. There's a neem tree at this window. Peepul at this one. Yesterday morning there was a shah bulbul sitting here. This is the spare room. If it gets too late you can just stay here. This is my bed. You can comfortably get to the bathroom at night. The wall itself gives support. Sleep worry-free. But this one doesn't sleep, she's always getting up to light my way with her torch. Her work is suffering for it.

Why is it suffering? asked Bahu, in that tone of false concern that families use: who can ever say it's a barb? She has your company! Mother-daughter special time! The hawk eyes glance about for inspection: *Poor people pots and pans. What slovenly pictures. If they're not nonsensical, they're filled with nudes. These are the only two possible outcomes in art today. Prehistoric chairs. Dishes of all different colours, no attempt at collecting a set. Rubber banana leaf–placemats instead of a tablecloth. A mat made of grasses and such, instead of a rug or carpet, strings of birds horses camels instead of curtains, boat-shaped cardboard bowls filled with wal-*

nuts and fruit. A fridge painted in unmatching colours. An open kitchen so the servant is always in front of you. Sofa and seats made of bamboo and jute. Walls look like they were smeared with cow dung; seems like she wants it to look like a village hut. Her ever-so-slight smile, ever-so-snide too, rests in the curve of her lips, like *you can't catch me out* and she can claim, *Oh, no, of course I'm not laughing. This room-less home. This junk-shop furniture. I would never accept such a home, even for free.*

But Bahu said no such things out loud. She gave her Overseas Son a missed call and as soon as he called back, she began singing the praises of his aunt's home. How it was completely unique, like the photos of homes printed in magazines and newspapers, like that article about the house in Udaipur that was built around the trunk and branches of a living tree. No, this one doesn't have a tree, but everything is turny-twisty. Fine for you young folks, she said. I would just fall right off these crooked seats. Everything is so low, if you don't keep your eyes to the ground you're bound to trip over something. Actually, the doctor forbids it. For the back, for the knees, it's not good to sit down so low and bend over for every single thing.

Yes, what else? She must be agreeing with Overseas Son, your Daadi is not in the habit of all these low-down things. Don't you remember, we put bricks under the legs of the takht on the veranda to make it taller for her? But she must like the change. He's saying he'll bring you a walker now, keep it with you, use it when you feel like it. The furniture is a bit too artistic, though. You do walk carefully, don't you? Please don't fall.

Arre, no, if Beti could say it, she would. It's not the low-swinging things here that trip you up, it's all the bells and whistles.

Oh, it's great fun, said Ma, still showing off the house, turning it over and over like a toy, whilst Bahu flips it about, judging it sternly.

Take out the amla chutney as well. Oh, but first drink some buttermilk. Will you have some wood apple sharbat? The gardener got some from somewhere.

Wow, all this, here. You've really set up house—mooli parathas? Wonderful. You've got a good cook. And the house is sparkling. You've also hired a maid? Well then. That hoovering once a week doesn't fly in India. Bahu sang praises. Ma has turned your house into a home.

Amma is looking so happy, Bahu praises further, looking very happy herself. So her sister-in-law has fallen to earth from her perch. All those airs about how her life was different and free. Now Beti's become one of us. She wobbled, she cracked, she slipped, she popped.

Bahu did not envy this zesty lifestyle. Sisters-in-law do not desire the sort of life another leads. But they are pleased to see another deprived of the life they themselves wish to lead.

Who knows if Bahu actually thought this, or if it just gets filed under the stereotype of sister-in-law relations. Family relations have their own beaten paths which turn into ritual relationships, roles performed accordingly. They are carried forward in the expected way without any thought, almost out of inertia. Has the relationship popped out of its worn groove? Who is going to trouble themselves over analysing that?

Beti's heart sank. *Yeh voh seher to nahin jiski aarzoo le kar / chale the yaar ki mil jayegi kahin na kahin—This is not the dawn we'd hoped to discover, my friend / when we set out, sure we would find it somewhere*—she thought, recalling the Faiz poem.

Your Sari. He bought it on Holi. I had the fall stitched on.

Goodness, I'd have to stuff half the thing in at my waist, you take it, you wear it.

Why, don't you like it? Why not? And some scent for you. Mitti—attar. I got it in Chandni Chowk. Here's a cheque. He said to sign here. On this paper as well. Do you need money? Keep some. We don't take from daughters. When will you come back? Why are you digging in your ears? Can you hear okay? Please don't leave home, something invariably goes wrong. I have to go to an ENT specialist. We'll go together.

What is Bade doing that he can't come here? Ma scolded.

Beti is watching as a spectator, listening. Like it's a stage. Is what's happening right now the play or was that the thing that already happened?

Just then another bell rang. *Door? Bird? Cooker? Ma? Heart? Phone? KK? I should say, Come, now, let everyone view my lifestyle, you won't find your ostentatious morality here. He must have arrived from Vishakapatnam.*

It was Ma's phone.

Hello.

Hello.

Ma ji?

No, it's me.

Arre, this is Rosie Bua.

Namaste, Rosie Bua.

Are you back? Hello. You were gone so long this time. Yes, yes, come. Whenever. Beti will give you directions.

That one? The hijra? Rosie Bua? Bahu asked. She comes here too?

She's coming.

Beti listens to Bahu listening. It's no problem, Rosie Bua. Ma is here. She's fine now. Yes, do cross both bridges. The road goes up from the bus depot, after that, there are shops, Le Marché is to the left. *Le Marché*. It's French. Everyone will say *La Mart* or *La Marsh*. After that, there's a round chowk. Come straight.

Everything is simple if you stay within the grooves of tradition. By that reckoning, Beti's mood will improve now. *There are no silly taboos at our place. And look how liberated Ma feels. She doesn't lie lifeless here.*

It appeared that Rosie had made short work of the Reeboks. Now who's the boss?

Only Ma. But no one realises.

★

It was on one of those days. Or nights. Yet another bell rang. Beti's half-slumbering eyes opened with a start. It was not a bell-like bell. But what bell is, these days? Was Amma adding to her invented language? Beti began to stare into the semidarkness. Ma was sleeping. But that made no difference. She heard the sound again.

Jingle jangle jing.

Bangles. On Ma's wrist.

Just two bangles. A few safety pins swing from them. This is what woke me?

Beti turned over irritably.

But the bangles were bent on disturbing her. As if to say, Why wouldn't we be thrilled to jangle? Or was this Ma playing a trick—a bangle manoeuvre—to get Beti to sleep separately and deeply?

It wasn't that late at night. Most of the night remained. And two bangles had started to jingle. Just as Beti was about to sink into sleep. Thin, shiny glass ones. Ma had removed her chain, her kangan, everything else, but who knows whether it was on purpose that she hadn't removed these bangles, or by mistake.

Perhaps they'd also found freedom from the surrounding world and so begun to jingle?

Heedless of thousands of other reverberations, Beti, who had slept through the snoring of several lovers, and once even a husband, began to feel defeated by these two small bangles. Ma's getting up, slipping her feet into sandals, the *squeeeaaak* of the door opening, the *pop* of the light turning on, the release of a stream of liquid, all these things kept her awake, and now to those got added these two naughty bangles. She had somehow endured all the other noises, but this time she cracked. Hasn't Kamala Jharia sung something like this: *In kashtiyon ka kya hai, aksar ye hi hua hai, majhdhaar se nikal ke saahil pe dub jayen— What of those boats* (how often this happens!) *that sail out of deeper waters, only to sink when they reach the shore?*

Were they jangling or chattering? Was it a joke or a conspiracy? *Let's keep this woman awake!* As though they'd purposefully made themselves so light that they jingled at the slightest movement. If Ma stirred a little or started or turned. They could rob you of your sleep and keep you up. They could stay up singing and dancing all night. The more Beti twisted her body, covered her ears, the more delightfully the bangles bantered. If Ma lifted her hand as she slept and placed it somewhere, they would clink as though Ma had purposefully wiggled her hand to make them tinkle.

They bicker-banter with each other, a sound someone else might call a light jingle, ringing relentlessly in Beti's ears. As though she had antennae, which had pricked up at their faint rattle. The two bangles waxed so garrulous they became the very definition of noisy, the epitome of the absence of quiet. What do noisy and quiet have to do with soft and loud? Something large becomes largely ineffective, something tiny becomes teensily ear-splitting. The soft tones of Khalil Gibran. Gulliver's Lilliput. An ant playing with an elephant.

And during those sleepless nights, Beti became convinced that some evil spirit had snuck in under the guise of the bangles to finish her off. She'd been so proud to be free as a bird: a working woman and a leader in women's rights. *So take charge now.* She hadn't wanted a more domestic life. *But you've got one now, when you're no longer fit for it. Now you're no good for anybody.* Na ghar ki na ghat ki—*no fixed abode; a flighty floosy.* Not alone, not with KK, not working or playing or waking or sleeping, though she wants sleep all the time, and *We'll kidnap her* and *jingle jangle jingle jangle whisper whisper whisper.* I don't know their language but they're definitely cooking up mischief. Sometimes it seems like they're clashing together and squabbling. *I'm prettier than you—no* you're *the pathetic one.* No, no, the two of them have a single goal—don't let me sleep, ring in my ears. *Jingle jangle cling clang clang cling.*

Beti passed the night in the company of the garrulous bangles, and Ma's proposal began to invade her mind, that she sleep separately, go into the guest room herself; can't send Ma there, after all.

When Beti got up, Ma, usually spread across the rest of the bed like a vast nation, was absent, but her daughter's ears were still filled with the din of the two bangles. And had those wretched things filled her nose with the smell of crushed garlic too?

★

At the scent of garlic, Beti opened her eyes and the bangles echoed in her mind. Amma wasn't there by her side. It had started to be like this in the mornings: she'd finally fall asleep and Ma would quietly get up and set off by herself. Beti would make her way unsteadily out of the room and Ma, on the balcony, would look up and call out to her. She'd have the tea nearby and be patting the plants or digging her hands into the dirt.

When Beti entered the hall confused, there were Rosie and Ma, goods and chattels spread out before them, the breezes bearing a strong scent of garlic.

Ooooh, careful, Rosie Bua warned. Baby, you'll fall.

I don't like it when she calls me Baby. It's not okay for Ma to get up so quietly. Did she make tea again? And garlic? She opened the front door too? The breeze is so strong. She's snuck in, the sly thing.

She found out that Rosie had suggested a home remedy for the moles and skintags that kept cropping up (which Ma didn't like). Just crush garlic and smear.

Ma sat with her arms and legs stretched out. The paste was smeared here and there on her body. The droplets of garlic stuck to her skin. Insides out, flipped up and over, inside faucets and entrails all gushing blood breath life. All exposed.

Beti didn't like Ma sitting around exposed like that.

Look how she's sitting, Baby, your Amma, Rosie laughed. Like girls who sit around helplessly after their mehndi's been put on.

The garlic burns it off, see, Baby, Rosie explained. Look, I pressed each one with a Bandaid. Smell gone!

Not in the slightest. How are you? Beti tried to smile and, after picking a garlic skin up off the floor, turned towards the kitchen.

She was feeling angry with herself: *Why can I never fall asleep until early in the morning, and why does Ma secretly sneak away? She's also getting stealthy in the middle of the night, so I won't wake up at her every breath. And now I'm the one who reaches for her clothing and body in the dark to reassure myself. Ma thinks I need room. She slides away to give me space. And then I slide towards her to make sure she's okay. She reaches the edge and I'm right next to her and the rest of the bed is vacant. That's why she's getting up before me.*

Later she kept wondering if the guard had called, what must he have said. And me still asleep. Ma must have answered the intercom. That's what woke her, maybe. Well, and why shouldn't Rosie Bua come? No middle-class hypocrisies here, demanding they take care of hijra business outside on the lawn.

She sat deflated on the balcony, watching Ma and Rosie Bua from the corner of her eyes. Maybe Rosie had come to get her Holi bakhsheesh now. Hadn't Amma been saying, *Oh, you were gone a long* time?

And thus began the visits of Rosie Bua. Barrelling in like a fresh gust of wind.

★

She could slip in at any time. Chiming like the wind. Making the whole house chime. Even after Rosie Bua left, she filled the house, leaving her mark everywhere. Sometimes she brought a plant. Or a bunch of fresh coriander. Or papadum from old Delhi, or badiyan, or pickle. Filling the house with new aromas. Her smell lingering within them.

What scent does Rosie wear? Beti asked Ma. Yes, that's a strong perfume. Damn it, it even gets into the rotis. And the garlic on you.

Not anymore. I just washed my hair. With that herbal shampoo. That's what I can smell.

Then why do you wrap your head in a towel? It's sunny, sit outside with your hair down and dry it, advised Beti.

No, Ma responded in a wise-old-woman tone. Rosie told me one should wrap one's hair in a towel for a while to dry it. Otherwise the natural oils evaporate with the wind and sun, and the hair looks dull.

She didn't tell you to dye your hair black? Beti didn't mean to be rude, but why was Rosie always meddling with Ma about hair skin moles?

If I wanted to, she'd suggest it. She's worked in a beauty parlour, that's why she knows all these remedies. Here, taste these mungauris. Nice and hot. They're soft now. One shouldn't put them in the karhi to cook them, they get hard. You should just put them in when you're about to remove the karhi from the flame.

★

27.

Every morning Beti saw Ma in a new ointment mixed by Rosie—amla, bhringaraj, brahmi, and a spoonful of henna. Rosie boiled them, ground them, blended them, then poured the mixture into a glass bottle. Ma would take it from the fridge every day and rub it into the roots of her hair with her knuckles, then pull out loose strands, wrap them round a finger and hand the coil to Beti: Here, throw this away. And she said, less is falling out since yesterday. After this she kept rubbing the blue colour from her fingernails with lemon peel, and she waved Beti away: There's still pith, don't throw it out. And the rotting blue lemons peer at Beti from the table and teapoy day and night.

★

28

A new posture for life. *Ow ow* from Ma, and Rosie guiding
and chiding.

Ai hai, you're acting like a touch-me-not, Baji.

Arre, it hurts. Look. It's turned blue. Ma bursts out laughing.

You must've run into something.

No, I just bumped into the door.

That's called running into something. Oh, Baji. You look all
beaten up.

Arre, I've been beaten all over. Even the air from the fan
beats me.

Listen, Baby, said Rosie, looking at Beti. Your Amma is
sixteen all over again. Even the air injures her fine skin. Did
you hear, Baby?

Of course she heard. That Ma ji had turned into Baji.
Where was I? Where am I? The language changes from one
thing to another and I don't have ears to hear it? How can
Ma ji become Baji? Should I start calling her Chamma,
instead of Amma?

★

29

She arrived at the crack of dawn carrying a sack. When Beti emerged that day, rubbing her eyes, bolts of fabric were spread everywhere between the balcony and the bedroom. Rosie was right in the middle of it all, but where was Ma? Then she saw that Ma was wrapped in a bolt of white and gold fabric, looking every inch Tutenkhamen. Her tiny head sticking out. Or a tiny replica of the Egyptian sphinx.

Ma like this! Beti was dumbfounded.

What's going on? asked Beti. Why are you hidden in this bolt of fabric?

Because she's Baji Goatearking, chuckled Rosie. She's hiding her ears.

Beti had no idea what Rosie meant, but the joke sounded crude to her. Rosie was getting a bit too free.

Beti learned that Rosie had suggested an antidote for liberating Ma from the height-shrinking-daily sari-wearing frustration of having to double the fabric over like an old hold-all and constantly take up the petticoat hem: wear a gown. I'll get it made.

By a tailor. A certain Raza Tailor Master.

Now you're going to wear a nightie day and night? asked Beti with an awkward laugh. She laughed, because at her house there were no middle-class concerns about how one must act like this-that in front of others, but felt awkward because these decisions were being made outside her orbit. They didn't even want her opinion. They just left her asleep and did as they pleased. She'd have to get used to Ma spreading her wings each day during the drawn out mornings.

(After returning from America, Sid would also drop by after his morning jog, and KK would show up as well, not heeding her refusals).

Not a nightie, Baby, a gown.

A dressing gown, said Beti, as though this too were unconscionable.

Evening gown, day gown. Wait and see; you'll want one too.

There will be pockets, too, for me to put my hankies, proffered Ma.

Yes, for sure. Hankies, cardamoms, pens, said Rosie, extending the list.

Elephant, horse, palanquin.

Lovely embroidery.

Nothing flashy.

They were selecting fabric and making sure there was nothing flashy, something in a sober colour, with a fine border or maybe some light embroidery.

You'll also get one made, Baby, when you see how she turns into Queen Victoria. And it will also be easier to use the bathroom.

No fabric getting bunched between the legs.

She just says whatever she wants. Queen Victoria, Eargoatking, now this.

Whatever happened, Ma's attire had been decided. Rosie pencilled in the design on the fabric and cut it out to bring to Raza Tailor Master. Scissors, thread, needles and pins and measuring tape could be found on the balcony at Beti's house now or on the swing or on a table or even on the desk in the study.

Because one thing leads to another, and a bolt of fabric leads to cut-up scraps, about which Ma said, don't throw them away, we'll start making little bags, sacks with pockets, handkerchiefs, stuffed cotton dolls, the parrots and monkeys of childhood days, we'll give them beaded faces. We'll make houses and cars out of matches, and we can use bottle caps for wheels. The children of the gardener and maid will get toys, Beti and the other family members will get all different bags, and the rest is all for Rosie's profit—she'll know what to do.

But one thing did lead to another, and so it was that other people living at the society also caught the bug, and arrived to donate their own odds and ends to Ma and Rosie and happily departed with snacks and handicrafts in exchange.

To tell the truth, trash was no longer trash. Because everyone was forbidden to throw anything away without Ma and Rosie's permission. Boxes, bottles, cartons, broken cups, plates, buttons, peels, wood, rocks, feathers, coins—all were kept and revitalised. They were turned into animals and who knows what.

Even a donkey's tail was fashioned from Ma's hair. Her hair had been trimmed to get rid of the split ends, because otherwise how can hair become beautiful, thick and long?

And Ma began to wear lovely embroidered abayas, or gowns or whatever you want to call them. She was like a breath of fresh air as she wandered about the house. She began to go downstairs as well, and sometimes she'd sit with the neighbours on the lawn, but best of all, she liked to sit with Rosie on the steps of the medieval tomb in the green belt across the street.

★

30

Beti remembered how Rosie Bua used to visit on holidays. If she happened to go to Bade's home at the same time, she'd run into Rosie too. Chairs would be set out on the lawn for Ma and Rosie, and Rosie would come in by the gate at the back of the lawn, the small one, or by the garage side, palms pressed together, and whenever she saw Beti, she'd pat her on the head without fail and say something like, Arre, Baby's come, may you live long, when did you get here?

Back then, Beti hadn't minded being called Baby.

Sturdy Rosie Bua always wore a colourful sari or shalwar-kurta, or maybe some type of sharara outfit. These would invariably be embroidered with gold thread and stars, and the blouse or orhni bordered with brocade. Or embroidered with twining vines. And her pointy brassieres, like the ones worn by heroines in old films. But Rosie Bua didn't sing or dance, and she didn't perform for a living. Her voice was a bit deep, but only the way many women's voices are. She sat with Ma. Ma would speak, give her gifts, snacks as well, and that's as much as Beti could remember. How much can you remember about a sight you've only seen occasionally?

But that was Rosie then, and this was Rosie now. Now she came bearing a large bag, like a toy hawker. Truly, if Beti had still been a little girl, she would have asked, Kabuliwallah, what's in your bag? and an elephant would have emerged.

But what emerged was an idol, not an elephant; this Beti would only learn many days later, when she climbed the ladder to search for a book on the topmost shelf. This? Here? Who put it up here?

Rosie did, came Ma's blunt response.

★

31

Daily life drops a veil over what's actually going on. What's really been happening only becomes apparent when much of it has already occurred. Beti reacted a little here, a little there, but usually the thing that came to her mind was, *Poor Ma, how broken and defeated she was as she lay there in that traditional set-in-its-ways-house, I'm not about to leave her forgotten and shrunken, and then, after that, getting lost, and thank God nothing untoward happened, otherwise everyone would blame themselves forever more. All these peaceful precious moments here, these mother-daughter moments, and I'm happy Ma's clank-clank-clanking about with her colourful cane, floating about in the open with the sunlight, and this is a space where one can breathe freely. Live, Ma, live to your heart's content!* These thoughts burst from Beti's every pore.

At which we can recount another story, whether we actually recall it or not. There was once a person who was very fond of trees, who always praised them, and exclaimed, How they grow bloom flourish! And this person spoke to them morning to evening, and never experienced loneliness on account of the trees. The cotton trees were well pleased and began to bloom everywhere. Huge flowers fell all around. That same person's car stood below the trees and beneath the car lay a paved driveway. This became a bit of a problem in terms of daily cleaning. Who would even think twice? This tree-loving individual had them all hacked down, those deeply beloved, much praised trees.

Or we can recall another type of scenario, if we wish, in which the type of people who go on and on about what a shameless country America is wet their pants in excitement and pack their bags to go at the slightest beckoning from that same nation.

And since we're recollecting stories, I mean, if that's what we're doing here, there's also the one about the woman who called herself a writer. Her life revolved around lavishing abuse on cities. I must get out; I want nothing, just my pen, my notebook, a couple of books, and nature. And she did escape with these to a forest rest house in a jungle to write her novel. A bungalow on a lovely hill, an airy room like a pagoda suspended from the sky. She uncapped pen, took out paper, and sat down, imagining the new life that would come to her: life, and plenty of it! And it did come. New life. And plenty of it. Because in this pagoda, where the wind came whipping through, everything else began to come and go with the wind as well. The beginning begins at the beginning. With an inspired heart, the lady writer watches her ideal embodiment bloom and blossom. With a puff of breeze, leaves, stalks, bits of grass, flotsam and jetsam catapult in. Yay, jungle! Yay, nature! Her quill thrills at its skill. But she did not realise at the outset that nature is not some dead thing; the pagoda is not a coffin. Everything here is alive. And that which is not will likely need only a nudge. The way new plants can grow from a corpse. Memory can raise an moribund tale. And so on. And so forth. Inspired by inspiration, the authoress can neither believe her eyes, nor her ears, nor her foolish brain, that everything is alive now. What she'd been considering a bit of dirt is actually a bug, which suddenly begins to scurry along. A leaf turns out to be a creature with wings. Even a stick, like a small child's first stick figure drawing, suddenly flips over on the wall and scurries off. And on top of that, the mice play hide-and-seek in the ceiling, and when they see the blank page from above, they fill it with their own writing *splaaattt*. The authoress is scared witless. Her breathing gets stuck right where it is, nothing coming in or going out. If anything died in that bursting burgeoning atmosphere it was her. Her love of nature, now on the lam, and her memory of her hatred for all things urban now filled her with longing, as though hate were a synonym for love.

But what does all this have to do with our story? Beti was improving Ma's life in every way. She did not forbid anyone from coming or going. She smiled at Ma's new styles of eating and dressing. She was allowing her to grow a jungle on the balcony. Later, she would even allow KK to sneak in without permission, as when she would go out, and return to find him chatting with Ma and Rosie. Rosie of course cheerfully visited all the time, and what did it matter to Beti whether she's this or she's that. Yes, perhaps she found it a bit unsettling when she found her cutting Ma's toenails—just a tiny bit—but only because, oh, hey, she could have asked me. These two were having a wonderful time while Beti was off busy with something. She was also in a bit of a quandary as to whether Ma should be so free just because she's found a free helper? But.

And everything beyond that also fell under the heading of *but*.

Yes, for Ma to leave the house to give her Buddha to someone, that was a bit wrong. And Rosie, in a hurry to get somewhere, bumped into Ma on the corner and told her to go back home, with Bade's house still in sight, and Ma turned back, but missed the gate, and continued on to the next one, and from then it was all next after next after next. But what need was there to get the idol out of the way? Or to hide it? Beti had needed K.M. Munshi's *Jai Somnath* and was wondering where it was, and so she'd climbed to the top shelf of the bookcase on the ladder, and was shaken because the missing Buddha had been placed right in front of the Munshi. The idol from her childhood. Which she had wanted, and which Bade had forbidden.

Did I steal it? she wondered to herself, stunned. Amma! she screamed.

All stared at the idol in her hand like thieves. From below, neither the idol nor Munshi had been visible.

I put it there, said Rosie.

Because I said to, said Ma. She reached out her hand. Rosie took the Buddha and placed it in front of Ma.

Both of them staring at it. The idol as triptych.

Beti watching this trimurti from a distance. Distance doesn't come from physical expanse, but from the gaze and the heart. She'd wanted the Buddha for so long; Ma could have given it to her. And here it was in her own home, brought here without her knowledge or assent.

This absence of knowledge and assent were precisely the things that sometimes awakened an emotion of displeasure in her, else she'd begrudge nothing.

And all the different winds and breezes blew and blew and blew.

★

Wind changes its disguise again and again. Memory pain desire faith charisma beauty imagination fragrance. One puff and the earth spins. The seed sprouts and climbs towards the tree. A flock of birds descends on the soft grass, believing themselves to be lotus flowers, the grass to be water. In this way, water becomes grass green. The wind weaves night into night. It spirits away the sun under cover of clouds. When the wind tickles the sun, it skitters away, and the clouds double over with laughter and expand fatly until they burst and transform into rain. And this becomes Ma-time so that she joyfully cries *ow ow* at every puff of breeze, delights in the marks left by the breeze on her skin, her joy reflected in her eyes, intoxicated with the pain, her life and breath sending breeze bubbles down her skin.

No one wonders, but in case they did, they would wonder what happens if the wind stirs up the juices inside your body. When a plane drops from twenty-seven thousand feet to seven thousand, the air blocks your ears. With every lurch, the blockage follows suit, and the wind rushes in and lurks in your ears. Then, at the next lurch, the air leaks out with a soft painful whistle. Sometimes it gets trapped in the ear for a long time with no way of getting out, and then the whistle stirs up a huge uproar deep inside, and it goes gambolling about somewhere below, and maybe it becomes a vein in the cheek and starts to pulsate, or it goes chug chug behind the eyelids, or flaps like wings beneath the brow. You get scared and call the doctor, the hakim, the vaidya, who tells you that your fluid balance has been upset. But who has upset it, if not the wind? Even a fluid that has remained still for centuries cannot stay static forever. The breeze moves it, shakes it from its atrophy and then begin its tiny stirrings and whirrings. Do memory imagination pain rebukes take to spinning about when Ma becomes a scrap of floating wind?

A body is also a home. Wind plays about the body just as it whips about a house. The wind skirts about whatever comes in its path, hops over it, and in so doing, bumps into it, and sometimes whistles through, creating a tunnel for itself, or at other times, it storms about. It sways dances gyrates.

When you open the windows after they've been closed, the direction of the wind changes and new types of wind begin to stir up new ragas. The walls become instruments and resound like the musical pillars at the temple in Hampi.

★

So now the story has come to dwell in Beti's house. Whoever comes here will be most pleasing to the pen. Bade's calls came, but not he himself. So why should the pen stray to Bade?

Because it's like this: it's an old custom when it comes to families that everyone comes to the eldest son. But not all divine the meaning of this. What it means is that whoever meets with Bade, wherever he may be, they are the one going to him. For example, when Bade is returning from a tour of the provinces, an inspector, a type babu, a panchayat babu, might request of the big boss, please stop by our place and dine, and then even if Bade has actually gone to their home, it will in reality be quite the reverse, they are the ones approaching Bade, hands clasped, greeting him with a grateful smile and standing in attendance.

And if you speak of those living with Bade, it would be something similar. Those living with Bade, wherever they may go, for however long they may leave, still live with Bade, and will surely return, once they've completed their leave of absence. Amma is living with him, no matter where she may be staying. All arrangements to do with her money, her care, her living and dying, are his responsibility alone. Whether it is said aloud or not, thought about or not.

So the pen can still travel to Bade because wherever the family or elderly Ma or the door might be, Bade will also be there, no matter what, whether he is physically present or not. The door joining the walls together has already gone to the other house, the post-retirement flat. It may look different, but it's the same. And Ma may not appear there right now, but she's there as well. It's like she's just gone on a little trip. Where Bade can still call and keep tabs on her.

A phone call came from Bade.

There are few eldest sons who know how to talk with their family members, i.e., how to call to ask how people are, have heart-to-heart chats, converse intimately. Giving orders, suggesting ways and means, or if not that, teasing and joking, these are the ways eldest sons speak. Outwardly attired, as it were, in the tough exterior of his father, even if his heart is his own and soft to the core. Bade's tone could be rude, dictatorial, sarcastic, fussing, worrying, talking of this and that. Because how would eldest sons know how to speak straightforward words of love?

(Talking to outsiders is another matter. In such cases, there can be political debates, talk of poetry and films, and other sorts of sharing).

Amma, what was the license plate number of Papa's car?

Papa's car? Ma began to sway as she held the phone. On the swing.

You know, that one he got in Fatehpur.

Yes, he did get a car in Fatehpur.

What was the number?

It was a pink Fiat. You don't see those anymore.

I'm asking for the number.

We used to drive to Lucknow to see Gautam Sahib in that one. And his daughter had such a wonderful nickname: Ek Cheez.

Amma, I'm asking for the number.

Why do you need that? We went to Kanpur too. Swaroop Nagar. A dog bit you there. You had to get huge injections. But it was a pet dog.

So what? Do you remember the number or not?

Name of Adgadaanand.

The dog? Bade had to laugh.

No, no, the one who owned the dog, his name.

Amma, I'm asking for the number of the Fiat.

Goodness, why would I remember that?

But you remember Adgadaanand?

Of course I do; you were bitten.

By him?

I wonder if he's still living? He was a nice man.

Even if he bit?

Ah, you won't quit. Find out the number. He was with the Water Department. Let's go some time.

When are you coming back? We'll go then.

Bade's conversation was intended to get to this very point. You've had your little vacation, now please come back. The house is all set, he said. You and D can stay in the big bedroom, *D* being the name husband and wife shouted at one another, an abbreviation for *darling* in the beginning, and later for *duffer*. Otherwise the side room is also fine, it's a bit smaller, and both rooms have attached baths, with a door on each side.

Why, Bahu was saying, you haven't opened all the boxes yet, just the special-special items, and even in those, you're not finding half the things, and everything is covered in dust, and

Bahu was saying, there's no time to sleep or eat for you, you don't even bathe, and you come outside the house in your undershirt, is this what retirement means, and have you had your sugar checked? At which Bade said, Okay, bye bye, and hung up the phone.

Bade does not know how to express himself in a straightforward manner. He just calls because he feels sad that all the stuff is still being fitted into the new flat, but Ma hasn't been fitted in, and it's not as big as before, with fewer servants, so how will she like it, but oh well, until then let her be distracted by change with my sister, let her get a taste of that bizarro lifestyle; that will also make her happy to return. She's feeding her properly, that's good, and Ma's demonstrating some proper etiquette to my sister's rag-tag shoulder sack-toting gang, so that's great too. The people in the society will also learn she comes from a good family, so that's good, isn't it?

How could Bade realise that these days, Beti's rag-tag shoulder sack-toting gang was being kept at bay by Beti herself? And that there was, in fact, a sack-toter in Amma's own gang. Rosie. The first time Beti had opened the door, Rosie stood before her with a huge shoulder bag and next to her, the guard, curious, somewhat uneasy. Now he doesn't come. But everyone else comes, bringing their detritus, and they watch with pleasure as Ma and Rosie create things. With which Rosie will set up shop and run a business, under the name *Odds and Ends*. And she'll come on summer evenings and bring Ma downstairs and the two of them will be spotted seated at the tomb, sometimes just sitting quietly, as if in some new posture of acceptance. Detritus-acceptance, hijra-acceptance, does Bade or anyone really know what all is accepted in this life?

*

___

34

A home humming with floating cotton threads and plant clippings. Wind blows and brick knocks against brick, creating a fresh idiom.

When the house had been solitary, it had understood Beti's work. It had sat by quietly and respectfully. Beti would lean over an open page for an age. In obeisance to the Goddess of Work. At any given moment, the Goddess may be pleased and slip in softly to sit down beside her. The pen rises by itself and begins to move across the page. An article a story a book begins to take shape.

Nowadays the house has grown brash. Each brick reaches up and stretches. Chits and chats occur. If someone particularly boisterous shows up, the walls think it great fun. They play with the visitors. The walls resound at their light taps. As though air has been puffed into them. At Ma's touch, relatively softly, but when Rosie Bua's portly figure flits about, one doesn't even know whence the jingling starts and where it's an echo. The pillars, in on the gossip, also jangle at the threshold. And Rosie, really! She might slap her hand down, or secretly scratch her rear, or smack her forehead in jest, causing a thrum, as though she well knows the walls jingle, resound at her touch.

Ma tries it too. At the tap of her fingers, instruments are summoned and notes emerge: *sa re ga ma*. At the thwap of her foot, the panchtaal plays. A jaltarang from this brick, an able from that, a veena from this column, a mridangam from that, knock with your legs, you get a ghatam, if you rattle the chains of the swing, bells ring, a shehnai from pulling the sliding door, blow on the dust: a conch; shake a flower pot: damroo.

The Goddess of Work peers in. She is frightened. Here's a party in full swing. But I am the Goddess of Solitude. She slips away.

★

35

Ma said, you don't work, you don't sleep, look at the black circles under your eyes, you must start sleeping in the guest room.

Beti didn't agree with what Ma said, but relented, exhausted by the heat.

Ma said, now it's not so hot, it's getting close to monsoon. She was happy just to open the windows, but not Beti. Beti turned on the AC and went to lie down in the guest room. The bangles had won at last. They had kicked her out. She pushed away Rosie's and Amma's Odds and Ends flotsam and jetsam and cast her aching limbs and spent nerves onto the guest bed.

The bangles will not jingle in the guest room. Beti took down the jangling bamboo chimes which she had brought from Bali with KK, wrapped them up so they wouldn't ring, and stowed them with the mobiles Rosie had made of tin feather cut-outs suspended from strings.

I'll go check on Amma in the night. Anyway, she's fine now. She's got better since she's been living with me. She walks around, eats, drinks, chats merrily.

★

One night after summer had receded, there'd been hours of rain, and now the sky had cleared. The moon weaved in and out amongst the clouds before alighting on a branch of the tree overhanging Ma's flowerpots. Ma was seated in her chair, looking up at the moon, and she began to speak. To herself. Or to the moon.

   Beti wanted to move closer and listen quietly. But she didn't get up.

★

37

When she did get up, it was at the aroma of coffee. She came out of the guest room rubbing her eyes, and a coffee cup producing the aroma appeared, and proffering it, KK's hand. Where am I? Beti looked around in confusion. As though she'd gone to sleep at home and awoken elsewhere. The thief of sleep had lifted her up, bed and all, and plunked her down elsewhere. But no, this was her own home, the one decorated just the way she liked.

Keeping KK away had worked until now. He went on long journeys. She'd been avoiding him on the phone. Not today, I'll tell you which day might be suitable, it's not about Ma, someone or other's always showing up, everyone will be awkward with each other, no one will feel relaxed and enjoy, what's the point.

Why are you forbidding me? What could she say? What will you do if you come here? She couldn't quite say that. He used to come and work on his laptop and Beti would work on hers. Peace all around. They'd cook together, eat. They'd relax in between, wrapped in one another's arms. Sometimes they'd invite other people over in the evenings. When KK had to leave, he'd leave, if he had to stay, he'd stay. He had the spare key; if he ever needed to go to the airport or somewhere early in the morning, she'd keep on sleeping and he'd let himself out.

But now none of this fits.

But we'll see each other's faces. We'll look at each other with hidden passion.

Beti found this crude. These were private matters, not to be played out in public.

Am I only myself when I'm alone? In public, I behave as others wish? But these were questions for other feminists. Beti no longer had the leisure to turn them over and examine them in her heart.

Yes, of course I'll introduce you to Amma.

And here I've been, sleeping, and he's out here already getting to know her. He came here straight here from Kenya?

Had Ma opened the door, or had KK let himself in? Beti wondered, feeling a bit cross. Why does Ma get up alone? They didn't have a battalion of servants to take heed if she fell. You could just be lying somewhere, alone, she scolded Ma. In her mind, she added, *the way you were lying elsewhere, alone.*

Hello, hello! said KK.

The two of them, he and Ma, relaxed; Beti, trying and failing. She felt put out.

She stays awake all night, manages some sleep in the morning hours, said Ma, spraying a fountain of water over the freshly washed plants, a cup of coffee near her, KK standing close by. She's always getting up and shining her torch for me. That's why I get up quietly in the morning.

Beti felt exposed.

The layout of the house had subtly changed. What had once been kept outside was now part of the internal layout.

But the rains have already started. Why water the plants? Beti objected, raining on Amma's picnic.

You didn't tell me you had such good coffee in the house, was Ma's reply.

What have these two been telling one another? Beti felt upset, as though one of her secrets had been revealed. She felt unclothed, that's why she averted her eyes, embarrassed at being caught so. She went to the bathroom and got her dressing gown, which she had taken out because of the new threat of visitors showing up at any time. The gardener, the maid, everyone showed up early in the morning or at any time, the family, or even outsiders, people from the society. Beti couldn't wander about in a state of undress as she had before.

I'll drink tea, she said with annoyance. Then she added, for the sake of formality, I take coffee with breakfast.

Not even a hello? whispered KK in her ear. He'd left Ma on the balcony to go make coffee.

When did you get here? Beti didn't ask that, because she didn't feel like it. *Why did you come?* She couldn't ask that either. *How are you?* That would require an affectionate tone. *What are you here for?* That would be downright rude. *When are you leaving?* Beti felt a bit out of temper.

Relax. KK put his arms around her. She's cool.

You go outside with Ma, I'll be right there, she replied sternly.

She did sit down with them when she was drinking her tea, but the conversation was just between Ma and KK. Ma had suddenly become extremely interested in Kenya's Rift Valley. Beti left them gossiping and went inside to get ready. She took a shower and then stood by the window. When monsoon was in full swing, the sweet scent of the tiny neem flowers wafted in through this window. After the neem fruit sprouted, it dangled in bunches. Then the fruit would ripen and fall—*plop plop*—as if there were small animals hiding in the leaves, mischievously taking aim and hurling the fruit at the heads of passers-by below. As soon as they hit the ground the neem fruit burst open, even if no one trod on it, and released a heady sweet-sour scent.

Would that scent rise to the window now, or would the fennel, garlic, coffee vie for attention and come out on top? The poor neem fruit would lie smashed and forgotten.

Beti turned at the sound of KK's voice. He stood at the door as though he'd never walked through it. *Well, at least he shows that much respect.*

I came to get my scissors, he said softly. Take a look, I called, you probably have some missed calls. When you didn't pick up, I thought, I'll go out in the morning and get them. Otherwise, I'd have to go to the barber to get my moustache shaved off. I couldn't find scissors like those anywhere else!

He was clearly a bit offended at having to explain. Beti smiled as she walked by him, and he pinched her lightly from behind. She jumped.

Right at that moment, a bell rang.

The arrival of Rosie, and the departure of KK. Beti was at a loss: should she introduce this one to that, she wondered with irritation, or that one to this? As she dispatched KK angrily, he tried to give her a secret kiss, but was annoyed by her jerking back and pushing him away. My God, you're acting like I'm a lech. He moved away. If you say to, I'll leave the scissors, there's a hair coming out of your nostrils, it looks terrible, do cut it off. Saying this, he left. As though his taunt had made them even.

★

Mothers know their dates. Oh, that happened the year Pappu had his mundan, or that was around when Munni fell off the ikka and broke her front tooth, or that happened the year the Ganesh idol began drinking milk at the temple in the village and then Ganesh ji began to drink milk all over India. Or that was the season when Jamman got smallpox. Or a long description of that time when Uncle fell from the roof and broke his leg, when the flood came and all the grain in the household and all the trunks and we ourselves went and stood on the roof and there were these huge snakes floating by in the water, which had turned the whole village into a pond, and the government brought flying beds—udankhatole! And lifted us up on rope ladders to shelter us at the hospital at that city nearby.

But this is not that sort of time, nor that kind of Amma. Here, where everyone is coming, the old, of course, but the new, too, to speak a few words with Ma, collect the bags she'd stitched, give her odds and ends from their house so she could make something from those too, or have a snack or tea break, it's no surprise when Sid shows up as well, always the type of kid to appear unannounced and for no clear purpose. At the first opportunity, that is, as soon as he'd finished his assignment in the US, he showed up to scold: Granny, Granny, first you vanish, now you're partying away at Aunty's! Mischief, the moment I leave?

Historians are always hypothesizing about which date which event occurred. They scurry about trying to classify events as major and minor. Who knows, they might get interested in researching which day Sid arrived to shower Granny with love and scolding. Before Rosie or after? Before KK or after? Before Ma fell, or after? Before the hospital, or after? Storytellers are a thousand times better than historians, they describe whatever draws their interest, whether it's the small moments or the big. So Amma's grandson did arrive, on whatever day it was. His aunt opened the door and again stood flabbergasted, as though she didn't recognise the person standing there. How could she be seeing her nephew in the house from which she usually departed to see her own parents?

But we can also ask how long it will take for Beti to grow accustomed to the fact that it's common Indian behaviour for people to show up at any time, you may not recognise them all, and anyway they are coming more to see Ma than you. If you don't even say much of a hi hello to the people at your society, what would you know about relations built on borrowing a cup of sugar and a daub of curd? Or exchanging plantings and clippings? Ma had created a garden on the balcony. A neighbour visited: *Mata ji, can you just tell the gardener to look down when he's watering the plants? We put our chairs out on our balcony and have breakfast at the table down there, and yesterday evening water sprayed down on it.* Watering—please forgive me! Oof, silly old me. Useless old lady! So blind, so stupid. And the complainer burst out laughing, and sat right down and snacked on something with Ma, and examined the garden, and later came back to get some stalks that you just stick in the dirt and they grow thick with fine leaves and red berries, Ma told Beti later. Meaning, the neighbour had come to complain, and only left after nabbing a bite and swiping a plant.

What's more, every single year there was a fight over whether any trees needed to be cut back, but the society residents didn't even have that fight with Ma. In that city, where *park* meant *car park*, Ma was delighted to see so many flowers and foliage. She forbade the gardener from cutting back the tree branches. He laughed, Mata ji I'll listen to you, Behin ji is also always arguing about it, but they still go and get them pruned every year. Ma was astonished. Arre, but why make enemies of the nice, innocent trees? Who knows, Mata ji. They say trees bring in all sorts of pests. Bugs. Cockroaches. And spiders. Then lizards. And squirrels, mice, and birds. They climb the trees and look in and see the juicy fruit on the tables. Cats sneak in to hunt for them. Monkeys are so greedy anyway, and snakes have been slithering through for centuries. Thieves then catch on and commit thefts via the trees.

Indeed, said Ma, glowering at him. So that's why all this go get rid of them, cut them down, trim the branches. Come on then, do the pruning, I'm standing right here. She stood by, like a sentry, brandishing her cane as if it were a gun. No, we don't want more sunlight. Yes, we want thieves and snakes.

The gardeners, the guards, everyone laughed. But Mata ji was Mata ji. The society could not fight her. Everyone came to see her. Beti just opened the door and made way as though she were stationed there to welcome guests into someone else's home.

Yes, Aunt, Sid laughed, it is I, your favourite nephew, Sid, US-returned, Sid, fresh from the American oven.

That's America for you. Some stay just a couple of days in its oven and come out an American loaf, they forget all other languages and tastes, sound even more American than the Americans, but others stay there their entire lives and still remain Bhojpuri breads—baati and litti: some are frosted with American icing, some remain smeared in sugar cane, gur, cow dung. One door stays forever open, another closes but then opens again, and the insider stands and stares foolishly like an outsider.

Ma looks like she's unfurling the sun all over the house: it's a bolt of fabric, its golden strands strewn about in the process. The sun shim-shim-shimmering.

This I saw. I'm telling you. Taking the mic from the people saying nonsensical things about desi and American accents, so they'll stop talking and I can begin my own narration. Because that's how life goes—sometimes one person narrates; sometimes another; rock, bird, tree, water, too, narrate; sometimes we think we're sharing our take, but it turns out to be yours; and sometimes it's me and my take on whatever, and I'm the one saying it.

What happened was that we had just left the airport when Sid had an idea: Come on, let's go surprise Granny. His aunt's house was pretty much on the way. So the two of us went swinging straight into the house on fragments of sunlight, smeared in the dust of America. The guard, seeing international tags on our bags, didn't make us fill out the register, nor did he phone ahead, we just popped up at the door. Buzzed. A maid opened it. Sid's aunt's head, bent over the table on the other side of the bookshelf, popped up like a balloon, followed by the rest of her. She didn't seem to recognise us.

But Granny was wandering about the house with an entirely different ebb and flow. A bobbing-along balloon.

Early morning walk, Granny?

For my belly, my child.

Granny embraced him, then me too.

Great to see you up and about, I said.

Yes, it's happened. I've barged my way in again. After promising I'd be gone for good. I know full well this world will go on without me, that it'll keep on keeping on. It's not like I'm some kind of witness to a murder. Although we could start a separate debate about what exactly counts as a murder nowadays, or a witness, for that matter. Who saw Salman Khan kill that deer? Did he himself drive his car over the poor people sleeping on the pavement or was it his driver, and what was the crime and who was the criminal? And who were the criminals and who the upholders of the law in the Dadri lynching, and among those cow protectionists? To the point that when it comes to patriotism and treason, the law is awfully confused as to who what where when which books which punishments, what manipulations, what tweakings, and so on and so forth, so who's been murdered, and who's the witness?

But wait! There's no murder here, just a rainbow.

It's possible that if it weren't for me, it would have gone unnoticed yet again. But I immediately took note. And anyway, he who's got nothing to gain or lose from the story can see it because he stands aloof, unlike the characters standing in the middle. Silent, external, what else has he got to do? Just look listen sniff enjoy. Even more neutral than Nirmal Verma's famously detached characters.

Me. With Sid. I'm going to leave, how can I not, but until then I'll continue to gaze at the scene.

I wasn't there when Grany went missing, nor when she came to Beti's home, the home of Sid's aunt, for a change of scene, and so that the government bungalow could be vacated and the new house set up for her in the meantime. But I was there then, when she was cheerfully telling Sid all about her constipation problems.

If constipation is the problem, Granny, then a small stick-sized solid is the equivalent of a pitcherful of water: Sid was going on with his usual bullshit. At which I laughed, and Aunty said shut up, what is this icky stuff you're saying. Granny looked pleased, as though her constipation had improved just by talking about it.

I liked Granny's new groove. Bobbing along. Bob up, bob down, haloed in Sunshine. A kite or a balloon? Perhaps the thing she was wearing, that ankle-length gown, was what made her look like a balloon. Or a kite. We found out that Rosie Bua had them made for her. I vaguely recalled her coming that evening. We heard she was dropping by fairly frequently, doing a lot for Granny, and that these boxes lids rags carton pots baskets buttons trimmings were from the whole neighbourhood, and Granny was planning with Rosie Bua to turn them into containers fruit bowls toys bags. I was given an ashtray, but instructed not to smoke. The rest Rosie Bua takes to sell somewhere, 50 percent of the proceeds goes to the children's home, and the rest Rosie donates for the needs of her community.

Sid suggested a name: open an online shop called *Odds and Ends*. Why not an Indian name, Granny asked. Not a chance, Sid told her. Look around you. Velvet Hotel, Sweet Dream Guest House. Snow White Beauty Parlour. Comedy Nights. And I added one of my own: Sid, instead of Siddharth. Rosie liked the name. When she came. She wasn't there yet. At that moment it was just us, and Granny informed Sid's Aunt and the maid that since the kids have just arrived from abroad, today we'll have real Indian food, the works! Sid's father was also reached by phone, informed that we'd arrived from the airport and would go over there after our feast.

First there was bathing to be done, then an unplanned but fully expected nap: we both lay down and fell asleep. On Granny's bed, because the trinkets and such and odds and ends were all laid out in the guest room. We fell asleep and didn't wake up until evening.

Actually, *wake up* is kind of a stretch, more like we were woken up. Aunty said to get over jet lag we needed to return to this time zone as quickly as possible. Otherwise we'd never fall asleep at night. And in the pink rays of the setting sun we feasted on Granny's stupendous lunch-turned-dinner. That was when Sid took out the wine we'd bought on the plane. He poured it into glasses and said, let's celebrate the return of Granny.

And of you, said Aunt.

A drop for Granny, said Sid, as he lifted the glass to his lips. And then that thing happened that had happened before: the last ray of the sun bounced off Granny's eyes and a rainbow floated in the wine.

I saw it. I looked up to see if there was a rainbow in the sky too. Was it reflected on Granny's face? And I became confused: had I imagined the one I saw before, at that lunch party, or was I imagining the same sight today, that is, a spilling rainbow?

This is the final frontier for me! Granny objected, throwing her head back. No, no! But pretend-like. It will be bitter, she said, making a face.

How would you know? Sid teased. Busted! So this is what you were up to with Grandpa?

Is the taste of alcohol something you can only know from actually drinking it? Granny laughed. She took a sip, seeming pleased.

And now, said Sid with his signature bluntness, Granny will tell us where she ran off to.

Just like that. He said it casually, in a way no one else could have pulled off, what with all their vagueness.

To put the Buddha in Rosie's care. She had a train to catch. She left me at the corner and ran off. She said, you can see the gate from here. But Granny walked right past the gate, passing gate after identical gate.

Incredible! said Sid, and held up his glass.

I'm pretty sure Granny sneaked a few more sips. Perhaps in the heat of the moment. Or because everyone was feeling so free. As though nothing was forbidden anymore. Or, I'll give everything a try on my way out. Or because everything was so interesting. And the rainbow was the result of that effervescence.

Aunt poured her a bit from her glass. So I did too. Sid joked that we were being called the drunks when in fact the real drunk was Granny.

Granny raised her cane to smack him. Rainbow and butterflies leapt with it.

It's possible I'm giving the rainbow special importance out of a sense of guilt, to justify my return to these pages. Therefore I feel obliged to say: *I saw the rainbow.* So what if I did or didn't? Whether the rainbow started in the sky or arced into the sky from Granny's eyes, how does it matter? It's normal for colours from one place to spill into another. If everyone's happy, that's fine. Nothing else special was going on. And I didn't choose to come. Sid and I had returned together, he hadn't even consulted me, just brought me along, otherwise I would have gone back to my place from the airport. If everyone welcomes me, I'm happy to go along, otherwise don't I know they're the ones who belong here and I'm just a bit player?

Dammit, no one else is saying anything, I'm cursing at myself for no good reason, and tying myself in knots. As though no one else ever went anywhere for no good reason.

From now on maybe I'll just say no to Sid for my own peace of mind. See? I bow deep in a farewell salaam. We shall not meet again. But the shorts and t-shirt belong to Sid's aunt's ex; those will have to be returned. And the clothes I took off and put in the laundry basket when they told me to, I'll have to get those back as well. But I'll send someone else to get them. Or even if I drop in, I'll keep my distance from the domain of this story and beat a hasty retreat. Life goes on outside these pages too; I'll just leave my clothes where they lie. Stories often have huge gaps, no one will ever notice this one.

★

39

People who extol murder and mayhem consider peace and quiet tomb-like. Some may call a river wet, a desert dry. They consider a groping molester a macho dude. And they call fortunate the woman whom he controls and beats to a pulp. If something is all gussied up, it's a shop, and if it's crammed full of stuff, it's life. Streetwise things stay on the street, homely things stay at home. The layer that forms on ghee is called chaadan; on milk it's cream. You mix dew into cream and get a Benarsi malaiyo; whip cream into yogurt and make Punjabi lassi. Rain falls in the rainy season; the loo blows in summer. The body of the mother speaks a new language; the heart of the daughter twangs like a busted drum. The shrinking woman compresses herself ever smaller, ever lighter. The growing-bigger woman gets stuck in her wrinkles, which makes her slow to fall asleep at night, and slow to wake in the morning.

The rainy season's here, but that doesn't ensure rain. Wilful weather becomes man-ipulated, and man is a know-it-all who actually knows very little, just struts about, but ultimately returns to God, because everything is God-willing. When the breeze doesn't sway gently like Ma, it whooshes viciously. Then it doesn't, but raindrops cascade or drip drop in tiny streams and wander about the house. Beti, this side or that of sleep, starts when the lightning flashes zip zap and the clouds thunder crash bang and the branches scratch and scream and hammer away crying, let us in, why have you thrown us out!

Oh, the majesty of nature! It contains all the expressions in the world. One need only catch the melody from nature. Heart and soul entrusted to the wind. When the clouds lower, the heart of the heroine is filled with longing as in Kalidasa's play *Meghadutam*. When blossoms bloom the foot dances and evokes Chaitanya Mahaprabhu. In a drop of dew Tagore discerned the cosmos. In the lull of wind Aristotle's philosophy wakes.

If you cry, your heart trembles like a paper boat in the rains. A robust heart swings gaily on the sunlight and the moonlight and the rain drops. The drops shimmer, swaying like streamers, and play on Amma who has risen from lying prone. She walks about peacefully, but everything around her is frisky, frolicsome, and fun.

Ma walks; peaceful though grave, happy though quiet. When she sleeps, she's serene, when she speaks, then too. She rests within the new uncurling place which has begun unfurling from inside to out. And the birds get to know her as they fly into her orbit.

★

40

One bird comes daily and whistles. Swooping up and down with its tune. Coquettish at times, mournful at others.

Hey Baji, who's that dude whistling? One day Rosie jumped up, as if to say, Hoo boy, lemme at him!

Come now. It's a bird, Ma scolded.

A whistle. Long. A changed tune.

It's a black bird. A blackbird.

A storytelling whistle invoking the past. Like a call coming from far off.

Amma purses her lips and blows. Rosie imitates her.

Both attempt to whistle.

The bird falls silent.

Rosie and Ma fall silent. The bird whistles again. They too produce another whistle. The three in unison.

Beti turns the key in the lock of the house...Is that whistling coming from my home? The door is already open. Rosie and Amma are the ones making the whistling sounds. Then silence. Then the bird. As though the bird is teaching them. Another whistle.

You see? Rosie's voice.
Sprinkle it. Ma's voice.
And the sky fills with stars.

★

41

There was no longer any reason for Ma to fall. Which is why she fell.

She whistles.

She blows kisses at the plants and tenderly caresses every leaf on every tree branch. Earlier she had done so to wipe them clean and make them shine, but now the rains have come it's just because—to shower them with love.

Sometimes she rubs fennel in the mortar or crushes garlic or pounds roasted spice. The fragrance wafts.

She rises on her own. She bathes on her own. She makes tea herself. She feeds herself, feeds others.

She greets people passing the house below with a *namaste, ho ho, hello*.

She sits alone chattering—with herself, or the sky and the trees? But it's a strain on the ears if you're trying to listen in. And she produces all sorts of other noises. Moans, sighs, sobs, shrieks, all filled with the joys of pain. Of course she speaks to others too. Mother-daughter time. Rosie-Baji time. Hello-goodbye time. And if Sid's there she even takes a few sips of beer or wine. One time KK opened the cognac and poured some out for her. First she made a face. Then she added honey, at which Beti raised a cry of *Cognac murder!* But Ma licked her lips and went on to develop a taste for her invention. To the point that when she had emptied her glass she would say, pour a little cold water into my glass, we shouldn't waste any drops.

But the story doesn't end here.

Now that she can move about on her own, she starts putting her cane to non-cane uses, like fishing sandals out from under the takht, pushing the window shut, shooing away the lizard on the wall outside, itching her soles, waving it to make a point as though delivering a PowerPoint presentation, making music on the walls and floor like a conductor waving her baton, as though she's Yehudi Menuhin, straightening out flipped mats and rugs without bending down, tickling ants, etc.

She talks on the phone. She's telling someone how she feels pain right where the shoulder joins the torso, just a bit, and maybe that's what they call *frozen shoulder*. I lift it this much, but further, *ow*, I can't do it. She's explaining this as though there were a pair of binoculars at the other end of the line by which the listener can see what parts of the limb she can and cannot raise. She's explaining as though every pang is filled with sweetness. Worth caressing with words.

The same with the ear. Stop, I'll sit down. I'll put it on the left ear. The right one's blocked, no, no, it's not the monsoon air, they just shrink with age, they say the hole gets smaller. I hear fifty percent less than I did. Or rather, sixty.

Same when she shows the swelling in her feet and legs. Look, the right one is different from the left.

Same when she says her bonetail hurts. By which she means her tailbone.

Same as how she tells people about her constipation, and how much more came out this morning. It's the same routine all day long, continued attempts into the afternoon. Get up and go, drink tea and sit down, go again after strolling about, have some fruit and give it a try, after breakfast, back on the throne. I take bel, I've tried everything: Triphala, Gastromone, Softovac, Looz, isabgol. I only eat boiled vegetables. Always feel something is heavy and hanging there. The flesh itself has started to hang, that's what gives me that feeling as well. Yesterday I took Looz both times, and then Rosie kicked up a fuss and rolled her eyes and asked, Are you going to administer the whole cure yourself, or will you leave the doctor something to do?

These are daily occurrences. Who would bother giving them the *something's-up* label? Like how pollution growing more horrendous everyday has become so commonplace, there's nothing worth remarking on. Hitler's gas chamber drama was not a quotidian affair, so yes, something did happen there. When we say *something happened* we mean something a bit dramatic: when notes suddenly become a useless piece of paper, when there's a twenty car pile-up on the Agra Expressway, when Bangalore Lake catches fire, when an expert guide carefully shepherds tourists along a narrow snowy path in Kashmir and then suddenly flips over backwards himself and lands spread-eagled in the snow, or when a mother falls down in her daughter's home.

There was no reason for such an occurrence. It happened just like that, for no rhyme or reason.

★

42

Why did Ma fall? This question sparked a furore. Which doesn't mean that everyone sat around a table and discussed it. Accusations arose behind backs then slid around, ending up before bellies.

Beti's thinking eventually became that *he*—no, *she*—no, *he* —no, *she*—was the reason for the fall—meaning Rosie Bua. Behaving absurdly with Ma, the sound of their whistling— quite tuneful, too—all the time from the tomb, which they began to do with increasing frequency and tunefulness, so the whole neighbourhood could hear and wonder what on earth was going on. So Ma really was bound to fall sooner or later. Rosie Bua can even scold Ma and is constantly with her and brings a tiny sprig of mint in exchange for wolfing down their food. Amma has got a brand-new atmosphere of freedom to lead her own life of her own free will, so the poor thing, in her simplicity, allows Rosie to plunder from her with equal freedom. All the rubbish of the neighbourhood comes here, and they design and make things, and it's obvious who's profiting and who's losing in that equation. Amma does too much, she's bound to feel the strain, a complete set-up for a fall. Earlier too, it was because of Rosie that Amma got into all that mess in the first place, got lost and was all in pieces for so long. It was probably Rosie who had told her that many people had their eye on the Buddha, that Bade himself had said: We can sell it for lakhs. Beti had already asked for it, and others were also noticing that Ma was busy giving away all her worldly goods, by chance if someone expresses a desire for it, you, Baji–she calls her Baji!–are hardly likely to be able to say, No, let me keep it safe for you. And Amma would have agreed, simple soul that she is, not knowing her own frailty. And went who knows where. Into a slum or a hut or some such. We go out, go to work, but Amma always stayed home. All for her Buddha, she wandered off into some germ-infested area. Ever since then some weakness has taken hold, it isn't necessary for an infection to show, and I brought her here, I didn't allow it to become full blown, but she came with weakened immunity. There was no advance plan for her to come here, otherwise perhaps she'd have told me to bring the Buddha and keep it safe for her. Now it's come here, but not for me, it seems. I'm the thief and Rosie's the guard. She really made a laughingstock of me. And she still is, and cleverly making a profit too, even though Ma's the one supplying all the ideas, and doing so much bending walking pulling cutting swinging at this age, and she's started to wobble and hobble, it's only natural she toppled over.

KK did not agree that anyone could be blamed for this, for any reason, thereby reducing his already low current sex appeal. Why did he say, *for any reason*, Beti fumed. *Any reason* was not where the blame was falling. And what exactly did he mean by *any reason*? At first he tried to answer this, then he admitted defeat and threw down his remaining card, i.e., if your sister-in-law were to say such a thing, how would you react? So that would mean something then, why not, said his current ex, looking sarcastic. And indeed Bahu probably was saying some such thing.

Which was a correct guess. Bahu was indeed saying just that. That if you send Ma among people who have such a bizarre lifestyle, a fall is bound to happen. So was Bahu blaming Bade as well? It seemed so. You didn't even go yourself to see how she was doing, how would you know? True, it was meant to be just during the home-shifting process, but then to leave her there so long! There's less to eat there, too much to drink, less medicine, more booze, she gets nothing on time, the fridge is always empty, you have to double over to pick anything up, take a single step and you trip over a wall, and if you need to get fruit from the fruit bowl, you have to lunge forward on the swing and grab it, and you're likely to fall at any moment. Your sister's furniture is made of grass and twigs, which one can get for free, and it fills the house with dust and dirt. And all the trash from outsiders is handed to Ma so she can make stuff for someone else to sell. How did it benefit anybody to send Ma there; she's there, but we're the ones who have to come running? We have to take her to the doctor, we have to order the medicine from CGHS, but who takes credit– Beti! Even the tea Amma gets up and makes herself. Here, she didn't have to get up for any reason. She ruled from her bed, she ordered whatever she wanted, her word was law. Now it's all so spare and bare, and that too she has to organise by herself, and at her age, because at that home, if you can even call it a home, there's a mistress who's busy conquering the world, she's handed Amma over to the servants, and who really knows what sort they are, really how could she not fall? And we are the ones defamed as though we turned her out, when I myself said she can't stay at Beti's home, whether she's unmarried divorced alone whatever. Every day my son explains on the phone that you can't bring Ma back by force, Beti's her daughter not her enemy. But I feel so anxious. She's her daughter, but she doesn't know how to look after anyone, she's a mess herself, so shabby. When Ma was here I was worried, and when she isn't, then too, and my son explains that you can't live another person's life, if Ma falls it's not your fault, but my heart trembles so, and you just sent me or Sid and said, go, go, and have her sign this, you didn't even consider it appropriate to go one time to see for yourself what condition she's in and bring her back.

How could I go? glowered Bade. He didn't say: Amma fell because of the saris, who says I didn't go and who says I didn't see?

★

Because the truth was that Bade had gone. And seen. When the rustling of the leaves had begun to change. Because the wind blew restlessly, and his mood had followed suit. Everyone remembers that Amma got lost at the very end of winter, and was found again in spring. It wasn't easy to figure out how many days had elapsed. Each year, at the end of winter, the trees shed their dry leaves and new ones sprout where the old fell out. That is, winter melts into spring. The dry crackling of the upper layer of leaves as they fall and crunch on the earth, and the light breeze in the tiny new leaves underneath, murmuring like soft green grass. Sighing above, singing below.

What with house change, work change, office change, atmosphere change, Bade had felt discombobulated. All this changing had flung him *crunch* on the ground, like so many dry leaves. Amma had disappeared, the leaves dried more, the heart smote more, hurt more.

But Ma had been found. The heart sang tenderly. Soft, fine leaves and buds grew in.

He'd sent Ma to his sister's for a little while. Those leaves that must fall, let them fall, those which must grow, let them grow.

No one noticed when the leaves changed the season of the heart yet again. When the monsoon was at its peak. The leaves grew fat. Hanging heavy on the trees. They hung, dripping sadness. Even when they're quiet, they hang heavy. There's beauty in their fullness, but there's a core of grief, dark and deep. The raga of grief in slow tempo, extremely slow, a despondent alaap, a prelude. Or is it a vilaap, a lamentation?

The super literate ex-bureaucrat Bade did not understand. He was unable to comprehend the sorrowful raga of the leaves playing in his mind. He drooped. His wife said, everyone ends up like this—the post-retirement malaise, you no longer know how to pass your days and nights, you sit around sucking on the corner of your undershirt. She too is educated. But she does not realise that his melancholy comes from the leaves, which were first buffeted by a harsh wind, then a springy breeze; then it turned damp, now it was oppressively humid.

No one understands the leaf-born wind-ragas, and how they gesture towards the heart.

And what is understanding, anyway—no one really gets that—where does it dwell? In the brain, which plays its tune as we smite our brows? This is what we've all been taught. That the rest of our mind and body and soul just hang loose like goop from that jalebi-shaped brain. You're like Alice and you go missing, and only your brain remains, suspended in the air as a smile? Nose eyes lips neck shoulder elbow knee ankle fist thigh runny funny tummy back plaque sac, all of it knavish slavish, all of it clueless mindless useless. If only we knew that all our other parts were so much finer than the jalebi brain–the most regal of sweets, compared to our simple tiny curly jalebis. They are balushahi rajbhog motichuur shrikhand saffron halwa kulfi basundi, and that silly little jalebi could never grasp all they contain. So understand if you can, how many brains hearts souls you have, all of which hardly exist in that itty-bitty jalebi, and that's why we should be proud of how many moods we each possess. That's why a child can become a pandit reciting the Veda by heart before the text has even reached his tiny jalebi brain. Vocalists like Bhim Sen Joshi and Sarafat and Latafat (both Hussains) understand every sur with every part of their bodies, and they release them into their musical compositions. These are not the capabilities of that gasping greedy sluggish rag-tag stagnant jalebi brain. The bandit Dasyu Ratnakar's jalebi was clueless as he mindlessly chanted *Ma-raa ma-raa*, dying dying. But behold the glory of bhakti worship, that *ma-ra ma-ra* became *Rama-Rama* through the subtle vibrations and reverberations of sound and meaning, and thus the dacoit was transformed into the great sage Valmiki. The jalebi is but a bull-headed morsel, hardly capable of any such things.

To put it plainly: what is a brain? It's where thinking happens. And what is thinking? It's what is felt, tasted, waved, flaunted, spun. The jalebi imprisoned in our brow cannot do all this. The other limbs and parts and pores do it, it is they that are the mind's eye, the true mind. The jalebi in your skull is simply a warehouse or godown or grocery. It's just a place to store stuff, that's all.

The brain resident in Bade's knees, wrists, and various other parts and pores, as opposed to the one in his skull, and along with his heart, liver, et alia, experienced a rustling. He felt morose. Despairing, sometimes. What should I do? As the breeze blows through the lamenting leaves, a memory comes, but of what, he does not recall. Of when Ma was with him in the bungalow before he'd retired, when the bell-like breeze played among the tiny leaves; the thought that this might one day torment his mind would never have entered his wildest imagination. What was this itch that made him scratch his head again and again, sit first crossing this knee and then switching legs, then stretch and spread his arms, searching for something in the void. But he is unaware of all of this. It just happened one day, as he was running an errand at the bank, which was the only sort of errand he left the house for: to put money in this share or that FD; and chitchat gossip, lemon tea, prognosticating about politics with the manager, who was his buddy from his working days; and when he was returning in his car after doing all that, he inadvertently turned left onto the street where his sister lived. Well, he hadn't really turned all the way, he'd just headed slightly to the left to go back home and then such and such a street appeared. He did not go to his sister's house. But yes, a little beyond was the home of Jamal, whose engineer son had been shot in a hate crime at a pub in America the previous week. He thought of going by to offer condolences, as he'd already half-turned in that direction anyway, lost in thought as he was. But he should have gone to the bathroom before leaving the bank. Well, now he'd stop the car and take a leak along the way.

So Bade stopped his car by the green belt and thought: right here, in the monsoon dusk. He looked up—the rain could come at any moment, but the last flecks of sunlight were still in the sky. He also noticed that over there was the house where Amma had gone for a bit of change. That one, on the second storey, next to that tree, yes, that balcony, aha, flowerpots, that must be Amma's doing. Beyond that, a light. During monsoon it comes on early.

Someone came out onto the balcony. Bade cowered behind a bush. Amma. In a long gown. Taking deep breaths as though inhaling a rich sweet scent. She was speaking to the pots, to the plants. She examined them, reasoned with them, tickled them with her cane. Then she raised her cane to the sky and said something, Ma did, and laughed. But what if she fell over in that slobby burnoose? Strange attire indeed—his sister dresses oddly herself; is she dressing Ma all funny now? Dervishesque. Scruffy.

Just then, Ma turned. To go inside. Her back to Bade. Had given one tantalising glimpse of herself and disappeared! Bade felt cheated. He locked the car and went to the other side of the street, the side where the house was. Near the tree, whose trunk was between the small rocks and whose branches reached out towards that very balcony. Who knows what got into his head, but he climbed onto a rock and jumped into the tree, amongst the leaves.

There was a traffic jam in his head-brain; since he had no awareness of his other brains, there was nothing to guide his understanding. He was up in the tree, peering inside where the light was on to see better. No one saw his seeing.

But he was seen. By the crows. Whose meeting Bade had disrupted with this game of hide-and-seek and hoppity-skip.

★

44

Bade wrongly imagined that Amma was talking to the sky when she waved her cane around. In fact she was talking to the crows, in a menacing tone, after their gang had suddenly flown in, cawing above her plants and trees. What is this hooliganism! she scolded. What's with all the noise? Greedy things, the entire group has descended on us, what do you think, I'll throw you some bites? Nev-ver. And look here, if a single eyelash of one of my plants goes, I'll pluck your eyes out, I'll twirl this cane like so, and I'll turn you into manure and feed you to the plants. And you, what a smart aleck! She flourished the cane. Are you glaring at me? Come! Come! she challenged, I'll clap a dog collar on you and turn you into my pet dog! She laughed uproariously at her own joke: Are you a crow, or some kind of dog? Oh, I will crow you down! She laughed so hard, Beti came out and Bade dove for cover. And Ma went inside, still not leaning on the cane; swinging it about instead.

Observing Ma loudly addressing the heavens was an unpleasant experience for Bade, which he attributed to some sort of sister-related phenomenon arising from Ma's bizarre clothing. *Good God, she'll fall, what happened to her saris!* Bade was consumed by worry.

There was an unpaved street between the second-storey flat and the green belt. It was the guard's job to forbid passersby from spitting, urinating, or shitting there, but these days he got his kicks letting young couples wander in alone, then suddenly bursting in upon them, separating them with his staff as though they were two grasshoppers stuck together, and thus he'd grown rather lax about other matters. But it could also be that Bade's bureaucrat-style grandeur was weightier than the guard's staff, and so the staff-holder could not bring himself to say, *Hey, Mister Officer, do not spit pee shit here.*

But for the crows, everything had gone awry, in terms of both their meeting and the air. They'd amassed a flock on that day, flying in from far-off lands, through rain, over mountains, through pollution, over buildings. Those who had noticed them would have had wondered what was going on and why the sky was blanketed with black wings.

The crows had rallied in huge numbers. The organisers were quite pleased, and a bit of a hurly burly broke out as they wondered how everyone might be squeezed in. They hadn't considered the need for a loudspeaker, nor even a CCTV. But that wouldn't have been right as their focus was this: the problem of the spread of pollution in the name of science. So the fatter and more aged crows seated the smaller crows in their laps. Like when a kangaroo plops her joeys in her pouch, or two nuts nestle in a shell, or when there are two bananas in one peel, or a double head on one torso, so too, two heads bobbed atop each crow body, sporting four eyes rather than two. The mounds and trees were filled with these two-in-one crows. The trees rustled with wings as though the crows had thought them naked and rushed to clothe them in crowments. There was a festive air, and even with all the cawing, there were no attacks from outsiders, whether by means of eyes or sticks or unwanted attention, because in the clamber of urbanism, who really cared about crows anyway?

The crow meeting was underway. Regarding the horrific problems they were experiencing due to climate change and the science-worshipping humans. There was much cawing as the environmentalist birds pulled their prepared speeches from under their wings and read them out. Those who were particularly skilled delivered speeches extemporaneously. The assembled crows cawed approvingly, or shall we say that it would have sounded simply like *caw caw* to humans had they been listening, the way every language does to an unfamiliar ear, be it Hindi, Marathi, Tamil, or Morse code. They engaged one another in lengthy debates in their various dialects, and since it's crows we're talking about here, let us set aside politically correct questions such as whether these were actual languages or regional crowlects they spoke. Suffice to say that the heavens echoed with their versions of Bhojpuri, Maithili, Avadhi, and Braj.

The era of debate was still extant among the crows, and conversations proceeded boldly. They were not in the habit of shooting point blank at those who put forth their own understanding, whether from their own experience or their own ideals or simple incomprehension. The mass of crows was a sight to see. Old birds, whose blackness had not turned to white, but bore a whitish tinge, high school and college student crows, male, female, all openly debating: about how the entire cosmos had been thrown into a muddle, even our sharp intellects have begun to fail us. We used to know without any help from a barometer, compass, thermometer, agrometer, Google, Twitter, that the rains were advancing, and the jungle animals were coming to hunt, the wind won't stop just yet, babbler birds will not stop babbling, the mouse will turn lion, the cloud a dancer, and so on and so forth. We knew a person just by seeing their face, which crook will snare you and gobble you up, which yogi will give a quaff from his water pouch. Now men have destroyed our capabilities by interfering in the natural environment, they rush about with their stethoscopes and telescopes croaking wrathfully, and we can't even be sure of providing for our children any more.

The conversation had turned to El Niño.

One young jackanapes, rather bored in his youthful zeal, as well as a bit self-enchanted, asked with curiosity (but also just to rile), Nina who?

Nino, corrected the one next to him.

El Niño, said another knowledgeable crow.

Le what? asked the jackanapes, twisting his beak to pronounce it.

El, el, replied the elder crow loudly.

Like Al-Biruni? Al-Azhar? jested the jackanapes.

Pay attention, don't turn everything into a joke, retorted an elderly lady crow.

And just then, the featherless, heedless entity arrived and threw a monkey wrench into the proceedings.

The shades of evening were deepening in the abated rain when a car stopped and a humanoid got out, onto the unpaved road across from the gathering of the crows, along the green belt. Said humanoid unzipped his trousers and proceeded to augment the pollution.

Hey, hey, blockhead! Young Jackanapes sat up like he had a mind to hit him. Why have you come here to spread filth, caw, caw?

Arre, after he spreads filth, he's heading towards us to chase us away!

Jackass! Jackanapes cried again, just because we pick out our food from rubbish heaps, you think we like garbage and trash?

As he yelled, all the other teenaged crows got fired up. What this punk doesn't know is, we never forget a face! He'll get away this time because our peacenik parents are chanting *om shanti shanti* over here, but show your face anywhere around here in the future...he raised a foot like a clenched fist, brandished his beak, and pretended to execute his eye-slicer move in the air.

Let's undertake a Swach Bharat campaign for a clean India, said the son of the meeting's chair. All the office bearers are here, let's pass the proposal right now. We'll elect some young people and give them cameras so that if anyone spreads filth in public places and disrespects nature, they can take a picture and we can put together another team to print out copies and shower them down all over the place. So these guys will get embarrassed and cut it out.

Shame is in short supply these days, someone cawed morosely.

So an I'll-do-you-one-better teenage girl crow began to hop about and cried, let's tie stones to all the photos and bust these losers' heads open when we drop 'em. Cuz I love dropping stones on bald guys!

It was at this very moment that Bade jumped onto the hillock and then into the tree, utterly oblivious of the crows rustling amongst the branches. An uproar broke out in which the elders shrieked to the crowd to maintain order and fly up in single file to make the sure the elderly and children didn't get jostled, but the worrisome thing was that Jackanapes and his gang were at boiling point, because at the sudden turn of events they'd also got startled, and the one who has frightened you automatically becomes the enemy, but also, the thing about fear is you don't like to see yourself feeling it, because it makes you feel less awesome, so it's either sink or swim, dude.

So imagine this: the tree and hillocks began to bounce with livid crows, and thence arose voices calling out, please, everyone settle down, and those youths who have snatched mobiles, whistles and drums—damroos—please refrain from playing blowing beating or bleating on them, so that the proceedings can continue quietly.

But the crows were stirred up. A whoop arose to rally against it all. Such a cawing broke out, the tree began to shake like it was dancing the fierce tandav, as though the double heads that had grown on it had decided to perform a ceremony to Shiva.

Hey, caw caw, make your own homes dirty, why have you snuck into ours to spread filth? Our home is the cosmos and nature, and this wingless community is bent on destroying our home to build their own. If they have such an appetite for suicide they can go for it, but why drag us into their mess? Where are we supposed to go when they fell our sky and our trees? We had no objection to excrement or urine as long as it was organic. Our trees knew how to separate milk from water. But now it contains poisonous chemicals that burn the roots the earth the air, which is what's happening, and we intend to protest all this.

There were many presentations that began to burst forth from the mouths of the crows, after that wingless being had moved, following his p(ee)-is-for-pollution ablutions, to the tree surrounded by mounds and rocks on which the meeting was taking place. And not only did he jump onto a rock, but he hopped up and landed on a branch of the tree. As though all these double-headed crows were invisible, and he had the right to butt in wherever he wanted to. Surely he looks down on our colour too. He has dishonoured us! The cawing of the crows transformed into a roar: So what if we're black! We're crows! *Ham ale hain to kya hua, dilwale hain!*

And thus, their honour was now at stake: you don't care about our business or our lives, and, what's more, you don't notice us at all. You don't even see us! Not just one, not just two, every single one of us is invisible for you. It's like we don't even exist. Arre, we are going to watch him. You know how we get together and poke our beaks into giant clouds, crease them, then hold a pleat each in our beaks and take off flying from one place to another tugging the clouds along with us? Let's stick our beaks into this guy's flesh and fly off with him and then smash him down somewhere far off, then he'll fall and explode and his remains will scatter all over so that no one can possibly gather them up and send them to Haridwar.

Everyone began to hop about in a rage, and that rage rose up from the soles of their feet to the hillocks and branches and it turned into droplets of burning flame, which a human might have mistaken for the last rays of sunshine.

It was a sight of polycrow magic: the jet-black crows dancing upon the burning embers and amongst them—but separate—a wingless sacrificial beast, neck stretched out taut turning this way and that, steering and staring, gyrating left and right, as if part of the crow yagya. A fearsome ritual.

The shrieking chant suddenly subsided.

Because according to the new instructions, the location for the acknowledgements portion of the meeting had been changed. It was shifted to the dome, ledges, and portico of the old tomb inside the grove. The black mass rose up and burst forth from the trees and hills. Yet, all the young crows kept leaping up and diving down towards the plants behind, which was why the tiny flapping fluttering gowned woman shrieked at them, I'll crush you if you come over here! And then flying by, screaming abuses at the head of Bade, there you are usurping our place in the tree, and the old lady is yelling at us, *Don't shit on my flowerpots!* when spreading shit all over the entire world is what you people do, not us, it's *your* special skill, turning everything to shit! The crows cawed menacingly, then flew up. Into the green belt.

★

An elderly crowess with the heart of a poet began to remind everyone of the crowlaw. She had been one of the most badass feminists of her time, one who had fought and won the right for mothers to attend meetings, and also take part in community decisions. Also: that none should leave their egg in the nest of another out of crowpathy, nor should they throw about stalks and straws willy-nilly to build a nest—we too will live in an orderly fashion, and the mancrow will also warm the egg, since the babies that will be born will be his as well. She was still outspoken and said her piece elegantly. She was more than ten years old now, getting on. Her eyes were as peaceful as a cow's and there was a certain wisdom in her wings, as in the sagely drooping roots of the Barghad tree. She hopped slowly, and few knew that she hopped like that on sunny days so she could soak all the vitamin D into her joints, and now it was simply the way she rolled, and consequently, when all the others started hopping about like mad she walked forth with proud, measured, dignified steps. No hurry, let bombs burst, mountains crack asunder, there was no such panicked expression on her countenance, only a supreme calm.

Whilst the other crows flew about in the air agitatedly, she stood by the human and watched him closely. Then she approached the old archway in the green belt with a pensive air. In awe and reverence of her majestic stride, the ones in front handed her the mic, which was made of pale green bamboo stalks, and her voice rang out with gorgeous elegant crowchantment.

My dear children, do not behave in such a manner that the crow becomes synonymous with mischief. Soften. Rain down from the sky like gentle flakes of snow, so the world spreads out tenderly beneath your cottony whiteness. Observe from your heart; not with unkindness. See how the two-footed one does nothing against you. He is experiencing a deep sorrow as he gazes thither, within that home. Perhaps he is missing a dear one. It is possible that woman is his mother, and that she does not see him from there. If you were right in front of someone and still not seen, how would you feel? You might worry you did not exist at all. The other must be her daughter. We have changed our ways, but they have not—that a mother should dwell with her daughter when the son yet lives: that is a mark of defeat. Have you gazed upon his face? What a forlorn countenance, like a wistful moon.

And you, Crowess stared at Jackanapes, why does absolutely everything incite you to violence? Bathe in the rain daily to cool yourself down a bit. It's too easy for you to stray, get worked up and lose your judgment. Just because you have ambitions of flying beyond the crowthority. Birds like you are the ones that get caught every other day: someone gives you a bomb, and says, take this, fasten it to your belt and go to festivals and fairs and press the button; daily your mug will appear on the front page. You just take off thoughtlessly and do what's asked; only your beak remains in the newspaper, which you can't even see. You're a crow. Don't be an ass. Or a kite or a falcon or a crane either. Patience, child, she said, patting him on his bowed head.

After listening to her speech, all the crows calmed down. They crushed red ants and rubbed them onto their bodies to get rid of the onslaught of the mosquitoes due to the deepening darkness, because formic acid is more effective than Odomos, but they did this calmly, the way a ganja addict crushes hash before softly puffing on it. The rest of it was, well, that they'd gone from jeers to ears and could now hear the silent cry of Bade's heart.

The poor lost sad moon of a human was murmuring something, and all the crows' eyes brimmed with tears. Jackanapes's as well; by now he had decided to abandon his plan to take revenge by throwing stones and was deep in thought as to how he might lighten and mend Bade's heart.

So much so that, after giving thanks, those who had to return to their homes and nests set out, but Crowess, with Jackanapes and his comrades right behind her, all returned to the old tree in newfound sympathy.

To listen to Bade's heart. Because they had special experience listening to words of the heart, especially if the speaker has fallen asleep. Standing on a tree branch.

★

45

Something moved inside the flat. Bade leaned over quickly, thinking less of him would make him less visible. A light came on inside, and the darkness was deepening outside, but who would tell him that this was the reason it was less possible for him to be seen? Even if you don't have a beard, a straw will stick in it if you're feeling guilty! He leaned over in the attitude of a criminal, and then, ensuring that there was no one to the right or left of the road who might see him, he executed an acrobatic manoeuvre, jumping up to a higher branch. Here the foliage was thicker but he had a clear view of the flat.

His ridiculous sister had left the balcony open, and the whole house was lit up as though it were Diwali, so that anyone could ogle her lifestyle under cover of darkness and leaves. Beti had never worried about Peeping Toms. She was right there on display, and had seated their mother on a swing in a dervish-type outfit, to make her a laughingstock. Swing swing. *Look, everyone, have you ever seen such a lifestyle, and look, clothing that swishes as she walks, and Uff, what if Ma falls! She used to wear beautiful saris, tied them smartly, and now?*

Bade began to remember Ma in saris. *Which she has thrown away*, he thought forlornly. And such a storm of grief arose in his heart that he grew exhausted and fell asleep.

The man slumbering in sari-memories was no less expert in the craft than any sari merchant. And so he began to unroll them all, bolt by bolt, the entire stock, in the forlorn courtyard of his mind, and since he was in a tree, he also began to hang them from the branches. There were the saris that Ma wore in his childhood, and then the ones he had bought for her on his official trips or transfers. Ma was Ma only in a sari. On the Dashashvamedh Ghat in Benares, descending the stairs from the Vishwanath Temple with the other women, tiny clay lamps alight on her tray, wearing a silk temple sari from Mysore. It was vermilion, with a thin gold-striped border. She wore the pallu over her head, her face framed by the golden stripes. The women leaned down to set the lit diyas adrift in the water, and the starry sky descended into the river, a shimmering Milky Way sparkling coquettishly. Ma lightly wiped her cheek with her pallu, and her son, sleeping in the tree, seemed to feel her buttery touch.

Then it transformed into a slap on the cheek. Which Ma had given him as she came out of the kitchen. He couldn't remember the date, or the city, but the air was fragrant with the delicious scent of pakoras frying in mustard oil. It was rice and karhi day. Amma had filled a small bowl with pakoras for him, but the tongue is the tongue and the hand is the hand and the feet the feet, and her Bade still small. He simply had to return to the kitchen again and again and grab a fistful of pakoras from the platter. Piping hot, tender and fluffy, here and there a crispy beak or tail protruding. *Chomp chomp.* Amma came back and saw; dragging him by a bush-shirted arm, she cried, And what will be left for the karhi? You're spoiling dinner for everyone else! She'd slapped him on the cheek with a touch that felt so sweet as he sat in the tree, as

soft as a Mysore pallu. But that day she'd been wearing a
cotton sari, and she'd wrapped the pallu around her front and
stuffed it in at the waist, making her look like a warrior
heroine as she patted her heated face at times, and smacked
her little Bade at others.

The son, sleeping in the tree, rested his hand lovingly upon
his cheek.

By then, the Crowess had returned to the tree with the
gang of youngsters.

We don't care if you don't understand anything else, but do
learn about the saris, the elders crowspered.

The young crows, eager to attain knowledge, took out their
notepads and each ripped out a feather for a quill, dunked it in
tree sap, wrote down name and date, and sat at the ready.

First, they all wrote: *he is sleeping.*

It was a strange sight in the tree: a human, sleeping with
his hand on his cheek, and loads of crows gathered about him
like students, seated on each branch in rows as they took
notes, listening to the words in the human's mind. The
Crowess was their preceptor, and when they didn't
understand something the sleeping man was thinking, she'd
clarify. Saris unfurled, softly swinging from branches. The
crows watched in amazement.

The man's heart-whispers unspooled onwards.

And eventually, a grown Bade had begun to bring saris for
Amma. When she heard he was going to Kota, Ma herself had
asked for one of the famous Kota-weave saris, the Kota Doria.
It was a light calf colour, overlaid in checks of the same shade,
with a thin gold brocade border. *Was I right to get white,* Bade
had said, questioning himself, but it was so lovely, and it was
not mourning white. Ma used to wear the sari on summer

evenings, when she strolled out to the cantonment with Papa, he remembered. Sometimes Brigadier Dhillon would ring up and invite the two of them to dinner with his own parents in the cantonment.

Kota thread, the crows crowspered to one another.

Then they noticed a magenta sari bolt that had just unrolled in Bade's mind. The whole tree was absolutely dazzled.

That was a Patola sari, the son remembered.

A Patola, the crows were breathless in admiration. Take a look at that colour, wow!

It had been printed with a design of ecstatic maidens dancing the raas leela—*A Nairkunj-patterned sari,* Bade remembered. He'd got it from Charminar in Hyderabad. He'd bought one for Bahu too, but she'd been more delighted by Ma's. Ma had said, you wear it, how can an old mare like me wear something so dancy-flirty? But Bade had insisted she wear it, and how darling she had looked. It must have been his wife's burning envy that had turned into sparks and burnt a few holes in it when the washerman had pressed it with a hot iron. Even so, Ma mended the holes and continued to wear it. And for at least three or four years, Bahu would ask for one just like it every time he went on a business trip, or if anyone was coming or going from Hyderabad. As though that Nairkunj consumed her with envy both waking and sleeping. Perhaps now it's hanging in her closet, but it must be even more threadbare by now.

But no sari was as regal as the Gadwal, he said in his thoughts.

Regal, a young lady crow noted, thinking this to be a type of sari.

It's a *Gadwal, silly owl,* her elder sister scolded.

I'm a crow, not an owl, she retorted, rolling her eyes.

As he unfolded the sari in the tree, Bade began to think, *See, thanks to Ma, I had the chance to learn about the skills of weavers.* How many men were likely to know what a Gadwal sari looked like? The main body of the sari is cotton, but the pallu and border are silk, embroidered with gold and silver threads. This one was a yellow sari with a parrot green pallu, and it was—Wow! Lovely!—loaded down with mangoes in every ripple and curve. They were printed from designs on blocks of stone and wood carved in the Gadwa region of Andhra.

At this, Bade's thoughts turned to mangoes, the juice of which he'd spilled on Ma's Pochampally Ikkat sari. Then, too, Bade had been small, and he'd wept mightily. Ma had kept trying to calm him, saying, Look, son, there are so many colours in this sari, see? Maroon, dark red, henna, turmeric— the design blends them all together, so the stains don't even show. Whenever Ma wore that sari, little Bade performed a circumambulation about her, holding out portions of the sari, looking for where the mango juice had spilled, but he couldn't distinguish it from the design, and everyone teased him for his anxious obsession, but he continued to worry. *And the Kalamkari...*

Kalamkari, one crow girl cried, and began scribbling away.

Before that Pochampally, and after that will come Kanjivaram, the Crowess with cow's eyes spoke softly, as though completing a multiplication table.

How do you know? Jackanapes asked excitedly.

Shhhshshsshh, she motioned and smiled.

She wore Kalamkari saris quite often, our Ma. He had seen the artisans tie hairs to a bamboo stalk to make brushes for painting mosaic patterns onto the fabric. *Call them artists,* Ma had

scolded. Those saris truly were something. The colours were
all unique and came from natural materials. Brown, dark red,
deep copper. They came from roots, betel nut, metal, copper,
turmeric, flowers, leaves, and there was even indigo in one,
*What essence must that have been made from? I've forgotten if I ever
knew. And Kanjivaram.*

At which Jackanapes glanced with surprise at Crowess.
Wow, how did you crow that out beforehand? he asked, and again
she smiled her secret smile.

She had a black Kanjivaram, with the story of Ram and Sita
depicted in white all over it. So full of designs, yet simple and
elegant at the same time.

Because there's no colour like black, Crowess explained to the
youths. *Aha!* everyone chorused back.

They carefully stroked the lovely sari as it swayed from a branch.

Not with the beak, she hissed. So they switched to their wings.

Bade had bought it for two thousand rupees. His first trip
to the south. He'd bought one for his wife too, but she would
also borrow the one he'd brought for Amma. It was very
expensive for those days. But even more costly than that was
the Paithani sari.

Pathaan, a crow crowed.

Pathaani, a girl crow corrected.

Oho, the senior lady crow hushed them both… P-A-I-T-
H-A-N-I.

He'd found it in Vadodara, at the home of the Gaekwad
family. A man had come from Aurangabad bearing a bundle of
saris on his head. After all, where else could you find a better
Paithani sari than from a royal family? Show him this one, the
Rani said, pushing it towards him. Take it for your wife. *For
Ma too*, he had thought. The Baangri peacock one or this lotus

one or this Ashavali. The sari seller told him that each and every fibre of those saris was spun and woven by hand. It takes a year and a half to make one sari, Sahib. I'll reduce the price for you, since you are the guest of Her Highness. He picked a purple one, and one grass green.

This too was hung from the tree, and one of the crow students carefully wrapped it in leaves so it wouldn't get caught on a pointy twig and tear.

Then everyone turned and gazed at Bade with curiosity, because he'd begun to laugh as he recalled his trip to Tamil Nadu. He'd been driving along and had chanced to see a brick-red sari displayed in a shop window. He'd asked the driver to stop, so he could just take a look, and gone inside to ask about it. The salesgirl had said brusquely in English, *No sale. Damage.* He was about to turn away, but his heart pulled him back. Please show it to me, he said. *Damage, damage!* the girl had shouted, as though speaking to a deaf person. But I can look at it! he yelled back. The girl looked at him as if she would swallow whole this time-wasting fool. She removed the sari from the window and practically flung it in his face. Bade could tell right away that this was one amazing sari. Tamil Nadu silk. The colour of red bricks. Peacocks all over and a den of lions on the pallu. Such fine work and not a single empty space. But so serene nonetheless. Such high quality. And the silk so refined. He touched it, weighed it, caressed it, put it down, then picked it up again and asked, how much? The girl was like, *this guy is nuts.* Damage! she now shrieked as though handing down a sentence, and began pointing out the damage to him: there's a tear from here to here; here too, it's ripped; here's another. But Bade had already understood that this was the only sari of its kind in the entire world. No problem. And in that era of low prices, and for a reduced rate at that, he still had to pay a few thousand rupees for it. Oh my, oh my, but that sari! His mother had worn it and so had his beloved wife. The tears were mended. The mending in those days was brilliant. Ma used to roll it up like a small carpet, then wrap another sari around it, then wrap that in paper and tie a ribbon around it and stand it up in the wardrobe so it wouldn't get torn any further.

At this, Bade suddenly remembered the sari that had been wrapped around that sari. It was made of tissue. The colour of clouds, with gold dissolving into it. Real gold. So fantastic, when he hung it from a branch the crows went wild with rapture: *Gold!*

That's right, the elders explained. People even have this kind of sari melted down to extract the gold.

We would never do such an inexcusable thing, said one, touching it, enchanted.

Careful! another yelled. This one will tear too.

Hey, look at this one, another crow directed everyone's attention elsewhere, to where the son was very carefully unfolding a different style of sari. A small one.

What does his remembering heart say?

The crows began to listen.

This one I did not buy. I had seen it in the temple of the Tamil minister's wife. Her father performed ancestral priestly duties there. It was a sari used to dress the goddess. And what should happen but that I took a liking to that one as well. That too was red, but not at all showy.

Crowy? In a temple? one crow asked with astonishment.

Not crowy, *showy*, another attempted to explain.

I'll explain; first listen, Crowess interjected. And take a look.

The sari was covered with golden checks.

It was rather narrow, Bade thought, *but Ma was delighted, and she paired it with another sari so it would be long enough to wear. Truly,* he remarked to himself in a congratulatory tone, *I had no idea what a sari aficionado I was!*

Crowess now explained this to the little ones: the language that rings out all around you fills your unconscious mind, and then shocks you and makes you wonder *when did I learn all this?* That is why one should wander about where people speak well.

Bade's sari class was going swimmingly. It was altogether separate from the sight across the way, inside his sister's flat, which he had climbed up in the tree to spy on. He was unfurling sari-wrapped memories in an orderly fashion in his slumberous state, hanging them up in the tree one by one. His students were absolutely ecstatic themselves, and Bade's heart-whispers continued anon.

It suddenly occurred to the sleeping Bade's heart that there had been a kind of sari tug-of-war going on. Bahu always liked the saris he brought for Ma better than her own. She would insist that Ma wear them once, to inaugurate them, so they would officially be Ma's; after that, she would borrow them for herself, without fail. Sometimes Ma would say, Why don't you keep it now? because Bahu would step all over the edge of her saris in high heels, since she wore her saris flush with the ground, and then there would be holes in the border. For her part, Bahu complained that all the sari blouses were cut to Ma's measurements, so she had to make do by mixing and matching. The sari conflagration between the mother and daughter-in-

law was of an on-going nature. Their household always
resounded with it and both would dress up on special
occasions, although Ma was more inclined to plain saris, and
she had started wearing less colourful ones even when his
father was still alive.

Oh, he suddenly remembered, *that deep blue sari I brought
from Shantiniketan.* It was a designer sari from Gayatri ji's
business. It had a print of Mughal design. Bahu had been with
him and she had chosen it, saying, Ma doesn't wear the over-
colourful ones as much. It was almost blue-black; printed with
kohl-black wine goblets. How dull it is, said Bade, finding
fault, but Ma had liked it very much. She had worn it to an
awards ceremony, where she'd handed out prizes to the soldiers
and their wives. There were even photos of her in that sari.

This sari is completely different! The crows gazed upon it
admiringly. Crowess reached out a wing and draped the
garment over a lower branch.

In the heat of the debate that Monday evening—or was it a
Tuesday?—they had waved their wings and feet about
animatedly, but now, under the tutelage of Crowess Aunty, they
climbed into the tree and began to gaze calmly upon the saris
unfurling from Bade's heart. They were astonished at the
variety. Several of them wished that crows could swan about in
such elegant attire, but they were crows not swans, after all.

And so, as night fell, a sari mood spread across the tree. A
sleeping person is enriched by dreams, where he sees sights
about which he has no idea when conscious. That is to say,
some saris about which perhaps Bade never even knew also
fluttered into view. On top of that, there were the sympathetic
crows, eager to listen to the heart-whispers. Now who could
stop the tree from becoming a full-blown festival? Bade's heart

billowed along with the lovely saris, and he slept comfortably upon a branch. In the meantime, surely by mistake on the part of some municipal authority in the Forestry Department, some soft streetlights came on, and the countless saris hanging from the tree twinkled spectacularly in the pleasing light. And the crows touched the saris, examined them up close, even wrapped themselves in them, becoming so mad for them they reeled and spun like tops. And they marvelled: *Look at that, the tie-dye! And the gold and silver embroidery of the zardosi, and the Bandhej, the Tanchoi, the Ikkat, the Ajarakh, the Jaamdaani; the one with chikan-work, the Chanderi, the Madhubani, the Maheshwari, the Mooga, the Kosaa, and that Baalucheri that has women smoking hookahs on it, and that white Dhakai, that Tasar from Bhagalpur, that Bengali Shantipuri made on a handloom, and this one from Bastar that's sandal-coloured with drums printed on it and was cut up later and turned into dupattas, and this one is just as lovely, a Lugda brought from Daang, light pink with a turquoise border—a bit short, but Ma wore it quite often at home; the colour was not fast, and then my sister, who only likes unstylish villager-type clothing anyway took it away—but, of course, she is patently ridiculous...*

Patently, the crows noted.

Paithani, Crowess said sternly.

We already got that one. A crow picked up his notepad and showed her. Then he stopped and, propping one cheek against a wing in the attitude of a promising student, turned to the cow-eyed Crowess and asked, but why, Aunty? Why did Ma renounce such beautiful saris and start dressing in sacks?

Because, child, she has peeled away all her outer layers, and now she is opening the inner ones.

Just at that moment, Bade, who had been gazing upon his mother's former sari-swathed self, awoke with a start, as though recalling the new Ma's mono-layered attire. Quickly he began brushing off his own clothing, in which all sorts of ants had begun to frolic. Actually, one must crush them by rubbing them, thus killing two birds—i.e., ants and mosquitoes—with one stone. He had not been taught this in school, nor at university.

What's this that's happened? Bade glanced at his watch and, stepping from one branch to another, tangling and untangling himself among the billowing saris, jumped down. A whirlwind of saris arose in which the Tanchoi, Tangail, Gadwal, Benarsi, Maheshwari, Kantha, Pochampally, Kattak, Balucheri, the embroidered one…sprung up anew and a shimmering cloud of dust flew all about, glistening like beads of sweat.

But Bade had climbed down. He glared angrily up at his sister's flat. He could see Ma walking about, swish–swish.

Good God, her foot will get caught in something. She'll fall! he muttered.

And fall she did. Just not right then.

★

46

The first messenger was a crow. Whom no one noticed because those days are gone when a person would see a bird and realise that it was Jayant or Jatayu, the one who recognised Sita and passed on the details to Ram, etc. Trees sky rivers birds, the honour of all these has been flung into cement. Water is a stinking drain, the sky a roof of smoke, and the bird, if it is a crow, has surely just come to steal or leave droppings.

Of course, the thought of theft did occur to him the moment he arrived, though truly, he had come simply to deliver his message. Seeing the fried toast on the table soaked in rajma and cooked in a sauce of nice red tomatoes, the heart did patter. A struggle with greed ensued. *Hunger*, he told himself, but his recently awakened conscience agitated him by providing the name *greed* instead. It really is hard to distinguish, he thought. Everyone—whether good or evil—gets hungry, but since nowadays the tummy begins to rumble at the sight of a tasty morsel, one has no idea whether it's one or the other. When he tried to avert his gaze, he suddenly wondered what difference it would make to anyone's well-being anyway if he just tried a nibble? *The window is open, I have both foot and feather, I could hop over, or I could skip or swoop. After that, I'll inform him his mother has taken a tumble. But are they in any state to hear?*

Husband and wife were bickering.

On that day, the exact date of which is no matter, because this is not a history, just a herstory, Bade was squabbling with his wife. Where are Amma's saris? Bahu, whose threshold was near zero after so much shock, as her Overseas Son understood, started crying, What did I do? Hide them? Do you see me walking around in them? I certainly didn't take them; don't I have my own, and was I the one who became the Wishing Tree, and said, *Take it all, take my whole life, all my worldly possessions*, and who is all this food being cooked for anyway if all you want to do is eat bread and ketchup, and why do all the glasses smell like whiskey, my friends don't drink that flavour of juice, and you're just hoarding all the money when onions are selling for a hundred rupees a kilo.

Is this your answer to my question, or are you purposefully changing the subject and calling me a money-hoarder?

So I'm a sari-hoarder, and I'm the one putting all the money in shares?

Did I touch your money? It's Amma's.

When a quarrel flares up, the agitation of the adversary can be a source of satisfaction. The moment Amma's name came up, Bade's anger hit the roof. Even more satisfying is when the adversary, in this case Bade, loses control in a fit of anger and babbles something from that height of rage which Bahu can then broadcast, What a low thing he said, how coarse, how petty, and the offspring across the sea will hear of it, and will wring his hands with despair and worry, What shall I do, should I leave my work behind and come home to take charge?

Everything's in Amma's name and the other names are your sons', what will I get?

And what of me? And what of your mother, has she given nothing to her beloved bahu?

Look, you better stop talking about my mother. Okay, enough. Take her saris next time, threatened Bade.

You won't go yourself, I have to get her to sign the cheques, as if I get anything out of going to that house, where not even tea is served properly!

Stop this sari check chuck chick, gasped the crow, controlling his saliva, *Ma's taken a fall!* he cawed.

This was Jackanapes, the same crow who had jumped up and disrupted the meeting and threatened to do this and that, when Crowess had reasoned with him and made him understand. First he'd been intent on busting Bade's head, now he wished to caress that same pate, having learnt of the tale of mother-longing.

Such is youth. Impulses leap. One moment we are ready to give our own lives, the next we are bent on taking the lives of others.

One thing leads to another. The question of how the young crow had gone from ill-wisher to well-wisher could turn out to be a long story. He too had had an amma; one who had died in childbirth. An egg burst in her womb and got stuck and she had wasted away, her breathing had slowed then stopped altogether. His aunt had spared him from wandering from door to door, or rather from nest to nest. His hard, youthful heart had melted at the mention of mothers, rendering him like a mother himself. As in the song, a show of *khuli palak men jhutha gussa, band palak men pyaar—false rage in open eyes, true love in closed*—this too was gone with the wind.

That's the thing. Both emotions are surging inside, but which will be dominant, and when will it spill over, this has been the concern of kingdoms, governments, leaders since forever, unless they make use of it for political ends. Which is always a temptation.

Here, the deciding factor that is emerging, despite being unnecessary, is that of youth. Youth could make the crow the instrument of others' self-interest. Act now, think later, is how things shake down in the storm of youth. Context and environment will determine which way the puppet jumps—into shove or into love.

And since greed has been mentioned, let us return to the toast with beans. Greed is present in both love and shove. The way that a dove is present in love. So the crow, forgetting hostility, became eager to be of solace. His heart swelled so for Bade that he made his way to the latter's new post-retirement home after asking the way. And he began to tap his beak, not on the door but on the window, right by where Bade was sitting. To tell him, hurry up, your most revered Amma has taken a fall! But neither husband nor wife saw or heard, and the crow could not help seeing the food and salivating for it.

Attention is divided when so many provocations and proclivities occur at once, and for a moment the crow might have felt disoriented and wondered why he had come. Like colonial amnesia. The ear over there, the heart somewhere else, one eye looking this way and the other that. But recalling his feet and feathers, compassion again surged in him and he considered how the poor things don't have feet or feathers like mine, and they never even managed to fully conjure a beak, so really what good are they? With this surge of sympathy, all the pity returned which had brought him there today, that is: Amma has fallen, I've seen it with my own eyes, I've come all this way asking directions to your house. Please come.

So there's still more left to the tale of our young crow, Jackanapes. But since we've said *so*, there must be a *just so* tale as well. Such a tiny word, *so*, but nonetheless not as insignificant as one might think. Important linguists, since the time of Sanskrit to the present moment of Annie Montaut, have been quizzing the meaning of *so,* wondering what makes it so puzzling.

But despite the immensely amusing qualities of the *so* tale, Amma has had a fall, so it does us no credit to linger over fun. Thus we shall cast aside this and countless other fascinating topics. But of course, every single topic is endless, and no tale is ever complete. Not even life. It is foolish to think life finishes with death—even in death, life is infinite. Today life is in danger because scientists have been born who are busy trying to put an end to death, who want to find a way to live for all eternity. They are surely about to put an end to life. Perhaps they don't know that. When Yayati received the boon to remain youthful forever, he himself became eager to disown it. His enmity was not with youth but with forever; if anything lasts forever its value is wiped out. Life exists because there's death, and joy because there's sorrow. And *so* on and *so* forth.

But this is a thinking matter, not a laughing matter, as the great Bade Ghulam Ali Khan once admonished, when he sang the line, *baajuband khul khul jaaye—see how her armlet slips away*—and explained that the armlet of the woman in love keeps slipping off because she's grown too thin with pining for her lover, and then his audience burst out laughing. And going forward, incidents keep occurring; even when they're over, they're not over, they remain entombed, entranced, in samadhi, and it may only take a puff of breeze to bring them back to life.

Something always remains. Whether a so-tail or a crow-tale.

At any rate, the crow must go on. He knocked, but who noticed? Important news, important, important, he called out. Who has the time? What with a world war afoot. The crow cleared his throat and began to speak verrry sloooowly, like an elderly person. Look, today, I returned to my meeting venue and you will be pleased to know that I thought I'd take another look at the saris you had hung out there, touch them, smell them, and also check up on your mother's health. So the saris, after you woke up, they must have floated away and vanished. So I turned around to take a peep at your Ma ji from the balcony. The morning was damp with dew, the sky blinked lethargically, opening its pink eyes as it slowly spun them round the world, and a pink haze spread all about. Even my own dark reflection took on a reddish cast, as I noticed in the balcony window. But before I could rejoice, prance, I saw something else and became terrified. The scene began to unfold before these very eyes of mine, as though it was just waiting for me to get started. Your sister was standing there, holding the tea tray, and your Ma ji was entering the room.

The crow was on a roll, but then he noticed that his announcement was having no impact on the flames of war. The toast was also still sitting there. He came hopping a little further in from the window, but nothing changed. No, no, he said after listening to Bade's words, it has nothing to do with the saris, nor with her tent-like attire; that only arrived yesterday, the hijra had it sewn and brought it by. Your Ma hadn't shrunk so much in just one night, and the cloth was above her ankles. That's why I could see her ankle turn. The fault belongs to the shah bulbul that came to perch on that branch in the rosy dawn where you had hung the Pochampalli sari covered in mangoes. Your mother saw, and she was misled, as all wily shahs are apt to mislead. Power is false but whoever begins to feel vain about his own power starts to believe in his own invincibility. Such a shah becomes arrogant and dictatorial. People are fools, allowing such power to accrue to one person, believing he stands for law and order and beauty and will make the world the greatest, when really he will only do so for himself. Do not consider this to be evidence of my own hurt ego. I'm black, so what, I have my pride, and I harbour no mad desire to become a shah bulbul, or a swan or whatever. But your mother has entered a brand new life. She sees all with new eyes, body and mind agog with excitement. She tottered. She wanted to soar towards the shah bulbul, but we're the ones who fly. If she turned fast, the bird would fly away, so she wanted to turn that way slowly. Understand?

They got not a jot. But by now husband and wife, worn and weary, ran out of steam for their quarrel, so one went here and the other there. Bahu arranging the breakfast on the table, Bade back in bed, eyes closed, obscuring his melancholy in the trappings of anger. The crow thought, *All's calm; now they'll listen.* He ratcheted up the tapping. *Tap tap.*

Bade opened his eyes. The crow was before him in the window, bathed in a soft light. He reached out slowly so that he could pull the curtain aside fully. In the eyes of the crow the agility of jump hop. The two of them face-to-face, eye-to-eye.

Would Bade know that this crow had been there on that sad evening? He probably didn't know he had narrowly avoided his skull being cracked. Who knows, maybe Bade thought all crows look alike, the way Americans think all sardars do, and Germans think all Koreans do, and white people think all black people do, and crass people think all amazing people do, and coarse minds think all clouds do, and lechers think all women do, and humans think all ants do. Anyway, he looked as though he sort of recognised him. The crow began to chatter fulsomely now that he thought Bade was listening.

He who does not understand simply hears *caw caw,* but there were in Jackanapes's speech the cadences and stylings of language, the expressiveness of feelings; everything was present. Please think, the crow told Bade, if the heart leaps up like a crow, and the feet are like a tortoise, then doesn't it just follow that the elderly will fall? Your mother's heart and stride were moving on two different tracks, one leg went forward and the other back. The shah bulbul must have wanted this, the crow said, offering his political analysis. For the footwork to get muddled, and that is what happened. Ma's sandals slipped, and in an effort to right her balance, she began to turn backwards. Your Ma cried out, Oh no oh no oh no, your sister freaked out, and me totally helpless. By the time I thought of jumping forward and stopping her, I mean catching her, she'd already gone *splat.*

At that very moment Sid popped in and said, in his typical style, Good morning, Pop, look the crow is also saying good morning, is there anything to eat, Mom?

And everything came together.

The battle cooled. Sid sat, Mom handed him the toast and beans. Also the fried mushrooms. She tried to scoop them up with a fork and pop the first bite into her eldest son's mouth, but it dropped under the table, and the crow son immediately jumped up. Pop saw the crow pop up and he leaned over and picked up the piece and tossed it through the window towards him. My husband will never improve, Bahu shook her head, but Sid had dissolved her anger. Bade said, he's better than you, he's listening to me quietly and not talking back. Sid laughed. Young Jackanapes's eyes flashed crowishly and were a sight to see, but the news was important so he gave it again: Eat quickly and come, Amma's had a fall.

I'm going, Sid jumped up. The crow thought he meant, because of his message. But it turned out Sid had an important meeting with the International Olympics Association members; if this thing worked out, his life would be made.

First go see your grandmother, she's had a fall, said the crow, swallowing his crumb.

When will you go to see Daadi? Bade asked. The crow looked at him with gratitude.

After Sunday, said Sid.

Take her saris, so she doesn't fall.

She did fall, she's already fallen, but it's got nothing to do with saris, as the crow and later the doctor explained to Bade. But there's no worth attached to the cawing of crows, and with doctors it's either all ears and yes yes yes, or no no no to every word they say. And some say these are matters to be pondered and not laughed off, and others feel it's all to do with heart-whisperings, and these are two entirely different approaches.

★

47

No, said the doctor. Beti was answering each of his questions promptly, becoming more fearful at every response.

It's easy to frighten those already frightened. Where had she gone wrong? Had she mistakenly considered Ma completely healthy, heedless of her advancing age? Beti would come out of the guest room now and again to take a peek at Amma. If the bangles jingled from far off or she heard the light switch go on in the bathroom. If Ma saw her, she'd say, Uff, go, I'm fine. If she didn't see her, then her daughter observed Ma's complete takeover of the bed. Beti would smile, thinking, *See how contented she is with me?*

But what had happened today? It was as though fear had demanded Beti learn a lesson. In the morning, she had been standing making tea so the two of them could sit on the balcony, when Ma began sliding backwards, senselessly ceaselessly, instead of moving forwards. *Arre arre arre*, sort of singing laughing like a ship flowing backwards *flop flip* turning her sandals like paddles.

A second or two became an eternity. Beti set the tray down and jumped to shield Ma's body, but by then the body had lurched backwards, slid against the wall and fallen to the floor. Beti's hand sort of pulled Ma back, probably keeping her head from banging against the wall, but the rest was nothing but shock, because Ma was lying on the ground, staring up in astonishment, wondering, *What happened?* to which she herself responded, *Arre, I fell.*

Beti shrank back. She'd grabbed but also failed to grab. Did you hurt your head? How could she lift Ma? Suddenly heavy as a rock. Beti dragged her along the ground looking for something useful to help with the lifting. Ma's body left a wet mark along the floor. Was it sweat? Pee? She'd slip even more on that. Beti's fear was all-encompassing. She simply couldn't lift Ma. Ma was now laughing guiltily. You get out of the way, I'll get myself up. *But if she slipped!* Beti ran to get a towel, wiped away the moisture, spread today's paper out on the floor. Ma looked around, what could she rest her weight on so she could pull herself up? Get me a chair, she commanded. Ma dragged herself along to the chair like a baby. Using the chair as a support, she somehow turned herself over. So she was back up, belly down. Then two arms on the chair, two legs on the floor; and waited in that position to catch her breath. She'd transformed into some sort of four-legged beast. Beti tried to give her a hand here or there, but Ma was lifting herself up on her own. Like a nanny goat. Her quilted coat swung beneath her like a belly that's borne oodles of children. Beti was terrified. *I can't do anything on my own, should I phone KK, or Bade, but I can't leave Ma like this either.*

Ma's flipped body lay there long, then she made a big push and lifted her hindquarters, gripped the chair one hand at a time, and scooted herself up, saying, *No, no, stop, stop, ah, ah*, grabbed Beti, and swivelled around slowly, after which she sat a long while right there on the chair, sprawled by the wall. Beti could have thought: *Look, after all those snipes about our low chairs*. But all that was ground to dust now. When Ma was able to get up, she said, all is well, but my pinkie got twisted, and in a fit of Brahmin-ness added, first I will bathe.

Beti kept peering in: Ma, a tiny little cotton doll, unclad, steadying herself as she washed and wiped.

Beti called the doctor. *She didn't get dizzy? She didn't faint? Does she have pain in her knees? Does her head feel heavy? Wet floor? She wasn't sweating? What had she eaten? Does she feel a burning in her throat?* Blood clot or blood pressure cataract ear pressure heart—the charts began to flip open.

No, said the doctor. He suggested Beti bring her to the hospital. Ma kept refusing, but Beti took her to the hospital Bade recommended, which was connected to CGHS, where she would have an examination and treatment under the governmental scheme.

★

48

Ma lay on the hospital bed. She was fine, but listless, as though to say, *You've put me back in bed*. Arre, it's nothing, she said. She was embarrassed; peevish too. My sandals slid backwards and I fell.

Mornings are a phenyl free-for-all in the hospital. Outside the OPD a group of sardars yukked it up. Loud congratulations, jests and guffaws. When the doctor emerged and snapped: This is a hospital! An elderly sardar held out a box of sweets: Doctor Saab, I just had a grandson, here, have a sweet treat. The sardar youths at his side raised their hands balle balle and did a bit of bhangra.

When mothers fall, all the characters in a story come crashing in and gather in one place. In a single gust, or not so much a gust, but a slap: *whapwhapwhapwhap,* everyone lurches in one direction.

It's the same MO in all families. Everyone shares the worry, even if they're annoyed with one another. Whether or not they get along, Ma is the tie that binds.

Each person is a reflection of their own time, but also separate from it. A mirror has so many angles and bends and corners, so many unthinkables, one has no idea whose reflection one sees and how it came to appear there; if you don't know how to look at it crooked, you'll never guess. In the silver of a mirror shines a sliver of time, and in a snap of the fingers there's the span of time, and where the image seems to steady, there, another snippet, another wrinkle, another baggy bit. The twisty-turny crackle of the glass is also time. Every speed is also time, even if it's swinging swaying slipping spinning soaring swimming, and women: what to say of them? They die daily but live on in books, and everyone has arrived at the hospital hovering around Ma, and here she is saying, *Get me Rosie.*

Perhaps Bade misheard this as: *Get me a sari.* Amma had fallen in her bizarro swishing canopy-cape thingy. For the first time since his sister's misspent youth he now addressed her directly, handing her a package he said, *They're here, take them out.* And out came the saris.

Bahu's eyes popped as she wondered when he had taken them from her wardrobe, and this, in turn, chafed at an old wound: *My things are never mine, whatever my in-laws want they just grab, they didn't even let me raise my own children, they were entrusted to their aunt's care, or to the grandparents, and the house was a watering hole for the whole world, do I even know what it's like to have a home of my own, my sister-in-law drops in to stay whenever she wants, Amma gives her my nightie without even asking, and says, Just stay here overnight, and on top of that, whoever feels like it just comes and sits in my window seat, where I like to sit and do my reading and studying while keeping an eye on the kitchen. And then they accuse me of no longer taking an interest in household chores. Then my sister-in-law sees the car and driver are setting out, and to save the petrol in her own car or scooter and using Ma as an excuse, she'll say, you should get Knorr soup in the nearby market, it's organic, since she's so fussy about eating let her have that, she just needs to drink it, and off they go. And she comes back after accomplishing a ten-minute task in an hour, and picking up her dry cleaning, and meeting and greeting, accomplishing god-knows-what-all. She'll fill our car with petrol once every hundred days, and then, for two hundred days Ma will bring it up every chance she gets, and mention that Beti filled the tank. They're all so clever, come here to serve their own ends and protect their own space as though it's sacred, they don't allow any interference in their own homes and work. Anyway, she lives such an outlandish lifestyle no one would want to go near her!* The whole history billowed up in Bahu's head like smoke, but on that sensitive occasion at the hospital she kept her mouth shut.

If you have to keep quiet but aren't quiet inside, sounds come bursting out of other places. Ew, ick, look at the cobwebs on this window, clean it off, ugh. Eeks, she won't eat this fodder, this sawdust, come, Amma, enough, now come home. Fuss fuss, oh my, you do amaze me. She'll wear this sari here? Shocking pink! And she's got a hospital gown anyway, and amidst these voices, Bahu took out the saris and counted them, to see which ones Bade had brought, and which of them were hers. Seven saris for the hospital! she exclaimed.

So that's why she fell, Bade told the doctor. But the doctor disagreed. He kept asking all sorts of questions, none to do with saris. How is her vision, check the eyes; did she feel weak, check the heart; the ear pressure gets unbalanced, check the ears; why did she twist her toe, check her bone density; she could be anaemic, blood, haemoglobin, platelet, thyroid, look at all those; ECU ENT MRI, this test that test, he wrote it all down. When he learned there'd been stones in Ma's gall bladder on occasion, and that they'd been removed in the past, an X-ray as well, to see if maybe there was some leftover swelling that might burst.

Ma was plopped in a wheelchair. Age. The demands of age. Have her admitted, look for a private room, she'll be comfy there, run tests, Ma had laughed when she fell but now she was tired, getting all those tests done that had been proposed the moment they set foot in the hospital and which took three days to complete.

KK and Bade stood side by side. Talking not to one another but to the doctors and nurses.

Do you wink, Ma ji? Asked the doctor reading the file.

Sometimes, said Ma, after some thought.

When you sing, do you feel hoarse? Is it like singing in khadtaal?

But I don't sing, Ma said after some reflection.

Is your coughing deep—mandra or soft—adhya or slow and drawn out—vilambit?

Taarsaptak—high octave, said Ma, tuning into her thoughts.

And if you itch your foot, Mata, do you lean over, or lift your foot?

I reach with my cane, Ma explained.

Do you dream? he asked.

A lot, said Ma.

Check her… the doctor wrote down some more tests in some unknown language. He was the Head Doctor.

The nurse spoke up. Doctor Sahib, at night…she opened the register pages and double-checked…Yes at 12:03 a.m., and then again at 4:52 a.m., the patient whistled.

What. Get rid of the whistle, she could get an infection.

No, no, laughed the nurse. She whistles with her lips.

Interesting. The doctor looked pensively at Ma for a moment, holding up his pen in indecision, but perhaps the whistle didn't seem an especially serious matter.

Get it? It's got nothing to do with saris. He spoke dismissively to Bade, who wanted to discharge Ma and bring her home as soon as possible.

★

49

Draped in medical gowns, stethoscopes hanging, clutching files, they come and they go. They're giving her this pill that pill, shots, even a saline drip. But discharge is in the hands of the Head Doctor who's coming in the evening if it's morning, or morning if it's evening. Bade will keep paying, everyone will come and go all day, Beti will stay the night because her work is of the type—if it is work!—that can be done anywhere.

Everyone looks frightened and anxious. Beti looks depressed. *I couldn't handle it alone and if this is what was to become my lot then I too should have done what others do, they who have the advantages that come with not living alone, here I have to deal with the disadvantages of being alone, but also the disadvantages of being with everyone by force of circumstance, without my having chosen so.* Bahu is also upset: *there's no one to share my burden, there's only one person who really listens to me.* She steps out of the ward to phone him. The son who is there for her in her time of need: Overseas Son. From that distance, he worries about how to help and console his mother. We let her go somewhere for a few days, and then look, she had a fall; if she has to be cared for, we have to do it. Overseas Son said: You should give Daadi Electrol, she must have had a dip in her sodium, and take some yourself as well, every half hour or so, Ma, take a sip or two, you can't tell, but you can get dehydrated due to a shortage of electrolytes. Yes, son, sometimes I feel sort of dizzy from all this to-ing and fro-ing, and these days I can't even get to my yoga classes regularly, Mom told Overseas Son, feeling emotional tired defeated cheered. Bade stood aside, sick with worry. But he felt relieved to find himself in his traditional role as he thought to himself, *NowAmma will be with me again, I had all the tests done, everything is fine, straight home from here.*

The lustre in his eyes full of pride-in-duty dimmed when Rosie Bua entered the hospital. That morning he'd been in the same room with that fellow KK. Bade was somewhat taken aback that a girl from their fair and lovely family had been fated for this black-skinned Baingan Bhatt. Heavens, if she married this guy, who would the kids take after, has she thought about that, and what if she got unmarried again, he doesn't seem very dependable. And now another scourge had arrived.

Rosie strutted in, chest out. First off she rebuked, I just found out today! I went to the house and the guard told me. What's this? You look so down! Baji, if you've got life you've got love, if you've got zest you've got zeal. Otherwise, end of story, game over.

The doctor and the nurse glanced up, then considered it better to bury their heads in their work.

Rosie took a small comb from her purse and stood to one side. She unfastened her bun, stuffed her hairpins in her mouth, gathered up the windswept wisps, refastened her hair, and sat down by Ma's bed. Three whole days, Baji? Rosie's eyes wide. She discreetly reached beneath her chunni and tight orange kurta with its black and blue flowers to adjust a twisted bra strap.

You were missing yourself, you good-for-nothing, Ma smiled.

Baji. Rosie's voice echoed. Good-for-nothings are the best. They always stick with you. It's the good-for-somethings that leave you high and dry.

The nurse burst out laughing. She took Ma's temperature and turned to leave.

How hot is our Baji? asked Rosie.

Normal. The nurse wobbled her head South Indian style.

That's because I'm here, hmmm? All is normal. Now I'm here, I'll see to it, otherwise who knows what might have happened?

I might've died, what else! said Amma cheerfully.

Baji. Rosie Bua turned with a sharp swish. It's not so simple. One must live through thousands of days to reach the dying day.

The hallways of the hospital began to echo with this aphorism of Rosie's, like a favourite film dialogue. Her *One must live through thousands of days to reach the dying day* became as popular as Gabbar Singh's *Arre, oh, Sambha, kitne aadmi the?*

No one knew how the discharge papers were prepared, perhaps because Rosie was running about creating a spectacle in the hospital, or because the tests were all completed anyway, and Bade only learned afterwards. Rosie had been doing the paperwork whilst Beti took Ma and returned home. Bade's son-ego was shattered again. And the most popular of all of Rosie's dialogues amongst the hospital staff was her very last quip, when Baji had said, Let Bade come back first, and Rosie had feigned incomprehension and cracked, What kind of bade, dahi bade? As though Ma was waiting for an order of fritters bathed in yogurt.

★

50

People came running from all directions on Ma's return, to ask after her and bring her little thisses and thats. The guard opened the gate and salaamed, the gardener opened the car door, the cleaner, the car polisher, the newspaper man, the maids and the other drivers and residents of the society coming home from the office, all stopped by. It was nothing, my children forced me to go, I agreed just to make them feel better, quoth Queen Ma. Age is treacherous, always up to mischief, people sympathised. What age! exclaimed Beti. The doctor was asking what does she eat, she's got the heart of a child and the belly of an oldster, cracked Ma, twirling her cane and causing multicoloured butterflies to dance on their heads.

A sea of bodies formed a procession to deliver her to the flat. When they opened the door, Ma whipped inside like a whirlwind and rushed about getting all the windows opened. At which the squirrel hopped, the sparrow fluttered, the ant tiptoed on tiny feet, the rabbit rabbitted, the deer leapt, the precious elephant waved its trunk, the cat padded, the mouse zipped in and the dog ran out from behind the almirah, tail wagging and tongue out, slobber-ready, all disguised as sunlight and wind.

When Beti saw so many bodies, something happened to her. Their scent, redolent with earth sweat soap food fragrance oil petrol all tumbled together went straight to her head. She snuck into the house, shuffling along, as though she was the patient returned from hospital.

You didn't water the plants at all, the soil is completely dry, Ma chided as she pulled up a stool, sat down and plunged her arms into the dirt. To grow back with the plants. To crackle back into her body.

★

51.

And here we go again: a girl going on sixteen, not an old lady nearing eighty? When a young girl bathes she gazes upon her body, at the buds on her chest, the roundness of her navel, the growing corn silk on her pubis, with delight on her face. Both bashful and lustful, there's mystery, there's fun. And if her own hand touches somewhere, then a thrill. It slides, glides, making light waves leap high. And then, and then? The *ow ow* of Ma resumed.

The hospital with all its poke-stab has freshened the sensitivity and woundedness of the body. Grab an arm, thwack a back, she lets out a whimper, Ow, it hurts, it leaves a mark, look, they gave so many injections at once, the nurse couldn't find the vein, she kept poking and prodding everywhere. A staining gel in one place, a needle stab somewhere else, a stinky ointment elsewhere.

Everything aches, she said happily, rubbing a hand and an eye over her slackening mottling dangling body. Look, this grew at the hospital.

My, Amma, do you really have everything memorised so you can tell what's new?

Why not, don't I know my own body? Look at this, touch this, *eeh, aah*.

Scratch rough edges, trying to smooth out and remove craters wounds blisters.

The cure for which no doctor of any kind possesses, but Rosie does! She brought thornapple leaves and tied them over a mole. She rubbed potato skins on Ma's face. The house filled with odours and again grew garrulous, the wall pillar corner rattled and peered, knock anywhere and check if you doubt. Ma's eyes bulged as she stared long, ascertaining that, yes, truly it has flattened, and look, look, the circle has shrunk a bit, and it's also paler. Fluttering butterflies with her cane, totally unaware that her daughter was wondering, *Who cares, who's going to see?*

Why do the young alone possess the right to passion for the body? As if one's life after youth is only intended, day by day and bit by bit, for sloughing off one's skin, growing more and more unconcerned, detached, nondesirous.

★

52

The body is a mystery. Beti pondered Rosie's, as she watched Amma go down for a walk to the tomb, leaning on her (his?) arm. What *is* that body holding onto Amma?

One with pointy breasts, which jump eagerly from behind the orhni when Rosie raises her arms. Crossing a boundary.

In the fine arts and in popular culture, it is a different body that crosses boundaries. Where the boundary is crossed, a confluence forms. Man–woman mash-up. Birju Maharaj and Kathak, Jayashankar and Sundari. Shankar and Parvati. Their union forges magic, becoming other, making the other their own. Sitting legs tucked to one side in a womanly pose, Gandhi crosses a boundary. Lacchu Chacha wins all hearts when he cooks.

Lachhu Chacha was always in the forefront with women during weddings, he fried puris and kachoris, and roasted and ground the spices for stuffed bitter gourd, tinda, and ladies' fingers. He covered his head with his dhoti, stretched out his legs in the courtyard, and for new mothers he poured ghee into the roasted wheat and gram flours, kneading them in a large thali with sonth, gond, boora, and nuts to make the large, round sithore which danced with his palms, and no one laughed at his effeminacy; in fact, new mothers felt revived by the fragrance of the laddus: Chacha, let me taste too, the men and children would demand. Chacha would laugh and ask them if they too had given birth? Then I will give you some. Looking every inch the grand matriarch. And happy titters bounced across the courtyard. But not at him. Nor would anyone call him unmanly or a eunuch. They had great respect for him. He enthusiastically broke bread with the women after all the men had eaten, smearing each piece well with ghee, for he belonged to the joyous world of women.

If you don't know Lacchu Chacha, what would you know of the gingery laddus? Or Radha Pehlwan's lassi and cream, or Mausa's balushahi sweets, and Laaloo Chacha's shakkar-paare. Timak Tau's millet kheer. Barnakku's imartis and the sweet lavanglata by Nacchi Kaki of the juicy curses. In which case, you are soul-deprived of the essence of all life and joy.

But there's no need to reconstruct that era here, but rather tell the tale of one family, in which there are different kinds of bodies and emanations, different fragrances and ways, and one is flummoxed by those of the likes of Rosie, and Beti who is realising her own incomprehension, and that she's losing sight of her own contours and becoming just an outline of herself, a faded sketch. Just about visible, lots of her invisible now.

Ma too has become newly embodied in the company of whichbodyRosie. She washes her hair and comes out head wrapped loosely in a towel because Rosie has issued the edict that if you leave wet hair loose the breezes spirit away the nutrients, leaving the hair brittle. Now she's loosely braiding her hair. Ma is seated on her chair and Rosie stands behind her, touching her hair, but with what fingers? Attached to a body, but what body? It's hardly nice to let anyone and everyone touch you; what else can Beti think.

Come, Baby, I'll do your hair too.

You should make a loose braid, says Ma. Had she read this in the magazines that KK kept bringing her, or was it again the lure of Rosie's sickly sweet concoctions?

Yes, Baby. Your hair is dry as a broom. The way you just coil it around like a snake on your head, hood up.

I don't get to oil it, nor comb it, nor brush it; I can't find the time I need for work, what with all these new responsibilities that have invaded my routine, you people will only be happy once you've robbed me, bit by bit, of all my old ways, Beti remonstrated in her head.

I'll make your hair so strong you'll be able to drag a plough with it and sow a field.

Oh yes, just what I always wanted, ploughing, farming, tilling, Beti said to herself sarcastically.

Why not? Rosie winked, as though she'd heard. Will the duck swim? she asked Ma.

At which Beti stared at Rosie Bua like an idiot, what sense does that make, but Amma laughed as though she was in on the joke.

What was all this topsy-turvy talk? Perhaps there was some clue to help Beti understand this turvy-topsy body. Strange how whatever one said of Rosie, the reverse too was also germane. Like a body engaged in challenging all stereotypes and definitions. A body unrecognising of the legitimacy of any borders. Flowing this way and that.

There was once a flowing river. A hermit was disgusted by a prostitute and scorned her, at which she retorted proudly, if I have followed my dharma, the river will switch directions and flow the other way. The woman pressed her palms together and performed the mangal archana, and when she opened her eyes, the river was flowing in the opposite direction.

So people will always be in a quandary over which direction is the right one, for only then can we know which is the opposite, in other words wrong! But flow both ways, this way and that way too, on this side of the border and that one too, how then to be clear about anything?

And where the water flowing this way meets the water flowing that way, what is that moment, that fleeting moment of halting together before each resumes its course in the opposite direction?

★

The halting of Beti's body. When KK sneaks in. A halting that steps away and stands at a distance.

KK is pleased. He had run into Rosie and Ma downstairs.

I sent them to go wherever they wanted in my car, there's no one here, just you and me, and I have the key.

Where? Beti is anxious.

Here. KK pulled her close.

Where is…Amma…? she asks between his forced kisses. A strange situation: if she completely pushes him away, he might be offended, but she's also annoyed that she's given up even the freedom of *no*.

They're going to a festival by a lake, KK whispers between lustful kisses. Nowadays there's quite a bit of water there, he added, his lack of control growing.

There's no water in the Yamuna, what lake has water?

His lips felt dry and sticky to Beti. Get back. She pushed him away. Someone will come.

A cat, a mouse, a crow? KK rolled her onto the mat.

Amma…she tried to say.

Is she hiding in here somewhere? KK's hands are insistent, joking on his tongue.

She's everywhere, Beti's body said, but her voice burst out: Get away, what if she comes back?

KK leaned over her. A long string of saliva fell from his laughing mouth onto her face. So stringy you could wrap it around your finger like a thread.

The thread wrapped around KK himself and he was deflated. A kind of revulsion leaked into the air.

The two of them stood up; Beti embarrassed, KK petulant.

She won't come that soon, he said, and began to straighten his clothing.

What if they've forgotten something? Beti tried to speak normally.

You're the one who's forgotten something, i.e., what we once were, and how you liked it.

Well. He turned to go. I must respect your wishes. As though giving an assurance that he wouldn't force himself on her, but also an accusation: you no longer wish it.

And she didn't. Her whole house and household was on the move, proceeding agreeably, amiably, properly, orderly, so that thing which they call desire, i.e., libido, had clicked its heels together and set out in search of more open terrain, longing for the razzmatazz of lighting and rain. Libido has no place in such an orderly household.

★

Beti's face looked blurry in the morning haze, as if her outline had been erased.

But more on that later.

Which means right now.

When she jerked up her head just a teeny bit from her work, which she wasn't actually doing, one could see that a housewife was emerging from the blurring outline of her face. Beti rose to start preparing dinner. Ever since she'd noticed that the maid just washed everything by sticking it in the sink under the tap, whether rice and dal or vegetables, and then took it out again, Beti had taken on this task herself. The maid neither knew nor cared about the proliferation of contaminants nowadays. Beti paid special attention when it came to greens. Fenugreek, chaulai, spinach, bathua, beet greens, dill, lettuce. The maid just cut off the roots of the spinach bunch. Beti had pulled the leaves apart, and showed her how some of the leaves can get cut off that way, and you should separate them over a newspaper and spread them out, tearing the stalk from each and every leaf, but in response the maid just stormed out. If I must be the one to do it, I'll do it, Beti decided. I'll also get the wheat flour out. What, we're out of onions already? We seem to be running through sugar rather fast. What items should I remove from the kitchen, how much should be kept under lock and key? Why do maids always insist on adding too much salt? And making everything swim in oil? How can I keep a constant watch? Will she cook the bhaji with too much water and make it soggy? And when I told her not to use so much water, she burnt the food so she could say, look, it burned! If you don't cook it slowly, how will the flavour come, you'll make it watery. Beti watches silently and the maid whines and complains. Might as well start doing it herself. But how can she make so many things all by herself? Rosie says, even food needs companions. If you make dal, then it wants the roti and sabzi to join in. Then they all demand the company of ghee, chutney, salad, raita, and a little rice. All of them come together and call out for sweets. Amma says, there should always be a little in case someone shows up, so you can offer it to them.

Even food has a joint family!

Aah hai, mumbles Beti to herself as she putters about. She removes the weight from the pressure cooker and blows in the hole to make sure it was cleaned properly. She removes the rubber sealing ring and runs her finger along the edge to make sure there's no dried food stuck to it, Hey prabhu, she murmurs to herself. Should I go and check on her? she asks herself. Yes, go check, she answers herself.

She opens the door for the maid. Now she'll ask me what she should make.

Tell me what to make, and Didi, give me some money, I have to get mustard oil, Mata ji says if Bahu Madam comes I should make sagpahita the way I made it last time, then she can take it for your brother.

Sagpahita? Beti stared into the void. Sagpahita, affirmed the maid. Dill, spinach, split urad daal. You want to get all this? No, we have them all, the maid explained. Then what are you asking for? snapped Beti. For mustard oil. To put in a tadka of garlic and oil at the end. Then why are you shaking the duster in my face? Arre, Didi, the maid laughed with embarrassment, putting the dusting cloth to the side, I was showing you that it's torn, I have to get one of these too. Then get one, Beti agreed. Money! cried the maid. Don't yell, I told you not to ask for an advance, and you just asked for ten thousand to go to a mundan. No! I mean money for the vegetables, the maid cried even more loudly. Vegetables. Had Beti forgotten? Sagpahita, the maid leaned over and whispered into Beti's ear in a loud clear meaningful voice. Beti felt her fate too had turned to sagpahita. In other words, to mush.

Beti goes to lean over her work again. All she's written in a long while is a small and lifeless fragment, on Aloe Vera, which one has begun to find on the roofs and balconies of every single middle class home, or in the gardens if people are so lucky as to have one. In my childhood it was called gwaarpaatha and considered worthless. A weed. But now it's become a gift and party favour at kiddie parties and anniversaries. It's carefully tended and blossoms happily. People rub its gel into their locks or their cheeks or their necks or their pecs, and they also swallow it to make themselves fair in the right places and dark in the right places, and basically it's come to represent living and loving life.

Your luck has turned, Aloe Vera, and so has mine, but in the opposite direction. Beti was dozing at her table. If Madam Inspiration were to pay a call, she'd awake, Beti and her work. But unlike Rosie, Madam Inspiration is not a daily visitor. Beti hears her sometimes even now; she starts and turns: surely it is she who peers in? Yes it is. She walks forward, wondering if she should enter, if Beti is alone, then she'll sit nearby; but without fail, she sees someone else and retreats, flitting away like a wraith.

Half-asleep-Beti is sad. Bangles jingle in her sleep. Amma's bangles. Ma must be up. No! They jingled on my wrists! She sits up. I'm wearing the bracelets I brought from Thailand. Leather ones. How can they jingle? They can't. It must be my ears. Or those other wily bangles have turned into ghosts and possessed them? Will my wooden plastic straw jewellery also begin to jingle and ring?

Beti gets up. Slips her feet into her sandals and they start to *tap-tap clap-clop-clip swish*, just like Ma's. Hey, is it me, or is it Ma? She looks down. Of course; that's why! She's wearing Ma's sandals. When did that happen? She hadn't realised. She'd been complaining about these chatty sandals and here she was wearing them herself? They chat up a storm amongst themselves as Ma walks, and argue with Ma's soles and heels. *Clippety cloppity*.

Beti begins to walk with the sandals pressed down, to avoid walking like Amma. (Op)pressed, they become voiceless.

Which is different from being quiet, something Beti had worked so hard to achieve by living alone. There was quiet and peace in finding one's voice,. She longs for quiet: empty, dark. You reach music in silence, sound in emptiness, vision in darkness. You touch the earth in solitude. You hear the grass grow. Watch the flowers blossom.

Weeds were growing within her. Dry and prickly.

★

On that day too, Beti sat up when she heard the jangle of a bangle. She saw that her wrist was her own, so it must be Amma's jingle. She felt affection now for the first time for these bangles that jingle in their proper place. But in the bathroom when she washed her face and was about to look up into the mirror, she felt a rush of fear: *What if Amma's face stares back at me?* She'd heard you begin to resemble the person you live with, husband like wife, dog like master, mistress like cow parrot cat, so Beti like Ma? Seemingly quiet Beti grew disquieted. She quickly cleared her throat and gargled, then she remembered that Ma cleared her throat in just the same way and lustily spit out her mucus. But I did that before her too, Beti admonished herself. What's this anxiety leaping at every sound?

Just then voices came from the hall. Ma's bangle chimed in again. Beti put on her dressing gown in the guest room and tiptoed out in fear of sandal sounds. Amma stood at the ready, with Rosie at attention. KK was giving his driver instructions.

Where are you going? Beti asked.

The sky is clear, Amma said, and left. As though she were going for a drive in the sky.

Ma would fly up wrapped in her new embroidered cloak. Free as a bird. The sari, with its leg-tangling folds restricting mobility, had been cast aside, and now she'd gone straight into flying. At home, in a straight-up-and-down non-pleated cloak or maxi dress or kaftan or aba or abaya or tent, her body easily performs gymnastics with no one the wiser, unless they know to look for it. Raza Tailor Master sent her this free and fun attire via Rosie, tricked out with old Belgian lace or antique Parsi borders or soft embroidery, and Rosie said, have fun, Baji, spread your wings and fly, raise the hem when you want to scratch an itch, let it fall and it becomes a mosquito net, if you can't control the pressure then just sit down anywhere and relieve yourself, as though you're inside a tent. There once was a burqa, Rosie explained, which reached the ears of not-working Beti, and the lady hidden in it darted among the cars in a three-wheeler, got out, walked along and sat right down by the side of the road, and no one saw anything, not even her face. If it were a sari then you'd have to stick a leg out here, fix a pallu there, what a bother!

KK looked oppressed regarding what he would do until his car was returned. Will you drink coffee? he asked.

Beti didn't retort that she drinks tea in the morning. She just walked forward, avoiding eye contact, and sat down for coffee. She felt that to speak, she'd need to translate what she said into some other language, but how?

Translation isn't easy. If you think you need only take two sips of English to be able to translate, and that you'll understand Bihari Satsai simply because you heard Braj as a child, you are sadly mistaken. Translation is a tricky business —tedhi kheer—trickier and twistier than our little jalebis can handle. Stories contain meanings that aren't always apparent. In an academic translation you get exhausted trying to find the right technical language. In literature, there are moods and vibrations. And if you want to sell the translation, the translator and writer must ask the publisher for money so they can do the work, otherwise why bother? And what can the publisher do once he has locked up his money in a place to which he himself has no access? So translation can turn into an absolute catastrophe, where *smile* means *knife,* and *eat* is *feed* and *you've arrived* is *why don't you leave* and *of course* is *oops, I'm trapped,* and *because, why not, andcertainly* means *I'm done for!* and *et cetera* becomes *infinity*, and Amma transforms into *childishness* and Beti into *maturity* and even more terrifying: then how to find the right words? She gazed *sadly* at KK, and *anger* rose within her, as though in translation.

She smelled sweat. The maid? Or was it Rosie? She hoped it came from KK because nowadays she disliked physical smells. She felt alienated from her own body in a kind of distaste for anything physical. Her body becoming a soul. When KK reaches out his hand, it slips through her soul like smoke. Then he persistently searches for the body, wondering where it's gone, and this looks like a scuffle, at which they grow annoyed with one another.

But KK was sunk within himself, pouting perhaps. Beti felt morose. How to make some kind of peace with him, be normal, share things, she fretted. Say the house makes a lot of noise. So did she want a coffin? No, but all manner of creatures come sneaking in. No, I don't mean Rosie Bua, she's fine of course, she looks after Amma free of charge, if you don't count the profits from Odds and Ends. But creatures run about in the guise of sunshine and air. What nonsense are you talking? No, not nonsense, no, but new ragas. What's wrong with ragas? No, they just come at the wrong time. Ma decides what we'll hear according to her mood, and she'll put on Darbari in the afternoon and Fado in the morning. Rosie has stuck a red bindi on the play button so that Ma can keep the music going even with her eyes closed and Amma plays Sufi-Fado-ghazal out of order according to her mood. Now you're complaining about Amma? No, about the different resonances and vibrations; the rhythms and the rhymes; about the dhwani. But how can Beti explain that dhwani is the hardest thing to translate of all. I mean, just look! The whole house is quivering as though it's not made of mud plaster wood in the walls, glass in the windows, but rather veins nerves breaths eyelids.

But now the house is quiet. Ma has gone out, and the mosquitoes, flies and spiders have all gone to sleep.

Beti is not speaking. The silence is heavy.

When will Ma come back, she asks. Outsiders will tell her now about her housefolk. KK is making himself very much at home. She's looking for an excuse to ask for the key back. He enters fearlessly, turning the key from the outside. What must Ma think? She must wonder if he did that before too, and why did he come then? Rosie and co must also be concocting juicy tales. And Bahu has got fresh masala for her chew crew.

Rosie's taken Ma over by the lake to the Saturday Market to buy lightweight sandals. You can get them in every colour.

This information seemed weighty to Beti, and exceedingly dark. *Where is the lake?* she wondered amidst her gathering depression. Daily a new beginning. There's no pressure to follow set customs in my home, so new beginnings are easy here. And Amma is enjoying it immensely. But I could have got her sandals, and why across this lake or whatever? The allure of the cheap. Rosie's cheap thinking.

The prices will fall by the evening when the shopkeepers hustle to gather up the market. They'll light their lamps with the generator and emit pollution and Amma will come home coughing, she said. Attempts at conversation.

Why would they wait until evening? They'll be back by lunchtime, said KK irritably. I'll leave.

Beti's depression increased, as did her anger and the sense of being an outsider to every decision.

No one saw it. Because who understands everything just by seeing? A sight passes right before us and even when we see it, we don't, don't see a catastrophe approaching, nor a beloved departing, nor a dot turning square, nor a cheetah becoming an ant, nor the stemming of the tide. If we do notice things occasionally, then what we see is what our imagination has formed for us. Outside same as within.

Silence fell. Should Beti scold the maid for spending so long cleaning the hallway? It doesn't occur to you to do so much cleaning every day! She saw that the woman was dusting the Buddha. When was it taken down from the shelf? Right in front of her and she hadn't even noticed? Do I have no idea what comes into my house, when it goes up and when it comes down?

Beti got up and spread out mats on the table for lunch, the way Ma liked them, and Hathrasi bowls, the spoons with the red handles, the coloured plates—she laid everything out just so, for the sake of doing things. She looked in the fridge—a pink chutney of amla and onions. Slivers of ginger, chili, and raw turmeric, jamun vinegar, white radish, turnip, cauliflower, carrot mixed pickle, rice vinegar, bhuknu, what to take out and what put in which bowl? Just plunking them all on the table as before now seemed a coarse custom, for which she sometimes now even screamed at the maid. *You're renouncing your own customs to march to the beat of others.*

Beti sat at the dining table staring straight ahead. She was gaining weight from all this sitting and staring. When one stares, the hands also begin to stare: at the carrot halwa and the gram flour laddus, and then the tongue begins to stare as well. Then the weight begins to increase even from just sniffing the okra eggplant cauliflower cabbage spinach or any old thing.

I'm getting fat. She pushes the tin of chocolate chip biscuits towards KK.

You're getting old, KK tosses back cruelly, and leaves. Saying, I'll be back in a little while, leaving her forlorn in her sagging spreading body.

But all other body types are left behind when Ma, with a new drama, draws attention to hers.

★

The mysteries of the body frighten. Those who consider the body insignificant are foolish. The Sufis and wise men have said that the body is a mirror a home a fine shawl a rainbow; clay fluid deep blue sky; it is a snake a lion probably a cow and a deer too. That you must worship it and dote upon it. It is a diamond mine, a coal pit. It zaps with lightening, it snap cracks the whip of darkness. The body is mind, the mind finds its path via the body. When the body has withered and surrendered to the fire vultures and dust, then all of existence will wander in the cosmos with the mind becoming mere memory. Memory is the soul that wanders the earth, we reach out to grasp a wisp only to feel it slip away.

Thus, to understand the body one must first know the earth. The mind coils within the body, earth. It is the fluid in solid. Reflections swimming within the whimsical mind. Its pace, its gait. Lying closed, if you open it, then it's open; shut it again, it stays closed. The capacity to crackle and flow lies everywhere. The slightest crack, the slightest bubbling: the earth slides and the liquids inside fountain flame rock and boulders course about. What has been thrown outside? The scientists come running with their tools determined to learn everything, once and for all. Under the hard earth all is soft bubbling raging fire, boiling spluttering water. If you must turn to God then do so, because the earth hangs in the void, and within all is aquake and ashake. And if god doesn't come, you'll definitely get dizzy, and you'll be like, Ha, I'm flying, falling, straight up swinging down, or maybe not, maybe swaying backwards, hhhhelp! help! ha hey ho what if something spurts from these mysterious inner spigots and hoses…from my mind, from my body…

You just hope that was merely a small tremor, then all becomes peaceful. If a great tremor, that would be an earthquake. The breathing is stirred, the inside drowns.

The rumbling rising from the earth far below our feet, thrusting itself forth, ready to burst forth at any moment, first emerges as a puff of steam, then a cloud, then a fusillade, or rockets. It boils over violently flowing with lava and spitting out sparks, and all the rest, black petrified fossilised remains, which will be romanticised in art centuries later, what amazing sculpted creations, or the doctors and scientists will try to guess what sort of steam it was puffing out from between the legs through which the hidden desires emerged into the open.

One hundred stones, Kaurava-esque. Sang-e-marmar. Stone-of-Marble. Marble. Rising from smoke. Ling-e-marmar. Phallus-of-marble. A phallus.

★

This time Ma didn't fall, nor did she get lost, but when she called out from the bathroom, Beti came running in fear, and rushed in, because Amma did not lock the door.

Amma was holding up her dress, feeling with her hand between her legs; caught red-handed. *Go away, go away.*

Why did you call? Beti is torn.

First go outside.

Once she was outside, Ma said, it's something thick. When I press it, it comes out; then it goes back inside. I touched it to see. A body part. Like this. Ma drew a shape in the air. Like water trapped in rubber. It's shiny. Swollen. This big. She showed with her fingers.

Show me, please, said Beti, at which Ma said, Never.

Beti blushed. Let's go to the hospital.

No. Let's wait a few days.

It's hardly something to protect, half-joked Beti, why would we wait?

Ma laughed in embarrassment. No, no, okay, let Rosie come.

When Ma said this, Beti said, That decides it, we won't wait another minute. She'll come up with some catechu powder potion bundle, she'll cover it with a balm, and it will cost us an arm and a leg.

KK said, Don't do anything silly, a growth is a growth, make an appointment immediately. Every moment is precious.

Sid drove Granny to the hospital. Once more the entire horde descended. Again the doctors fell upon Ma. Hospital hospitality, all over again. Outside the OT, a woman on a stretcher wept, My child, oh, my child. The nurse snapped, She didn't go pee-pee, get her down, and at the door of the OT the nurse sat the woman down on a bedpan, right on the floor. The woman crouched over the bedpan saw Ma coming in a wheelchair but she kept weeping, My child, oh, my child.

Rosie was missing.

Ma said, Tailor Master's shop is in the bazaar nearby, go inform.

Perhaps she was intent on Rosie recommending a cure before the doctors reached a verdict. Leave my body in my control. Or else, she feared, it would turn out like in factories, where there's no human hand or breath that moves things, only machines, as on a conveyer belt, where you can't get off once you're on, until it's stopped. Like when they mix milk cocoa sugar and *chug chug* along comes a container and the machine *puff* dries it *smack* flattens it *stamp* brands it *zip* plastic wraps it, and *boom bam* stacks it and *whoosh* flings it out into the market.

They took Ma into a super-duper deluxe room. They fastened her onto a chair with a seatbelt, stuck her feet in the pedals, and told her, okay, now we'll leave you alone, you pull your clothes up to your waist, no one will be here, hold on to the handle. Somehow she managed to press a button on the remote. The chair sprang to mechanised life and began making *zhzhzhzhzhzhzh* sounds. Bands clapped onto Ma's arms. *Zhzhzhzhzhzhzh* a curtain swung over her lap to cover her nether regions. *Zhzhzhzhzhzhzh* the chair reclined fully, with Ma's lower half on the other side of the curtain. Body parts served up on a tray. The tongs snatched, lifted with the little spoon, smoothed with a knife. *Zhzhzhzhzhzhzh* suddenly the chair straightened, the curtain lifted, the cloth covered. A throng of doctors entered. They thrust Ma into a wheelchair and dropped her back into her family.

Is everything okay, Doctor?

All, as if they stood before God.

A flood of faith ready to plunge into a flood of tests. Test by test we'll learn what it isn't and eventually it will become clear what it is. Then we'll decide what must be done, upon which, more tests will be undertaken, to see if the lungs and all other parts can withstand the treatment. Is the growth a jackal or a lion? asked their fearful eyes.

It is a cyst, the doctor told them. About two inches long.

Shhhh, the other doctor, standing nearby, stopped the head nurse standing in the corridor from talking too loudly.

What is this, *shshshsh,* in the OPD?

Any way you slice it, it's a…*shshshshishan*…it's a penis…!

Sshshshs…shishan…Ma whispered. In my old age I am growing a *pee*…a *pee*…a penis!

Yes, of course, but is this fiction? Because clearly Ma did not say this, since how could she say such a thing? But maybe she thought it?

How did you find it, Auntie ji, asked the lady doctor.

I have constipation, I feel pressure, I pushed down.

So then it came out?

Yes, it comes out with a sneeze and also with a cough.

So with anything?

Ma told Beti with some embarrassment that when she had gone to get the injection the nurses had come and shaved off the hair down there, and then they'd put her in that strange chair.

Then she asked, Will they operate?
Then she insisted, Call Rosie.

★

58

This wasn't the moment for charms and amulets, so Beti paid no attention to what Amma said. When the household horde arrived, she herself went home to freshen up. But just like when you yell *Snake! Snake!* and then a snake appears, so too, she kept repeating, *Not Rosie, not Rosie*, and the fear hidden in her heart was bound to appear and

Oh, Rosie Bua! Beti blurted out as she parked the car at the Madras Café to get idli, since the maid must have already come and gone, and Ma had put an end to the practice of keeping leftovers in the fridge.

Rosie was waiting to cross the street. She turned, stared straight through Beti and continued on.

Then she slipped into the shop on the other side of the street.

She must not have seen me, thought Beti, getting out of the car. *But now she's appeared before me, how can I ignore Amma's wishes?*

It was a tailor shop. The person who cut receipts and looked after the money stood behind the counter. The hum of machines emanated from the inside room. Thread, cut pieces, and bolts of fabric lay scattered at the ready. An odour of new fabric pervaded the shop, and rows of stitched clothing hung from hangers. The tailor was giving instructions to the others, a measuring tape hanging from his shoulder.

Arre, this is Rosie Bua! Arre, this is the one who was outside!

Rosie Bua, said Beti spontaneously peering in at the door. The body turned. The eyes of a stranger.

Arre, but this is a man! In a masculine Punjabi suit. Did I not notice that before?

Same height and build. Same face. But eyes of stone. Lips sewn shut. A cigarette packet peeking from his pocket. A small pencil stuffed behind the ear. Hairy toes. An embroidered Islamic cap on his head. Surma rimming bespectacled eyes. Measuring tape slung around his neck, swinging from his shoulders. Scissors in hand.

Who are you looking for? Polite, but cold unrecognising eyes.

Beti was startled. A man's voice emanating from a man's body.

Yes, but…

The man watched silently, then went back to drawing lines with chalk on the fabric spread out before him.

See what Madam wants made, he loudly instructed the youth standing at the counter.

Nothing. I wanted to see…to meet…she…Amma… hospital…Rosie…

The icy eyes of a stranger.

Rosie Bua knows me, she added by way of clarification.

And?

I wanted to…Rosie Bua…she…, Beti stammered.

Just then another woman entered growling, Tailor Master ji, my suit.

The tailor turned and called inside, Is it done?

From inside, a voice: No.

You had said Tuesday.

Come get it on Thursday. The stitcher has gone to his village. We have two people on leave.

Arre, Master ji, she reproached. And my dupatta?

It's not wide enough. I told you. There won't be any cloth left.

But the cloth seller was saying…

He sells cloth, I tailor. What will we accomplish by saving bits of cloth? Should we be making handkerchiefs? Raza Tailor Master doesn't do cut-piece work.

But Master ji…

Please come on Thursday. Right now… The tailor perhaps turned towards Beti, but she was already outside the shop. Was this Raza Tailor Master or Rosie's twin or Rosie? Already she was a river flowing in both directions, wasn't that enough? How many directions would there be now?

And now Ma facing in two directions as well?

Beti's eyes clouded with tears of anger and confusion. Or because *will anything be in my control anymore.* Or because *will nothing ever be the same.* Or because *why don't I understand anything?*

★

59

They all stood around. An unmatching set: Bade, Bahu, Beti, KK, some other people, friends and such of one or the other, everyone avoiding eye contact but deeply immersed in intimate worry, related to the intimate body part of an intimate human: Ma's vagina. Or penis.

Enter Rosie Bua, panting like a horse. What, Baji! What, Baby! Why didn't you tell me? Don't make this a habit, Baji!

Old age plays games. Ma was pleased the moment she saw her.

This has nothing to do with old age. Even little girls get cysts, boils, pimples. This is your youthful old age.

Everyone averted their eyes, darting about.

It's nothing—just an infection, said Ma proudly. Where were you? Off on your bossing rounds? she scolded.

Practicing my art, Baji. I practice reciting thirty-four poems every day, seventeen facing in one direction, seventeen in the other. And what is this you're wearing here right in the middle of a crowd? Rosie pointed at the bangles on Ma's wrists.

Ma looked at her with surprise. Only two, said Ma.

Baji, this is India, where people steal the chained tin cups from railway toilets while they're taking a shit. And here we are at a hospital, where they strip everyone naked.

Eyes again darted about.

It's not like I've come here to stay. Ma closed her eyes. When she opened them, she took off her bangles and lifted Beti's hand. You wear them.

There are four people you must steer clear of, said Rosie, revealing the perspiration in her armpits as she raised her arms to unfasten her bun, twist her hair back up and re-pin it. The lawyer, the policeman, the doctor, and the butcher. Those four are always busy sticking people, either with cases or with knives.

It's just going to be an ordinary little puncture, not some kind of knifing.

I know everything, Rosie Bua snapped back. I've just come from speaking with the head nurse. I'm here now, she said, leaning over Ma, waggling her finger. This is where they make the sick sicker, she said menacingly, so you'll keep coming back for more. They just make sure not to kill you because then you won't come back. Operate indeed! Why operate? To poke? Prick? These doctors do love a good poke around. Prick the boil. She flushed with anger. Then laughed. Especially the men.

From then on, Ma dubbed her new growth the Boil. Which had grown within her, and popped out at every twist or shake. A cheery phallus. Whose eruption date the doctors had designated for the coming week. Until then it would periodically emerge in secret, peep out at the world, then return to sleep in its cave.

Or was it Shiva's throbbing lingam that Parvati had pulled within to dip in her cool waters, and extinguish its burning? *Shshshsh...shanti...shanti...*peace...peace...the yoni poured soothing water over the boiling desires so they might be stilled: nirvana, meditation, samadhi; just as you see in every Shiva temple.

The yoni and the yogi.

★

60

The growing-smaller woman was mesmerised. She'd gathered every scar freckle movement moan from the earth of her body and replanted it in the clay earth, as though she were removing all the forgotten stones, twigs and thorns from the earth to make it smooth and fertile again so a new crop could grow. And a phallus had grown!

Perhaps Ma was fearful. It can be intoxicating to recognise and remap the body, but if others interfere, like doctors, it's no fun. My earth is my own. Shoot leaf stalk cluster or this most auspicious lingam or even if it's merely a lowly cyst which must be removed, then so be it, but it's for me to do so. The moment the word *operation* springs into the air, the conversation reaches its apogee. Some are stunned, some despair, some are enraged, some return to faith, some are carefree, some are end of story. Some feel the need to lecture: *Arre, even an injection is an operation, do not fear.* Some hold forth with their knowledge: *Not even a needle, they don't actually use a needle, they remove the pus from the cyst with a syringe and then it dries up on its own and falls off.* Others remind that when you clean, you just scrub the encrusted dirt off, don't you, it's really just exactly the same as that. No worries! Stop fretting, don't stop the operation. And Bahu declared that Overseas Son had reported on the phone that this digging cutting twisting is quite a minor procedure, and after that you'll learn whether the thing is *benign* or *malignant*.

Perhaps Ma felt angry. Once Rosie was by her side, she became more powerful. It could be that the two of them had sat down face to face and cursed all cysts and cyst-poppers so vehemently that exactly two days before the surgery, something bizarre occurred: a stream of blood trickled down Ma's thigh, like a young girl's first period.

What's this? Beti was alarmed and wrapped cloth around cotton to make a pad, called KK, and told Bahu, who swirled in like a dust storm with Bade.

Bade was the most silent and most worried. On the one hand, he felt they should get Amma fixed up as soon as possible and take her away, and on the other, he worried that before she went into the operation theatre they should have her sign some cheques and share papers, some for the land outside of the city as well; the final instalment still needed to be paid on that. Amma would also want this. If the house were finished, the one with a lawn and sunlight, then Amma would be happier. His wife didn't want to leave the heart of the city. If she had her way, they'd sell the new house and let their sons invest the money themselves. But let's sign, so there's no danger of late fees or cause for worry. And just in case, one or two signatures on blank paper too. But when was the right moment to push the papers forward, and how many? Bade stood by looking utterly defeated. Which is, after all, the fate of all eldest sons.

So Ma was taken for the third time from Beti's home in a blue gown and a wheelchair for tests, and the entire worried throng wove about here there separate disparate near and dear, and seeing the doctor arrive they amassed asking, *wh...wwha... whattt...what happened?*

Congrats, the lady doctor said. No, she did not say *It's a boy!* or *It's a girl!* or *It's a bicycle!* She said the cyst had burst all on its own, as sometimes happens, and all they had to do to heal the wound was administer one course of antibiotics, And everything will be hunky dory, said Rosie.

And now, with everyone's approval, Ma returned to Beti's home. It was a lady problem like menstruation, who better to handle it than a daughter? For the next few days the thick oozy flow continued. Beti purchased sanitary towels, feeling as though she were buying them for her daughter, and paper envelopes and old newspapers were placed in Amma's bathroom and she was told to wrap them up and throw them away, just as Ma had once taught her to do.

Once again, Beti wondered if it wouldn't have been better if she'd married? That is, if she had, and the marriage hadn't ended up ended. She'd have heaps of children, people of every age coming and going through her home, and there would be her own siblings and his siblings and uncles and aunties and their Gabloos and Babloos and mother-in-law and father-in-law and helpers and workers and authorities would all be there and perhaps there'd be a two-storey house and a room on the roof, which she would have turned into her study, where sometimes she'd nip in and someone or other would be with Ma so that she could sit worry-free with no fear of sudden events.

Amma, what's that ooze that stinks so, what is it? she asked, bending over the wastebasket outside the door to throw away the paper packet.

My infection, said Amma proudly, which we killed.

God, please end these strange days. Where did they come from? These awful horrible days.

*

One should not say that. Nor think it. Because time is the great one-upsman. Whatever you say, time insists on one-upping you. You could say, Oh, what a horrible time this is! and then it will go ahead and make things even more horrible. And no one will say, but these are good days, acche din! Except for the government, that is.

Anyway, since Beti had said these were strange times, you know it won't be long before they turn much stranger.

First there was Rosie, whom she couldn't find, but found Raza instead. This had made Beti anxious, and now, he who had never appeared until that day began to appear with regularity. He appeared at the paan shop and the same thing happened, where he turned and didn't recognise Beti. His face frozen, ice in his eyes. Then she saw him smoking a cigarette and sipping tea with the truck drivers at the dhaba on the main road. One time she was buying sago and she turned to see him right next to her buying a packet of cornflakes. Her head tilted in hello. But his did not. The gaze that pierced right through her said: *You're smiling at a strange man, what's this?* Furthermore, she found him standing outside the lift at the newspaper office. The two of them entered together and the lift ascended silently, and they both got out on the same floor. He politely held the door open-button so that she could get off, and then he got off. He nodded slightly at her *thanks*, but all of it in a one stranger-to-another sort of way.

She was already used to Rosie, the way she would come home from somewhere and find her in her house, or she'd bathe in the morning and come out and Rosie would be sitting in the hall. So it was not her voice but Amma's that stunned her. Not the voice, but the conversation topic.

She heard: *No less than two inches.*

Goodness, Beti flashed hot with a mixture of shame anger humiliation. How could Amma say such things to Rosie? And now the two of them are chuckling over Amma's two-inch lingam?

Beti came out, as she had to, to face the music.

And then the displeasure in her heart was replaced by a wave of distress. Before her was Raza Tailor Master, not Rosie. In her home. With Amma. Gabbing about *two inches*?

She saw that here was the measuring tape pencil glasses and Amma was being measured for a robe.

Two inches less will be too much, Amma ji.

No, no, Ma insisted. You don't know how quickly it gets too long and I trip. I'm shrinking.

How can that be, Amma ji? Master smiled politely.

Well then, the cloth must be growing on me.

Thank you, thank the Lord! They were talking about something else; Beti's anxiety rose and dissipated. But the horror subsided only to rise again, not a wave but a snake, regarding her, hood upraised.

My daughter, Ma introduced her. Tailor Master, Amma told Beti.

The snake nodded his hood. May you live long, Bibi, he hissed.

Should I be afraid? In my own home? Beti didn't reply, only continued to watch quietly. Tall and hearty. No, perhaps Rosie didn't look such a pehelwan. But was it her? How can one body take two forms? Or perhaps we're all alike, we just look different depending on our clothing, gait, manners, our standing straight or slouching, limping or strutting; one gesticulates like a dancer, the other is pillar-tall, and that makes them look different.

Beti brought two more cups of tea with her own and set them out. Rosie—*sorry*—Raza, said, Bibi, what was the need? He smiled. His mouth opened. His teeth were showing. Those same front teeth, ordinary, the front two a little crowded, one on top of the other. So that when the light fell on them there was an uneven flicker of light and shadow. When Rosie comes, I'll look more closely. Beti moved away.

Is this Rosie or does he just look like Rosie? They look alike and then they don't. It was all a bit frightening.

Fearful, always fearful, this was Beti's new life. It's one thing to be alone. But to be alone with a person between whose legs there is a puffing hissing steam rising from the earth that might erupt like lava, and her guests, flowing in every direction, and what use are you, when you can't lift an elderly doll-like woman, smaller than yourself, up off the floor?

She began to feel weak. If only there were someone who could give her a hand and lift her up, then she would eat a banana or something. She'd go over there, but only after Master left. When this RosieRaza looks at her she feels naked. Clothing flowing in all directions in the hallway, and the people wearing it. Was I wandering about naked all this time?

But it didn't matter, since I was alone, who would see then, but now everyone's watching. Beti trembled.

She continued to feel anxious.

No one else is anxious. The cloth is being laid out so patiently and traced with chalk. And then he went out onto the balcony and puffed on a cigarette.

Rosie doesn't smoke. She doesn't chew paan. After all, she is not a man.

★

Let us pay close attention to the shady dealings to get a sense of what happened. But the what doesn't jive with the why. Whatwhy: what a wacky pair. Misleading, deluding, arbitrary. Be a believer; have faith, or you'll rock the boat. Don't be a prisoner of two plus two is four. Don't be Gandhi's three monkeys, which were actually Mizaru, Kikazaru, and Iwazaru, inhabitants of the Tosho-gu temple in Nikko, Japan. That saw no evil heard no evil spoke no evil. If only we had chosen to speak what we see and hear. That's why we didn't realise that maths is full of twists and turns, and two plus two is simply creative counting. A pair can be anything, flowing in every direction, like Rosie. And finally, is there a Shakespearian method in madness or no? Shakespeare did ask, but he got no answer. And he won't get one, in fact. Nor in fancy.

Stories and tales are dreams that create meaning as they move along. Borges reminds us of this. All is Maya, he says that too. Which, just like everything else, originated in India: this too had already been said before. A dream is like a tree, where each branch twig leaf shoot sings its own story, lifting its vast arms and tiny little ones too, holding hands and emerging separately as well. A story joins, and what it scatters rises from the air earth sand and weaves a new warp, a new woof. If it hasn't yet woven one, it will.

Cells also join. An entity emerges. Of a human, of a collective, of a part, of parts of parts. And if half-human half-tree join together, that too becomes a full-fledged entity. Like Bade and the crow. Amma and the cane. Rosie and the river. Beti and prone.

Then it is not false or a myth that wolfman, fishgirl, bugbrain, butterflyheart, tortoisehead, colourfall garbgrabbing borderhomeland are all matched mismatched personalities, whether complete or incomplete. And all infinite, if evanescent.

★

The guard isn't worried either. He buzzes the intercom and tells them that Raza Tailor Master is coming up.

Is there any irony in his tone? Does he, too, wonder if this is Rosie coming in Raza attire? Or does he actually think that the one comes to look after Mata ji, the other to stitch and hem Ma's clothing and also take orders from other residents of the society. One of them brings Ma downstairs for short strolls and takes her to sit by the tomb where the peacocks cry, and returns bearing peacock feathers in her hands, which Mata ji dangles from her golden cane as if to announce that the days of butterfly-peacocks are here. The other, after showing the fabric and discussing the stitching and listening to Ma's wishes, goes out onto the balcony and lights a cigarette, and if KK comes right around then, he goes out and puffs with him.

KK comes infrequently, but come he does. Before going to the office, or after. As though challenging Beti to get up the nerve to demand her key back.

What Beti objects to most of all is why she deserves no prior notice or anything. Even the voices she hears deceive her. She thinks it's Rosie but finds Raza, or she's sure it's Raza but it's Rosie. Is there one voice? Or do we all have one voice, which comes out feminine for a feminine body and masculine for a masculine body? Some femininity, some masculinity.

Here, too, a mixture. Here, too, the river that flows in both directions.

KK also flows in every direction. Ma, Rosie and he all sit together. Ma, Raza and he as well. Rosie the medicine woman, Raza the booze man. He brings it even on dry days, and KK pours him a peg with a thank you. Ma, she who was wont to nurse a lemon honey brandy, also partook. Even without Sid.

When they call out to Beti she's always busy. She's got in the habit of steering clear of everyone.

Unaware of her wishes, the party goes till late.

Do stay, Amma says to KK, one evening after the hospital days. Without wondering where he'll sleep. Now that she sleeps alone in the large room, and Beti sleeps in the guest room. Or did she mean like before…?

★

Being sick of one's self is worse than being sick of anything else. The absolute worst. Others are at least other. You can get away from them, for good or for a couple of hours. If a wife is sick of her husband, she can offload to her girlfriends. She leaves home and begins to breathe again. Outside the gate she starts off at a trot. When she gets to the street, she breaks into a run. Now fly soar fall, as is your fate. If getting out isn't in the cards you can still fling the tiresome party from your mind. If that doesn't work either, then them down in your mind, smash them to the ground, enthrone yourself on a peak. If you put them below, you'll automatically end up above. Feel pride that will blot out the oppressor like a cloud. Delude yourself into a state of smugness. And the best solution of all: turn every intolerable thing into a huge joke and laugh it from your mouth. Hahaha hohoho.

Laughter is a gift that humans have learned and taught. There must have been some time in the past when humans didn't know how to laugh. Nor did they feel joy at the birth of a child, nor sobs of sorrow at the passing of a loved one. Then the two had to be strained apart so they got joy from joy as well as a method for removing sorrow. Then humans became happy even after they weep, and when they laugh, they're just plain happy. The animals too learnt these tricks by their side. Not just the dog's tail, but his mouth too began to laugh, although the ones on the street still make frowny faces. The cat refuses to belong to the house, else it too would be having a chuckle. Alice's cat strove to smile. It's all about self-confidence, which springs from laughter. It's another matter that just as all things have an ill use, so too has the smile, and today, the smile roams the streets, as evil doers, villains, scoundrels, toss their horrid smiles about, causing harm, and laughter remains but compassion is gone.

But Beti's smile has already turned upside-down, and all mirth has gone missing; only fed-upness remains, which is what she felt in regard to herself. Because in adding a garlic-chili seasoning to the dal, the question rose to the lips of her mind, Is this me? Then who am I? So when did I become me? When did I come to live in this house? Who is this, or who was that? This she who's enmeshed in running the house in an efficient manner, and catering to the needs and desires of her offspring—no, mother—and feeling repelled at KK's kisses, and getting annoyed at herself. From backstage, where she listened to the conversations of Rosie Raza Amma, or watched relatives opening all the drawers and cabinets, taking out napkins, glasses, paper, pans, evaluating and pricing the things that lay within (without objection, she watches), and Amma's instructions spring from her own mouth now to the maids, neighbours, guards, gardeners. She fries pakoras for Sid and his troops, rolls out papad: so then, what is she?

When did I become me? Am I me or a mouse? Diving behind furniture, scurrying about the house.

How can you be happy with yourself if you imagine yourself a mouse? You can't even run from yourself. According to Borges: The world, unfortunately, is real; I, unfortunately, am Borges. Or as Confucius said, Wherever you go, there you are. That is, wherever you go, there you'll find a mouse!

Beti sits among her books pretending to work, and when she lifts her pen the bangles on her wrists jangle, the ones Amma had given her, and at this, the question jingles afresh: When did I become me, and am I me, or have I become Ma?

★

65.

Bells and whistles. These are things that pierce not just the air but the heart, and bump into the body. Those that live in houses understand this, because their hand shakes suddenly while writing something and their body lurches suddenly while doing something. Some flee their homes. Many, mostly men, stuff cotton in their ears and crawl inside themselves. Those who can't do any of these things learn the trick of swerving about so as to avoid the bells and whistles. These latter are women, of course. When Raji Seth translated Rilke into Hindi, she pressed the bells and whistles between the lines and created a new kind of punctuation. Sheela Rohekar counted the pressure cooker whistles as she wrote, making her lines gleam with a fresh calculus. Maitreyi Pushpa forged her own path, which she populated with a band of women calling themselves villagers, who pushed aside all those who stood in their way. As a result, when bells and whistles trilled, they collided with the village women and collapsed. A fresh new dhwani, a vibration of wobbling bells and whistles rang out, and Maitreyi's writings were as killer as her pakoras.

This is what we call *bell and whistle writing,* it's a style of writing that contains fresh artistic resonances. It's the secret recipe for success for those who must work in the midst of everything. It's something that can't be learned in a day, and those who don't learn it won't, but for those who do, they whistle a different tune to their whistlebells and slake everyone's thirst in so doing. To give a final example, Sid's wife (who won't enter this story because she's not a character in it), at some point in the future, did an amazing job with bellwhistle punctuation whilst climbing the corporate ladder in the company where she worked, and raising her darling daughter to boot (with Sid's cooperation, it would be miserly not to add).

Or think of it this way: once you've fulfilled your social duty, such as getting married, giving birth to children, caring for your in-laws, go ahead and start wearing Reeboks and witness how their decisive gait falls like a hammer on the shrill squeaky shrieking of whistlebells.

Some are able to learn nothing. They jump at every ring, so words remain incomplete, sentences limp, and they themselves are crippled. When the pressurecookerdoorphonekettlewashingmachineoven whistle a long *thweeeet thweeeet* they make the whole house dance. The reverberation is so powerful that if you haven't grown used to it, you'll rattle as though you've collided with a heavy object. The way Beti does.

Others get up and turn off the whistle, but here it's the whistles that are turning off Beti. The punctuation of her work is not coming together. Work has become attempted work. In the midst of peering out at the comings and goings from behind her books. At the daily arrival of Rosie. Which is not true, but truth is in the seeming, not in the being.

Rosie had been mentioning she had to go somewhere. She kept going away. Sometimes to Janghai, sometimes to Vyara.

She'd phone Ma from Baksar, from Mewat, Karnal, Bhondsi, Bombay too. She was setting up a function, arranging a charity sale, making money.

Beti's ears perk up from behind the books as she listens to all this talk of going abroad. About Pakistan. About her passport.

We'll get Bade to take care of it. Amma's voice.

Will he agree? What will he think of getting such a passport made?

For female Rosie or what? Beti smiles snidely to herself.

She removes a book from the bookshelf, peers through the gap, and sees it's not Rosie, it's Raza. As if in retaliation for Beti's sarcasm, she'd morphed into Raza Tailor Master. The deception of those two was wearing Beti out.

Is it Raza Tailor Master who wants a passport? In his passport it will say *male* without doubt.

She can see one of Rosie's—no, Raza's—eyes between the books. Beti imagines s/he has closed the other eye, as though winking, and she makes a sketch in her imagination, he must be so crooked behind his fine manners. He looks at Amma with a deceitful eye.

Was this Rosie's cunning or Master's? And this new mischief about getting a passport made.

KK Bhai will get a passport made, she heard Raza saying. By now KK was his bestie.

KK's lustful eyes blinked in Beti's soul. Although now he didn't so much as glance at her. Otherwise the two of us would be chatting away about why Rosie had become Raza. They are one person, aren't they? Or two? One is flat-chested, the other is flat between the thighs. Or they are two in one, Jekyll and Hyde. But which is Jekyll and which is Hyde? Who is who?

One day she asked Ma. Not like that. Like this: About how the smell of cigarette smoke had started getting into the house. Ma was silent. Why does Master ji smoke? Ma was silent. He also has crooked teeth like Rosie. If a person keeps quiet at every turn it gets awkward. What is their religion?

Whose? Ma then asked. Rosie Bua's and Raza Master ji's? Ma began to laugh. You're actually interested in someone's religion!

And Beti shut up. As though Ma had cautioned her not to dig too deep, leave them be. One religion or two? One person or two? Forget about it.

*

66.

That's how forgetting works. You can forget whatever you wish to. Even that you had wished to forget. A border is drawn all around that memory and no method remains to reach it any longer, provided that you don't stagger across. On purpose or not. And even if you do stagger, that initial memory doesn't remain, it's a reinvented memory. A bit like when they say that before becoming a foetus you were someone else who was born again, but now, in this life, your personality has been made anew by the day-to-day. The one who was reborn, that's not you, you're someone else. Bound to that other by memory. If the memory comes. So the mouth falls open gaping and eyes pop at both the forgotten and the new. Because there's a new world over the border, whether you go backwards or forwards. As when the two women in the story arrived in Khyber, it was the same Khyber that had been there before, but also completely new, and the dangers were new, even though they said it had also been dangerous before.

Lines get crossed like conversations, if they're not a presentation in a seminar. Time and order get jumbled. Breaths and sights and smells and tastes and wheels and Catherine wheels and prose and poetry too.

This is why the wind roars—because it knocks into everything, then gets wounded and falls back and there too it collides with wind.

Wind is memory. It is a question. One should definitely remember. And also question. Where? How? That which was. Like that. So then? There is questioning and memory in walls. In words. In sights. They are cracked, they've fallen, they get up again. What's it to me, who am I, which way to my village? What are you staring at so hard? These aren't the questions whose answers you memorise, pull together and write down in your exam booklet, get your results. Real questions don't have answers. Where is our India? This is spouted on and on, but even those who go on and on with this hardly know the answer themselves.

The thing is that the question isn't about the big and great. Vast, great, outspread, large. The question has to do with smallness. It's in the territory of little and slight and details. In fact, it really isn't a question at all. One must look, take note, pay attention, study, notice detail. One tree standing apart in the jungle. A face flickering in a large group, the memory of malice that arises for a moment on a sympathetic face. A tiny wrinkle peeking in the elevator from amongst the make-up and paint. The rest that's talked about is for covering up what has been said, obscuring detail.

That which is far is hidden faraway. Look up close if you must, that's the only thing that will take the sight far—the ant slips through the wall; it sneaks into the crack, and crosses over to the other side by digging a hole with its breath, beyond the border, passes the Khyber Pass into another world. Past the pass. Close to the close.

If the family had looked close, they would have noticed the intentions of others. If they hadn't been so wrapped up in themselves, they would have noted many details. Questions would have arisen or they would have raised them. Of course they noticed nothing, entrenched as they were in their own preconceptions, sure that Ma should come back here, or that she should stay over here. How could they have foretold that one day she herself would say, I must go?

★

67

Beti fell.

The sun was setting, and Ma had pulled her chair into its orbit to sit with wings ruffled out like a hen warming her eggs. As she fussed over her plants with her cane, butterflies too began to fly up.

Beti heard KK's voice. When she peered through her binoculars, that is, through the gap in the bookshelf, she saw he was out there blowing smoke rings with Raza Tailor Master.

KK came inside with a plate of onion, green chili, coriander leaves, and kala namak on fried peanuts. He put it next to Beti on the table. He neither looked up nor said a word.

She was irritated and tearful, both. She leaned over her books as if engrossed. When Ma called out, she said, Coming! But stayed sitting where she was.

Beti's stupor was broken when Ma called out again. The party was breaking up. The voices were still loud, but she didn't recognise them anymore. She rose, a bit startled, when she heard a door being closed. Had KK left without saying anything? She got up and her foot, asleep, slipped, and she fell. She twisted her lurching body to protect her papers, so the papers were saved, but nothing else. There was a cacophony and then Ma screamed What happened! and Raza Master came running.

He pulled her up and steadied her, and she leaned against him, limping.

Amma came behind them, walking quickly.

Just don't ask, don't ask, thought Beti, sobbing quietly. What happened? asked Amma, panicky, and then Beti began to sob in earnest. Raza Master practically lifted her up and sat her on the settee in the hall, a pillow behind her back and under her feet as well, and he massaged where her ankle had twisted. Does it hurt? Here? Here?

At Ma's instructions, Raza Master took ice from the fridge and asked Beti, Bibi, tell me, where's a small towel? He took one from the drawer and wrapped her ankle and pressed it gently, administering first aid.

Oho, said Amma, now you won't get up at all until your ankle is better. Look, it's turned purple.

It's not broken, Mata ji, but she's pulled a muscle. See? A bruise has formed.

KK would have already left for the airport. He wouldn't be back until tomorrow. What to do? You mustn't move, Ma scolded Beti. I'll check if Siddharth is home.

Ma ji, you sit please. Why are you worrying? Someone will stay the night. KK Bhai will be back tomorrow.

She can't even go to the bathroom. Ma still anxious.

I'm fine, said Beti. It doesn't hurt as much.

May I go in there? Raza Master ji asked, motioning towards the guest room. He picked up the bag he'd brought that contained his sewing fabric and went inside.

When he re-emerged, it was Rosie, in a tightfitting grey shalwar suit with a pink border. Bun, sandals, handbag, Jaipur bangles, which she hastily removed as though she'd put them on for the sake of removing them, and then she began examining Beti's ankle again, and had taken everything over in a moment.

It's just ordinary swelling, Baji, everything is going to be A-OK.

It was as though someone had sprayed a water gun in Beti's eyes; such streams of tears. As if to say, *My body doesn't listen to me. If I stand up, I just fall down.* Beti doesn't know how to do anything at all, how to brook no opposition, how to live life in technicolor.

Does it hurt? Rosie Bua asked. The touch of her hands was different from Master ji's. His was strong but careful, hers was intimate, soft, knowledgeable of the secrets of each place. I won't massage it, I'll just bandage it. She took out the herbs and remedies from her bag, heated the turmeric to prepare a salve and also applied a lime powder. She rubbed it in lightly and wrapped the whole in a crepe bandage. Then she poured turmeric into milk and fed it to Beti, who promptly fell asleep. Truly!

★

68

The next day KK came and Rosie left.

In the evening, Raza Tailor Master returned to see Beti.

All A–OK, Baby? Raza Master asked, becoming Rosie again to make her feel less anxious. The bone is okay, you're fine, Bibi—turning back into Raza. Beti looked at him gratefully and clasped her palms together. For looking after her in so many ways.

Master ji placed a hand on her forehead. Her hair was untidy, and he smoothed it back. This triangle formed by the hair on your forehead is a sign of beauty. Please don't hide it.

She gets it from me, Ma laughed, touching her own forehead.

Where the hairline ends, the pointy triangle in the middle that dives towards the nose.

You, Aunty, are beautiful, extremely, KK said.

Mata ji is Mata ji, Raza Master also smiled. But Bibi, cheer up, get well soon; don't worry, be happy.

Beti's heart was set afloat. She felt like opening her whole body and stretching and making loud sounds, just like Amma. She liked the touch of Master ji's hand on her brow. She thought of a joke from her school days. In school we called this a widow's peak, she said. This triangle, and we said, whoever has one, her husband will marry twice.

Well, yours did, KK laughed.

Mine probably did as well, said Amma.

Oh, Mata ji? Raza Master looked at her solemnly.

Beti and KK laughed together. How conversation flows into absurdity. Ma also laughed shyly, as though she felt exposed and the laughter hid it.

★

She (Rosie) says, there are no red-faced rhesus monkeys there.

She (Ma) says, must we take one of those too, laughing.

She (Rosie) says, only chironji seeds and you.

She (Amma) says, letttt's see iffff....

She (Rosie) says, what do people like me need a passport for? There are advantages to not existing. We aren't counted among the Muslims and Christians nor the Jews Parsis Hindus nor the men and the women, they won't take our name, won't recognise us. What does 'real' mean to us, they want us to stay disappeared from imagination itself. So we can sneak in anywhere.

Ghost, she (Amma) laughed.

Ghosts you will worship too, sometimes you will call on them to learn the way to heaven, you'll pester them with a broom to leave the bodies they've entered, indeed a ghost is multitalented, immortal, ever young, omniscient. We are not ghosts, we are impurity. (Rosie)

What on earth are you talking about, Rosie? (Amma). Humouring her.

We are the grotesque, Baji. Keep us away. If you see us, punch us. Did she die, or did she survive, don't even turn around to look. You can't see what you didn't see. We've always been missing, we're forever missing, *yeh gulistan hamara hamara—this garden, ours, oh, ours.*

Such folk disappear easily. Who bothers about the nobodies in society?

Baji, the children of Nithari. Look what happened with them, but who cared? Who cared? Who knows, perhaps a demon awoke in that man at the revelation that no one cared. He lived alone, he must have felt lonely, his home must have been a wasteland, he must have come out and stood by the gate to watch the passersby on the street, on the lookout for a caper. And there was a poor little girl, downtrodden, wandering about all day. She must have passed that way. She must have seen his loneliness. She must have been the one to say, Uncle, toffee. Or, pen. Or maybe it was a boy. He must have seen uncle smoking a cigarette. Then tossing it away. Ran and picked it up so he could get a puff or two from it. The next day, said, Don't throw it away. Or said, Uncle, cigarette.

Or might have seen the man alone snacking on roasted chana. It doesn't take long to link up. The first day he must not have given or taken anything. The next day they might have felt a false sense of acquaintance. Then chana cigarette pen toffee. Not out of generosity. Just. Indifferently. Heart in one place, hands in another. If no heart, then the mind in one place and hands right here. Thank you, the child must have smiled. About which, who really cared? But the link was forged.

The next day the man must have smiled. For no reason. Just because. The link grew. The man might have got a fleeting sense of his own power. Well here's the caper. I smiled. No one knows. No one knows I gave a toffee. No one knows anything. Nor cares. Merely a link. Shall I do something? Who really cares? No one is accountable. Who cares about these kids? Who would blink at this link?

Scram, he must have said, and the child must have scrammed. Power. He must have smiled to himself. The next time, the child must have watched, wondered, will he say scram or will he give me something? The kid fears me. Power! Come, he must have called. He must have given him peanuts. Or he might have had a cigarette and it was the little girl. So he must have said, come, and he must have turned towards his house. The little girl stared for a moment. Then slipped under the gate like a cat, following the loner. The loner turned. The girl stopped. The loner continued. The girl walked. Power! Inside, the man gave her something to eat.

One day the boy, or girl, opened the gate himself—or herself—and went in. One day she sat on the chair beneath the tree and began to eat. One day she was discovered sleeping on the veranda outside the door. She has no one to ask after or search for her.

What man, these kids have no one ahead, no one behind. Eh! He bared his teeth in a grin. The girl was frightened, stood, fell. He burst out laughing. She too. A game. Power! No one knows they exist; no one knows them, nor me; anything could happen, anyone could do anything, I could do anything.

What should I do? Power! The rush of power, the rise of demons. To taste his power, he began tasting the child. He ate, tossed them aside, grew bored, then told his servant, come, grind the spices, prepare the feast, sit with me.

Who cares about us, Rosie told Amma. We don't even belong in their markets, they have no need to advertise for us, open shops for us, earn a profit. Even the greedy grocer doesn't want our business, so imagine what a vile invisible afterthought we are. There are no films for us, no literature, no art, no clothing. We wear what you discard. We count for nothing. Toss me away in the lake, Baji, and no one will notice there's one less.

Who cares about us? We don't even exist, and if I don't then what do my rights matter, and if they don't, then why a passport, when I'm already on both sides of the border?

Like we are a sort of demon, but this society, this world, those who don't know don't care that children are disappearing, are they gods? Killers, all, Rosie had speechified.

She had plaited her hair, and her pink paranda swung coquettishly as she spoke. Her shalwar suit was navy with a pink rose vine embroidered on it. The chunni was fuchsia with a pattern of green flowing leaves. Just as Raza Master behaved decorously and dressed plainly, Rosie was sassy and her clothing sparkled. If she were to disappear, the world would be a little bit less fabulous. Whether or not anyone cared where she had disappeared to.

The lake. Amma broke her silence and rose.

The lake. Amma practically ran out from the house, bewildered, dragging her cane and her daughter along with it.

★

Mother and daughter stood by the edge of the lake. They had arrived via GPS, and thus had gotten lost. Where was a lake in this city, and where must the water come from when even the beloved Jamuna was all dried up?

Far from the city was a layer of snow, which was not snow but rather a lake, which would burst into flames in just a few days.

The lake peered out, black and murky, from beneath a highly noxious white haze. Into which drained sewage and factory waste from cities all around. A toxic stew of oil and phosphorous bent on combusting, which it soon would. Flames would leap up, twelve feet high, and another apocalypse would come to pass. What looked like a sheet of snow from a distance was proven up close to be a layer of foam, in which shone destitute splinters of the setting sun. Time was that the moist earth of the wetlands here had worked as a filter, but now the entire area had been filled with cement buildings. A sheet of toxic sludge covered everything, and Amma stood observing it all peacefully, as though her gaze could cut through the lake like a knife, and as soon as it did, Rosie would float up from wherever she was hidden, like a fish.

One of the nails fastening the notice that hung from a pillar had fallen out and the paper hung crooked, tap-tap-tapping as it flapped, intensifying the desertedness of the scene. If you bent sideways, you could read the rules written on it. Beti bent sideways.

Playing cricket alcohol gambling cigarettes dogs forbidden in park.
Hiding in the bushes is forbidden.

Picking flowers and plants: forbidden.
Fighting: forbidden.
Urinating: forbidden.
Riding a bicycle: forbidden.

But there was no park in sight. Like the lake, it had swathed itself in toxins and disappeared.

Someone would fire up a bidi and set the foam aflame. Far-off countries would tremble at the Wonders of the Third World. The headlines in the papers and on TV would be heady indeed.

But nowhere would there be the news that Rosie was missing.

But Rosie goes away all the time, Beti said at Ma's anxiety.

But she calls.

She will when she gets back.

She does when she's away too.

She must not have connectivity.

It keeps ringing. But she doesn't pick up.

Maybe she went abroad somewhere. She'll hardly pick up her phone from here when she's over there. She kept talking about passports.

She was talking about mine.

Beti was confused. Muddled.

She wanted to bring me along.

Where? Beti asked anxiously.

There are no monkeys with red faces there.

As if taking Ma would fill that gap. Beti's muddle muddied.

She'd manage without a passport.

Then she must have gone. The whole thing seemed bizarre to Beti.

But she left the chironji. The chironji is still with me.

Beti had grown accustomed to her own incomprehension. She did whatever Amma told her. She called wherever she was told. She left a message at Tailor Master's place and she asked Kantha Ram if Rosie had shown up? Sometimes she does, he said. The phone just kept ringing into the void at Master's place.

Have the two of them disappeared together? Amma asked enigmatically, at which Beti shook her head with a no, in ignorance.

I don't understand, said Beti, defeated.

That's just it, said Amma, making her cane dance. I don't either. As though the two of them were in agreement.

And she'd brought her to the lake that would burst into flames from someone lighting up a bidi or cigarette and tossing a match into it.

If the lake were to burst into flames, would Rosie emerge like the Loch Ness Monster?

It's about to get dark. Beti put her arm around Amma's shoulder. Let's go now.

Do you know, right here...? It was unclear if Amma was speaking to herself or to her.

Yes, you came here to the Saturday Market, to get sandals.

...she had bought a house, finished Amma.

She lived out here, so far from the city? But I thought… But Beti got all tangled, wondering whether they were they speaking of Rosie or of Raza? She had always assumed that both of them used to come from somewhere nearby. The shop was also close. And during Bade's days as an officer, Rosie had also showed up in the area.

She had rented it out. Amma's cane was roving about as though it was part of her body. She'd been talking about moving.

So then Beti had her answer: who phones while they're moving? People's phones just ring and ring at such times.

Beti shivered. Two youths came and sat on the slope. They stared at their mobiles silently. Could be porn. Or they could be stoned. They were the only other beings for a long way off; gaseous clouds hovered about hazy buildings in the distance.

Let's go.

Yes, let's, said Amma.

What Ma meant was, over there, in the direction of the buildings. Where the toxic clouds were drifting from the lake, which would burst into flames in just a few days. Think about it: a lake would catch fire.

One building after the next. They set out searching for a needle in a haystack.

★

71

There are agencies that help you find registered helpers. They can come for a full day, give Amma her tea bath breakfast head massage comb her hair, take her for walks in the garden downstairs or to the nearby tomb, Beti said.

No one was listening to her. Amma was busy with KK in her search for Rosie's address. Some small room behind the mosque in the area next to the cemetery. KK took Amma over there. Where they learned she'd said she was going across the border, but before that she'd come by to put some things in her flat by the lake.

I told you, didn't I, she's gone abroad; she probably can't talk, Beti reminded Ma triumphantly.

But Amma was lost in herself. She stayed lost for a bit, and then suddenly seemed to tighten her belt, tie her shoelaces, ready herself for a tussle with fate.

It's a strange thing to worry about, Bade said anxiously. Bahu got busy with spicing up the issue. Kantha Ram just smiled and said, Mata ji, don't get so worried, Rosie Bua has one of those unsettled lives, running all about. But no one could openly dismiss this outlandish obsession of Ma's. And no one could bring themselves to say, you may have a screw loose yourself if you're getting so worked up about searching for someone with address unknown, gender unknown, precise role in the household unknown, what do they tell, so who knows, and at your age, not the time for going to cemeteries in disreputable neighbourhoods, wasting your time and tiring yourself out.

This time, when Rosie's phone rang, someone picked up.

Who is this? Rosie? KK turned when he heard Amma's voice and Beti got up and left her desk. Sid was there, and since I had driven him there: yes, me too. And another one of our buddies. Who has not previously entered the story. Nothing shall be said of him. He's even more unnecessary to this story than I am, even more tangentially present than me, but even if he weren't there, others can bear witness. His name was Raheel, but really, why do we need to name him?

Sheela. Or Shakeela? Ma spoke faintly. After the call.

Now how many forms is Rosie taking, Beti wondered.

Let's go to the house on the lake.

Everyone went.

★

72

The door opened as though our pounding had forced it. The woman behind it stood flabbergasted. She'd meant to open the door for someone else. Sheela or Shakeela had.

Rosie? Sid's Granny looked searchingly behind her.

Sheela (or Shakeela): Who are you?

Where's Rosie? asked KK.

Sid and his aunt both squeezed in past the woman.

She left, Sheela or Shakeela said. She looked behind her, and at those standing at the door, and couldn't figure out whom to address.

That was you on her phone, how did it end up with you?

She left it, said Sheela. Or Shakeela.

Who are you, where is she, when will she come?

Suddenly the sentences began rolling furiously from SheelaShakeela's mouth. She wasn't rude, but totally startled. I'm a renter. I've stayed here for a long time. She went to her home. My husband will come. We're about to go out. We have to go somewhere. Our scooter is outside. There's nowhere to hang clothes so we put them on this. The machine runs over here, they've opened a factory in their house. They make plastic lids. It makes a huge racket *slapslap* in my head. I have a headache.

She talked and talked until she began to explode. Her anger exploded. Who are you? Who are you to ask anything? How should I know? You think she'd tell us anything before she left? It's not like we're best friends or anything. How could we be? How should I know when she'll be back. She forgot her phone. She was sick.

If she was sick, how could she have gone somewhere?

She must have gone to the hospital.

Did someone take her?

I didn't notice if she went on her own or someone took her. Why would I take her? Who is she to me? We pay her rent. She increases it every year. The expense is sky-high.

Why did she leave her phone?

What do I have to do with her phone? She left it; she must have got another. Whether it works or not, she must know. It rang, so I picked it up. I must have picked it up without noticing. I have a fever. You're disturbing me. Why are you cross-examining me like this? She adopted a combative stance. Her hair was red, and loose, as though she'd been sleeping. She had black circles under her eyes. She stumbled and her head rolled forward as though a noose had tightened around it.

We have to go. You go away! she barked hoarsely.

Ma turned. Let's go.

★

Everyone said they'd felt weird the moment they set foot inside.

There was the stench of stale pickle, said Sid.

It was a two-room flat. A small veranda in back strewn with stuff.

I saw her pink arranda out there, said Beti.

Ma had circled about the entire home, tapping her cane. SheelaShakeela had followed along, grumbling. One room was completely swallowed up by an enormous takht-like table, the other with an enormous double bed.

KK said he had felt scared.

Everyone had noticed paan splatters on the back wall that could have been blood.

Did Rosie chew paan? Raza sure did.

Under the double bed, someone remembered. Behind it, someone else remembered.

How could we accept that these splatters might be blood?

★

73

It's good to have an idea of the zeitgeist. People get bored. Something must be going on at all times; there must be drama, otherwise it seems like nothing's happening at all, like life has come to a standstill. If life moves along at its own pace, everything feels motionless. If you sit behind your books or computer, far from the pace of life, you feel like you're dead. Stillness frightens. What if sitting calmly turns me to stone? A terrifying thought. Better that the days lurch and sway, the ground flips beneath your feet, routine is upended, heart lungs desire jump, stir, churn, as you wonder what's been broken what's survived, and every morning you're forced to march out and grapple with life.

That's why mutiny is more fun than harmony; salaciousness trounces salubriousness; desecration beats devotion, destruction wins over construction, kerfuffle over unruffled, panic over picnic, cruel over cool. Thus, as in Tolstoy's story, the wife tires of her nice calm doctor husband and runs after her hedonistic good-for-nothing lover. Sometimes people embrace their own ruin. They abandon dependability and go all in for whatever sets their pulse racing.

The pace of nowadays is on-your-toes, keep-on-moving, and sometimes even break-into-a-run; people forget to keep their feet on the ground at all. How long can you keep your balance when you're on your toes: Look out! Splat! You fall flat on your face.

It's just that sometimes the calculus gets scrambled. Amma stood on the same earth as Beti. And then, splat! Everyone fell; for most people a fall was just a fall, but when Rosie fell, she died.

★

74.

Rosie died.

*

75

And the lake burst into flames.

That shape-shifter? The inspector stared at Sid and Beti and burst out laughing. Nothing happens to him. He's always out and about and sometimes he comes this way. Everyone around here recognises him. Of course, there's no recognising him *really*. Every form he takes is counterfeit. Bring tea.

Then he turned towards Amma. So, Amma ji, what's this? Whose sway have you fallen under? You're an innocent. Decent folk worry about everyone. You're old, so you get worked up. My Daadi's just the same. She lives with us. She starts up early in the morning, *Has Hariya come*—our servant—*it was very windy last night, get him to sweep the courtyard, it's six o'clock, turn on the water, pump, arre Bhaundey isn't back yet,* Bhaundey, that's my nickname at home, Ma ji, the inspector told Amma with a laugh, *It's past five*, when in fact the bell on the clocktower is striking five right at that moment, *call the station, worry worry, since Bhaundey's job is to straighten out crooks and scoundrels, danger, all danger,* oh, my darling Daadi.

Inspector Bhaundey proceeded to create in his mouth a mixture of yawns paan tobacco katechu digestive powder and phlegm, and then went on as he chewed lustily: These people don't disappear, they're always on the move. He didn't come over here before, but then he bought a house, God knows where he got the money. What don't these people do in their line, they really make a bundle, you and I can't afford it, but these people just snap it up. But whoever sold it to him, how did they sell it? Nowadays if they get the price they want, people forget everything—black—white—everything. Or maybe they didn't know who they were selling to. Probably didn't even show an ID card to buy. Look, he said mixing wisdom with the sludge in his mouth, these people can't even be properly identified; they can call themselves whatever they want, and they take advantage of that, no papers, so they escape easily.

Bhaundey waxed morose: Once these people start coming and living among the rest of us, it'll be a disaster. Anyway, he rented out the flat. One time a bunch of dogs suddenly attacked him, the inspector laughed. He's just standing there, next minute he's flat on his back. Even the dogs can tell this is someone no one recognises! The kids chase after him, throw rocks, we scold them, be good, don't hit people. Anyway, he showed up now and again. Must have been making a packet. This is an expensive area. It used to be a village, now respectable people are building houses here. It's open. There's a lake. Buses. The metro's coming out here too. The fire will go out. It's nothing—a pointless uproar, the government's investigation team came by. Someone threw a bidi into the lake; dry trash'll catch fire anywhere. There was a layer of trash on the water. There was plastic garbage on the bottom so the trash on top didn't sink below the surface. That's all—no big deal. But it made my job harder. It's all on me—I have to take care of it. Anyway, you can rest easy. Mark my words, he'll pop up somewhere.

I'm always busy, said Inspector Bhaundey, leaning over to Sid. I could also hear, because I was with Sid that time too. But forget about me. But the folks in the neighbourhood say he's been coming around in men's clothing lately. That way, the dogs and the children probably give him a pass. He burst out laughing. Truly. Even monkeys and langurs avoid men, they'll threaten women, they'll even snatch their purses glasses mobiles. They quickly make off with bananas bread bhaji. There aren't any monkeys over here, not even langurs come, sometimes to the lake, but just a few, they wander in from somewhere. But take a look at the temples. At Sankatmochan they stand in line, or sit, so the devotees'll share some of their prashad when they come out. Why not, they're Hanuman, we worship them, I'm a devotee of Hanuman myself. I recite the Hanuman Chalisa every day, and on Saturdays I go to the temples and offer ladoos. I exercise because of Jay Bajrangbali —I joined the police only later. Shree Hanuman is our favourite deity at home. Everyone's happy and peaceful. There's no fighting among us brothers, we don't even quarrel with our wives—laughter bursts forth from the mixture in his mouth like tiny bubbles—Hanuman himself is a renunciant, but gives blessings to devotees who fulfil the life of a prosperous householder. And my heart, don't ask about my heart, it just keeps on ticking. Who knows what a heart attack even is! Everyone's having them nowadays—the boss had a heart attack and now he's gone. Recite the Hanuman Chalisa, Mata ji. No attack will dare come near your heart. Look at this —the inspector pressed a button on his mobile—my father recites it all the time. His father's voice chanted from his mobile: *Jay Hanuman gyan gun sagar jay kapeel tihun lok ujaagar.* His heart's even fitter than mine, Ma ji, what you should do is recite the Chalisa all the time, then your days will be well spent, and your life too.

Amma twirled her cane. Please, make a missing persons case. Amma had not relaxed a whit since meeting that SheelaShakeela. She'd brought us to the police station. Not the station where she herself had been found after she went missing. This was the station next to the lake. The one that had caught fire and was belching fumes.

Inspector Bhaundey grumbled: What are you people thinking? You don't even know if anyone's missing; where's the case? If a grown up person disappears from somewhere in particular, then it can be said that they've gone missing, but he hardly had to tell anyone where he was going, he had no one to answer to, and what does he have to do with you, Amma, do you really want to get yourself all mixed up in this? Making the rounds of the police stations and courts at your age? Chewing on his melange of yawn cough sore throat paan tobacco katechu chuna belch as he spoke, he added, You know what he is, don't you, whose sway you've fallen under, dancing singing begging who knows what line of business he was in, these folks wander all over the place, weddings theft begging and things I can't even say in front of you—they do it all, I know all about it, we crack the whip a bit when we catch them and then we let them go, no one wants that filth in their station and how are we supposed to arrange a separate cell for them, there are so many crooks here, there's no room for them and there'll be such a furore if we throw them in with the rest, so we give them a bit of the old stick—a froth of laughter burbled up from his mouth on to the police guy standing nearby—then we let them go. Amma ji, if something's the matter, write it down, but how can someone with no fixed abode go missing? Bhaundey ji began to feel himself very mature and wise.

And you know the lake is on fire! he grumbled.

In the furore over the fire, those missing remained all the more so. The reputation of the country was at stake. NGOs reporters national international the people and the government itself, everyone piled on. On one side were those who were seeing the end of the world in the fire, on the other, the government saying that this was only a minor bidi accident. The first group said that this is the consequence of dangerous interference in the environment, that chemicals were burning on top of the water; and the second group asserted that the lake had been dry, and that stuff had collected on the shores during monsoon and an illiterate villager had thrown a bidi on it. And this was a mishmash of perspectives bound to spread unrest: anyone can tell that those who revel in fomenting trouble are behind this, unable to separate the accidental fire on the banks from the smoke spiralling up in the middle of the lake.

The police cordoned it off so that no one could get close without a permit, and they were stationed there day and night to keep tourists from crowding the banks on one side, whilst clouds of smoke and fire amassed on the other.

*

But Amma was Amma: she got KK to take her back.

We can't even rest at night, and you've come again to ask if we've found that shape-shifter? You tell me: how on earth are we supposed to find someone when we don't know which part of them is real and which part is fake? Is the creature a human or a jinn?

His manner was joking, but this time Inspector Bhaundey seemed tired. As though he didn't have time for the Hanuman Chalisa nowadays. Because the lake catching fire had caused such an uproar.

He'd begun to prepare his juicy mixture in his mouth when KK's press card went on the attack against his heart. The police had not yet managed to fully escape fear of the press. Inspector Bhaundey choked on the swirling juices and diverted a small portion of his force from lake duty, sending them over to Rosie's new flat.

★

Lovers adore romance, bigots love weapons, butterflies love canes, tricksters love the government, you and me love barfi and laddu, and newspapers love masala. That's why you'll see their pages stuffed with crime and the bazaar full of crooks fooling customers. Theft robbery Nithari December 16 Jessica Lal havala Harshad Mehta Neeta Tandoor Shobhraj cheating Zeenat Amand beat-up Kapoor-Shapoor's heat-up. In a world of the right to do this and the right to do that, newspapers also have the right to dislike the farmer suicides and deem them beneath their notice, nor are they sufficiently fond of the beatings of Adivasi forest dwellers that they should deign to turn their eyes thataway. So their pages are a reflection of the latest shiny objects that attract their attention. Some news items are plastered all over and especially up front, whilst others are swept into the corners like tiny insects. In the court there was a hearing about how one goat had snuck into the grazing area of another for a munch, and there was another case in which it was discussed whether or not, in the age of rising nationalism, a person might remain seated in their wheelchair during the national anthem. The press is free to choose who gets space where, and which stories shall be graced with pictures. KK decided he would give the Rosie tragedy its due place by writing an article, and he was lucky to get space on a page. Thank god for small mercies!

Whoever happened to cast a glance there would have found out that there was one Rosie, hijra, who had laid down capital and created a charity organization for her people. She'd run away from the Anjuman-e-Islam Orphanage to the Langar Khana at the Gurdwara and from there she'd reached the home of a Christian Missionary, who'd educated her a bit, and when she grew up she'd become master of her own livelihood. Sewing, embroidery, making all sorts of handicrafts, preparing jam jelly chutney, sending tiffins for workers, such was the work she did. She had bought a flat near the lake and rented it out.

When the inspector arrived there he found a lock on the door, and when he encountered the lock again two days later, he broke it and entered. Sheela or Shakeela and her boyfriend with the black slicked-back hair were caught outside the house, preparing to take a long vacation somewhere, and Rosie was found inside, stuffed into the box portion of the box bed.

In the newspaper it said that Rosie had wanted to get rid of her tenants and live there herself, and a dispute had arisen over this. First SheelaShakeela had asked for some time, then she said she was willing to pay more rent, then she'd expressed a desire to purchase the flat, then she'd brought in her boyfriend, then they'd started trading insults, and SheelaShakeela and partner had said the same thing Inspector Bhaundey had said.

That is: that you have been taken in by that faker, this person has no proper papers or any such, we were cheated, we had no idea she was a fake, first she came as a woman then she started coming as a man.

When the criminals and the police both fully agreed there was no reason to get involved with a faker, the issue was dropped for some time.

We're decent people, this is a neighbourhood of decent people, ask anyone if we've ever caused a disturbance, we had a faucet installed in this house, we built that wall with the neighbours' permission; they're good people, the boy works in an electric shop, the mother gives us coriander, mint, green chillies, she grows them in pots, once they even grew aubergines, if we didn't get a bit of cover from the wall then anyone could peep in, when he goes to work why would I want everyone to walk by and see in while I'm alone? The ceiling was also leaking, we spent thousands of rupees, we even coated it with waterproof paint. But she never lifted a finger. We told her, whatever happens we won't drag you into legal-illegal now even though we could put you inside for the crime of imposturing. You're not like the rest of your people, clapping, vulgar dancing and singing, you don't do all that, we rented a house from you, we'll acknowledge that. You come from time to time, you may stay with us then. Look at this, we put up walls around the veranda and created a space. You can live with us, we gave her permission, otherwise who would want her to live here, respectable families stay around here. We've already paid, she'd told us she was going home for a long time, that's probably why you can't find her.

But she was found. In the box. In the iron mortar in the kitchen they found a pestle covered with the same blood that splattered the wall like paan spit. Stuffed in with some shards of shattered rotting skull.

One more shape for the shape-shifter, Bhaundey did not say.

The newspaper said she'd been a respectable hijra whose tenants were trying to get her to sign papers declaring them the owners of the house, to promise to leave the place to them upon her death, and they hoped maybe she would go away and never come back. But Rosie had no desire to sign the papers, nor was she in any hurry to die, so they'd whacked her with the pestle, and then whatever happened happened.

KK wrote all sorts of things in the article about equal human rights under the constitution and how finally these days you could declare yourself third-gender and you too had rights, but in reality it happened rarely and social acceptance was even rarer. The editor considered this bit useless from the perspective of reader interest, and told him he could write a long article about it for an academic journal. The reader would get bored of the story if he took it too far. So that was it, that was as much as anyone read of the tale. End of story.

Nowhere was it recorded that they'd requested an identification, nor that Amma had again said:

Come on, let's go.

Meaning, this time, to the morgue. To Rosie's corpse. Head covered with a sheet, two feet sticking out. A shapeless form with a toe tag bearing the corpse number.

A price tag. Cheap.

★

77

Fog spread before Beti's eyes. All the longings in the entire world, all the grief of separation, all the memories resentments deprivations joys rose silently from the person lying before them and evaporated into smoke. Beti felt tearful, as though the corpse that lay before them was not Rosie's but her own. We'll all end up like this, we'll all go like this, look like this, what will become of our beauty and what will be our price tag?

Rosie's feet were as green as the lake had been that night, blotchy, protruding from beneath the sheet. She was loosely sewn up in it, so it looked swollen, as if what lay beneath it was bloated.

Had Rosie's stomach become distended, swollen, burst, spreading ooze on the covering fabric? The blood in all the limbs must have turned to pus and was seeping out, breaking through like a flood.

Amma wanted to see the face.

When Sir says so, then, said the attendant.

Ma paid no heed and pulled aside the sheet. Rosie's hands were stitched up. Rotten branches of a rotten tree, like the legs. Don't touch, said Beti, trying to stop her. As if they would start dripping like pressed beets.

Let Sir come, please, admonished the attendant lethargically.

Amma touched lightly. KK gently placed his own hand on hers, either to stop her or support her, who knows.

The sheet had become crooked. Beti stood on tiptoe as though preparing to flee.

Rosie had already decayed. The sheet was redolent with the stench of death, mingled with the acrid fumes of formaldehyde. The digestive juices that dissolved the foods and such inside the body were now dissolving Rosie, since they had nothing else to consume; they were fermenting her morsels. A festive feast that continued on in Rosie's entrails.

The heart had stilled its pumping. The blood had congealed in the hanging parts which had turned rotten swollen repulsive. The pus had burst through the skin and begun to ooze. Like when you roast an aubergine to make bharta.

Sir arrived, pressured by KK's card. Cover the face, he scolded the attendant.

Push back those hideous eyelids, thought Beti as she clenched shut her eyes.

Rosie, said Ma calmly, as though to confirm identification. To recognise.

Open that mouth that has been silenced, Beti wished desperately. Seeing one glimpse of the congealed ooze from Rosie's nose, which was either blood or worms that had not survived.

Hospitals and morgues are in a hurry to extricate themselves from unclaimed unidentified corpses with no future no past. Provided that people like KK and Ma don't see them.

Why wasn't Rosie washed, scolded Amma.

Straighten the sheet, Sir rebuked again.

When the attendant jerked the sheet to straighten it, it slipped further.

A putrid stench rose in the room as Rosie's naked body emerged, covered in waxen skin which had shrunk and begun to crack and was full of deep green blue dark red stitches splotches and blotches. Here and there the cracks were sewn and filled with embalming masala.

Artistry. A curiosity. A monstrosity.

And those? Breasts or boils? And was that a penis at half mast?

They call it *rigor mortis*, when a bygone body stiffens like that. Near the scrotum the penis goes wooden. Boils bulge.

Why is the body unclothed? Amma scolded, looking pleadingly into KK's eyes.

Sir looked a bit flustered.

The body almost looked as though it were clothed in the oozing chemicals blood scurfy wounds stitches and hues and rotting shapes that covered it.

As in the home of a prominent colonial gentleman on the great festival of Christmas, when a large animal is roasted whole and *dressed* with delicacies, soaked in chutney, basted in butter, filled with colourful dried fruit and nuts, sprinkled with garlic ginger petal leaf, and set out fully decorated at the great table. Spice and sauce as attire. The fork and knife neatly arranged on a napkin nearby.

Rosie bequeathed her deceased body to the hospital for medical research, Ma announced, and it was no less than a legal bequest.

This was Rosie's last rite. Religious rites were thus absent.

★

78

The cane bellows and roars, then stills. Breath rises falls, then comes to a stop. Eyes stare aghast, then dry up. One dies, another becomes lifeless. When lightening zaps a tree, it snaps like a straw. As a dust storm abates, thatch cracks. When a song is lost, the throat is reduced to coughing.

Melody is important. Whether love affection friendship are madness or no, there should always be a melody in one's heart that plays throughout life. That's why, in Sara Rai's story, P Sundaram is distraught when he loses the thread of the melody.

The return of history. Ma lay lifeless, began to cough, lost the melody, this time in Beti's home.

In which breeze did the microbes come a-buzzing, do you know? The unclaimed just fester there, admonished Bade's doctor. Who took Ma ji to such a place? She was bound to come down with some type of allergy.

Coughing took the place of melody in her throat. Ma forgot how to speak. Move her frame ever so slightly and a dry crackling *cough cough* slumped her over. Emptiness echoes and is mistaken for a cough. Beti has to help her straighten up and each time she does, Ma's grown a little smaller. Small, smaller, much much smaller, as though she intends to dig a tiny chink in some border and come out on the other side.

In the morning, when Beti seated her by the blackbird, the two looked to be about the same length and width, because size has no relation to actual measurements. If a banyan is the size of a bela bush, it's tiny; if a butterfly is the same size as a crow, it looks huge. Ma sat vacant, and the bird, seeing the entire family drowned in pity for her, felt moved by pity herself. Observing this distraught woman, bent over, smaller than herself, she'd come and sit on the tree branch and sing, then stop, then sing again, as though she were reminding Ma: Ma, this one is your melody, come on, don't you recognise it? Here it is. Ma must have been abstracted, lost, besieged by stories that jostled knocked thronged together inside her. Ma swallowed whatever Beti put in her mouth, and started coughing every time, as though something might fly out, breaking her samadhi.

There was a light chill in the air and Beti, seated on the balcony, wrapped Ma carefully in a light shawl to guard against the cool morning. All of Beti's love, all her Shravan Kumarness burbled up in a flood as she thought about how Rosie was not here now to take Ma downstairs for a stroll. How tragic Ma looks, and if I didn't think of it, it wouldn't even occur to her that it's time to eat now, time to get dressed. She who had shrivelled up in a corner on seeing Ma happy and busy with Rosie and the others now reemerged as important and necessary to Ma. The worm she had become crawled into a corner and died with Rosie. Now Beti was a soft velvety sunshine, spreading out warm like a shawl over Ma to protect her from the coming chill, softly cosying her.

As Beti became sunlight, she began to feel powerful, and one day she even sympathised with KK's desire and found she desired him herself. So much so, that when the two of them went out together to submit an article, they stopped on the way back at one of their favourite ruins, a place seldom visited, because no one likes the jungle if there's no McDonald's or Haldiram's nearby. The two of them rekindled their romance in the dark on the bough of a mango tree that reached all the way to the ground. It could have been dangerous, not because of snakes or tigers, but, as has become more prevalent, humans; yet Beti had a newfound strength, and because of this she took the risk.

Love for others also bubbled up as compassion. The door of her home opened wider than it had before. If someone relapses after getting well and doing fine, near and dear ones feel especially anxious. They show up in a panic, wondering how they themselves can bear to breathe without first ensuring the other can?

Ant brigades began appearing in search of the scattered crumbs of snacks and tea. Sid and the rest of the family, servants, friends, battalions of community members, began showing up at Beti's and suggesting remedies: try this, this will make her feel better. Remedies were suggested from far off lands as well, via Bahu: Give her chamomile tea, it's soothing and everything also gets messed up with gas, give her mint, it will settle her stomach, and her coughing too, and half a sleeping pill is fine at her age, she'll get better if she sleeps well. The guard's daughter-in-law was from somewhere in the mountains; she brought a type of oil and said let me go to her, let me massage her head with it, it'll draw out the poison that's got inside. There was a green-coloured oil in the bottle, and the stalk floating in the oil looked sort of like a centipede, which the daughter-in-law said was a worm that's found in those parts and dropped live into the oil and its essence keeps oozing out, which has immediate health benefits. The doctor wanted to run tests in the hospital to see first if all the parameters were in place, after which they could think about other tests. What he said was that uncommon viruses had been dormant in the ice for eons, and they were now making their way into the world with the melting of the ice, and that coughing diarrhoea weakness were no longer the simple illnesses they'd once been, when they would quickly go away on their own. They'd actually become rather difficult to cure: let's check her into the hospital and put her under observation and come up with some solutions. Global warming is what's behind it.

The family was not, at least for the time being, willing to take Ma back to the hospital. As though Rosie had gone but she'd left her vote behind. Sid said bring in a house doctor, but no one agreed with that either: there was no pain, no dizziness, no shortness of breath, no sweating; the cough was also improving, and they were hardly GPs that they could just diagnose the whole thing, they'd already seen that every doctor needed the other ones, each had to have their own separate tests to decide that it's not this, not that, and finally get to what it is. Rosie would have said, *No, no one's taking Baji to the hospital. They kill people there instead of helping them to live, but they also don't let them die because that would give them a bad record. You just tell me and I'll come running to look after her. I don't need a passport to come.*

But Rosie was gone and with her, her spirit. Amma just sat quietly or coughed. And the family became the quilt that wrapped her, the blanket that covered her, her magic carpet, her cane, her every support.

The family understands all, since time immemorial. Before, too, they had understood that when her husband had departed, Ma too had departed, and they'd worked to pull her back, and now again they were busily pulling her back, because Ma had departed again.

No one says it happened because Rosie left. Bade and Bahu believe that it's because Ma left their home that she's now exhausted and sort of finished, and Beti believes that it happened when Ma relinquished her care to others. The family doesn't give up its ways, and nor does it stop seeing itself as the great guardian of all. Families love a half-dead bird. If that's what you are, you'll get endless love and sympathy, and the one who made you half-dead will face the family's wrath. How they love to help, puffing up the decrepit wings of the bird, come, lean on us, move, slowly, try to fly, try a bit more, we're right here, holding you, supporting you, don't worry, yes, yes, open your wings a bit, careful, slowly, no, no, not too much, no, no, absolutely never without our help, you'll fall you'll get trampled.

How could they know that something else also goes on in families: in their self-gratifying super-sympathetic worry they do whatever she says, thinking it's charity, and they humour her kindly at this last phase of her life, little realising that she'll get them to do things they could never imagine in their wildest dreams.

★

———————————————————

Hearing a sound at the open door, Beti stood up in shock. Her brother stood before her. She before he. Their eyes locked, as though there's you and me and no one else. The earth gaze air mind body stirred as though all was turned fluid and splash bubble melt puddle.

A masterful mien hung over Bade's face like a curtain. A way to hide anxiety and also wipe away the sweat. Raza Master had made costumes from cloth, but this one was woven from demeanour.

Amma was seated on the balcony, cloaked in stillness. Bade went straight over to her. Come along, he commanded, if you sit outside your health is bound to get worse.

Ma slowly lifted her head. She looked at Bade, looked at Bahu, who'd come in behind him, looked at Beti standing behind them, looked at the open door behind her, over to where the neighbour's shaggy dog had started barking with joy at making eye contact with Ma.

You left me behind, said Amma.

Bahu leaned over to touch her feet.

What are you talking about, Amma? You left us. But enough is enough, now come along. Let's go now.

Let's go now, Amma repeated vacantly.

She's had her outing. Ma's had her chance to try out this crazy quilt. Time to return to comfort, said Bahu. She's had her little flirtation with weirdo lifestyles. Time for her to return. Where else could she find what she gets at our home, sooner or later she has to return to us. Overseas Son has also called to say please look after yourself, please don't neglect yourself, hire a nurse, and tell her all of Daadi's needs: that she gets constipated, dissolve half a spoon of Isabgol and give it to her with every meal and Nebicard in the morning and I am sending figs from here via a colleague, and also a foot massager that you should also have Daadi use, okay?

At which one remembers Paul Zachariah's story, if one has read it, where another overseas son thought of all the tiny ways in which his elderly Ma lying alone needed to be cared for. This overseas son explained everything in a letter to the lady who responded to his advertisement for a nurse's post, after telling her about the amenities, salary, and so on. All the rest of his siblings were stationed about the globe, and he wrote: I have taken on the responsibility of darling Amma, and I come with my family to see her once every two years. So, Nurse, you will stay with her. You will wake Ma in a soft voice at 9 a.m. Not by shaking her. By patting her palms lightly, and her forehead. If she awakes and recognises you, smile sweetly. If she doesn't recognise you, smile and remind her who you are. Then raise the head of the bed and sit her up with a pillow to lean on, pull her body forward slightly, and massage her back and shoulders softly but thoroughly. Then with Sosamma's help —another character in the story—seat her on the commode. But smile the whole time, because when Amma gets up she should feel good cheer and affection, this is good for her health, both mental and physical. When Ma is on the commode, then, Nurse, you should keep patting both her hands, or her back, with one hand. At 9:20, give Ma a sponge bath. Continue to talk to her throughout all this. On sweet topics: make a connection with happy experiences in your life. Or about us children, that is, Ma's children, or about our own children, and continue to say sweet things.

In short, there are instructions for the future nurse for every moment: when Ma goes to sleep, when she awakes, in bed, on the potty, in the wheelchair, everywhere. Such detailed instructions, such as to position her wheelchair on the balcony in the evening when the sun begins to set, and turn her face towards the horizon and lock the wheels and put down the bar, so she won't slump forward, and then leave her there alone. Allow her to enjoy the pleasure of solitude.

Alert to the smallest details, even when far away across the seven seas. And then Paul writes that the son in the story instructed that at night, at 9:30 p.m. to be precise, you should lay Ma down and look into her eyes and say, *Good night, sweet dreams*, and see if she smiles or not, and give her an affectionate kiss on the head, another on the cheek, and another on the lips on behalf of us six, her sons and daughters, and say to her, *My dear Ammachi*, and thus it seemed that truly the nurse becomes a medium, and it's the children who are giving her their love.

Having set all these conditions, the son in the story ended his letter thus: If you agree to these terms, we will interview you for the position of nurse to our mother.

But no one had read Zachariah in this family. Yet sons are sons, whether they are in stories or outside of them, so Bade's wife said, look how much he thinks of Daadi even when he's far away, and of me too, and how my life shouldn't just be spent in caring for Ma and the home, and he makes sure to leave his work in the middle of every other day and call me, even from over there, he's doing all these things so that I never feel truly alone.

Pack her things. Bade's first words to Beti after eons, and they were words of command. Was it any wonder she minded?

Let her health stabilise first.

I'll go. Ma said softly.

Why do mothers always think of their sons' homes when they're dying? Krishna Sobti showed us this in her novella *Listen, Girl*.

Ma began to cough, resting her cane on the floor, bending over it.

Let's go inside, said Beti.

Ma lifted her cane, coughing coughing trembling trembling. And her head. When she lifted her cane, it was like a long thin matchstick that took the spark from the redness of the setting sun to light the candles hanging in the shade of the nearby tree. Soft red flickers swung about. Ma rested her cane upon a branch, as though it too was a branch of the same tree. The blackbird hopped up alone at this glad tiding. The sun was moving upwards as the bird perched upon the cane-branch before Ma and turned blacker, eyes redder. Chirping its long *tweet tweet tweet* it tried its best to help the melody return to Ma's voice.

Over the border, said Amma.

For some reason everyone fell silent so they could hear the song of Amma and the bird. The whistling one. The love-in-separation lament, the cry-for-meeting, that one.

The blackbird whistles. Before a small woman. Wherever it may be, it is, before this tree or this bush, in this light and this moment.

Then the bird flew away.

And Ma began to whistle as though she were not in the bustling home of a populous city, but in the wilderness, in a desert, where a whistle echoes in the void and slowly dies away.

★

80

Thud. A tear falls like a rock. Or a drop of rain.

There's so much one hasn't an inkling about, yet one doesn't even believe that truth. Everyone running after the cause of this and the reason for that. One body has many different lives. If it weren't so, could a great heavy Taj Mahal of solid rock waft in the breeze like a feather?

A rock floats up like a sheet of paper. A droplet falls like a rock. A rock is only a rock as long as it's a rock. Heavy solid unmoving unshaking. A breath rises and the rock trembles. Then it turns to paper and floats. The paper flaps and a story flies upon it, new and fresh.

The red glow of the sunset spreads over the frontier like words flowing from a pen.

The frontier, which is the border of another border, beyond the border.

There's sand at the border. As in a desert. The sand awaits. Paused. The vigil of the sand, the arrested desert. That's the border. Some on one side, the rest on the other. This side or that side. Commerce, boundless.

Dramatic. But this can be understood. There are answers. Wherever I am, there I am, wherever you are, there you are. Over there: you me; and over here: me you. Waiting for these to meet. If they do, a romantic meeting. Body mind plunge into sand, sinking.

The growing-smaller woman whistles like the wind in the desert that flows without colliding with anything, and slowly the layers of sand fly up, and forms meditating in samadhi are revealed.

★

81

Like a game where the children take running leaps, and right at that moment, the word *passport* jumps in, and everyone nearly falls over.

Ma is asking Bade for a passport. Not to go to his house: she's cooking up a plan to go elsewhere. Everyone in shock.

Ah well, she's at the end of her life—they justify it to themselves—let her have her dreams and fulfil them. It's good she's interested in doing something. Otherwise we feared she'd just lie down again like last time. We'll take her on a trip.

Pakistan. When Amma said it, everyone thought they hadn't heard right, and no one even paid attention.

Even at this age, desire is desire, and why should anyone die without giving it a shot. They go to Kashmir Goa Kerala. If she wants abroad, then try Singapore or Shanghai. When Sid's planning his events there, he'll take her along. When would his boundless group of friends come in more handy? If she wants, we could even arrange for Sri Lanka or Mauritius. Jhumman went there too, the walls of his hotel were made of glass and the sea flowed about on all sides. Yes, one can surely dream of London Paris New York, where everyone nowadays has some child or other who's gone to study or marry. But one must take age into consideration when planning a journey. And if you really insist, then come, let's get up the courage and go to Australia. He's always calling his mom and saying I'll show you around here. Let Bahu take Ma along, she can travel too. Become foreign-returned. Take a trip abroad.

Because: Pakistan. Pakistan? Pakistan! Why fling Ma into the swirl of the noisy slogans in Krishna Sobti's *A Gujarat Here, A Gujarat There*?

And how far Pakistan is, Amma, t's so far!

At which Amma got a bit annoyed—It is where it is. We're the ones who are far.

Yes, but all the same, if you really have it in you to go that far, then why not Australia, it will also be home. But Pakistan? Who goes to Pakistan?

Rosie. Amma's response.

What does this have to do with Rosie? everyone shrieks, and they're all startled at one another's shrieks and jump.

This is what you call an obsession. Or spirit possession.

Rosie had to go.

She's gone.

But she didn't take the chironji.

So what?

I'll take it.

Bade, Bahu, Kichaluu Taya, Doctor Mirasi, KK, Beti, everyone jumped and bellowed and then fell silent and began to think: *so what is to be done?*

Bade talked to someone and got Ma's passport made. Bahu said, let her feel happy. Sometimes it's enough just to make a plan, then you don't need to go.

Beti analysed the matter compassionately and open-mindedly and decided that whatever one may feel personally about Rosie, after all, she always stood steadfastly by Ma, and if now

Ma wants to do this in return, to deliver the chironji to someone for Rosie, then I will absolutely support her. This is the LGBT age, and I am no reactionary.

Shall I come along? KK gave Beti a surreptitious punch. What harm if we too take a trip, with Aunty providing the excuse, we've been planning to go for ages with the peace group, he said.

Amma was sitting there too, but as though indifferent unaware displeased with everyone. For her birthday party. KK and Bade were both there, saying to one another, have another drink, what can I get you?

Have another drink, Bade said to KK on Amma's eightieth birthday at the Officers' Club.

Brandy, Aunty? asked KK, seeing her subdued look, but Beti motioned for him to be quiet.

You, Ma lifted her cane and pointed it towards Beti, You will be the one to go with me.

It was an order.

Let's go now.

Ma stood up, more or less right in the middle of the party, and turned her face away from everyone. There was a slight chill in the air with winter coming, and she shivered, but she allowed the shawl Bahu had wrapped about her to slip unceremoniously to the ground.

As though she'd removed all her layers, one by one, wife mother aunt this that, now at last she was simply herself, laid bare, apart, her own, untouched by the thoughts and concerns of any other.

At eighty, Ma had turned selfish.

★

It so often seems as though preparations take an eternity, and yet the outcome appears finished even before one starts. For example: exams, speeches, life, dinner, childhood, Ma falling then rising again, and to a whole new beat, contrary to the expectations of all. Emerging beyond her husband, then beyond Rosie, then yet another new border.

India and Pakistan play games. One says, it's cricket, let them come, the other says, it's their singer, don't let him sing. This one says our fishermen are sitting about catching fish over there, drown them; that one says he was in the army before, now he's a spy, skin him. And amidst all this my turn no mine no mine, visas are granted or not granted. The diplomats are such deities, they can sometimes finish the game with no preparation at all, and sometimes they keep hitting sixes and losing anyway.

Bahu had gone to Rashtrapati Bhavan for a dinner, all dressed up. All sorts of ambassadors were to be present, so she wore formal black pants with a cream top and black jacket from Australia. Not with Reeboks, but high-heeled Christian Louboutins, bought at the imported shoe shop. A pearl necklace, a brooch flashing with diamonds, and on her wrist a sparkling watch worked into a bangle. Today she was capable of anything, she could get anything done. And look, she said to Bade, that girl was my yoga student, she's the daughter of the Pakistani ambassador.

You are welcome in our country whenever you wish, the Ambassador said. You have taught my daughter.

See. Bahu was head over heels with her own outfit.

The very next day, Sid went to the embassy to get forms, etc, and filled them out every which way and *You sign, it's fine, please,* the official said, so Sid signed for Granny and for himself as well, and also for his aunt. In the *where you plan to visit* portion, he filled in what he could remember: *Lahore, Karachi, Islamabad*, where else?

When a country divides, enmity jostles amity and visas and borders depend on the mood—be it slighted, delighted, even far-sighted. Or meditative. In a state of samadhi.

Bade came as far as Wagah, dividing his attention between Ma and Beti as though he himself were a type of border— slighted, delighted, far-sighted. Entranced. In a trance. Samadhist.

★

PART THREE

BACK TO THE FRONT

1.

Here we are at Wagah, where the tale is drama and the story is partition. Is this the chronicle of the getting-smaller woman or is every story really a Partition tale—love romance longing courage pain-in-separation bloodshed? It's an absent presence: lost souls flitting about in the ether. Or sitting: the group of Partition writers has come to sit in a row, and every person has a name card at their place like at a formal banquet. Bhisham Sahni. Balwant Singh. Joginder Pal. Manto. Rahi Masoom Raza. Shaani. Intizar Hussain. Krishna Sobti. Khushwant Singh. Ramanand Sagar. Manzoor Ehtesham. Rajinder Singh Bedi. So many, one could go on and on. And crowding around them, actors, bobbing and swirling like acrobats as they read lines from their scripts.

Mohan Rakesh's character Ganni is seated on his pile of rubble.

There sits Intizar Hussain Sahib writing *Basti*. His heart is filled with sorrow: We young bloods emigrated towards a new horizon that had opened up to us; we were the chosen ones, but no one wanted to leave their homes—how could I turn my back on my hometown of Dibai forever? Did we know that once we turned our gaze from there, we unwittingly turned it from here, and the path to our return would be cut off forever?

Maulana, an actor, reads from his lines: Everyone has wronged us. Strangers have done it and our own have done so as well.

I wander about listlessly hollowed out on the inside, disaffected on the outside, reads an actress from a page.

When Intizar Sahib turns to look at her, she taps his shoulder and reads aloud his own written words as though they're hers, and Intizar Sahib is the reader. It's sad when lanes birds trees no longer recognise you, if they do, you feel depressed. You wander about looking for the neem tree, Intizar Sahib speaks listlessly. Over here, the situation is that the neem, tamarind, mango, peepal, all stare back at me blankly

And over there: the pages of *Zindaginama* riffle by and an actress stops to shuffle through them. Krishna Sobti emerges from the pages looking fabulous in a brilliant purple garara and kurta studded with silver stars, a warm vest and Chitrali cap to top it off, uncapped pen still in hand, ink not yet dry. As she moves the pen across the page, she draws a line between *Zindaginama* and *A Gujarat Here, A Gujarat There*, and keeps forging ahead, as though fashioning new borders—all of which she will cross—and thus it is never closed and never shall be. One character walks along by her side, dazed, and remarks softly, after opening the book:

Hind Rao had sons—four:
Siyo,
Thiyo,
Dhiyo,
Why bother naming the fourth?
He was a Dalit meant to pick up the trash.
Islamuddin also had sons—four:

Arab
Pathan
Turk
Mughal

Other characters hear and come crowding around from all over, as though these are the sounds of some game in which one can form all sorts of words by stringing syllables together. Together, separately, one after another, on two sides far from each other, the slogans rise dance stir pause in a strange theatrical manner as if experimenting to see which permutations are the most fresh and invigorating:

Then, a voice:
Why just your voice?
Why not mine?
If not mine, then not yours
If not yours, then none

Krishna Sobti is drawing lines with her pen, joining them from memory. The voices pierce one another, turn to steam and bubble up among the populace.

New border, new crossing.

Just then Bishan Singh from Manto's "Toba Tek Singh" comes somersaulting along and with each turn, a security guard immediately shoots at him and a thin stream of red shoots from his body, and with each of his dizzying turns, red fountains arc in the air above the stage. Some laugh, some shake with fear. Bishan Singh relishes them watching him, and he executes more manoeuvres in the air in a showy manner, at which the shooting causes more red circles to spring forth and he begins to recite his beloved gibberish: Aupad di gad gad di annexe di bedhyaanaan di mung di daal of di lantern.

The actors are delighted and recite with him *Aupad di gad gad di annexe di bedhyaanaan di mung di daal of di Pakistan Government.*

Aupad di gad gad di annexe di bedhyaanaan di mung di daal of di of vahe guru ji da khalsa and wahe guruji di fateh.

At this, the assembly abuzz with both the drizzle of red and the fizz of mirth.

Just then an announcement is made: This is Wagah, quiet down! Everyone halt whatever you are doing. Sit down. Calm down. The writers sit like statues in their chairs and the actors freeze in whatever pose they are in. Bishan Singh too, one hand cupped to his ear, the other shading an eye, adopts a listening watching pose, attentive to the voice. Then he asks in a serious tone, Fazaldeen, where is Toba Tek Singh?

Manto replies softly, Where is it? Right there, right where it always was.

Bishan Singh leaps up. But his voice grows serious and is suppressed by the words, This is Wagah! echoing in the air.

Suddenly many, many people, some dressed up, some villagers, and many in military regalia, come running forward. They pull the chairs out from under the writers, push their pens into their pockets, and hoist guns and swords, brandishing them at the ready. It takes the writers a while to understand that the chairs have been pulled out from under them, so they remain sitting in the air for a time.

Actually, this drama belongs both to those from the future and those from bygone years, such as Krishna Baldev Vaid. Some will say, two dramas side by side. Some will say, two dramas mumble-jumbled. One appearing to all, that same one about giant soldiers in khaki uniforms on this side of the gate, black uniforms on that, the black and the red, turbans decorated with tall plumes on both sides, as though they are roosters, which ratchets up their height from six feet to seven: a drama consisting of Jai Hind—Vande Mataram—Pakistan Zindabad—Quaid-e-Azam Zindabad. The other is not visible to everyone, and in this we are the writers, who still exist today, and will always exist, even after Wagah is gone, whose chairs are pulled out every other day and they stare about vacantly.

And this is also because they have never been able to understand whether they have to go to this side or that side, and what is this side and what is that, so their necks are sore from turning their heads thisawaythataway and their eyes are questioning and they themselves, lost, go sometimes that way then stumble this way as though carried by the changing of the winds. What everyone calls a border: they gaze out at the sky that canopies both sides and can't detect the border anywhere, and because of this, either they are mistaken, or they are actually the ones crossing the border.

So they were sitting there, these wise, lost travellers, the bewildered writers, saying to one another, listen my friend, time and territory are all mixed up within me. Sometimes I have absolutely no idea where or when I am.

They're in their desolate jungles and their empty halls, so they hadn't even known their chairs had been pulled out from under them and a new audience had asserted itself. Such a crowd there was, and such patriotism, that a shortage of chairs was a daily occurrence.

But what mutinous mood was Bishan Singh in that day? On other days, his circling drama ran on a parallel track, but today it was like he'd got himself properly sozzled to totally confound the frontier dance-drama. Well, how is one to tell why on all other days the two dramas chugged along separately, side by side, and then one day they became combative and collided? Suffice it to say that's what happened to Bishan, and no one could quite tell what was happening, but what they did see was the tempest spinning and the tell-tale cascades of red shooting up, swirling designs messing up the Wagah staging. Orders came from above to arrest the troublemaker immediately, but they could only do that if they saw him, right? And if they couldn't catch him then, how would they do so now?

Everyone certainly heard the harsh commands, in those tones for which, even today, Krishna Sobti has zero tolerance. She stood straight up, such that the guards advancing towards her got intimidated and stopped in their tracks. She waggled a fierce finger at them: You, sir, that is enough. As if to say, do you dare clash with Toba Tek Singh?

Over there, the guards on both sides of the gate, in their high-crested turbans and their handlebar moustaches, grew somewhat ruffled. How to look sharp, stand tall amidst these streams of red? It rains down on their eyes and ears, but they can't lift their hands to scratch nor can they bow their heads this way and that to duck.

A chaotic interlude of to-ing and fro-ing. Then another announcement echoes: the sun is about to set. Begin. The vast gates between the two countries clanking open, and quickly the crowd sits down on this side that side of the Hindustan Pakistan gate and the tall dramatically costumed soldiers march to the fore in their tall boots, the high-crested fans on their turbans flapping like flags.

By then the writers have stood up, but they wander about in bewilderment, wondering where they're supposed to go, and Bhisham ji stands at the gate staring in astonishment in the other direction and then falls right over. Arre, they've bashed in the General's skull, he laments. Behind him, an actress reads from Bhisham Sahni's *Tamas*: *his cane, his dark green, moth-eaten turban, his worn-out sandals—all were scattered...* She falls silent and Bhisham Sahni takes his book from her hand. You, he says. I, she says. You want to know, don't you, if something happened here. Listen, he says sadly. He reads as he writes, tell, don't tell, makes no difference.

But Khushwant Singh, growling like a tiger, leaps into no-man's-land, looking neither to the right nor left. His turban unspools like a third flag and flaps in the breeze. At this, Bishan Singh jerks his head towards the sky to cry out in Punjabi, ahoy, bird, are you flying up there? His voice echoing into the present.

Who knows if anyone saw him or not, but everyone heard the flapping of the wings of myriad birds and everyone stopped right where they were to stare upwards for a few moments and see where the birds were, and their wings. But they're nowhere to be seen. This is noted in the newspaper in the report on the drama that day as well: that no one knew if they were birds or UFOs or voices returning from a past massacre.

Both moustachioed fellows on each side of the gate also throw their heads back, then hurriedly jerk them straight, worried that they are going to get it for this too! And their eyes meet in shared camaraderie in a moment of worry before their show. But this is out of sympathy, companionship. During the show, their eyes will lock in ferocious enmity.

Whatever happens, the show must go on. It's an atmosphere of patriotism, the crowd is already seated and only the stupid writers still stand stupefied; women in military uniform who can see them but don't recognise them are scolding them, as they're herded about like cattle this way and that but reasonably respectfully, and then seated amongst the people.

Only Bishan Singh eludes everyone's grasp. The sound of birds' wings flapping continues unabated.

So the crowd sits and the writers are bewildered and except for them, every single person has a mobile in their hand which they hold up, outstretched, and the final flames of the sun reflect on every screen, but the flames have shrunk in size to fit the mobile screen and so it's like each person is grasping a burning candle. Is it a prayer, the writers are about to ask, but everyone's senses are focused on the two enormous guards on each side that have leapt on to the road that runs betwixt the seated crowd, stamping their boots.

It becomes clear from the roars of patriotism that rise from the seated people that this drama is no candle-lit vigil.

Rahi Masoom Raza writes: *This street is silent; it has not asked anyone, who are you, why have you come, where are you going?*

One actor reads the line again: *This street is silent; it has not asked anyone who are you, why have you come, where are you going?* At which Rahi Masoom Raza glances over at him. The actor greets him. Raza salaams back, *Neek rahilan na vo puchta hai. Will you stay a while?* asks the actor. *Abhin rahi ke hoi, what's the use of staying now*, responds Raza, turning sadly away.

The crowd goes wild. How long we've been waiting! *How long we've been waiting! Kab se intezar tha?* they cry to one another enthusiastically.

At his name, Intizar Sahib stands genteelly. He wears a closed-neck coat and seems not to see anyone. His voice is sad. Now we must die. We've witnessed enough. We've even seen what should not have been. I have no urge to see what lies ahead. He speaks in a tone of hopelessness as he stands in their midst. My good fellows, is anyone in their senses at this moment? People have lost half a country and they still haven't come to their senses.

Who sees him, hears him? People have time and money to burn, and so they've travelled to Wagah, they've been waiting, and no one will stop them from seeing the show!

And then the not-to-be-missed performance begins. Such a crisp martial dance! So sharp! Both parties must have rehearsed thoroughly together. No one is an enemy during rehearsal. There must have been laughter and joking. You'll kick your leg so high…as if you're going to kick yourself in the head, then I'll kick as if I'm going bust my own head. Then you'll glare really hard as if you want to gobble me up raw, then my eyes will shoot burning flames at you menacingly, like bombs and bullets raining down on you. But now in the show, it's all feints of animosity. The sword slashes through the air. The gun does flips crack-frack and they stare at one another in a scary way, and when they brandish their fists the fans on their turbans flap fiercely. Like any riveting drama, no one can tell if the emotions being performed are true or false.

Is it a fight or a game? the audience wonders as it stares. Writers too. Manto gazes down as though sleeping, or weeping.

Krishna Sobti of course continues to waggle her finger at them angrily, saying, Sir, that is enough.

But Bishan Singh is on a roll. He's busy throwing the laal salaam, amidst the soldiers' manoeuvres now, and there are other shenanigans going on as well. Everything is under control for the time being, still, one might say, with nationalism so strong, but he resorts to new and newer tricks to put a spanner in the works. Jumps suddenly from hidden places and startles the cries of nationalism soaring up to the skies. So the cries waver and behind all the military alertness, a nervous quiver: be alert, look sharp, catch the troublemaker out lest he ruin your performance. Because at any time, the birds, or whatever they are, flap noisily up there and the streams of red spurt upwards, and cutting through the shouts rising higher than in a cricket match, of the ear-splitting Hindustan Zindabad Pakistan Zindabad Quaid-e-Azam Zindabad Bharatmata ki Jai Jai, comes the voice echoing loud and clear: *Aupad di gad gad di annexe di bedhyaanaan di mung di daal of di phite munh.*

It seems a contingent of plainclothes detectives has been deployed. Their eyes dance about robotically but Bishan Singh evades their grasp. He swerves left and right of the plain-clothes and the uniform-clad soldiers and surprises them all by suddenly popping up somewhere in the midst of the populace and screaming out. No one is able to stop him from doing his hopskipjump antics on both sides of both gates.

Once he shouts Har Har Mahadev from the midst of the Pakistan zindabad contingent and the soldiers ran to catch him, but somehow he flew over or slipped under the gate and came out the other side, where he shouted: Aab-e-zamzam rutba shah! Then some person quick on his heels and deluded about his own genius hurled forth a blow, through which Bishan wriggled as though it was merely a plume of smoke.

But Bishan Singh was pleased by the punching idea. His invisible fist gave it to the demons on both sides, and he'd gleefully land a punch on their dangerous thighs, making their legs buckle and their uniforms lurch. And making them splutter. They couldn't turn their heads to look and see who was hitting them, so he could spring forth again and punch them again and they could lose their balance any moment. Everyone else was aghast too—is there a monkey or what, doing this and then vanishing like a ghost!

Bishan Singh's sudden appearance and disappearance—like a spirit—was going well for him today. Now one guard, turban fan dancing, felt himself tickled at the waist, so he bent to the side, but the fellow was clever and suddenly bent to the other side as well, as though this was simply a step in the martial dance. The man on the other side vigorously followed suit, so as not to fall behind in the competition himself. Synchronising their movements to make it look like part of the performance.

Now what shall I do? Bishan Singh picked up the books from the writers and actors as he pleased and started to read them aloud at the top of his lungs. When the mishmash of literary lines echoed amidst the usual slogans of the populace, the writers felt befuddled. They couldn't understand anything anyway as they stood about in confusion, and when they heard what they'd written, they gave respectful greetings as though they were supposed to humbly acknowledge their own lines. Like when he picked up *Sukha Bargad—The Dry Banyan Tree*— and the echo rang out in the wind, that even after being burnt to cinders in a riot, home is still called home, Manzoor Ehtesham turned around in a flurry, and stood up as though he were confessing his guilt, and then he felt more confused, and he crouched down as though he hoped it would render him invisible, and started tiptoeing away.

But he who had gone mad from the years of lunacy between the two countries was not in the mood for leniency today. What happened next on that day on that stage at the edge of the border, which is on the other side of the other edge of the border, was this:

The sun was setting, and the moment had come for taking down the national flags on both sides. The guards in the crested turbans were in a great hurry to execute their duty correctly, though they hid their haste. They'd already shaken hands with one another with excessive alertness, as if to say, Buddy, it's you and me together today; the enemy is some third party. The last section of the dance remained. They must lower both flags.

Slogans arose with great force, as though they were arms and legs that had climbed the poles with the agility of monkeys and would now lower the flags. When the noise outside rivals that of the drama within, then the spectacle can seem obscene, and so it did. But then something happened. The mischief-maker leapt up like a monkey. And jumping from this pole to that like an acrobat, began impeding the lowering of both sides' flags. The guards were at their wits' end. On both sides. If they jerked hard, the rope might snap. But why wasn't it working when they pulled? They stared at one another balefully, as if to say, Brother, we shall pull and tug together, it's up to us to protect our honour together, please help me out. Deep down inside, they feared the authorities would blame them and their jobs might be hung out to dry. But today the flag flew free. Pull it down, up it goes. Raise it, jerk it, it gets stuck. On both sides.

Then everyone sat up and took notice. The gawkers forgot their fulsome cries and watched in shock. Silence fell. Phone calls were made on both sides, messengers were hurriedly despatched, and in the blink of an eye the army's highest officers came marching in. Straight to the gates, barking orders in muted but firm voices. That the flag must come down.

The grandeur on the faces of the gigantic guards wilted pathetically, as if it had been drawn on with face paint that had melted in the sunlight. They'd been transformed into hulking lambs today. Disgrace and humiliation.

Everyone staring fixedly at their own flags. The flags doing their monkey dance. The guards able to do nothing. In place of the flags their faces had come down, then only their uniforms remained, and they themselves were as good as gone.

Then the birds flapped back and the next thing you know, both flags came fluttering down, and they hadn't yet reached the bottom when they leapt into the air as though some unseen hand had flung them here to there and there to here. The tricolour there, the crescent moon here.

Oh, oh, oh! A screaming, or hissing, rising from the crowd.

Quick, shut the gate! The command rings out as though the reality of what's befallen the flags can somehow be terminated. There's a shrieking of metal, and the speed with which the police round up the cameras, that is, the mobiles, and the journalists from both sides, will certainly be cited as praiseworthy.

Because there will be no news of this fiasco-drama in any newspaper or publication, no one will write that the flags had been laid low at Wagah and they'd forgotten which side they belonged to. No photos exist anywhere. Some police or army officer might have taken a shot on the sly out of curiosity or interest, and centuries later, some researcher or dissident may fish it out by accident, and may delve into the story behind it, in which case something might come out. But for now, noise, and then everything sinks unseen into the silence.

★

2

Who pays attention to the little people in these appearing-disappearing dramas? No one has any interest in the little people's line except they themselves, and even they don't understand all that much all that well, because they're always absentmindedly mixing up old times with new and youth with old age.

Among these proceed the small woman with her growing-bigger daughter.

Ma sitting in the car with Beti would not listen, and had got out insisting on walking the remaining path to the border on foot. As though it were not she but her deceased companion walking, who had had her dream of traveling to the other side with her packets of chironji snatched from her.

To follow the path of a soul, one must walk at a soulful pace. Ma walked softly, gently.

When they reached Atari, a milestone stopped these small people the way the Mona Lisa arrests one in the Louvre. On the milestone was written the distance to Lahore: thirty kilometres. The road stretched out in both directions; on both sides.

The woman walks as though traversing an entire century with each step. Her daughter's hand in hers, leaning on her cane. The son watches from far off, somewhat restless somewhat ruffled, as if to ask, *What's left now but to turn about, get back in the car and set off for Amritsar?*

As there was heat in the sun, there was cool in the shade.

Spacious yards, as in factories.

What sort of factories are these? Were they here before? wondered one of the little people.

Plastic chairs by the side of the road, on which uniformed men dozed with one eye open. Some types of birds can fly long distances half-asleep and half-awake; they must have got their training from them.

Were they here before? asked some of the little people.

A policewoman assessed the women. What's in the handbag? What's in this packet?

Small folk pass through large halls. Interrogation after inquisition. Immigration halls, brand shiny new. No one here belongs to anyone else. One's own long since forgotten. The hall is huge. The people small. The queue long. Destitute poor. Shiny rich. Bundles atop heads. Faces snuffed of light. Polio pill? Yes, taken, see? Certificate. You have passport, visa, or no? Suspicion in the officers' eyes, right left turn stare turn stare.

The officials scratch their heads wondering what to examine and what to evaluate: bundles of photos. No sensitive photos? Of our nuclear facilities, parliament, army area? A bundle of letters. Man, these are ancient, take them, take them. Pictures of trees? What game is this? Bhai, explain why are you taking photographs of these trees? Are there no trees on that side? They don't get it, that relatives trees rocks, someone wants to see, someone wants to show. They scrape the rocks, flip the trees over and examine: What is hidden in these leaves, in these layers?

Not getting anything. What they are trained to see is not here. What is here, they are not trained to see.

He's taking manure? What to do?

Is it dry or moist?

Dry?

It should be properly packed.

Pack it properly in plastic. Should we let them take it or toss it?

Arre, you decide for yourself.

Go, Bhaiya, take your hobby with you.

Chironji seeds. Smuggling? Drugs? Both women seem beyond such possibilities.

And this?

The Buddha? Beti stares in astonishment. When had Ma packed it? Had she feared Bade would take it in our absence? He's hardly going to break into my home. This Buddha has become self-willed, it shows up of its own accord, whenever it feels like it. Does it seek its own niche in the tale? The examining officer picks it up and turns it about. Beti's face goes blank. The officer is young. The Buddha is ancient, accompanied by an eighty-year-old woman. The final layer of skin moulded over the final bit of bone. Sunken eyes. Ribs you can count. The young man begins to count them, then tires. He still has much to do, no time for games.

Please go and sit on the bus.

He lets them go.

And so they arrive at the gates; the gates between Hindustan and Pakistan. From Hindustan gate to Pakistan gate.

As the gates clang open, some walk slowly, some start running. The bus stops.

Some continue by foot. They walk along, drawing their laboured breathing from the harsh brilliance of the sun. They stop. Then walk again.

When Ma gets down from the bus, her eyes too bear the signs of being lost that is visible in those around them.

Border to what? Do we belong here or there?

There are rows of flowers; Ma bends down and dusts off a few petals. She gets the soil on her hand.

Some people have only come to see someone. An old woman from here runs and embraces a little girl from there, crying out, My granddaughter, my granddaughter! The little girl laughs at the old woman's tears. Where are we? She blinks. What does she know?

Short kurtas, long kurtas. Plain kurtas, embroidered kurtas, some wear pyjama-like shalwar pyjama, some wear shalwar-like pyjama.

One has come for a cassette. Bebe can't walk. So she's sent her voice. Give it to me. Give. I'll listen to it every day.

Kuku, who was the younger brother of Shamli Devi and used to be Paramjeet, has come from Mauja Kot Khalifa. Now he's called Karimulla and has a wrinkled face. Shamli's son, who has never seen his uncle, leaps up on seeing him approach and says, oh you've come! Standing at the Zero Line, the brother and sister ask a question of each other in curiosity or accusation and start when they realise they're both saying the same thing: Where have you been all these years? But repeating the words over and over doesn't elicit an answer. If you don't know, you don't know.

Sarabjeet Kaur has come as well. She throws back her orhni as she searches: Where is my little girl? Who is your little girl? Four-year-old Amrit Kaur. A sardarji had been sitting in a bus on that side. Sakina's daughter Masooma sat near him, came up and called him *Uncle* and touched him. What's this? Uncle looked, and realised that Sakina was Amrit Kaur. He went back to his home village, where there was a mother who stared at the stars every day, wondering, *which one is my little girl?* A star would fall, and she'd cup it in her palm like a firefly. That was Sarabjeet Kaur. *This is my little girl. This is the little girl of my little girl.*

The green and white clangs to a close. People are treated as cattle. Some push this way, some that.

The tiny woman gets off the bus with her daughter.

The Pakistani ambassador has sent a car to bring Ma and Beti to Lahore. Rahat Sahib greets them.

The tiny woman stands at the thing they call the border, on the other side, spinning slowly like the earth, wondering where to go: this way or which way? It's as though she'd started wearing her dervish-style attire just for this day. The clothing makes her spin too. Her daughter stops the spinning and turns her mother frontwards. Facing the road to Lahore. The road they're on is called the Grand Trunk Road. It comes this way and goes that way too.

The small woman sets out swiftly, as though she's racing with the street.

★

3

The artist Swaminathan made a bird.

His friend asked, So why a bird?

I must have seen it somewhere, remarked Swami absent-mindedly.

Why is it sitting on a cliff?

It must have found that place to sit, he replied in the same fashion.

Then all the world looked up at all the cliffs and imagined a bird perched upon them. And large cliffs began appearing all over the place, all over the world, and on them tiny dots or butterflies or flowerlike birds. Resting so gently they might tumble as you watched, but they didn't and won't tumble. Solid, hearty, smaller-than-small birds that no one would have noticed had Swami not seen one such bird somewhere, and had he not waved his brush, and if the world were not a stage.

This is how the performance begins. The bird and the cliff! A large cliff. A teeny bird. An about-to-crumble cliff and a butterfly-esque bird. Now what will happen, oho, what oh ah? A rock will fall. The bird will die. No no no. The rock will rise, the bird will sigh, catch a fish. The rock will melt, the bird will swim. Ahaaaaah.

Then why wouldn't Swami ji paint a fish in water? And so he did.

One day he rose. It occurred to him to choose a new colour that day. He stretched out the canvas on the floor because he wanted the water to spread and the bird to swim. He picked up the tubes of paint. Which shall I squeeze, cobalt blue or letterbox red? His hand had five fingers, as usual. Which were adept at pressing out colour. But he is Swami, not a machine. A human, even if Swami. It's a finger, not some button you can set at the exact speed and exact force you want, exactly directed. He accidentally pressed a bit too hard. Too much colour spurted from the *squishing*.

On that special day paint squirted out of the tube, like extra toothpaste oozing with childish glee, and ran amok all over the canvas with immense delight. Swami jerked his dhoti forward urgently like an anchal, as mothers do, and used it to blot the foam of the frothing colour, as though it were spilt milk. But softly, so as not to suffocate the fish.

Handloom dhoti, white in colour, thin black border, Mrignayani from Bhopal. He printed it onto the canvas for all eternity, and that very moment a whole new world arose with another story in it. A story which contains a rock and a bird and a fish and water and myriad wanderings on handloom-pressed worlds.

The tale unhampered. Ma unending. Women in new beginnings.

★

4.

The road observes two women alight upon its surface. And off they go.

The road has seen many stories pass along it. Some trample, some hop.

The road has traversed centuries, twisting and twirling like a river, wandering from this country to that. It has known the laughter of humans, understood their haste, seen many fearful sights that flow through its veins like blood. It must have been offended when so much dust rose up that the green of the trees gracing its edges could barely peek through the layers of brown and grey, and the waters of the nearby spring, in which fireflies twinkled on summer nights, flowed red, a reflection not of the rising and setting sun but of the bloodshed of days gone by.

Once upon a time, a riot had broken out amongst the caravans of refugees that passed along the road. And here's the thing about rioters: they celebrate beating killing screaming shrieking as though they're at festivals (like, imagine there's this guy in Gujarat: if you ask him, *So where are we going today*, he'd answer something like, *C'mon today let's drive over to the Sabar-mati River banks*, and his fishy eyes dart about obscenely, as he pulls apart a hapless couple like fish with a fork. And he chortles: *Let's have us some fun!* And that too is a kind of riot, embarked upon purely for sport.) Whether or not the street watched, so many riots occurred here that everything got confused: who was running to kill, who was running from the killers, who threatened, who pled for mercy, who was alive, who was dead. As when one human saw the swords, axes and spears charging forward to kill him, he hurriedly picked up a dead child lying in the street and swung it before him madly, like a shield, hoping to be spared himself.

All this was also not entirely clear, because the fleeing feet and wheels and hoofs stirred the dust until the scene swam by in a whirlwind. In the gloom of the gale, a father cut off his own daughter's head and a husband pulled the pestle from among the pots and pans on his wife's head and beat her to death. There was deception all around and large trunks yawned empty, whilst diamonds and pearls lay hidden in tiny bundles.

The road looked on in wonderment as one band tied jewellery, money, and sparkling buttons and bars of gold into a pouch and handed it to the children in an oxcart, and whispered to them to go and hide in that tree and stay there.

There were two of them, the children. They got out with their heads down and climbed into the tree. Into this tree. Maybe onto this branch. Maybe there were more leaves then. They weren't as dry and dusty then.

The road must have felt maternal towards them. It forgot all the others and just gazed upon the children. One child accidentally fell from a branch, and the street and the other child both screamed as one, but thankfully the sound was masked by the hubbub of the dust storm. The child jumped up and climbed back without even dusting himself off, as though a bear were coming for him.

Or as if he'd left his life on the branch. After stuffing his life back in, the child laughed at his own naughtiness. Or rather, he laughed, because to calm him, his elder brother had motioned to him, *don't cry, did you see that? Ha ha!*

By which he meant: two men in flight, lugging an ancient woman wrapped in a cloth and suspended from a stout pole, as though she were on a swing, so she could go swaying along as they ran. Or as though they were villagers who had killed a hyena and brought it back to the village hanging from a pole. The children must be forgiven for their laughter, as they were at the laughing playing age.

But when the two men flung the woman swinging from the pole onto the road and ran off, the children did not laugh.

For a long time, the children crouched in that very tree, meaning this very tree, holding on to one another. They shrank back as they watched, their innocent eyes not knowing or understanding what was unfolding along the road.

The road was of course a road. It hardly had the power to direct what went on. It continued to lie there, mute, but it too had veins, had age, felt emotions such as joy and sorrow. Its long form wound on continuously for a great distance—if you tapped on it many miles away, the sound would echo here. Because a street or road is a silver river. *The river of life*, as an English writer has dubbed it. And like a river, it has neither head nor tail. Where is its beginning, where is its ending? This too is a giddy confusion. If we stand at this end, then this is the beginning, and if we stand somewhere else, then it begins from there. And who's to stop it continuing on and on.

But such matters all precede the days of the bomb. At least back then it seemed as though the road would keep getting longer, would keep on twisting meandering moseying. Horses, camels, mules, feet, whoever, whatever, walked upon it, giving it a festive air. Shady trees line its banks, which are dotted along the way with ponds. And many inns where one could relax if one had travelled from afar. Sing, play music, if you wish, take a nap, fill your belly.

But please oh please, stop all this brawling and battling, this murder and mayhem. If you're going to stamp on me and kill me, I might get wounded too, and I do. And those two kids, how long will they dangle from that tree?

But the cries were not prepared to stop. Run here, run there, one on top of the other.

Amidst all the bloodshed, an extremely old man sat silent in the middle of the road, hands clasped in prayer. He was praying with the road: *Please, oh please, make it stop*, or perhaps he was sitting there dead, his hands lifted in prayer.

Just then the smaller child fell from the tree again. This time someone caught sight of him and ran towards him, weapon raised. Run*!* screamed the tree, and the child rushed hither and thither, and the bullets came *pow pow* but not one hit him. But as though his younger brother's life was his own, the elder jumped down from the tree as well, and ran after him screaming, Leave him alone, leave my brother alone. And now one bullet hit the younger brother and felled him. When the elder brother reached his side, another rioter lifted his knife to kill him, but just then the rioter that had shot the younger boy arrived as well.

Leave this one alone, he said.

Why? asked the man with the knife.

I'll take him, said the guy with the gun.

He scooped up the child. Where did he go? What happened? Who knows? But the road must have recognised

Rahat Sahib many years later when he came and collapsed under this very tree. The bullets were long gone, but his face was buried in the road. The road listened to his breathing and sobbing for a long time.

★

5

Who knows if the women noticed the road, or it noticed them, as they walked along with Rahat Sahib.

Rahat Sahib was fond of the road.

Come, let's take a stroll along the banks of the canal, he said. The weather's lovely, you'll feel refreshed.

Ma also enjoyed the road. Strolling beneath the trees, speaking of the twinkling of fireflies in the canal in days gone by.

Beti had to laugh: Amma had certainly learned well from Rosie; she seemed to know all about what had twinkled where. Such enthusiasm, and at her age! It made her own relative youth look weak. Beti laughed and thought she would tell KK, don't you think youth comes at the wrong time? When we haven't lived at all. It comes and then it's gone, and we don't even notice. It should come in old age. After we've had all our experiences. Then, we understand desire and enthusiasm. The finer points of youth bring joy. One understands.

Rahat Sahib was walking ahead with Ma when she leaned down and touched the road with her hand. Ma was so small that the road was quite close; that is, it rose to meet her. As if to say, *Here, go ahead, touch*, and she reached out a finger to touch it.

Ancient rock is not just stone. The souls of ancestors slumber within. The first human would have laid his hand upon it, and this sensation trembles in your finger when you touch it. You too feel like you are the first human, just recently created by God.

The women fell silent. They stopped for a moment. The small woman wiped the faces of the leaves that bowed down from the branches of the tree.

She didn't seem fatigued anymore. Rather, Beti suspected that Ma was drawing Rosie down into herself, now that she'd paid her debt and carried out the wishes of her dear departed caregiver-friend. She was getting filled with Rosie-power.

Rahat Sahib watched from the corner of his eye. He smiled. You don't look tired anymore. There's a spring in your step beneath these trees.

Filled with delight, he meant.

Have I become a mynah or sparrow that I should start hopping about? the small woman laughed.

It's Rosie, thought the bigger woman. She has brought you here. The bigger woman felt anxious. How had Rosie hypnotised Ma so that she continued to live on in her, even after her death? It was thanks to her that Ma was becoming un-Ma-ish. Mercurial. Got the notion of going to the most difficult country stuck in her head. *How alone I have become.*

A boat, Apa, a boat, you are becoming a boat. Drifting about as though this is no road, but a river. Swaying. This is why Kipling called it the River of Life in *Kim*.

Ah, you're just putting a kind spin on the vicissitudes of old age. Nothing more.

Then the road lurched. Or swayed. Ma twirled.

The road hopped. Ma hopped.

Ohohhohohohh, Beti grabbed her. Why are you walking like this? You're not even holding your cane properly.

Like a queen, said Rahat Sahib laughing lightly. On the Royal Road, the Sadak-e-Azam, the Shaah-Raah-e-Azam.

It's a very ancient road, said the growing-bigger woman, just because.

Very. Chandra Gupta Maurya repaired it; Sher Shah Suri lengthened it.

Amazing, all of history has melted into the surface of the road, said Beti, just because.

Rahat Sahib's eyes remained wise.

This road spans two thousand five hundred kilometres. It sees ahead and behind, he said.

Like serious eyes, that see both ahead and behind, said no one.

It sees countries that were, that are no longer. Caravans of refugees. Tongas, bullock carts, trucks…

Blood, smoke, glass, gold, pus, riots, refugees, dried fruit, and nuts.

Rahat Sahib's eyes see forward, and back too. He stops by a tree. A huge shady tree. Full of many birds: as many as there are inhabitants in the two countries. The light of the sun filtering through the network of leaves and branches. Above the network, the Lahori sky. He looks with seriousness as though wishing to know where to throw the net.

Lahore's rising sun sparkles in his eyes.

He places a hand on Beti's head. You belong to a different generation.

Ma begins to tell Rahat Sahib some names and addresses.

Rosie took care of all the arrangements, thought Beti, standing apart; or finding herself apart. She begins to read what is written on the nearby signpost: *Lahore-Delhi Road.*

The road knows no restrictions; whether it goes this way or that, it needn't go through the bother of visas, says Rahat Sahib.

Everyone starts laughing. What else can they do?

★

6.

And Amma was in a hurry to visit Lahore. When she said, we'll visit the Inner City, Beti again marvelled at how well Rosie had taught her before sending her here. There was now a light chill in the air even during the day. Ma wore a shawl over her embroidered abaya. After having a nice breakfast with tea on the lawn at Faletti's, the three of them set out. We'll see the city, said Ma. Then she produced an address: We'll go there too, to deliver the chironji.

As Rahat Sahib showed them around Lahore, he told them about all the sights. We'll go wherever you wish; the car is yours. Lahore is yours.

He enjoyed Ma taking them from place to place and crying out like an eager tourist, let's see this, let's do this. We'll climb the minaret of Vazir Khan Mosque and look at the view. Amma climbed up, huffing and pausing, and beheld Lahore outspread below.

She used to look, she said, as though lost in memory.

She died, poor thing, said Beti, thinking of Rosie as well, and took a picture with her mobile.

We'll see Lahore Fort, she liked wandering there, said Ma. They saw it. We'll see Badshahi Mosque. They saw it. We'll go to the Ravi. They went. How it has dried up, said Ma, as though speaking of an old acquaintance. Lahore is green, but where has the water gone? she mused. She used to come here often, she said, as though remembering.

This too must be a quality of friendship forged in old age. And with whomever it is forged, be it human or jinn or animal, one feels pleasure only in that friend's company, and even after that company no longer remains, the pleasure lives on. Thus did Beti keep up a continuous train of pop psychology musings. *Okay, so this is what they were chattering about as they sat on the balcony of my home and at the tomb across the way, Ma and Rosie. They were cooking up a Pakistani kichadaa. Rosie would tantalise Ma with her knowledge and tell her, I'll take you with me, and you'll see this, I'll show you that. When Ma came to my home she began to dream new dreams, she began to think, Yes! I will go to Pakistan. Now Rosie is no more, so I'll take Ma; I'll show her what Rosie would have shown her. But our Amma sure has done her homework, she's memorised the whole list of things that must be seen.*

Amma said, we'll go to Montgomery Hall. And she learned it had become a library and was now called Quaid-e-Azam Hall. Then she said, where is Lawrence Garden? And Tollinton Market?

Then let's go to Mochi Darwaza and Mochi Bagh.

Then, oh, my, how has this dried up so?

Rosie must have told her it was lovely and green.

This is where the political leaders give their speeches and the children play cricket, but there are some attempts to make it into a park, said Rahat Sahib.

The shops too: it seemed there were shops on her Rosie list which they absolutely must visit. They looked the same as on our side, as did the goods: dried fruit, plastic containers and bottles, spicy foods, everything you find in Karol Bagh or

Chandni Chowk. But within Ma is Rosie, and through their four eyes, all is new, unique.

Then she said, We'll get khatais from that store, they make great ones.

Marching to the beat of Rosie's experiences. Each aspiration, each thrill is redolent with Rosie. Each step fulfils a desire left behind.

Now Beti watches with curiosity: it is as if Ma has turned into Rosie herself, who is now showing us, and Rahat Sahib too, the city of Lahore! Now Ma is walking ahead, the two of them behind. The *tock tock* of her cane. Rosie whispers into Ma's ear: *Now turn right, now left*, and Ma turns.

Cycles, scooters, the coming and going of beggars too, and amidst all these, Beti and Rahat Sahib under the leadership of Ma.

In Anarkali Ma says, she bought everything from Bano Bazaar. When they reach there she says, I don't remember exactly.

How much is a person supposed to remember of what they've been told, what they've heard? No problem, Beti consoled her. Let's go.

Yes, let's go, said Ma, agreeing to drink tea at a dhaba. They must drink tea at a dhaba in the corner in Anarkali. She used to drink tea here, she said. She must be pushing herself to remember what Rosie told her, that's why she's examining the whole area.

That dhaba, she points. Had she recognised it, or decided that must be the one?

She and Rahat discuss things. Names and addresses written on paper reemerge. Beti is surveying the gloss and gleam of Anarkali, she's already checked out a few shops herself, bought herself a pair of sandals, some jewellery, a chenille suit, an ashtray for KK, some ornate candle sticks, and a carved hook for hanging your keys. She hears the words, *Delhi Gate. Surjan Singh Gali.*

How fortunate is Rosie! She wanted to give someone some chironji, couldn't do it, and beneficent Ma took it upon her own shoulders. And I took Ma on mine. Let's go, can't be that hard. Even though Rosie is in it as well, I'm the one making it happen.

Tussi us paar taun aaye. You've come from that side, the shopkeeper says in Punjabi. He serves them free pakoras.

★

7.

When they arrived in Surjan Singh Gali, Beti notices Ma's eyes shut tight. She stands still at Delhi Gate. If you want to look at a map etched in your mind's eye, you must close your eyes. Or if you need to consult with the spirit that has journeyed by your side. Ma is talking to Rosie, though it looks like she's just talking to herself: Is it to the left? Shahi Hammam. The bazaar is up ahead. The men sipping tea from china saucers in the gali. They walk on ahead slowly. Old tumble-down homes, naked wires hang suspended. Above, the tangle of wires; below, the tangle of lanes. Pigeons fly. Cats appear. Ma keeps talking, as though explaining to the spirit where it is, what it is. Inlaid; etched. If the spirit agrees, take the next step.

A full about-turn. Advancing slowly into the gali, whispering with Rosie. What must the people of the gali think, the woman come from that side talking to herself.

Beti is about to interrupt, but Rahat Sahib motions to walk on quietly. As though it were normal to come across and chatter with a ghost. To become one from two.

The kite store, Ma says, and points as though she knows everything. Where's the tree?

Tree? What tree? In these narrow lanes? Where you can hardly walk single file? Your elbow catches here, your foot slips into the drain there.

Tree, Amma?

The tree with the sindoor on it.

Rosie, Rosie, Beti wants to feel angry, but why waste anger on the dead? And yet, what had Rosie been teaching Ma? Looking for sindoor? Here?

She asks this one, asks that one. Ma does. Rahat Sahib doesn't lose patience: she's come from that side, she's a guest.

Someone said, the Shia one? The Nauchandi Jummerat one?

Truly there was a tree with red tikas stuck to it. So was Rosie Shia? Beti had never been able to tell.

Ma stood there looking all about like a madwoman. Then she said, I can't find it, let's go back to Delhi Gate.

What wasn't she finding? The addresses Rosie had given? But those were written down. Just show them to someone and they'll send us there. Or is she looking for some other tourist spot now? Does she want to see absolutely everything? But why like this? Why the searching with a retinue?

Rahat Sahib brought them back to Delhi Gate. Ma stood again examining all around and then said, Don't go that way, go this way, toward that lane with the tree. Then she walked along slowly and carefully. Look at this, then this, she said, speaking to herself, or to Rosie.

Ma, the engine of the train, the other two compartments bringing up the rear.

Now Ma began to walk with her eyes closed. As though it would somehow be clearer that way.

Arre, does anyone even walk like this? Amma! Beti blurted out. Rahat Sahib pulled her back.

Ma in front, eyes closed, swerves, turning about, then left again. The two of them in the rear.

Shutting off *now*, unfolding memory.

Ma stopped at a flowing drain. It didn't look dirty, but it was a drain after all. Here Ma opened her eyes and watched the water a long time. She patted her body and her hand travelled down and stopped between her legs. Softly, she murmured, she used to pee in this drain when she was small and it wouldn't stop.

A woman among men, pressing her hand between her legs, standing heedless beneath the Lahore sky, come from that side.

★

Beti's ears felt hot. What sort of things had Rosie been telling Ma? She guided Ma's hand away.

Ma freed her hands and gazed off into the distance, into the galis and lanes, as though she could see far off. She had a vague look about her, as though she'd become a two-headed river, like Rosie, that can flow both this way and that. This was the moment when the two streams met. A moment stilled in time. Creating a border.

She decided to enter. The very narrowest lane. The walls on each side so narrow they reached out and grasped their elbows. What need for a cane here? Ma handed it to Beti. Nor any need to keep one's eyes open. So she closed them again. And kept them closed.

Standing waiting. The two behind her waiting as well. Touching the walls with her hands, as if to judge: is it rough and gritty to the touch like Rosie had said it was; and to feel reassured. Same wall, right? Yes.

Ma began to walk, eyes closed, hands touching the gali wall. As though she'd entrusted herself to the lane, which was leading her by the hand wherever it pleased.

And it carried her along. The wall grew older as they moved on. In one place there was a hole the size of a small window. Ma reached inside, then stuck her head in as well. Halting there. Without opening her eyes. There was also a hole in the ceiling on the other side. So that if you rolled from above, you wouldn't fall, you'd get stuck half up, half down. Over this lay a tarpaulin that Ma saw when she half opened her eyes. Still? She asked, addressing the hole in the ceiling.

And quickly she shut her eyes so that all that appeared before them would not be extinguished.

Ma stood there a few instants as though returning to a dream. But the way she moved suddenly; as though her feet had forgotten to walk and were moving in all directions. First move one, then another, not like that. Instead, both lifted at once to move forward together. As if fearing that one might be left behind, that if their connection broke for even a second and one went alone, the other would go. Like one life in two bodies.

Ma ahead, hopping or running. Where the wall ended in stairs and a small red stoop.

Amma, Beti tried to leap forward and snatch her up, fearing she might trip, but this time Rahat Sahib pulled her back by the shoulders quite sternly; she stared steadily at him with surprise.

Ma hopped up the steps in that same way, lifting both feet at once in a state of excitement. Stepped up to the red threshold and stood at the door.

A stout old door, green in colour, etched with network of cracks, fastened with a heavy iron chain.

And this is her maternal home, exclaimed Ma, but in a whisper.

The nameplate was not visible on the door, but there was a board fastened to it, on which it was written in Urdu, cricket equipment available here. Ma read out the words, and rattled the chain against the door.

The chain rattled this side, and at that same moment, an old man emerged from a small building on the other side of the lane. A one-hundred-year-old man. Long beard, spiderwebbed eyes.

Daktariyane da pind, from the doctor's family, he said gazing at the woman clasping the door chain. Daktariyane de aa gae, doctor's daughter is here! he shouted to the gali. Climbing two steps, he placed a hand on Ma's head as she stood on the red stoop.

At which the hairpins fell from her bun and her hair tumbled down, and people began emerging into the gali from every direction to pick up the pins, carefully, one by one.

★

8.

Many years ago, there was a painter named Bhupen Khakkar. He told stories with a brush. About women, although for himself he preferred men. He gave them feminine attire and manners. He knew that a story cannot be locked into a box, or a canvas, or a gaze. So he never tried. On the contrary he always left a small window, an empty space, so the story could move on at will and take another path if it so desired.

Because stories never end. They jump through windows and cracks or other such openings, or create them by shaking, causing the earth to quake. From Bhupen's unspoken unwritten unfilled space. Where do they go? This isn't immediately clear, either. Vanished. Unfettered, unworried. Customs thrown to the winds. Crossing borders. Like Ma. Over and over. Now with Beti, spanning boundaries. Arisen from samadhi.

Religious fanatics and governments do not care for samadhis, nor stories, nor Bhupen Khakkar. They like to shut them all up. In files, boxes, trunks. Imprisoned not just over bribes or other dishonesties. Imprisoned over stories too, especially if they're about women. If they don't move, so much the better. Make a grave, and that too, the sort that will never burst open. Make sure to put women in there, so their shine will dull, their colour fade, their skin wrinkle, their bones dissolve. Their fragrance waft away.

The fanatic does not allow the lid to be pushed aside because the women's flaunted fragrance is unacceptable to them.

But they are not gods, thankfully. Although in another story by Paul Zacharaiah, even God, who can do anything and everything, goes and sits before Babuka, the great artist, accepting defeat, and begs of him, teach me as well, teach me your music. This is the triumph of art which exists in music and in stories and lies outside the reach of God.

So even lids get knocked off. The perfume sways and the rising wave wafts up the image and the story takes off on a new path. Just as Europa arose from churning waters, just as the Himalayas rose, so too arises the story from the churning sand. New marks are scratched into old sand. Shapes form. Boundaries are erased.

The winds wander like tales. No one can stop them. They can't be suppressed by lids or shut up in boxes. The winds don't recognise such things as visas. Like stories, they flex and stretch. Is it wind or fire? Or smoke? Or fragrance? Its elements are not such that they can be cut into bits and stuffed into a box bed like Rosie.

And did Rosie even stay shut up?

She has arisen, walks ahead of Ma and behind Beti.

So a story is just so.

So there once was a king and there once was a queen. Both died. End of story. What does it mean?

The little boy bursts out laughing.

And there once was a king.

There once was a queen and so and so and so.

The little girl laughs: There must be more to the story!

Once there was a Rosie, and once there was a Baji.

He picks up the brush. The brush fills the canvas with colour. Then all the Bhupens stop. One portion of the canvas is unfinished; the colour ends in a muddle: how will he spread it? What else will it do? It is silent for the moment. It will jump, it will cross over, the story will not end.

★

9

But where is Rosie? Right now it's all Baji, and we've lost our *baazi*—our turn!

If you've been seeing something a certain way all along, and then it turns out you were seeing back-to-front, you get angry. As though a question mark has been placed on the accuracy of your perception. Wherever we thought we saw Rosie, Ma was there. We were the ones who created Rosie's ghost and saw only her. Whilst she wasn't there at all, it was all Ma. At Vazir Khan's tomb, at the drain, at the green door, on the red stoop.

The balance of life gets distorted. Who tied a cloth across our eyes, who babbled on and on, who is this woman? She reads Urdu, and says things like, the name of our Lahore station used to be written in four scripts, Urdu, Gurumukhi, Hindi, English.

Amma, you told a lie, accuses Beti, in their room at Faletti's.

No.

You said *she* did all this and all that...

And she did.

Rosie did...

No, *she*, the one who left here. Me. *She* was me.

★

10

Ma walked past, ignoring the person opening the green door, and slipped into the house declaring hora changi tarah laga de —lock up properly—in Punjabi, and began drinking in the home with her eyes, taking long sips, in the company of the elderly man. She blinked in slow motion. Her eyes seemed to close for an age, then open for an age. The people who had poured into the lane, one by one, gathered behind her and the one-hundred-year-old man. So many, one couldn't tell who had come from inside the house and who had come from outside.

Ma looked up. As did the entire group.

Goodness! Her mouth opened wide and she clapped a hand over it. Did the upper storeys collapse?

Everyone stared.

There used to be five storeys, she explained, then the roof. Look at that, even the second storey is broken.

No, there are still some rooms there. The boy that said this —had he come from outside or in?

You climb the stairs; then there's another entryway. Over here is the room where the metal trunks were kept, she said. The trunk room. There were quilts, mattresses, blankets, and sheets in it. Plates, ladles, bowls, notebooks, photos, binoculars.

This was her grandfather's room. She called him Taya. He used to play carom here. Everyone called her ghaseeta maar, because she dragged and pushed the pieces with her thumb.

The bathroom was here. Just one faucet. Not this geyser, nor this shower.

Above is the next storey. Ma began to climb upwards, and the neighbourhood folk and those who lived there followed. Avoiding the electrical wires dangling along the walls, tangled in old cobwebs.

The sitting room upstairs, Ma said as she entered. And this. Green woodwork. She showed them the green room. On the windows, red–blue–yellow panes; that's why it was called the colour room.

From here, she could see her classmate, Kausar. Then she'd go downstairs and leave with her in a horse carriage to go to their dilruba lesson. They also rode cycles. Raleigh Cycles. They went to study together.

This is the pillar room. Ma, the guide. They prayed here. The pillars are broken, she pointed out.

Across from here, Uncle's room. It's gone, she told them.

Above: the bedrooms. The iron grille is gone. From there she could see who had come home. Was Kausar alone or was she with her brother?

From above, throw down a basket. For purchases, fruit and vegetables. Eggs one anna a dozen. Two large loaves of bread for an anna. Four annas for a seer of fish. Four annas for a seer of meat. Raw. Six annas for cooked. Pai, how much for the rasgullas? Mai, one for one anna.

There was also a room on the roof. Did it fly away? This said somewhat accusingly; Ma turned to the assembled group.

That's where she studied. With Kausar, with Anwar. Their father was an English professor.

They'd come out on the roof; they were at the nonstop chatting age.

I was making phulkas. Taya told me to run up and hide on the roof. I'd fired up the hearth, the roti was on the pan. There was a commotion; he said, Jump up, get out. The doors fell, the stairs wobbled. Taya cried out, go, go. The house was on fire.

The house survived, Ma said calmly. I will tell him, the fire went out.

Let's go downstairs.

Everyone began walking down. Where all the cricket equipment was lined up. Bats, balls, pads, wickets, caps, all wrapped in plastic. For sale.

Uncle's dispensary. Over there he checked people's glasses prescriptions.

Her uncle, Ma told the people. Was an eye doctor. Khaki pants, yellow checked shirt. His compounder wore a Pathani shalwar and crested turban.

Someone pulled up an easy chair for Ma. She sat down.

She would sit with him here. She was sixteen. She was reading the Tribune. Uncle checked Anwar's eyes.

It cost five rupees. Read the line. *Lahore*, he read. But he couldn't see four or six. You need glasses, you're nearsighted. Such glasses will never break, will last your whole life. Thick glass, black frames, a rounded bow fit over the ears. Whenever he'd start winning at carom, she and Kausar would tease, Hey it's those ridiculous glasses, you see twice as well. Cheating. He'd put the glasses in his pocket and hit a piece again.

Tea came for Ma.

The green wooden door was open. Children, old people, youth, all gathered. Cricket equipment was written on the door, and the inside was indeed full of cricket equipment. The elderly man sat with her; if anyone could have understood the conversations that went on between them, they really ought to have written it down. Long. Tangled, without beginning or end. Like the people gathered in that green wooden Lahori house, who could tell whose words were from inside and whose were from outside?

Gurdaspur, Hoshiarpur…Layalpur…Duska…Duska is one hundred kilometres from Lahore…we were in Maja Kot Khalifa…my sister in Rajpura, Patiala…yes, yes I remember Sheikhupura well…talking to Gujranwala every day by phone…Shakargarh destroyed…he, ji, is doing business in Sutarmandi…may you live long, son…don't ask about Sabeeha, this kameez she sent, I'll die in it…Katra Munshiyan went to Ludhiana…Bhayyaji, Khalu, Mamu, Doctor Chacha gone…come to our home it's your home, stay with us…God be with you, this must be your daughter…come.

Hands on Beti's head, caressing, soft and still on the head in blessing.

Now it's so, each one is wherever they have ended up, said the one-hundred-year-old man.

Why are you people crying? asked Ma, laughing.

★

11

Sir, her daughter had started to get angry.

At what?

This was a phone conversation between Rahat Sahib and the Pakistani Ambassador, seated in Delhi. Menacing flames crackled through the wires from one direction; from the other bubbled a weak, whimpering whisper.

About chironji.

What am I asking you? You're chewing chironji.

No, sir, that was for the hijras to eat.

Huh? Such sparks flew through the wire that Rahat Sahib was nearly electrocuted.

She brought it for some hijra group.

Hijras? Since when do such topics arise in our governmental department?

Sir, the two of them were talking about it. They were saying, Let's go now.

To the hijras?

No, home. They had to go home.

Then you should say that they returned.

No, Sir. The daughter said, Let's go home, and the mother said, Yes, we'll go home. That's all I know.

So they came back here, that's what you mean, right? The Ambassador was sitting on the here side, that's why he said *here* for *there*.

No, Sir. She was talking about going to her home over *here*: this side, Rahat Sahib explained.

What the hell are you talking about? I know where their home is.

Sir, she said the home of her shauhar, her husband.

Her husband's home is *here*.

Sir, she's saying it's *here*.

Have you lost your mind?

No, Sir, it's the two women from India. They're the ones who are lost.

You were given a responsibility! Where were you? growled the Ambassador. What am I supposed to say?

Sir, I had a Karachi booking made, I personally got on board the flight and seated them there! My men over there took them to the hotel. Then...

Then? The phone wire throbbed like a palpitating heart.

Sir, something happened at Mohatta Nagar, that's what we've learned. Something about going to see the Chief Engineer in the sugar factory.

Will you say something more? The wire wobbled.

They said something about Hinglaj. About how there's sea there, and desert.

Now you're trying to teach me Pakistani geography?

No, Sir, what I'm trying to tell you is...

...is what?

Sir, they didn't have a visa, so our guy advised them not to go. He said, please stay here, and that he would talk to me and arrange for a visa. But they didn't stay.

Without a visa? The wire, enflamed. You know what you're saying?

Begum Sahiba said that she was from here, she didn't believe in the restrictions of visas.

And you don't either? sizzled the wire.

No, Sir, of course I do. The wire drooped. But they didn't agree.

Do you have your head on straight?

Sir, I'm afraid. It's just that Apa, the younger of the two women…

Put out an All Points Alert to search every corner of Sindh. But there shouldn't be any drama. Do it discretely. You know the infighting between governments here. If they find out what's up, there'll be a furore; they're our guests—please take care. Find out what's going on *carefully* and send out descriptions of both ladies and find them before word gets out in the two countries that they're wandering about without a visa.

Yes, yes, Sir, I'll see to it myself. No one will know of it, only us, wherever they went, in the desert, the sea, which country.

What the heck are you on about? You know perfectly well this has been a headache for both countries, that neither has been able to figure out to this day who has the right to live where, who belongs where, and whom the law favours.

★

12

Someone said they'd been seen in Mithi. Someone else said there'd been a sighting in Mirpur Khas. But the women were still missing.

An alert went out along the way, and perhaps didn't stay as secret as desired: If you see any sign of two women, one small, one big, from the other side of the border, in the Thar Desert, please inform the nearest police station.

The most concrete bit of news that came in was that a tire puncture had been fixed for a private vehicle in one place, and that two women deep in a dispute of some kind had got out of the car and hovered at a distance like twin shadows.

But how should I have known there was a search out for them? asked the lad at the garage. It was hardly written on their faces that they were foreigners. Even looked like my great aunt!

Both of them?

No, all three.

What three? Where did three come from?

The two Indians, plus my aunt; that makes three, yes?

Ass. Why wouldn't your aunt look like your aunt?

All three look like her, that's what I'm saying.

Whatever. Now tell me this, what were they saying?

How should I know, Sir? The boy dusted off his grimy clothing and fell into a sullen silence, as if to say, here I am giving testimony and you're giving me a scolding. No wonder everyone avoids government folk.

The mechanic standing nearby said, oh, you're searching for them? I overheard them talking.

How did you hear them?

Sir, I was in the bushes over there on personal business.

Where they were standing?

Yes, I was already there. I couldn't come out in the middle, so I stayed in there.

Fine, tell us what you heard.

Sir, they wore woollen shawls. It was cold. They seemed like a mother and daughter. I saw that…

I'm asking what you *heard,* not what you saw.

Sir. Yes, they were searching for someone. They were mentioning someone's name. Little Someone. Or Junior. Kausar. Shauhar—husband. Anwar. They were arguing.

Arguing? asked the man who'd come to sleuth.

The mechanic wore jeans; one leg was rolled up to the knee, making him look every inch a film hero. He also revealed that he was a huge cinema fan, a devotee of Amitabh Bachchan.

Sir, I was about to stand up, how could I have known I should pay especial attention to their words? If I'd known, I'd have written them down. See this, I keep a notebook in my pocket, sir. He grinned. I take down the lyrics of film songs and hum them, and that's why everyone says Imtiaz—that's me —is a cheerful chap. He turned a page and began, So this is Amitabh Bachchan's *Sala Main to Sahib Ban Gaya.*

Dilip Kumar.

Sir?

Who sang this one?

Probably Rafi or Kishore. The mechanic was a bit uncertain.

It was Dilip Kumar.

He sang it?

In the film, someone explained.

Oh. He understood. Oh. He scratched his head. Oh yes, I misspoke, sir. What I meant was *Khaike Paan Banaras Wala*.

The Very Important Official glared at his underling so menacingly that the latter quickly stiffened and spoke sharply to the mechanic: We're not here for a lecture on the films of their country. We've come to capture their women. They were not singing these songs, I trust? So then?

No, sir. The bigger one was angry.

Meaning what?

She was getting angry and asking, How long must we wander from door to door, or maybe floor to floor, or car to car, or Thar to Thar? And she yelled, I think the daughter to the mother, You've completely forgotten that you came here to deliver shatraonji or did she say kalaunji or was it chironji? Sir, it was clear they had come to deliver something. That we have already done, Rahat Sahib already delivered it, the smaller lady said. The mechanic spoke loud and high, to imitate Ma's response.

And? The officers asked trying to piece together the information.

That's it.

The mechanic couldn't decide what bits from film dialogues to bring into play next.

He went on: You are forgetting. *I remember well*. You are telling it wrong. *No, right*.

Then the two of them got into the car and drove away. I didn't read the plate number, forgive me, sir, I was in a hurry to get out of the shrub.

The people who had come to make inquiries were not interested in the mechanic and his shrub. They didn't need to know whether he ever got out or stayed in there indefinitely. They were there to hunt out two foreign women who looked like they were from around here, and to do so as discreetly as possible.

But even a small amount of fire will send up smoke. The smoke reached some other administrative departments, and then the story circulated that two women, one small, one big, have slipped into our country without a visa on the pretext of searching for some *sarvar anwar shauhar kausar*, and that nowadays innocent-looking women, even little girls and old ladies, are sent in for the purposes of spying and terrorism. This *Rosie*, this *shatraunji kalaunji* this *door-floor-thar*, they could all be codes for some dangerous undercover operation.

But beyond this, they found no trace of them. Just the Thar. And stillness.

★

13

The Thar, which is a desert. Silence, which is its voice. Devoid of noise or crowds; filled with echoes. Empty, meaning free. Desert, meaning sand. Thus memories came to the poet Faiz in the night:

> *Jaise virane men chupke se bahaar aa jaye*
> *Jaise sehraon men hauli se chale baad e Naseem*
> *Jaise bimaar ko bevajah qaraar aa jaaye*
> *As when spring arrives quietly in the wilderness*
> *As when a gentle breeze wafts over the desert*
> *As when the invalid feels soothed for no reason*

It is night. The moon is full. Night shimmering in moonlight. The sand was once an ocean. Spiny shrubs cast shadows over the sand. Towering dunes. Some as high as four- or five-hundred feet. The dunes shift. The roots of the shrubs and their tangled twigs peek out from the sand as though eager to gambol in the moonlight.

A gorgeous sight, a silent scene, two women in their own world and no one to witness, no historian to see and note down what is happening.

But.

This thing about noting down. When such companionship exists in the sand there's no need for historian or witness. The butterfly floats up to tell the tale. The particles of sand band together, the breeze blows gently, the moon flickers as if reflected on glass, the woman says, *Stop*. She gets out of the car and sits in the sand, becoming a sand shadow.

Her hands folded over the cane, she sits in the desert, and, oh, see, one of the butterflies painted on the cane flutters up slowly and alights on her hands. Lightly, between the woman's fingers, so lightly, like a dream or fancy.

The butterfly is black, its outspread wings dotted with white, which turn to lines in flight. Quietly fluttering open, it stares unblinking at the woman as it listens to her story.

The woman narrates in a flat tone. The butterfly listens, and to hear one does not need an ear but a soul, and thus it flutt flutt flutters now and again throughout the tale.

And with each flutter, a grain of sand floats up, invisible to the naked eye.

The words emerging from the mouth of the woman sitting completely still. Her fingers on the handle of the cane. Between them, a butterfly. The Thar all around.

The butterfly listens quietly to the woman's tale.

As she narrates. Then stops. Then starts again.

The First Tale: Tales

Chapati on the pan, hearth lit. She is on the roof. *Crash crash, knock knock*. Footsteps chasing her. *Uncle, uncle!* She calls her grandfather uncle. A man appears, his face masked by a strip of fabric. He seizes her, grabs her. Pulls. *Uncle!* Chapati. Smoke from the kitchen. *The house will burn down…*

She—like a sack. The masked man wrapped in a niqab, dragging her along. *Drag drag.* She is being dragged down the lane. *Bump bump.* Leaving her home behind.

Fire in the neighbourhood. Smoke. Coughing. Down the lane. *Drag drag.* One of her slippers breaks. It had been new. It had pressed against her big toe. *Wear daily. They'll soften up. An hour. Or two.* The nail of the toe presses further and further into the flesh. She'd planned to cut it, to pull it slowly away from the flesh.

Sky. Spin. Birds.

A tin of food thrown open, its contents scattered about the street. She is smeared in the gravy. Spicy gravy grinds into her wounded toe.

Homes, in flames. Dark shadows dance in the fire. Leaping out. Someone leaps out. Is picked up and tossed back. A potato into the tandoor oven.

Aunty. Aunty, Aunty! Jaddan Phuphi's shop. Jaddan Phuphi was everyone's aunty. *Help, Aunty, the chapati's on the pan! Oh dear, I've set the house on fire! Ashes. Aunty, Uncle, Uncle!* she screams. Coughs. Scrunching her eyes

Her hair is caught. On something pointy. Pulled from her scalp. The man in the niqab gives her a jerk. Pulls her. Blood.

A dog turns tail. Whimpers.

She knocks into burnt, brutalised bodies. Corpses. Or live bundles.

Anwar, Anwar! Anwar has gone to Lyallpur City. To look for a house. Then he's going to take her there with him. Until then she'd been left with her maternal grandparents.

Before the wedding she'd been to Lyallpur. Once. During college. Cinema hall in a tent. Stools and benches. *Maya's Town —Maya ki Nagari.* Film.

Kill kill kill!

Girls alive.
Screams.

Oh, bhabo ji, oh, bhapa ji!

Shoes and sandals: puffing huffing fleeing.
An overturned tonga. Was there a horse?
Someone's earring. Glasses. A crushed skull. Tossed against the wall like a watermelon. Brains and a single eye, popped out like a spring.
Dragged on and on.
Lifts her. Throws her down. Truck. Or what? One or two more masked men. In the truck, girls. Like her: sixteen. Seventeen. Eighteen. Weeping. Snivelling. One on top of another. Sheep goats. Insects. She bites a hand. The masked man slaps her. Terrifying eyes. Bloodshot. A lump on his forehead. Skin parched black like he got burnt dragging her through the fires.
Darkness. A tarp thrown over them. They are buried beneath. The girls scream. Clawing. Sink beneath the tarp. Darkness. Heavy things fall onto the tarp, *thud thud*. The girls beneath. Suffocating, suppressed. Dying. Unconscious. Some crying. Some silent. Blind. She too.
Noise. Or quiet.
Memory. Or guessing.
The truck stops. The masked men jump down. Pulling, pulling, pulling the girls down. Weeping. Silent. *I did nothing.*

Let go. Oh, God! Where are you taking me? Amma! Bappa! Big Brother? You? Your khala will not forgive you!

A graveyard. An open grave. New. Or broken. She tumbles in. Lies still. She'll run away. The one with the lump jumps in after her. Grabs her. Throws her. Pain. No memory.

Yes, pain. She remembers her toenail. She'd never got around to trimming it. It was growing inward, cutting into the flesh. How to remove it? It's begun to fill with pus.

He kicks. A door opens. A tiny room. In the cemetery. Girls stuffed in. Terrified. They threaten them. Shove them in. Choc-a-block. Like cattle. The door is locked. Darkness. Sobs. Be quiet. Tears. Blood. Sweat. Urine. Stink. Must've been, don't remember.

Day or night? How many days, how many nights? Who was alert enough to count?

Now loaded onto an open truck. She stands up. An open street. No wells to be seen to jump in. Two masked men behind her. She's shoved forward and made to sit. She falls.

Where will you take us? What will you do with us? Anwar! Where will you search for me?

Desolation.

A white sun.

A well, a well, her heart sobs. You can't die just by wishing it. Not by saying it either.

Wear two shalwars. That was Ma'am's instruction to us girls. Double shalwar left behind. Back home.

When they had snuck into her home, was she wearing one or two shalwars?

The chapati burned. The fire spread. I set my house on fire. Sobs. No wells anywhere.

How many days? How many nights? Locked up who knows where. Then loaded onto the truck again. Locked up again. Then the truck. The same one, or another. Who knows? Same set of girls, who knows? How many are there? Loads.

At some point in a tonga. Pressed down beneath the feet of lump-head and the tonga driver. Covered in something. And the other girls? Who knows.

Half a piece of toast. Sometimes some food and water. Sometimes only food. Sometimes only water. Some dates. Some chana. Four anna's worth of qeema, one anna's worth of chapati. *If only we had poison!*

She hears of riots. Of refugees. Thoughts shutting down. Speech shutting down. *Anwar. Uncle. If I see a well, I'll make a break for it.*

The girls are so quiet now. Someone says, *They're going to whore us out.* Someone says, *They're going to pounce on us.* Then silence. They sit clutching one another's hands, and sometimes keep apart.

The truck has changed. A military truck, kenkda. All stuffed in. New girls too, maybe. All girls. Why only girls? The fate of girls is rotten.

In a pen with cows and buffalo. With animals. Straw, cow dung, lowing.

At one point, in an old ruin of a fort. *If only I could jump from somewhere high and take my life.*

Slam on the brakes. Sudden. The girls all tumble on top of one another. The truck stops. Everyone is taken out single file. Inside. More girls. All locked up, prisoners. In a convent.

Abandoned. A bathroom. First time. But ransacked. Shouted at. Handed soap and clothing. Bathe. They bathe.

Hospitality for sheep on their way to slaughter. *Why don't they give us poison? Oh, God! Oh, Lord!* The girls grab hands and form a circle, quietly.

She tears at the sleeve of her old kurta to make a bandage; wraps it around the wound on her toe. Limping.

For the first time, a large place. A large prison. She wanders about the rooms in disarray. Limping. There was an idol in one room, a Buddha. She'd seen one such in the museum. With Anwar. Anwar must have put it here, to give her courage. A sign from Anwar. It was small—five inches or less. That ancient Buddha. *Anwar, where are you? How will you know I am here?*

She picks up the Buddha and holds it to her chest. She keeps it with her, sleeping and waking. *What need to die? I already have.* But she holds on to the Buddha. *Our last rites will be together. This will go wherever I do. This is a sign. This is Anwar. This is solace to my drowned heart. This is my compassionate stone-hearted one.*

★

14

The woman had stopped. The butterfly slipped back onto the cane. After leaving Karachi their driver had continued to ask search drive. When she'd seen the desert, the woman had again asked to stop the car. She sat down again in the same manner. Fingers wrapped around the cane handle. A butterfly slipped out when it saw her mood, and sat between two of her fingers like a fancy. But this time the butterfly was dark red with black stripes. On each side, two dots opened like eyes and the rise of its wings protruded like ears.

The woman began telling the second tale and the second butterfly sat perched before her, eyes open, ears alert. It listened, and it saw.

The Second Tale: The Buddha and the Girl

Bullets flew nearby. The roar of a heavy vehicle. A truck. Footsteps. An argument. Loud voices. The back gate screeched open. Girls crouched. Grabbed one another's hands and sat pressed against the wall. She hid the Buddha in her dupatta, pressed to her chest. *Anwar, Anwar,* she thought, fear rising.

Who were they? Arguing—*Your girls are all Hindu. That's not fair for us.* Guffaws erupted. *Hey, hand over a few.* More guffawing. *Friends, you've found a very convenient place. C'mon, let us have a bit of fun with them too.* Banter.

Then silence. The screech of the gate closing. The skidding of the truck's tires. The truck had left.

What will happen? What's happening? We're dead. No, the Buddha is her saviour. This is a sign. The first time she'd seen such a Buddha had been with Anwar. Anwar will sense it. We'll be saved.

Did she cry, or was it the other girls? We sat in a line holding hands.

She began openly clinging to the Buddha. When she missed home, she pressed it to her forehead. If she felt the silence of death she bowed to the Buddha.

For how long? Who knows? No clock, no radio, nothing.

After the arguments and lewd laughter, they were shifted from that old building. So lustful they aren't willing to share. They'll plunk us down in a harem. We'll be sold to some rich guy.

That's where they're taking us.

Far from the city. A deserted place, an uninhabited place.

A jungle. They lit a hearth, gave the girls flour and told them to make roti. *Do as we say, or else!*

Do you want to save your life or your honour, heart despairing.

There were no tongs, no pan, so they threw the dough balls into the fire, flipped them out with a stick before they burnt; the murderous beasts also ate the bread the girls made.

Were there two or three? There was the one with the lump on his forehead.

They whispered amongst themselves. Fire. Attacks on caravans. Karachi Pindi Lahore. Tandojam Umarkot Munabao. Tharparkar, Khipro, Tando, Alhayar, Khadri. Where are they taking us? To set us out in the bazaar. Statue. *My statue. My heart-of-stone.*

The wheel got stuck. The car wouldn't move forward.

Turn the steering wheel fast, yelled one.

Get out! Panic ensued. Not everyone has it in them to drive a car in the Thar.

In the Thar. Where are they taking us?

Wind. Crashing. Beneath the flap-flap-flapping of the tarpaulin: girls. Now when the girls wept and wailed it seemed out of habit. All wasting away. Sitting hand in hand. *But I have my Buddha.*

Skin-peeling wind. We all nearly tumbled out when the tarp flew off.

The roar of engine and wind.

The truck stopped again. A thorn stuck in the tire. Puncture. Long delay. They're filling it with air. *Fill it fast, yaar, it'll be Maghrib soon.*

She saw them praying. Maybe there were only two. Or were there three? The fluttering of their shawls is doubled by the wind as they kneel statue-still in namaz.

One girl had diarrhoea. They all began to beat the walls of the truck in unison. From under the tarpaulin. Kept beating. Screamed. *Let us out! Please! Untie. Belly.*

When the tarpaulin was untied, the wind came rushing in like an attack. The desert wind. Many girls fell over.

It was day. There was sunlight. The wind was dangerous. They couldn't stand up straight. They clung together so as not to fall. Sand-filled wind pricks bodies like splinters. A shower of pebbles in our eyes. Rivers of blood from our scrapes. The abrasion of sand. Tumbling girls. A gale. Sand sand sand.

The truck raced on. Then they were unloaded again. A station. Khokhrapar. *Built in 1870* said the sign. Small. Empty. Train tracks. Everyone was taken out and seated on the platform. Waiting for a train. To which market were they waiting to send them? What should the girls think, if they can think at all?

Me. My statue. My Buddha.

Were there two or three? In front of us and behind us. Raptor eyes. Letting no bit of flesh escape.

How long did we sit there like bundles? Were there clocks there for us to keep time?

Everything senseless. Everything stopped. Weeping screaming keeping quiet speaking all absurdities. A rat ran by, someone shrieked, someone laughed, someone laughed at the laughter.

A caravan of camels appeared in the distance.

One of the men with covered faces appeared, out of breath. *Get out—they've found out!*

Chaos.

They're coming this way. Run run!

Did the girls say it, or the masked man? The one with the lump. *They'll stop the trains. Get out of here.*

Crash, from far off. Wind. Heart.

Everyone began to flee, uncomprehending. It didn't even occur to them to wonder if they should run from these ones or the coming ones. They just ran.

They found a parked truck somewhere. They were pushed towards it and loaded on. Picked up and thrown in. She was terrified. Got up to jump. My statue? Where did I drop it? Someone threw her roughly back. My Buddha? A feeling of terror burst in her heart that this time for sure.

Truck. Full speed. No tarpaulin. Rush of wind. So strong, shrieking, knocking them all about and over. Me without my statue in a fleeing truck screaming falling not from the wind but from the pounding of my heart.

Someone's hand in hers. From fear. A small girl. Eleven. Or twelve. Terrified face.

The truck stopped with a jerk. *Get out. Get out. Jump.*

Scream shout feet hands abound.

Take this take this take this. The masked men were distributing whistles. The kind you get from the balloon man. *Blow on these.*

Run. They ran. Some here, some there.

Not this way, that way. Shove. *Towards the sand.*

Run separately. If you're seen together, you'll be caught. Blow your whistles. To keep track of one another. So you don't get lost.

Go. Quickly. We can do no more. Blow the whistle so you don't get lost. When you get there, gather together. Be careful.

It wasn't the sort of moment to understand anyone else's intentions.

One of the masked men came towards her. But there was no mask. The one with the lump. Can't remember the face. The statue in his hand. Mine.

Take it, Baji. People have gone mad. Run now. Then return. Quickly. To your home.

Baji, sniffled the small girl. The one holding onto her hand. As though she'd never let go. The Buddha in her other hand.

And I ran across the sand, pulling the child with me.
And that child was Rosie.

★

15

At some point, heaps of butterflies had climbed onto the fingers of the woman telling the story as her hands rested on her cane. Those that found no room sat about her on the sand, wings raised in rapt attention. No need to note what they expressed with the fluttering of their wings, namely: *Oho, such good people in bad times, saving the girls from the savagery of their own kin.* In the peaceful flutter some touched wings to express, *Look, no matter when, no matter how evil the times, never abandon the hope for goodness. Inscribe this on your wings. Imbue your wings' flight with this message.*

The butterflies knew that they were but brief guests in this world, scattered about like moonbeams on sand. In six or seven days it'd all be over for them. From beginning to end, they'd survive twelve days at the most.

But they also knew this: that it was they who spread messages of trust throughout the world, generation upon generation. As when they took the pollen from flowers and carried it to spread in other places, where they helped flowers sprout and blossom and disperse their fragrance. It's the same when they listen to stories—they enjoy the essence of a tale, gather it like stardust, and scatter it in the sands so that even after they leave, the stories will grow and blossom and spread their perfume. So what if we ourselves have died? Our roles as messengers never will.

One butterfly is enough to make a far-off flower blossom, and here so many are assembled. The stories could not be suppressed now. Nor could goodness.

And then? They sat in a circle, gazing rapt at the woman, their wings outspread in anticipation.

The Third Tale: Sea of Sand

Such a sharp wind, like a ship on a stormy ocean, and the people in it slide sometimes this way, sometimes that. We fell this way, we fell that.

Run separately!

We jumped this way, we jumped that. As from a sinking ship, not into water, but into an ocean of sand. One pursued us, another we pursued to save ourselves. Sandstorm.

All of us separate. The little girl and me, holding hands. We had whistles to blow to give one another the comfort of nearness. Arms and legs flailing, swimming in the sea of sand, we blew on whistles. A hollow echoing cry in the wind. Or a sand bird. Or our imagination.

There was wind, and particles of sand rained down in torrents.

You can never imagine it if you haven't seen it: a sandstorm billowing towards you from a long way off, towering to the sky, like a tsunami growing in the ocean. Barrelling towards us. A high yellow-black wall about to attack. The fearsome wave, leaping towards us, monstrous, high wide vast thundering.

Should we turn and run? But how? Behind us approached a frenzied crowd who had learned that some of their own had searched for girls from all over and hidden them so they wouldn't fall into their savage hands. They burned with rage. They were coming for us.

Fire behind. Storm ahead. Shapes waving in them, real or imagined? The images of ferocious murderous creatures galloping in the sand. A whole army. Thundering towards us. To swallow us. Animals running at a gallop. Thundering growling bellowing vomiting smoke screeching.

So much wind. So much sand. We were swimming in it. Flailing, trying somehow to keep ourselves from drowning. To not let go of the child, to not let the statue flow away, to keep myself from drowning. Arms slicing through the sandy waves like water. An earthquake of water.

I didn't know how to swim. Huffing and puffing. The sand cut into our lungs. Life ebbing out. Suffocating. Sand sand sand. Drown drown drown. Sand filling the nostrils filling the mouth. Flying into the ears the eyes. I swam, holding my breath. My mouth opened suddenly. Breath breaking, filling with sand. Throat rasping, painful breathing, smarting with cuts upon cuts. Just keep moving your arms and legs, keep pulling the child's hand, keep believing, keep hoping, she's still clinging to your hand, and the statue, my statue is here, yes, it is, isn't it, cling to it, don't let it fall flow away get lost, close your eyes, keep ahead, just keep on, where are the other girls, I blew my whistle, didn't hear anything in the din of the waves, don't let the rioters hear, but this noise, oh, not theirs, a whistle blew, oh, someone's body floated up ahead, like a corpse circling in the water and disappearing, that's how they forged ahead. And me too.

Ahead, the demon wave bore down to swallow them. Like a host of bestial jaws. And us, fleeing into them.

And then we collided. An apocalyptic collision. The whirlwind's yellow wall broke over us. Blotting out the sun. We heard a rip in the cosmos. Ocean, ocean, everywhere.

We broke into smithereens in that giant wave. We swirled in bits and pieces. The sun—blotted out. Sand and darkness everywhere. Our hands and feet surfacing and whirling agitatedly like fish leaves branches in roaring water. Reflections in the depths of the ocean. A person's half-eaten body. Or what? Something rippled by. A disembodied arm. Or a snake. Oh, are these innards, floating to the surface? And this: a holy man seated in samadhi? Like my statue. But the holy man's head is cut off. Headless samadhi.

Where are all the girls? Am I all alone? Whistling within the thundering. Blow the whistle anyway. Anyone there? Do you hear? Sand in mouth. Blow it anyway.

Maybe from over there, Baji. The child spoke. Had she really heard something? A whistle responding to a whistle.

Perhaps the storm had got less stormy. Perhaps whistles were blowing. The girls were blowing their whistles to escape drowning. One whistle. Then another. Feeling our way to one another. Calling one another close.

Fweeeeee fweeeeee…

Then the whistles grew faint. Fainter. As though someone blew on her whistle as she drowned; she is drowning, she keeps on drowning, she keeps on whistling. At every whistle, the breath sinks. Sink. Sank. Sunk.

The girls continued to swim in the sea of sand. They struggled in the yellow-black waves. They blew whistles now and then. Slowly their bodies lost strength. One by one they began to drown. One by one the whistles ceased. One by one the shadows sank, the whistles stopped. Silence.

★

16

Noiseless wind. The butterflies have returned to the cane and the one butterfly-fancy still sleeps between Ma's fingers. To listen to stories in its sleep. Dreams, nightmares, the breathing of folk, all these lift stories, and then they will spread all around the butterfly like peace.

The butterfly slept, and the story, spread out beneath it, began to flutter and unfurl in its mind.

The Fourth Tale: The Drowned

When they came to, they were tangled in a prickly bush. She, the child, the Buddha. If the bush hadn't caught them, they'd have fallen into the pond. If they'd fallen in there, they would have drowned by now, not in sand but in water.

The sun had set. It was twilight. Nearby were huts and wheat fields. This she was remembering. No one at all for a long way off. Ma and Rosie felt frightened and thirsty when they saw the twilit pond. Ma was the elder; Rosie, young and fearful, stuck to her side.

They looked around. No one at all. Saw the whistle was gone—drowned somewhere. Saw the statue was with her. It was fine, and that meant they were fine too.

Ma dragged herself forward, holding onto the child, hiding. Blood dry caked. They took refuge in the field. Wheat, she thought, but who knew, maybe some other grain? The two of them chewed on raw ears.

Ma sat the child in the field with the statue and went to get water at the pond. The darkness deepened. How to scoop the water out? She could only get a palmful at a time, but she did have a chunni. Ma dipped the chunni in the water. She poured drops of water into the child's mouth.

They needed to get away. What village were they in? What if they fell into the hands of attackers? Let's get away. Where we'll find the other girls. Or go it alone.

Oh, God. Ma looked at the Buddha. Oh, that man with the lump. A brother.

But where to go? Which way had they come from? What lay behind and what ahead? Perhaps there was a bit of gleam over there, lingering in the sky. The storm is ahead, the sun behind, so we should go that way. The older girl assessing. Pressing the Buddha under her arm, they continued on.

They kept walking. Silently. The wind had now abated. The sand was soft, it pressed gently beneath their feet. Bare feet. They walked on hand in hand. As though they were enjoying a night spent traversing cold sand.

What must they be thinking? What was there to think?

Sand all around. Roots and branches peeping out. Broken bushes. They kept moving in the growing stillness. Then they heard a whistle, first softly, then more insistent. *Fweeeee. fweeee.*

Whistle, Baji, said the small girl. She took out her whistle and gave it to Ma. Her whistle had survived.

Ma blew the whistle. *Fweeee.*

She gave it to the child. *You blow on it.* She blew on it. *Fweeee.*

From somewhere far off came a response. It rippled across the desert's peace.

Blow it some more.

The child continued to blow the whistle at brief intervals. The toy balloon man whistle. When she blew it here, an echo would return from elsewhere.

They both looked. Where had it come from? Over there. Let's go over there.

Perhaps they were pleased. Perhaps they didn't know where they were going but they got up their courage anyway.

Their mouths had filled with sand. Their bodies were filled with sand. They were coughing. Coughing more and more.

How long? Who knows. How many days did they keep walking fatigued starving surviving. When the sun was strong they'd sit in the shade of a bush. They'd even nap.

No one at all around them, far and wide.

In the dark, ripped up arms, cut off heads, broken fingers, shadows swaying in the sand. Or in the wind.

Very softly, the wind began to whistle like them. As though to encourage them.

It could be that it was only the wind. They whistled. They heard a whistle respond.

The two walked alone, they were walking alone. The little girl was her. Baji was me.

Once they sucked on some grass. The child's white, chapped lips.

Then no strength remained. The child asked Baji quietly, *Baji, did we do something wrong?*

I laid her in my lap. I patted her in the shelter of a bush. I told her a story:

Once upon a time there was a king and a barber. The barber was commanded to shave the king. When the barber arrived, the king sat with his head wrapped in a turban. The barber unwrapped the turban. He saw that the king had goat's ears. *If you tell anyone I'll have you killed,* growled the king. The barber went home, silent with fear. But he had a stomachache. It got worse. So much so that the barber fell ill. What to do now? He went out. He went out into the desert, where there was no one at all. No one at all. Then he saw a tree. He ran. He said to the tree, *Listen.* He told the tree about the king's ears. And then he felt fine. But the tree fell ill. Someone cut it down and built a sarangi. One day, the barber heard someone playing the sarangi and it sang, *goatearking, goatearking.*

The child began to laugh. *Goatearking goatearking*, she sang, and fell asleep.

When I awoke, I was in the hospital of a cantonment. Fever. Green phlegm. Coughing. My whole body a welter of wounds. *I won't survive this,* I thought.

The child wasn't there. The Buddha was on the table next to me.

Later I learned a border had been drawn, and that I was safe, there was no danger for me anymore.

★

17.

Soft sand, wind soft.

The sand swirls in the wind.

The wind shifts the sand. The sand wraps the wind like a blanket.

The blanket flaps.

The sand is soft. It leaps lightly in the wind.

Rabbits have snuck into the blanket. Rabbits run under the blanket. The blanket runs with them. Look at that, a blanket racing across the desert, hopping bunnies inside it, chasing the horizon.

The story doesn't end. A new story speaks. A sensitive woman's eyes are deep. A girl's braids are tied with two different-coloured ribbons. A butterfly has floated to perch on the highest branch. A single bird flies over the desert.

Where is it going? It searches for a perch. It rests. It looks all about. It picks something up. Its heart trembles.

Swami closes his eyes. He sees a far-off voice. He listens to its silence. Some sound some melody some flutter rests on a dune in the desert off in the distance.

What can be seen? A rock moves. The wind has changed shape. The butterfly soars. The tree kisses its brow. It giggles.

So laugh.

Open your eyes. Did you see anything? Nothing? Laugh all the same.

Because Intizar Hussain has said that the earth takes hold, feels hurt, the trees recognise, the soil retaliates.

The brush swished in Bhupen's picture, the story raced. Sometimes with the fresh crispness of an athlete, it takes a giant leap, full speed ahead, over the surface. Sometimes it swings, and at every swing a memory flies up, and in every memory some new twisty turn.

Then Khakhar came to a halt. He finished. He left the colours wet and smudged. Not everything is right here. Not everything is right now. It will arise when it arises. A new leap then.

That window. From which Ma leapt to reach the desert and create a story. Where did she go then? For the moment it wasn't known. Whether she was living or returnedtogod by murder or by herself and her daughter: so many questions.

The final piece of information was that they had been seen in a bus near Peshawar. The bus had been painted by someone named Bhupen, with that same colourful depiction of the desires of ordinary people.

But a drama did unfold. And it did so in Khyber.

★

18

Each day of interrogations brings the same whirls that are sending Khyber into a twirl. On one chair, the interrogator. Before him, the table stacked with files, passport, glasses. On the other side, another chair, for Ma, and she, sitting when she wishes, standing when she will. On a nearby chair, Beti. Beti's head covered, Ma's bare. Beti is sad, interrogator going mad. Ma is glad.

When they ask her name, she says Chanda. When they ask her husband's name, she says Anwar. When they ask her about her home, she holds up a handful of soil.

Who is this? He motions towards Beti. Sitting nearby.

My mother, she says laughing. And you are my grandfather. Oh, lord, son, can't you tell she's my daughter?

Madam, please give clear answers.

Son, first you have to ask a clear question.

What's your name?

If you ask the same every day, will I eventually tell you some other name?

Your passport says... He tries, but can't pronounce it.

Do you know how to read? asks Ma.

Where is your home?

In this soil.

For God's sake, please, stop talking about the soil.

Son, please don't speak of ignoring the soil. The soil will sulk. And Ma stands and holds forth, as though reading aloud, your land has put a hex on you. Dear sir, the land also curses and complains. Alas, if only in the excitement of settling Pakistan they hadn't uprooted us and made sport of scattering families to the winds.

Please sit, please sit, he scolds nervously.

You can read, but you haven't read? What do you do then? That was Intizar Hussain. *The Sea Lies Ahead.*

Madam. The man who's come to question stands. He has no idea what to do about her, and how?

Tell me, she asks, standing, what land is Intizar Sahib's? Tell me, son, is he yours or ours? Sit down, sit down, and tell me.

Madam, I'll be asking the questions.

And you'll also be giving the answers.

You, he mewls. The more upset he gets, the more his mouth protrudes like a beak. It seems as though in place of a mouth he is growing a bird. At first just a little bit of beak sticks out, then the mouth swells and now an entire bird has appeared, an irritable one, that jerks forward with impatience at every word spoken by Ma, this strange new woman. If it flew away, what would he have where his mouth had been? His subordinates stand near him and keep their faces expressionless, but they too are exhausted by this daily brain-racking.

What is your address?

Ah, son, don't you know the address? Really, someone tell him the address for this place. Landi Kotal. Deserted guesthouse. Birdhouse. Two empty rooms. Tiny veranda. Tiny yard. And these high walls. As though it weren't a birdhouse but a fancy fort. Above the walls you can see the minaret of a mosque and above that just a wee sliver of Khyber sky.

Ma'am, we're asking you for the address of your own home. This is a prison.

Prison, hah, perhaps it is to you. I came here of my own accord. Yes, it is taking time to get set up. You have tossed in two charpoys for us, and there was the stench of stale smoke—how many cigarettes you all smoke here! Stinking up the two pillows and that suffocating quilt. It's a stroke of luck that you have some respect for your elders, so when we asked for sheets and quilt covers, you brought them. The good thing about Landi Kotal Bazaar is that you can get everything there. Gun pistol airplane hashish, which, why would we want? Buckets mugs toothbrushes water jugs and drinking glasses. You've even had the bow spring of my spectacles mended and returned them to me. And naturally, curtains we could not do without. We don't observe purdah, but we do hang curtains in our windows. One needs darkness to sleep at night. Sometimes the sunlight is very strong by day. That is good: the mattresses and quilts needed to be sunned, good of these khidmatgars to realise that.

Ma gestures towards the four guards watching over them with kalashnikovs, their fingers at the ready on the hammers of their guns. Though, I dare say these kids could do with some sunning too, it's unfair to put them on military duty. Their huge, heavy guns weigh down their shoulders. They have nothing to do save twirl up the ends of their moustaches while they sit about guarding us. Hey boys, you don't even have moustaches, how can you twirl them? You have a beard. Is it real? Doesn't look it. Such a large beard on such a callow youth. Why are you making a fool of this broken-down old lady?

In fact the old lady was the one driving the interrogators up the wall. Never a straight answer to any question, long speeches whenever she felt the whim. And laughter. Otherwise muted silence.

Please understand, Madam, we are taking care of you fully. In deference to your age, we have not put you in the lock up. Otherwise.

Bravo, bravo, well done! How could you put us in the lock up? Your famous Pathan hospitality, your joie de vivre, what would become of that? Your Pakhtun-ness, which is renowned far and wide, of which you are so proud, how could you get rid of that?

We are doing absolutely everything respectfully. You please do so as well. We have everything sent to you: food, clothing, kahwa. Fruit, vegetables…

Yes, the cure for my constipation is fine and dandy. But our luggage that you disappeared? Is this your hospitality as well? And there's no mirror in the bathroom, no heater in the bedroom, the light is too dim to read by, and there's nothing to read anyway, does reading and writing mean nothing to you all?

If you're so educated, why are you wandering around without a visa? It's a double crime: no visa and in Khyber on top of that, a border area where even we can't travel without special permission. The interrogator tried to explain. Forgetting that he must maintain harsh questioning, and instead descending into puerile peevishness. We must do our work, you'll get your luggage, but we must clear it first. Then he remembered who was supposed to be giving the explanations, and he quickly followed up with a question. One of those that he and his colleagues came and asked every day.

Please quietly give the answers to what you are asked, Madam.

How are answers given quietly, son? Ma laughed at him.

Again and again she stood and held forth at length.

Please tell us, how did you get here?

Son, your memory is very feeble. Only yesterday I told you, when we were returning from Turkham one of your own cars came up behind us and drove around us, blocking our path. At which we were forced to stop, otherwise we'd have crashed into it. And then loads of gun-toting fellows popped out and surrounded us. At that time I was gazing intently at the hills of Khyber. Greyish-brown, as though carved with a knife, and the peaks of the mountain range sanded to sharp points. The street twisted and turned along, sometimes so narrow a one-humped camel could barely have squeezed through. An azure sky. Caves in the hills, like the closed eyes of holy men, or the sly sharp gazes of thieves or soldiers—what's the difference there— holding the final rays of the sun. The hills—deep black here, shading bright pink there. I was entranced.

The interrogator is perplexed. Please tell your mother to cooperate like you have. Give straight answers. Answer directly.

They come, then they go. Then they come back again. They sit Ma in the chair before them. Beti nearby, but instructed to remain silent.

When did you come here?

When you fellows captured us. Look. Ma crosses her legs and digs her cane into the dirt as she embarks on a lengthy explanation: We had arrived in Torkham. We weren't even tired. All along the way we met with such love from everyone; they took us into their homes—their hujras—and invited us to relax against bolsters, fed us dry fruits and kahwa, we went into the women's quarters and took care of our feminine needs.

Everyone urged us to stay. So much love. Those forts of theirs, built of mud, those gates of iron, numerous cars parked inside, slits in the wall to peep through from the inside, or push the barrel of a gun through to spray bullets. I'd never had the luck to see all this before.

Please tell us what you're asked. Why did you go to Torkham?

Why, because of your Special Officer on Duty: we'd heard he'd gone there. Some good soul had us to dinner and got his son to accompany us. Afridi. Michni Post, Torkham Post, everywhere, the sweet boy got out and told them, *These are my guests*, and we'd continue on. But you've shut him up somewhere. Where is he? Did you lock him up too? Why? He was showing us hospitality, the famous Pakhtun hospitality. Where is he?

We're the ones doing the asking, not you. You answer please. Please tell your mother to pull herself together. We want to settle everything quickly, insh'Allah, you are ruining your own case.

Amma, just answer them. Then we can leave.

That's what we want, we want to expedite your departure.

But we don't want to be expedited. We need to see your Special Officer. That's what we've come for.

What made you come to see him?

Look, son. Ma again tapped her cane. It's better if you write it out word for word. You forget each time. Listen again. This is how we got here: by car. After that there was a bus. The bus left Peshawar. People were sitting in it with their legs hanging out. Such a colourful bus. There's no colour that wasn't painted on it. Covered with paintings and engravings. And here were pine trees. Lakes, houseboats. Faces of film stars; fair and lovely Shammi Kapoor I could recognise. Chickens, swans, ducks.

Deer, bears, flowers, and bright red hearts pierced by the arrow of love—hush, don't interrupt, let me remember. Decked in colourful garlands, of flowers, of tiny lights, inlaid with tiny mirror patterns that blink when they catch the light; you can stare at them for hours and never tire. It was such a beautiful bus. The driver really laid on the charm. Nothing like this room in the wilderness you people have provided. Put in a lamp, why don't you, there's really not enough light. Again she motioned for him to keep quiet and let her remember. People walking all along the way, with their backs loaded down with heavy wares. TV sets, stereos, fridges, whiches and whatsits; they must have brought them this way? How hard would it be to set up a TV for us? We could watch the news. You've cut us off from the whole world.

Please Madam, do stop. Come, let's begin again, he says, as though giving her one more chance. Whilst it is he who is getting worn down. Ma is exasperating him. The bird on the interrogator's mouth protrudes more and more, and he runs his tongue along it, as though biding his time before he gulps it down.

Come, sir, make up your mind. You say stop. In the very same breath, you say, come, let's start again. Ma's little laugh echoes across Khyber.

Name? he asks, raising his hand to maintain order.

What should I tell you? When you people can neither read nor listen?

Chandraprabha Devi, please tell me your name, he says rather loudly. He must have been practicing the pronunciation in his head.

You take my name while asking me to tell it to you. She laughs. O Sun, tell me thy name. O Moon, O Chanda, tell me thy name.

Who is Chanda? Where did she come from? Why did she come into this?

I am Chanda, Ma says to him loudly. *C-h-a-n-d-a*. Chanda. From here. Now she presses her hand into the soil. I came of my own volition.

This name is not in your passport.

Chanda was sent off without a passport.

You have no visa.

Chanda was sent away without a visa.

Your address is in India, which is very far from here.

It is where it is, you're the one who's far, son.

I'm from here, you've travelled here.

No, son, I didn't come here, I left here. And she quotes the poet Mir Taqi Mir, bowing reverently to the sky as she speaks:

Vajah beganagi nahin malum
tum jahan ke ho vahan ke ham bhi hain
I don't know the reason for this estrangement
wherever you are from, I am from there too.

Bibi, please tell your mother to give correct answers.

Why are the only correct answers the ones you know, son?

Ma ji, he clutches his head as he speaks. Why have you come here, to call down disgrace on all of us?

Look. Ma again rests her cane as though she's about to tell a long story. She's standing now. This is Khyber, isn't it? She stops. When she gets no response, she continues. Khyber is Khyber. Everyone comes here. And she begins to enumerate all the people who have been drawn here over the centuries: Alexander, Timur, Babur, Ahmad Shah, Gori, Ghaznavi, silk, iron, gold; all succumb to the spell of it. Look at the splendour of this rocky land. Wonderful indeed! Wah, wow, you've carved a ring somewhere, somewhere a locket, bangles elsewhere, with which the Lord of the Forest of Khyber has lovingly adorned his limbs. So there's magic here. Anybody would be filled with a longing to come. She shook her head, and with it her cane, as she spoke.

My dear lady, you do know that this is a terribly dangerous place? Who brought you here?

But Ma cuts him off. When the sun is setting, she says, the hills of Khyber flash with pink. The sky fills with colour. Anyone at all goes missing here, they fly up and away—no one has any idea where they go. But what shall I do? She spoke in an innocent tone. When there's only one way to be safe here— by not coming—then one must take the risk, no?

We wish for you to leave, protected. But you need to answer our questions. Who brought you here?

My desire.

Name, please.

Chanda.

Not yours.

Aha, so you do recognise my name.

The name of whoever brought you here.

Ali Anwar.

Whaaa…? The bird flapped, agitated.

What is the name of your Special Officer on Duty?

Ali Anwar. The answer slipped from his lips involuntarily. Whaaa…Now perhaps he was kicking himself. The people who were with you in Karachi and after that too, tell us their names, he quickly clarifies. They brought you. Without papers. We need to talk with them.

Ali Anwar brought me. I need to speak with him. Did you send him my message?

Begam Sahiba, we desire your wellbeing. Please answer our questions.

Please answer mine.

Madam, we will have to make full enquiries. You are a foreigner, a woman, elderly. The people that brought you here are Pakistani, they knew they were doing the wrong thing even if you didn't, so we must investigate them.

The way you're doing with our luggage? You've simply disappeared it. Only the cane, you no doubt thwacked it this way and that before you returned it to me. Have you sent the rest of the stuff to the bomb squad? And you think I'll help you send those nice people there? Never.

Your luggage will be back with you soon. Now please give us names. As though he were offering a bribe.

Chanda. Ali Anwar. What do you have to do with anyone else?

The luggage came the next day. Ma jumped up and opened her bag. My statue. Where is my statue?

It's being examined. It's very old, and it will stay here, where it's from.

I too am very old. I too will stay precisely where I'm from. Boys, she said to the kalashnikov bearers, get me a nail clipper.

★

19

Who is this woman? I don't know her. Every day a new story. Can this happen? Has old age shaken something loose inside her?

I'm the one in whom something has come loose. I can't bear to watch my mother's daily transformations. I can't tolerate her constantly changing hues. I don't even know what she'll call herself from one minute to the next. I'm in doubt at every moment.

How did she get like this? How can someone be so many things, flow in so many directions, in just one lifetime?

She was my mother. I was her support in old age. I held her hand and led her to this side. When did I get stuck to the hem of her abaya, pulled hither and thither wherever she willed? Where has she brought me? Whom has she met with, and whom has she dragged into her loony quest? Someone is a friend in Karachi, someone else, we learnt, had gone to meet her Maker, but her daughter was somewhere in Sindh, and from there, we learned that the daughter's maternal cousin was transferred to Peshawar. We absolutely have to meet this cousin, so when we get to Peshawar and it turns out he's out on his tours, she insists that we set off immediately. And off we embark on a course about which the government says they can take no responsibility should anything untoward occur: death, accident, whatever. And she's slipped fearlessly into this dangerous place called Khyber. After Jamrud Fort, the Khyber Pass, and we're thrown on the mercy of the tribe of Pathans. A place where murder, mayhem, and marauding are the custom.

I'll go mad from fear here. But she—who is she? Fear simply does not touch her.

By now I feel nothing even resembling hope. I came along because I thought, okay, let's give elderly Ma some small shred of happiness in this final stage of life. But is this her final stage or mine?

I was tricked. I had thought I'd show her the way. Well, I was wrong. Every time I thought, okay, this one thing, just a little bit more, okay, I'll keep her company, she's old, but keeping her company is a neverending story! If you ask how much farther, you'll get *oh, it's just up ahead*. Every time with the *oh, it's just up ahead*. Over and over, *oh, it's just up ahead*.

And what was it that was just up ahead? Khyber. Stillness. Even the Khyber wind blows elsewhere. Nothing enters here. These high walls on all sides and a wooden door set into them. Which is always closed. Which opens only if food or kahwa or the interrogator come, and lets a slight breeze sneak in alongside them.

And this woman? Who is she? A shapeshifter with so many names homes tongues. Whom to believe?

This is the last place we need to visit, she says, just this one last person I need to meet. This is the end.

How can this be the end when she won't leave? Why does she keep making it so that they can't let her go even if they want to? After all, they do have to follow some sort of protocol, if only for show.

That woman, who is she? It's like she just doesn't want to go. I see her age, I point it out to her, but does she care at all about the years I've lived? Who am I, how did I get here, did this have to be my life? Whose life am I living? Is this the real me, or the one I left behind?

I miss KK terribly. I even told them, I'm a journalist and so is my partner. He must be getting worried, he must be searching for us. I said it with pride, but I hoped perhaps all these people would be frightened. Just a little. Of me too.

But who's frightened besides me? Not this woman, not these men who come every day, sometimes border police, or Pakistani government officials, or army officers, or the tribal leaders, and, who knows, maybe terrorists. Fear and threats are the game our two countries play. Anyone could become a pawn in it. They could turn two innocent women into political pawns. Agree to let us go if India does the same with their prisoners. Make the value of our lives equal to some dangerous spy, or the release of terrorists. Would our government agree? Only if the lives of us two women means something to them.

My life must mean something to my mother, right? This is not my story but hers, I have no part in it. Who is she, what does she want, why doesn't she do what they ask so they'll take pity on us and let us go? Instead of goading them.

I'm afraid. I keep my head covered to show respect for their customs, and so they'll respect me as well. They come every day to ask their questions, and every day I answer them politely. *Your name.* I tell them. *Your father's and mother's names.* I tell them. *Why did you come here?* With Ma. *Without a visa?* Yes, what can I say? *You're educated, you know this is wrong.* Yes, but we didn't have bad intentions. We're blameless. Please let us go.

How long will you keep us here? Our family will be worried. You can see Ma's age.

How would KK know what's happened? How would Bade know? There's no way, otherwise they'd have tried to stir things up. It'll take a few more days before they begin to wonder where we are, why there's no news, when exactly we plan to return. By then these four guards will have plugged us full of holes.

Which they've been itching to do since day one. I'm constantly anticipating the day they'll choose to blow us away. The four of them hover by us round the clock. When we go to sleep at night they stand at attention by our door. So that if our eyes drop shut for even a minute, they'll jump forward and shower us with bullets. With each bullet I'll sink further to the ground. Which bullet will do me in? Who will see my face when I'm dead? You, KK?

Why have I started missing you so much? Why don't we miss people when they're near? Next time we walk together, I'll look at you and imagine being separated from you, and that way, I won't make the same mistake of keeping aloof and ignoring what you say. I'll touch you again and again. As you wanted me to.

Why do each of us want to touch the other at different times?

And this woman who thinks of no one but herself. Does Ma not see the circles under my eyes? She even asked them to bring a mirror, and now I get upset when I see how I look. At my hands—how dry and rough. And this hair sticking out of my nose, I can't even ask for scissors to trim it. You'd be annoyed if you saw it, but what can I do? Where are your scissors, KK, in the guest room? KK, if you saw me now all your desire would evaporate. Eyebrows: a centipede.

Moustache: enormous. I'm turning into a man here. An old fogey at that. You'd hardly love this droopy sallow withered old man.

Surely they too can see that we're broken old women. Innocent, ignorant. Not spies or bandits or bombs. But these two countries…this is an insanity contest. They'll make anything retaliatory, revenge-worthy, a bargaining point.

And this Ma who used to be mine, she's bent on complicating the simplest things. Travelling without visas. Then refusing to divulge the names of those who helped us. I know them only as uncle this and cousin that, I couldn't testify against Ma even if I wanted to. And then there's the Buddha, found here, and apparently there's one just like it in the Lahore Museum, it's an ancient national treasure, and she's walking around with it like it's her personal property. They're not giving it back and she's kicking up a fuss. Come on, please forget it. Please save our lives—yours and mine. Let's go back.

Back? She said to me: I have come back. I must see Ali Anwar.

Ali Anwar Ali Anwar. I keep hearing this name, I get upset and try to erase it from my mind. Let him be whoever he is. Leave us be.

What's this? The guards are sleeping? Propped up against the wall of the small veranda. Sprawled out, kalashnikovs pushed to one side. Careless? Or have they finally realised that there's nothing to fear from prisoners incapable of fleeing or killing?

I'm staring. Right now they can't do a thing to me. Asleep, but powerful if awake. Should I jump forward and seize the guns? *Pow pow*, that'll take care of 'em. But even then, we wouldn't escape. I'd wipe them out first, then Amma, then myself.

What's happened to us so far is minimal. We're still together, mother and daughter. But what if they try to put pressure on us by splitting us up? Or by breaking our arms and legs? No, no, they won't lay a hand on us. But what if they call in the lady police?

The sound of a gun. Where? Bad to worse. Did they hit me? No, they're sound asleep. What about Amma? I've come running into the yard. They've mowed her down. What will become of me? Left alone in this hell.

The guards woke up. One of them laughed a gun-toting laugh. Seeing my terrified eyes. Someone shooting outside. Must be a wedding, he said.

How well he comforts me, my murderer. How am I supposed to take that? The guard is small, in height and age and in strength. Without his weapon, just a poor, useless fellow. Behind his beard he's just a kid. One of the others doesn't even have a beard. Probably doesn't even shave. But such a big gun. Does he know how to shoot it? It's a real Kalashnikov, after all. Guns have a habit of going off of their own accord, between these two blasted governments.

Is this a joke, or are our lives in danger?

There's a separate fear of not understanding. Nothing will happen to us, right? If we get stuck in governmental machinery, they'll have to observe legal protocol. If a case has appeared on paper, then the pen must be deployed: we've looked, we've listened, we're taking care of it. Inspect the luggage, ask us questions, keep us locked up—they're cogs in this system, just like we are. We can only get out once the process is completed.

But Ma behaves like all this is some sort of holiday. Sitting with her chair in the sun. And by her side, two guards stand at attention. They're laughing. Are my ears ringing, or what? *This guy bowls faster than Shoaib Akhtar*, is this what he's telling Ma? I sit down with a thud on the veranda, by the other two guards who are sleeping, the two guards I'm going to waste before they waste me.

It makes no difference to anyone at all, and the fast bowler laughs and puffs himself up with pride.

It's true, I did play club cricket in Peshawar. Javed Sahib saw me one time during net practice.

Javed Miandad, the other guard explains to Ma.

He said, Go on, bowl, I'm watching. He came wearing pads. He was retired by then, but he was still Javed Miandad. I got up my courage. I counted out the twenty-five steps to start and laid the mark.

How will you understand what he's talking about? By now all the guards have surrounded Ma.

I don't know, but keep talking, I'll get it. I've watched everyone else watching cricket.

It took five balls for Javed Sahib to admit defeat. Enough, man, I've shown myself a failure.

See how full of himself he is, Badi Ammi?

Badi Ammi? They've started calling her Badi Ammi!

Well then, child, why didn't you become a cricketer? Why did you pick up a gun instead? Ma raised her cane and pretended to give him a beating.

You go where poverty takes you, replied the child.

You tell us, the other said, is our Imran Khan better, or your Kapil Dev?

I know nothing of yours and mine, said Ma, and they laughed, ha ha, Badi Ammi is trying to avoid the question.

Badi Ammi! Badi Ammi?

★

20

Khyber remains silent. Every day is the same. And in this muchthesameness, every day is different. Life at a standstill but still moving on.

Khyber's sky. Khyber's statuesque hills. Their sharp peaks. Their peaceful lotus poses. A gateway encircled by sky and monumental mountains. Mountainous monuments.

But their gateway, their door, goes nowhere. It stands erect, surrounded by high mud walls, two rooms carved within, attaching itself to them. If ever it thinks of leaving it will drag them along like a railway car.

The door remains locked from the outside.

If you look from above, you can see the stillness of Khyber. Far off, on the street, screech the tires of numerous colourful trucks, but these leave nary a trace on the silence. The heavy black smoke billowing from the carburettors plumes up like a mute beast and disappears into the mountains. Like bullets from guns. Which shoot into the air in Khyber for weddings births deaths enmity love every occasion, and no one bats an eyelid.

Behind the door live two women. Mother and daughter. Look at the daughter and you get the sense of one imprisoned. She circles the tiny yard like a mouse in a cage. Casting suspicious glances at every single thing. Death seems to rush at her at the slightest twitch. And what with the same old same old, day after day, the twitches have come to lose their twitchiness and fallen into deathliness. Everything so motionless only death can animate it. There's no difference between one moment and the next, no difference between day and night: all is an endless death scene.

The door remains locked, but it opens again and again. In come tea and breakfast, fruit and vegetables, dal and meat, roti and naan, a sliver of breeze, police army government terrorists, chests out, to catch the thief. They sit Beti and Ma down before them and interrogate. Ma lets her shawl slide down her head to her shoulders and gives wackadoodle answers, or answers questions with questions; Beti wraps herself completely in a shawl like a burqa and cloaks the atmosphere with the peaceful utterances of the old and the wise. In exchange for Ma throwing off centuries of hijab layer by layer, it is now necessary for her to bow her head and veil like this. Lifelong bowed veiled. The life of lifelong in the custody of Khyber, even so. If death came to her now, so be it, the decision would rest with Khyber.

The questions have fizzled out by now. Same questions, same answers: they rise up over the yard, hover above the high walls and disappear into the tiny patch of sky above. Some fragments—tatters—get stuck, flapping from the lone minaret of the nearby mosque.

The interrogator leaves through the door. He doesn't fasten the lock. The chain just drops limp with a clatter. Beti is scared. He left it open on purpose. So that we would flee, and that could be used as an excuse for us meet our end in an *encounter*. They're bored of this drama, time to finish us off.

So that's why everyone's so calm now? All four guards are ready to pull the trigger, like robots; right now they're just lolling about, them on one side, guns on the other. They're discussing cricket and Bombay films with Ma.

Beti says to Birdmouth, so now you know we're not bad guys, please let us go. A tear rolls down her cheek.

Say, why are you so upset? You're our guests.

Prison guests? The plot thickens. We don't want to be guests here any longer. When can we go?

Insha'Allah—he says—what is this insha'Allah insha'Allah, some new threat? It makes the bird hop. That too will happen, we're waiting for orders from above.

Orders from on high? Who's up there to give orders? A very thick plot indeed.

And this Dilip Kumar-Madhubala, this Sunil Gavaskar-Imran Khan, this reassurance and soothing? What's it all about? More tricks to make us drop our guard? So then they can rub us out?

Beti has aged. The hair at her temples has turned white. She's experiencing shortness of breath like she's having an asthma attack.

Whatever you need, please let us know. Any complaints, please let us know.

Beti's breathing is getting stuck. We're finished. This is a carefully thought-out plan. For our defences to slip, so we'll cough something up; then they'll take care of us. We'll be offered in sacrifice. Until then: wine us dine us drape us with garlands of flowers.

The flowers have been prepared. Brought here at the other woman's request. What is this dry lifeless atmosphere you've created, she'd scolded Nawaz Bhai. Put down some grass, plant flowers. And so Nawaz Bhai has brought plants trowel manure watering can.

Does Ma not get it? That this is a prison? Catering to all your whims like this: it's all a ploy. For show. A conspiracy to weaken you. You'll get carefree and drop your guard, then in goes the knife. She's unwittingly aiding and abetting their tricks.

She's foolish. Tiny like a doll, standing about in a loose abaya, leaning on her cane. She's created a flower garden in a matchbox. While yukking it up with murderous dudes over cricket. Now there's greenery and clean gravel. She combs the earth soft with her hands. She pats it even. She lifts the plants, cradling their tiny roots with a trowel, and digs a small hole in the earth where she sets them down, patting the edges with soil. The beardless murderer fills the watering can and Ma soaks the newly bedded plants with water.

Nawaz Bhai has also brought flowerpots. The same kinds of plants. But large. The flowers have arrived. Marigolds.

I've seen goats wearing garlands of marigolds on Bakr-Eid. The plants in the earth have not yet blossomed; how long must they wait to garland us for the sacrifice? That's why they've brought them ready in pots. It's all a plot. Stupid Ma is actively participating.

Gulaurang, says Nawaz Bhai. Zafargul, says one murderer. Gulfishan, says another. Gulhazara, asserts a third. Marigold, says Ma. Genda. Then she adds: a marigold by any other name. You call it this, I'll call it that; it bears whatever name we give it.

Khyber quiet. As evening rolls in, a blanketing silence enfolds, as though this is merely the first layer of the many layers of night.

★

21.

Up flapped a crow, flipping through the air like someone shot him from a gun. He swung cawcawing from the minaret of the mosque, then steadied himself on a perch, panting.

Ma down below, up to her elbows in dirt, heard him huff huff puffing and squinted up. Eh? What? The crow saw her looking, saw her hands digging through the soil and thought, *You never know, she might be in search of a worm.* That's all it took for the two of them to see eye to eye, and also an eye for an eye, and after that, everything was settled. Just as it had been that other time. The crow might come and sit on the minaret at any time, piercing the silence with his cawcawing. Like he was saying *Ram Ram.*

Ma sits swathed in mud, Beti wrapped in her chunni. Ma's begun chatting with the crow, Beti with crevices and crannies.

The crow, wary, hops down to the high enclosing wall, eyes alert, wings at the ready to fly off in case of a threat. Ma waggles a finger at him, but there's a smile on her face. The next time she turns, Mr Crow is seated by her side in the mud. He hops two steps behind, watching Ma's sharp gaze. Don't even think about it, Ma says, don't even think of poking your beak into these tender leaves.

There are some buds. Ma caresses them with her fingers, folding shafts of sunlight into them.

Tap tap. The crow politely taps his beak in the soil. As if to say, no, your roots and leaves and buds are in no danger from me. What I need is worms. Or a roti. He eyes some bits in the dish placed by Ma's chair with longing. Ma follows his gaze.

Well, sir, you certainly are a busy beak. Are you planning to steal something? This is a jail, my dear sir, you be careful here. No visa? You too? Wish yourself well. You also will be presented before Ali Anwar.

Ali Anwar is out on official tours, Nawaz Bhai has told them. That same Nawaz Bhai who calls Ma *Amma ji*. Who leaves the door open a crack, chain hanging loose.

Whatever I have to say, I will say to him, Ma tells the crow, giving him a bit of naan.

Now she's talking to the crow, Beti tells the cranny in the yard. Now this is how we'll live. Half here half there. Until when? And for what? I need to see you, KK. At least once. Before I die. To say sorry. That I didn't see you when you were there. I played games. At least let me go, that's what I'll say to this mysterious Ali Anwar when he comes. If he comes.

Until he does, Ma won't budge. After that, if these gun-toters budge at all, it's curtains for us ever budging again. Oh, oh, hush, she snaps peevishly. Who knows whether it's at her chunni, or at Ma chit-chatting with the crow. She turns an ear to them. Ma talks and laughs with a crow but not with me. When he flies off, she'll find another conversation partner. She'll pick up a ladybug, put it on her palm and gossip with it. But me—I'm nobody. My life is nothing.

Ma even chats with these murderers. Guns sprawled out like extra arms or legs. Lazing about like this, they look less like soldiers and more like collapsed pillars and walls. Or gardeners. One of them is weeding the flower beds, following her orders. Dust in our eyes.

Come, come, Ma is telling the crow.

Or is it *caw caw*?

The crow pokes his beak into her hand.

Ma is talking to him. She's teasing him. Hey, greedy. Then she scolds, no worries son, take it, just don't disturb the plants. Then she waxes a bit filmy: Have you ever fallen in love, given your heart-of-love to anyone? Then she philosophises: Is true love always the love which we've lost?

Lost love is true. True lost, lost true.

Is she talking about me? Beti wonders with a start. KK. You and me? You are my true lost love. She recalls her nephew Sid. She imagines him picking up his guitar and setting this to a disco beat. *Looo-ooo-oost, troooo-oooo.* She imagines KK laughing, clapping to the beat, tapping his feet.

How alone I am. Beti panics. Where am I? Am I? Do I belong to anyone? To myself? Not to KK. Not to myself.

Beti is alone. Who is that woman? Beti watches from a far-off nook. How alone I am. KK, how am I to speak with you? What does Ma keep muttering to herself? That's what it amounts to, after all, speaking to a crow. Beti is fed up. From her far-off corner, she intervenes. Amma, she cries wearily. Stiffens her legs a bit and stamps.

The interrogators enter through the door, which is ajar. When they see the crow they step back out.

Or else they're worn out too. They all want this thing done and dusted, these crazy conversations buried forever within these walls.

But that too is a sinister twist. What if Ma starts singing like Anarkali—*jab pyar kiya to darna kya*—*what do lovers have to fear?*

Or else they're waiting for orders from above: what next step to take with the pawns. Are they themselves being wiped out as they wait to find out when to wipe out these women? Shoot your Kalashnikovs and get it over with.

And lo, the sound of a Kalashnikov shot rips the air. Nawaz Bhai bangs through the door into the yard as though he himself has just been fired from a gun.

Beti stands agitated in the corner. The crow flies up to hop on the wall.

Congratulations, Nawaz Bhai gushes, the big boss is coming to meet you. Him, the one you wanted to meet. He'll understand your situation. The order for your release, you can consider it done.

Beti runs up to him. Nawaz Bhai, let us go now. Please give us your phone number. I'll call you from our country. She's babbling uncontrollably.

Toba toba, Nawaz Bhai presses his palms together. Don't even do that by accident. Please just pray for good sense and divine guidance between the two countries, and greater maturity, so that we can all freely come and go. Otherwise, so many people will continue to end up in prison like this for no reason. On both sides. My uncle's been over there seventeen years. A single tear splashes from his eye.

Down the soft cheeks of the murderers too. Beti stifles a sob in her chunni.

Ma's hands are caked with earth. She slowly stands. Stands tall. Then she turns lightly, like a spinning doll. Another tear splashes from Nawaz Bhai's eye. So too down the soft cheeks of all four murderers.

Why did it happen like this? Why has this happened to us? Why couldn't we meet? She raises her downcast eyes and asks the crow. His eyes are burning coals. Where were you? she asks in a sad tone. Did you fret again, get scared?

Caw caw said the crow. Or maybe, *yeah yeah*.

Or *Ma Ma*.

★

An office has been set up. But whether it's for officer Ali
Anwar or for Ma, is not clear at first glance. A chair and table.
Seated at the ready, Special Officer on Duty, Ali Anwar.

Behind him in the small yard, arms crossed, Nawaz Bhai,
four innocent murderers, Birdmouth, some other bearded
dudes in dark clothing carrying Kalashnikovs; the crow has
descended from the minaret to the wall; and seated in the chair
in a nearby corner, peeping out from her veil, Beti. By the
table but not touching it, one chair, empty. Because Ma is
bending over her plants.

She stands up and spinning about like a doll on a stand she
turns towards everyone. Slowly. Stares the newly arrived officer
in the eye. The newly arrived officer immediately looks down.
Ma throws her earth-smeared hands in the air and announces
sharply, like the crack of a gun, Ali Anwar, a.k.a. Nanhe
Miyan. A shower of earth leaps into the air.

Nawaz Bhai hands her cane to her and she swings it like a
staff as she walks over to the chair, sits down, and says, sit,
because Ali Anwar has stood up.

Beti's eyes pop out. The words come bursting from her
mouth, she can't stop herself. But no one is paying her any
attention. Yes, once or twice the crow hops along the wall in her

direction, but crows hop to the tune of their own drummer, always wondering where they might find a tasty morsel.

Beti is beside herself, muttering to the enclosing wall: She's still doing it. Is this Ali Anwar? This is the guy Amma is calling her husband? I was so afraid, I didn't even let her words enter my heart. I only remembered by accident, her telling the wrong name in the police station, showing her widows peak when she heard what it meant, the echoes of such memories had alerted me. Out. Get out. Life is already complicated enough as it is. I shall not permit these thoughts to make it worse. Of course, I never believed. Clearly, she's confused. But a to-do is created when you hear a thing, that's why, out please, keep out. But today is proof she's lost her marbles. She's calling this guy her husband? Please! He must be my age. Or thereabouts. A bit older? Or a bit younger. She must have heard the name from somewhere and got it stuck in her shaky mind. Poor thing. Perhaps it's all been a bit much for her. Maybe her thinking has got foggy. Amma. Mine. I will have to take care of you. But how? What am I capable of here? Please God, Allah, Bhagwan, Rabb, KK, Bade, Rahat Sahib, Mr Ambassador, Sister-in-law, Janab Insh'Allah Birdface, someone, anyone, please save us.

Beti's acting a bit like Bahu today, bowing her head before every single deity, circling the aarti. The Remover of Obstacles has arrived. God Almighty. The Provider.

Arre, she blurts out, coming forward. As though freeing herself from her prison. We were waiting for you. You've come. We need your help, you're educated, please talk to that ambassador who arranged for us to come here, we've done nothing, please release us, she crumbles in the yard.

Birdmouth motions for her to sit down.

Your name? Ali Anwar is asking. Ma.

Oh my, you haven't even been told whom you've come to meet? asks Ma.

Ali Anwar looks down at the table, then up, but to Ma's left some of the time, and to her right at others. How did you get here?

This army of yours, Ma waves her hand at them, as though sweeping them away with a broom. They didn't even tell you? The soil still tumbling from her hands.

Ali Anwar says very politely, Madam, you've done a very bad thing. It's dangerous out there, you have no idea.

Then many thanks to your people who brought us here, smiles Ma.

You are speaking the truth, Madam, you are protected here; outside, if someone goes missing, they could fall into the hands of the Taliban or get buried somewhere in these hills. We want to send you back safe and sound.

But I have *returned*. Ma looks him straight in the eyes. Ali Anwar lowers his gaze.

Madam, you know you have no visa.

Why should I have a visa? I never had one before, why should I have one at this age? Ma says this as though she's one hundred years old, or two hundred. Or centuries upon centuries.

You know this is a crime. You've crossed the border. The volume of Ali Anwar's voice inches up.

Beti takes one step towards Ma and three steps back. The crow stays right where he is, head sideways, sitting perfectly still, resting his cheek against one wing so as to listen attentively.

Because Ma has rested her cane in the earth and has begun to rise. She is rising. To stand. After that she continues to rise.

As though she won't be small anymore, she'll continue to grow taller until her head reaches the Khyber sky. Now she stands tall and all look up and listen to her, cheeks resting on their hands.

Border, Ma says. Border? Do you know what a border is? What is a border? It's something that surrounds an existence, it is a person's perimeter. No matter how large, no matter how small. The edge of a handkerchief, the border of a tablecloth, the embroidery around my shawl. The edges of the sky. The beds of flowers in this yard. The borders of fields. The parapet around this roof. A picture frame. Everything has a border.

However, a border is not created to be removed. It is meant to illuminate both sides. You removed me. Should I leave? No.

A border does not enclose, it opens out. It creates a shape. It adorns an edge. This side of the edging blossoms, as does that. Embroider the border with a shimmering vine. Stud it with precious stones. What is a border? It enhances a personality. It gives strength. It doesn't tear apart. A border increases recognition. Where two sides meet and both flourish. A border ornaments their meeting.

Every part of the body has a border. So does the heart. A border surrounds it but it also binds it to the other parts. It doesn't wrench the heart from the rest. Fools! If you cut a border through a heart, you don't call it a border, you call it a wound. If you lock a heart inside a border, the heart will break.

Asses! A border stops nothing. It is a bridge between two connected parts. Between night and day. Life and death. Finding and losing. They are bound together. You can't separate them.

A border is a horizon. Where two worlds meet. And embrace.

A border is love. Love does not create a jail, it throws out stars that surmount all obstacles. A border is a line of meeting. It pairs this way and that way to create a pleasing shape. It happens when the two meet. It is a confluence. A sangam.

A border is a game. A delightful one. A line has been drawn. The two sides begin to play hopscotch. Jump jump. Like so. Tie a rope. Swing on it. This way and that. Like this. Slip slide this way and that. Like an acrobat walking twirling falling in both directions. Laughing uproariously. A game. Laughing and playing. First our side, then yours. Toss the ball, hit it, let it fly over the border, chakka! You've hit a six! Let it touch the border: chauka, a four! Everyone's happy. Hunky dory.

Fun times at the border. Sing songs, dance, recite poetry. Beautify it. All the way to infinity, fearlessly. All the way to the edge. The boundary, the frame. But don't get nailed to it, and don't be the hammer. Push the border forward, forward, further forward, forming a lovely serious fearless shape. Like tugging at an invisible rope. On and on and on. Without losing balance, without breaking, without being broken. Come out the other side.

A border, gentlemen, is for crossing.

A border says *jump*. It's there to tempt you to cross it, come back, play, smile, welcome, meet greet create.

A border is fun to cross. All give-and-take goes on there. The border exists to connect, one to another. If there's one, there's another. Through love.

If you hate, the blood that flows through arteries to deliver strength from here to there will flow out and away; each side will die bit by bit. What fool would want this?

But this is what you fools want. You've made the border a source of hatred. Not an exquisite border enhancing beauty on both sides, but one that kills them both, a murderous beast cutting the artery. Ignoramuses! Only dimwits like you could be deluded enough to say, I will kill you but nothing will happen to me. You children, borders running with blood can have only one consequence. The blood will burst their borders and seep away, and all the limbs will dry up and stiffen, but everyone will keep chanting *Allahu Akbar* and *Hare Rama Hare Krishna*.

This thing called a border is a matter of the difference between your time and mine. We never used to be paranoid like this. We did not imagine a bomb hidden in every single thing. In this cane, in that flowerpot, in my fingernail, and here you go wasting all your precious time on bomb squads, sniff sniff, knock knock, search search. The world was not like this everywhere we look, defining one another as strangers and foreigners. The air was clean, and every little thing sparkled. Straightforward, simple days. Dust was plain simple dust, not these invisible unknown poisonous chemicals. We knew our desires. There wasn't this debilitating obsession with fame money competition power. The sky wasn't this half-clenched fist you misers brandish before us. There weren't such walls that turn a house into a prison. Our doors were always open. There weren't just these narrow cracks and certainly there was none of this shameless stuffing of the muzzles of guns into them to shoot instead of looking out through eyes. What borders there were contained beauty on both sides. There was love and respect at borders. The border was a children's slide for you to laugh as you slid from here to there.

Armed with this knowledge, Intizar Hussain set out with the belief that home is back here, and also over there. Across a new border there's new joy. Why not enjoy it? Thousands of

Intizars set out saying, Come, let's go over there, and then come back.

How was he to know what a strange new breed you are? You think you're big shots, throttling the neck of the world. You believe the cries of ruin are buds about to blossom in the garden of life.

Not all the Intizars could return to their towns of Dibai after they departed; they were turned into strangers everywhere. And the border? It grew hungry for crime and bloodshed, let loose ruthless murderers in a place of sunlight and air. Besides shattered battered memories what else befell them this side or that, and Intizar Sahib grieved, *I am but a cotton-carder of memories*, and that is all that remains.

Where is the border? Sir, Pichwa raised a flag on a tree, and it became a border. Joginder Pal's crazy Maulvi Sahib arrived in Karachi, but there was no border for him, so he continued to believe that he was still in his beloved Lucknow. You created a border in your mind. You changed the names, but the places and the people remained the same.

Don't be a fool. Do as I say: flow like air through the thorny border. Become electricity, if there are electrical wires. Be good and play good games. If you stop the good people, how hard will it be for the bad to move in? You have created a game of fear. You've created a dogfight. *Bark bark*, this is my territory, you've made yourselves a piss-border. Now I'll bark bark at whoever comes, I'll chew you up whole.

Do not turn the border over to the greedy. For them, blood and crime come free. And sunlight, sky, air is for stealing.

Do not accept the border. Do not break yourself into bits with the border.

There's only us. If we don't accept, this boundary won't stay.

Ma drew a line with her cane and began to move from this side to that side. She jumped, she swung. She threw up her arms and legs playfully, stirring up the earth. Her voice rose, then fell. Sometimes her eyes glowed, or she laughed. And sometimes she stood on the line and twirled in a circle, her cane upraised, waving it slowly over everyone's heads, making them swerve and duck.

She enacted all nine rasas.

Everyone had got to their feet, coloured in every hue. Ali Anwar's face was red, the bearded men's faces were yellow, Nawaz Bhai's face was softened, the murderers' were flabbergasted, Beti's was terrified, the crow's was proud. And not a peep out of any of their mouths.

Ma fell silent, slowly began to sit as though descending deeply within herself. Even after she was seated, she continued her descent, as though to bury herself in the earth.

Go, she turned her face away, I feel sad. Many people have died.

★

23

It's not clear when he left, but it's very clear when he returned. Ali Anwar, that is. After prisoner Ma's border speech. Whether one day after or two, nobody could rightly say. What happened was this: the unlocked door opened and the entire gang entered, all in roughly the same state as before. That is, at a loss: Ali Anwar red, Birdmouth Insh'Allah and the rest of the beardeds yellow, the murderers appearing dazed, Nawaz Bhai's face soft, Beti's terrified, the crow's proud—not a caw from a maw. All standing there like statues, exactly as before, as though there'd been no intermission, and will time move forward even now?

Surrounded by plants, Ma slowly turned, took up her cane, made her way to the chair, rested the cane against its back, brushed the soil from her hands and said softly, sit, as she lowered herself down.

Ali Anwar sat. Everyone else remained standing. The crow, contrary to habit, flew noiselessly to perch alone on the wall. He placed a wing just so on his cheek, giving everyone else their cue to adopt the same contemplative pose.

Now all were quiet, as though none knew who would take the lead: Ma or Ali Anwar?

All silent.

Like they were stoned on ganja. Waiting for one to burst so all the rest could follow suit.

Ma, silent, lost in herself, making the atmosphere intolerable. But then she motioned as if to say: Go on.

Mohatarma Chandraprabha Devi, said Ali Anwar, looking down.

Mohatarma Chandraprabha Devi. Ma broke into an ironic smile.

A sigh escaped Beti's lips and fell to the ground like a firecracker.

Mohatarma, said Ali Anwar in a controlled voice. Please gather up your luggage. You will be delivered safely to the Lahore airport, and from there…

Where is my Buddha? interrupted Ma.

That… Ali Anwar's voice shook slightly, then he calmed himself…is not yours.

Then whose is it, bhai? snapped Ma. It stays with me.

It belongs here. It will remain here.

Then I too will remain here. With it.

How did it come into your possession? The museum has sent a report. It is from Sikri District Maidan, Khyber Pakhtunwa. It's from two centuries before Christ.

There's one exactly like it in the Lahore Museum, Ma told him, as though they were in agreement, advancing one another's arguments. The same layered stone, the same dark colour. We had seen it there. That's why I picked it up.

That is stealing.

What, son, was there an FIR recorded?

There's no mention of it anywhere, but the statue is real; that has been established.

I, too, my child. I, too, am real. Whether or not I am mentioned in anyone's report.

It has been found here. This is its country.

I, too, have been found here. Tell me, which is my country? Ask your father.

Ali Anwar's face flushed. Please do not talk nonsense.

Ask your father if what I say is nonsense.

What do you have to do with him? Speak for yourself, please, speak about what's happening here. It's better to talk straight.

I will talk straight to him, to your father. Let me see him.

Do not drag him into this.

Drag him in? He's already right in the thick of it.

Why are you talking gibberish, Madam? This is a government case, not a game.

A government case is a game: meaningless and shameless. Ill-fated and ignominious; ignorant and ill-advised.

Please be quiet.

Will *he* keep quiet? Call him, let's find out.

Why would we call him? What does he have to do with all this?

As much as a husband has to do with his wife.

What happened next? Everyone on one side, Ma on the other. Some stood, some fell. Someone's heart pounded, someone lost nerve or patience, something arose like a whirlwind. Ali Anwar grasped his head. The Kalishnikovs managed, albeit shakily, to keep the murderers from losing balance. Insh'Allah blurted out, My god. Nawaz Bhai took one step towards Ma and stumbled. The other beardeds turned to the left and to the right, then began to chew their fingernails. And Birdmouth's mouth opened so wide that the bird fell out and fluttered off somewhere.

Even the crow blanched.

Beti took one step forward, then three steps back, then began to cry and fill the yard with pleadings, her words a flood unleashed. To Ma: Amma, don't be absurd; they're letting us go so let's leave. To Nawaz Bhai: Please, explain to her that she should keep quiet. To the crow: Has she come unglued? She will die and take me down with her. To the murderers: Don't kill us, we're already dying as it is, I feel so weak I can hardly get myself up, but don't tell her, she'll say I have a deficiency in my blood, she'll say to feed me chicken soup, she'll say go get multivitamins from the bazaar. To the beardeds, addressing them each in turn: This is a jail, we've done nothing, at her age the mind wanders, you must have an elderly ma too, an elderly dad, if they were to say, take me to such and such place, it's my last wish, you would do what I did too, she's lost her way, she's even forgotten me, her own daughter, and her son too, she's forgotten our home, and she thinks this is her home, she's planted a little garden, sown flowers, but this is a prison, this isn't our life, this isn't my life, I'm a different sort of woman, I live alone, I had ambitions to live differently and I stayed apart from the rest, oh, my home...my books...my music...my nightly calm ...my friends...KK...my long necklace of old coins...always wore it...didn't bring it because we were to return soon...in customs I'd have to take it off over and over... here I'd keep taking it off at every checkpoint...If I'd known... that she...then I'd have brought it...it's a part of my personality...you won't find something like that in Landi Kotal Bazaar. To Ali Anwar: Why don't you understand, she doesn't know what she's saying, I'm also going mad, I'm suffocating, Ali Anwar ji, my brother, you are my brother.

Yes, said Ma, this is your brother. Go and tell Anwar, Anwar, your wife has come.

The crow had regained his cool. Wow, he said.

★

24

KK, I'm going. I'm leaving. Separating forever. Your love was so important to me, I just wanted to say that before I go. With you, I was truly living. Even our quarrels made us feel alive.

Thank you, KK, thank you for giving me those moments. It was what I wanted—you gave me what I wanted. But now I realise that the way we wanted to live our lives, falling asleep and waking up together in the morning—that just isn't meant to be.

I'm writing to you, my love. Feel it if you can, give me the courage to endure this separation.

If there were an ocean here, I would stuff this letter into a bottle, cap it, sneak out the door, and set it afloat in the sea so that it would reach you one day.

But in Khyber there are only mountains. Easy enough to get here, but getting out is impossible. Even the wind stifles and dies once it's snuck in. There's a crow, who's become Ma's companion these days. Like that blackbird before, remember? I wish it were a pigeon. Then I could tie this note to its neck and have it fly to you as my final wish. From me, to you.

But what use is a crow? It only annoys me more. It just flies about in circles as Ma spouts nonsense, as though taking it all in. This only encourages her. She doesn't understand that it's only hopping around her because it's greedy for dibs and dabs of food.

Perhaps it will bring dibs of me to you. A dab or two; it will arrive chewing on a bit of bone and drop it down in front of you. You'll start: *eek!* But this morsel of food is from a human! Maybe it will be my hand; you know how my pinkie is much shorter than all the other fingers? And you'll remember, why yes, this belongs to my beloved, who has departed this earth. Or maybe it will be a foot. Then too you'll have no trouble recognizing it: the big toe sticks out. If you've paid attention.

Where were we traveling? We were taking a trip somewhere, in a bus or a train, researching an article, when you put my feet in your lap, and said, They're not pretty, but they're very dear to me, my precious. You were teasing me. Remember? Where was that? When was it?

Do you remember anything? Do you remember me? Or have you forgotten everything, just like Amma? Have you moved on with your life?

All the same, I want to tell you now when there's no longer any chance of our escape, you wouldn't even believe what's happening to me, KK. Where on earth has she brought us? This is my mother. Into such a bizarre drama. That she's enjoying so much she's happy to die enacting it.

What does it matter to her? She's eighty. What does she have to fear? She can depart dreaming her dreams.

But I, I didn't want this, did I?

Yesterday I argued with her. I said, You're inventing one lie after another.

But it's like she doesn't even know they're lies. There's no lie, she scolded me.

I wonder if she started doing this to add some colour to her existence. Maybe I shouldn't have brought her to my home. She envied my life. That I'm the mistress of my own desires, absolved of responsibilities towards others. I can go wherever I want, bring whomever along, whenever. There's no one to stop me, nothing to get in my way. She started feeling competitive towards me. As if in a race to outdo me. Threw out her old clothes. Let it all hang out, and there she was, singing openly and lustily. With that Rosie. She made friends with Rosie, which no one approved of. Except me. I never stopped her. I encouraged her. When Rosie-Raza shapeshifted, I let it happen. The entire design of my home, of my whole way of life, got turned upside down, and even that I participated in. She began to cook up outlandish tales about herself, that, honestly, I thought were fabricated. See, I too have a widow's peak, which means that my spouse will marry twice. She invented a spouse in her head. Even invented his name—*Anwar!* We ended up here chasing after that name. Until yesterday, the story went that she had to meet with the Special Officer, her shauhar, her husband...husband. But that guy turned out to be much younger than her, so now she's looking for the father.

Do you not have the slightest regard for us? I ask her. How everyone laughs at us, how ridiculous we are to everyone. At least respect your age. Marriage-husband-love-shove; are these the only kind of outrageous tales you can cook up? Have you completely forgotten your own family, forgotten to think of their well-being? What sort of a mother are you?

And do you know what she said to this? What is forgetting, have you any idea? Think about it. The things that happen, do they happen on purpose or in forgetfulness? The things that happened, were they accomplished by thinkers, or by those who ceased to think? Forgetting is dying. I'm not dead. I'd buried everything from my past in the sand. Today I've returned to that sand. Something like that.

I screamed that these sand memories of yours, they've dragged us to the mouth of death. Go ahead and dream, think of those dreams as memories, enjoy your little game of make-believe, your days of restlessness.

No, I couldn't really be so shameless as to say, whatever was going to happen to you already happened, now either live in reality or in fiction. All I said was that I still had more living to do. I didn't have to live like this. I just can't breathe here. Arre, if I had to exist amid the struggles of home and family and others, I wouldn't have done it as others do: two or three children, household, servants, car, someone helping at every step, becoming a mother, grandmother, a rani, a begum. I'd wear Reeboks too, and show people, see, I can do this too. But I wanted my own kind of life. I just worried over you a bit, and what a tumble that took me for. Took the life out of me.

You leave, she said, at the first opportunity. As though she'd come up with a great solution. I'll tell Anwar.

Anwar, Anwar, who knows where that name came from; it buzzes constantly in my ears. The first time she spoke it was in the police station. Perhaps we didn't realise she'd truly fallen ill after Papa; she was so very depressed. Maybe then her mind got a bit confused. She was having trouble being alone, so in her weakness she invented another husband and got caught in her own delusions, in the need to revive herself with the help of the lie. She went on joining one lie with another, and this is where it brought us to. Prison.

Or a madhouse.

I've heard about people becoming children in their old age. But to start considering oneself youthful? How crude. And she has turned me into an old woman and brought me here to Khyber to die.

Yes, it had to be Khyber. The best setting for such an unreal drama. Timbuktu would have done as well. Or the moon. Or Mars. Places more rarefied than the real world. Ma is delighted with this drama she's created. If she dies here, it will be such a lively death. What a soliloquiser she has become. You should have heard her dialogues on the border that day and seen the plight of those of us in the audience!

Please be reasonable. Please observe your age. And mine. You were going to finish this with Ali Anwar. When that didn't work, you started in on his father. Now there's no hope for us. Did you see how angry he was when he left? Understandably so. If some lady came and said to us, I am your father's wife, would we take it lightly? I reasoned with her.

If she was your father's wife, then you shouldn't take it lightly, you should welcome her, she said stubbornly.

How could he be anything to you? I tried to reason with her again, KK.

He is not my *anything*, he is my husband.

KK, I reminded her, Ma, he belongs to a different religion, a different country. What will be gained by these absurd claims?

Gained! she cried so loudly that the murderers began to peer in. This is the word that deludes religions and countries; it divides them. Gain, by separating, by breaking apart. Make a country, save a religion. Is a country created or broken? Does a religion expand or contract? Gain? What is gain? Don't tell me. I haven't come here to gain anything. To demand my share, to cause one more partition; I have no interest in such things.

Then why did you come? I screamed.

A mosquito has come in from godknowswhere, to buzz in my ears. Remember, KK, how you used to grit your teeth and go chasing after the poor tiny mosquitos, yelling, This ass shall not escape me? KK, keep calling mosquitos asses: imagining you doing so will soothe my soul. But listen, don't tell Amma. Otherwise, next thing you know, she'll have made the mosquito her confidant.

The ass has made me forget where I was. Yes, so I yelled at her, then why have you come here?

To see my husband, she said, with an odd candour.

You're Hindu, he's Muslim: how could he be your husband, how could you be married? I wanted to expose her lie.

So, KK, she had that answer all teed up. She gave me an entire speech. What do you think, she asked, that relationships, love, only got invented after your generation showed up? Were there no people in the world before you? Did they not have dreams and desires? We too have lived life. We too have studied, met, wandered. We also created fashions and destroyed them. First we'd adopt them, then they'd be copied in other places. We also fell in love. And listen here, there have never been borders in human relationships and there never will be. There were conventions then too, yes, but also people who broke them and moved forward. Right across from our class was Jafri Sahib's class, he taught Farsi; we studied art. We used to get together and go to his house to eat haleem and meat. My maternal uncle used to tell us not to go there, but Taya never forbade it. My aunt said when you go to eat there, recite laillaha ilallah muhammadur rasoollallah on the way. Enjoy your food while you're there. On your way home, recite, om bhurvasaswaha. Do everything properly. When Kausar came to our home, she'd laugh and say om shanti shanti. Paths were forged through laughter and play. Everyone relented to love sooner or later. For a few days there was fighting arguing complaining, then we got married.

She says there was a special marriage act in 1870, that made it so two people could legally marry outside of their religion, if their elders approved, and they did. But that can't be, where is it written that you did such a thing, where is the record? When I boxed her into a corner, she smacked me on the shoulder with her cane, okay, not very hard, but angrily.

You're asking for a record? Those who moved everything from here to there, ask them what records still exist. Those who ran from fire chasing them, is there a record of that? Which home belonged to whom and what shards left behind belonged to hearts: has a record been kept of all that? Do you look for the papers to prove that? And this, that the two of us were blessed and accepted by Nana and Chacha, you're asking for the papers for that? Take it from the record, take it from the home, make a border of lies, and believe that we were not there? How much there is in this world that belongs in the pages of history but is never mentioned. It blows in the wind. If you can recognise it then do so. Don't throw it away; acknowledge it. When it is convenient for you to operate without paper proof then you assert the statue is yours, when it isn't convenient, you demand written proof, or else all is relegated to falsehood. There's no mention of this statue anywhere, not in any office, nor any museum; you're just looking at it and making guesses. Look at both of us too. We're our own proof.

She descended even deeper into her story. The more entangled she gets in her story, the more she enjoys herself.

The more she kills me, the more she feels alive. Arre, that's why you should shut up and let us leave so that I won't be ruined by this, the world is laughing, what's left for us now?

But maybe this too is caused by her envy, that not much is left of her life now. Please, do separate me from my life. From you. KK, a border has been drawn between us. If I'd known, would I have ever come to this side? So that I might never return?

You stay well, darling KK, keep calling mosquitoes asses. But one last time, I will ask you to stop shuffling all over the place with your sandals half on half off, it irritates me to no end, going drag drag. Please at least do that for me. Or in my memory. Or in the hope, even if false, that perhaps one day you'll open the door and I'll be there.

Will you wait? But why would you? Will you come here? But how would you? No one is waiting. Does anyone know where we are? It makes no difference. Thus shall I depart. And you won't know that I missed you, I missed only you. True love, lost love.

Yours,

Effaced

P.S.

Nawaz Bhai just came. You people get ready, he said, the car will take you back to your country. This Friday is a holiday. Then there's Saturday and Sunday. So the next day, on Monday. And, Amma ji, you cannot meet the Sahib's father.

Arre Nawaz, why can't I meet him, you just tell him I'm here and he'll come himself, he'll definitely come.

He can't come. He's paralysed. He can't get up.

I don't understand a thing. Ma is whispering with Nawaz Bhai. Nawaz Bhai places a hand on her arm. She's asking, why didn't Shimmi tell me? Shimmi, the daughter of someone named Kausar whom she refers to as her girlfriend. We met her when she was leading us around Sindh without a visa. She's the one that told her that her mother was no more and where her maternal uncle was.

Ma stands. Alone. Tiny. Nawaz Bhai has left.

She opens her mouth to say something. She opens wide as though to scream. She breaks down as though to weep. No sound emerges. Ma stands. Alone. Mouth open, wide, distorted, silent.

Her shadow grows on the wall. As though it does not belong to her. As though it belongs to history.

I'm tired. I can't sleep. I wish I could sleep. Stay asleep.

I'll keep on sleeping. Come and kiss me. Then I'll wake up. If you don't, I'll sleep forever.

★

25.

At some point later in time, in Sri Lanka, the ace batsman of the Pakistani cricket team starts hiccupping right before a match, and he just can't stop. They give him water, tell him to hold his breath, slap him on the chest, thwack him on the back, but he's hiccupping so hard the dressing room is jumping. Are you trying to kill me or what, asks the batsman, his red face damp with tears, and a bowler gets super serious, says that he once knew a woman whose hiccups would only go away when she was given a swift kick in the back. The whole team bursts out laughing. Fighting back hiccups and tears, the batsman says, Yaar, if you're so into kicking, then go ahead and kick. The other players start making fun of the bowler: We're not football players here, we play cricket. If you wanted a bat to the backside, or to hit a six, we would have helped you, they say.

I'm not joking, says the bowler in a serious tone. I used to call her Amma.

The players begin to enjoy this. And she must have called you son!

Yes, but her daughter called me *murderer*.

Why, son? chuckle his comrades. She saw you holding a bat?

No, ji, she saw me holding a Kalashnikov, that's why.

Oh my God, yaar! Listen to this guy! Too good!

But the cricketer is serious. It had been a painful time in his family. His father had died in an accident and the responsibility for his sisters and mother had fallen on his shoulders. He'd had to quit his studies and was accepted into the army on his uncle's recommendation. He was sent to Landi Kotal to guard political prisoners.

He told them there had been two women from India. One old, one scared. There was no special need to guard them all the time, guns at the ready, but orders were orders. So we set our guns to one side, he explains, and discussed cricket. He tells them that she told him that once she'd fallen down and her husband had rushed over to lift her up, but she fought him off from the ground, saying, Get away, get away, Imran will miss his six.

She'd been caught in Khyber without a visa. Her Pakistani hosts had brought her there on a tour.

At this, the team cries out, What's so special about that, yaar? One guy says he took his Indian friend last week to see Mohenjadaro without a visa. The rest share stories as well. They all begin chiming in about who has taken their friends and relations sightseeing where, without visas. Who needs a visa, come on, we just picked up a car and set out. To Karachi. Takshashila. Chitral. Mardaan. Indus. Hazara. We were going to go to Swat and Kashmir. But one evening before, my uncle called from Islamabad, don't be stupid, every authority cuts in on every other here, you spoke to the Brigadier, but ISI, Border Force and so on, if anyone finds out, your guests would be finished and so would you.

This is what happened. After all, it was Khyber, says the serious young man.

The chiming in starts up again: when we went to India we had a visa to go to just two places but still they took us all over: Bijnaur. Karnal. Moradabad. Vrindavan. Gujranwala. Ambala. Banaras. Atrauli. Bhopal. Khatauli. Malabar Hill. Park Street. Shimla.

Who gets caught for the way they look? But Khyber is Khyber. Your lady had become a bit too much of a tiger.

Tigress, says he whose sobriquet had been *murderer*. She said, I will not leave, and insisted she must discuss the good old days with the father of our big boss, and only then would she consider shifting. She got some kind of bee in her bonnet and wouldn't budge an inch. Drove our bigwigs up the wall.

And then? Whether they believe it or no, the cricketers begin to enjoy the tale.

There was a plan to deport them. Then…he falls silent.

Then? Someone asks after a pause.

Then she started hiccupping.

Hiccupping? Yes, we had completely forgotten that. But this time no one laughs. There's a peculiar tension in the air.

What the bowler tells them next is so strange that no one knows how to react. It might seem humorous, but for some reason they're having trouble finding it funny, even though the whole hiccupping part was hilarious.

So here's what happened:

That night…, says the cricketer who had been a guard…she starts hiccupping and just won't stop. It's so bad it's getting hard for us—there were four of us—to sleep. Finally we can't stand it anymore, so we go and knock on the door of the room these two women are staying in. *Everything okay, Amma ji?* When none of the big officers are around, we call her Amma Ji. Nawaz Bhai too. Who is Nawaz Bhai? someone asks, and he explains. Her daughter comes out and tells us, *Ma is having a hiccupping fit.* We guards give her water. But it doesn't help. *We'll call the doctor and tell Nawaz Bhai,* we say. At this, Amma ji says, *No, not yet. Just give me a whack on the back.* Her daughter gives her a whack. *Harder!* she says. After a couple times the hiccupping calms down.

So, all better? the cricketers ask after a silence.

Then it started again in the morning. Now all us guards and Nawaz Bhai start giving her suggestions of what to do. Drink water, but just a drop at a time. Hold your nose with one hand, drink water with the other. Drink from the glass, upside down and backwards. Hold your breath, count to a hundred, then breathe out. I'm bringing the doctor, I'm telling the Superior, we were going on, when she again instructs her daughter to hit her on the back, hard, and then she's fine.

Story over? asks one of the listeners.

No, says the storyteller, it's just beginning.

When the hiccups return, Amma ji has us drag out a mat and unroll it. She stands before it. Insisted her daughter should come diving at her and not punch but kick her, hard in the back, in the stomach, in the side, whichever side was facing her.

Did the daughter agree? The listeners are astonished.

Never, how could a daughter agree to such a thing?

And then?

And then she says to me, Hey, you're a cricketer, come on over and show your skills.

And then?

And then her daughter agrees.

Yes, everyone understands, if you're going to get kicked, let it be one of your own, why an outsider?

But then, we too kicked her.

Whaaaa….? The cricketers, agog.

As time goes on, it becomes a game we all enjoy greatly. And a crow she used to feed from her plate, he sits on the wall and cheers us on, cawcawing rowdily as if in applause. She gets the hiccups, we run and grab the mat, then take a running start and give her a kick, *bam*. The crow hops down and bounces around us, cawing. Day by day our kicks grow stronger. Amma ji falls every which way on the mat, and after a few rounds of practice the hiccupping stops. If it doesn't, she lies panting on the mat for a while, then gets up and orders us to kick again! The crow also eggs us on. I have the very best kick of all, and she started encouraging me in particular to go for it. I come running and somersault like this in the air, *whack*!

You behaved in this manner towards an old woman?

That's it, he raises helpless eyes, her insistence, her perseverance, her love, all were such that when she said, *do it*, we'd do as she asked. Without fail, she'd fall with a plunk when I kicked her, then jump up again. And he demonstrates such a mighty kick in the air, that the rest of the players reach out automatically as if to protect an invisible woman.

Wow, amazing, dude. You could have hurt her.

That's what all of us said. That's why we suggested we lay a mat out in front of her, to cushion her fall when we kicked her. So she wouldn't get injured.

Yes, that makes sense.

But she has something else in mind. She pulls the mat away so swiftly, it's like she's the youngster. And she berates us so much that none of us even has the strength to give her advice again. She shouts, do you want me to fall flat on my face? I will not fall like that. I will fall backwards, gazing at the sky above, lying on the earth.

No matter if the bullet comes from in front or behind or anywhere else.

You mean kick.

Or hiccup.

No, *bullet*. What she meant was bullet. The storyteller has grown serious—sad. She says, this is Khyber, a monument to two crazy countries. Anything can happen here. A bullet or a kick. Nothing is within our control. But I must fall comfortably. At my age, in my bed, I must lie down elegantly; I shouldn't end up like a broken old toy.

And then? someone asks, with a gulp.

And then we continue to kick, Amma ji leaps smartly into the air, folding up her cane *click click click*, and ends up lying back on the mat, laughing at the sky so hard we all start laughing as well.

You're making this up, ventures someone.

It truly was an unbelievable time.

And the hiccups? The cricketer who'd got the hiccups asks. Neither he nor anyone else has noticed that his hiccups have stopped.

She didn't even have them.

Wow, what sort of joke is this? It's not even funny.

It wasn't funny. Nawaz Bhai was weeping copiously. They weren't even hiccups, he says. She just started hiccupping so she could practice falling properly.

When she got shot? The questioner sounds angry, the way you sound when you think you understand, and then your understanding gets pulled out from under you like a rug and you fall flat on your face.

Yes.

And did she get shot? Someone whispers.

The one who'd had the hiccups makes a strange sound. Don't laugh, he says. I feel as though a bullet was fired in some other century but didn't stay in that century. It keeps hitting the people who came later, they keep getting mowed down. By now his voice shakes a bit.

Stop it. The captain scolds. What sort of mood are you people getting into, right before the match!

And in that match, the hiccupper established his record at 105 not-out. After 99 runs, when he hit the ball past the pavilion for a sixer, he leapt into the air and executed a glorious flip, landing so that he didn't fall: he simply lay down and gazed affectionately up at the sky, holding out his bat in friendship.

★

26

If you want to hear the buzzing of all, be a mosquito; if you want to be damp, be a cloud; if you want to headbutt, be the leader of a country; to dance, be the wind; to whimper, be the tail of a dog; a river, be Ma; a caged, pacing animal, be Beti; and if you need to put an end to a tale, then wind up here, because a tale doesn't end, but it can pause.

But a story can also continue on; sand butterfly birdie old lady pouch other lady, there is no stopping any of these. Yes, for them, there's nothing left that we can depend on in writing. Because here there is no Buddha, no marriage, no prison, no visas, none have documents to show. Some records were never written in the first place, some were burnt to ash in the sinful fires set by humans.

The other possibility could be that some among these documentation-worshippers can descend into the ear from the brain, and listen and listen to different voices, and guess where they come from. From goatear to caw caw, or God Above. But with these unbelieving intellectuals, there's the problem that they lump together rumour and chatter, and keep seen-said separate from imagined-invented. They have no sensitivity to where the real unreal is, in fact, they don't even know what language is. If they speak Hindi, they only understand Hindi, and consider all other languages gibberish or a cascade of pebbles. They would never dream that others might know something they don't, that isn't mentioned in their language or written in their files. The mere thought that birds bugs air darkness all have languages of their own is simply beyond their mental capacity. If they only knew that what happens on earth is heard and discussed on the moon! But don't bother hoping that they'll ever change their ways. If such understanding were possible for them, the earth wouldn't be coming to an end. Instead they smugly believe that floods storms ruin and destruction may rain down upon the Philippines and Uzbekistan, but never on Germany or America. One or two Fukushimas might have occurred, but definitely never again, and anyway, Japan might have Western pretensions but it's the East and always will be, and such accidents only happen in the East.

For people such as these, what is it that matters—the story thus far or the story ahead? No one can return to the scene we left, because even though those two women slipped in from outside, nowadays even birds are blocked from Khyber. The Taliban, Al Qaeda and their ilk are the rulers here now. All of Khyber Pakhtunwa has become one huge anthill from which armed ants emerge incessantly, to bomb and shoot-out and mow down young girls, and never pause even a moment to reconsider.

The crux of the matter is that those who haven't cared to read this far are advised not to read ahead either. But for those who relish colours and paths, why should they stop? Like musical notes that go in several directions in a single raga. Such pleasure, such pain in them. Another raga meanders in to join the first. The new tune makes one sway, so that the first becomes a sweet memory. Echoes and reverberations of melodies cross every border. Melodies change, music remains. Death comes, life goes on. A story is created, changes, flows. Free, from this side to that.

But those who wish to listen further will have to believe in shadows. Because shadows lie ahead. Shadows that someone saw, that someone heard. And the flying bullet that finally hit home, that too was a shadow.

This is what they call a crossroads. So which will it be? The path of shadows or of sharply delineated dark shapes? If you're game for the first, come along, fellow traveller. Prefer the second? Then stop right where you are.

★

27

That night.

That night, near the prison compound, the cook's fourteen-year-old son claims to have seen two shadows. He was busy urinating so couldn't see that clearly, but one was a rather tall, robust shadow, face lost in niqab; the only thing visible, a pair of frightened-looking eyes. This shadow was trying to hide the other one, which had the shape of a little girl, and periodically strayed from the bigger one's protection. According to the boy, when the smaller turned and the light from Nawaz Bhai's nearby quarters fell across her face, he couldn't recognise her, because her face seemed covered by a veil of freckles. He felt scared, but it was impossible to stop his urine midstream, so all he could see was the fear of the one, the spots of the other. And yes, there was a staff in her hand, which she waved in the air playfully, and up flew fireflies that looked like butterflies.

That was all the boy saw, but the stray dog sleeping in the veranda outside the bungalow of the Special Duty Officer also saw two shadows. It is surmised that these must have been the same that had appeared near the prison-house, one tall, one small; one hidden in the shadow of the other; the small one flickering out from the big one's cover. The dog heard the shadows glide by, which sounded different to him than the gliding of beings of flesh and blood. At this, he awoke, albeit reluctantly, cursing his own curiosity. Oh my, they were standing on the veranda! The dog blinked twice, his eyes crossed betwixt competing urges of curiosity and sloth. By then they'd pushed open the door and entered the house. If the dog had known the door was unlocked, he certainly wouldn't have spent the night on the veranda. But by now his tired body shivered in the Khyber chill, and he couldn't be bothered. Some long-forgotten notion of his breed's proud role as guard dogs did arise in his mind, and he even made a feeble attempt to limp to a standing position. But when he tried to bark savagely, it was a breathless shriek that emerged, due to the chill in his throat, and, like a ganja addict, he slipped back into dreamland in order to save face.

What happened next, whether the shadows melted into the darkness or what, was hard to ascertain. But there was a series of coincidences. First, there was the coincidence involving a chukar. At the very moment the shadows slipped into a particular room of the house, this particular chukar, which is a type of partridge, and had been spending the night on the awning above the window, opened an eye. Had he been ejected from a dream, or woken by an unfamiliar noise? He couldn't say.

Being the national bird of Pakistan, he thinks he's the partridge's pyjamas. But the wily greedy humans are always out to show what prodigious partridge poachers they are. For this reason, he'd started making himself scarce during the day, going on his rounds under cover of night. He'd had excellent experiences on this awning, so he usually ended up here. In the darkness, he'd often feel secure enough to take a quick snooze. Between snoozes, he'd open one eye and scoop up in his beak the grasshoppers ants bugs creeping up the leafy vine that climbed the window frame. Otherwise, these interludes would be used for general luxuriating. He'd never been much for flying anyway.

The night was extremely dark. So dark that Khyber's sky had all but disappeared among the stars. The partridge admired the stars with one eye as he searched for bugs with the other, and would have considered it a night and gone to sleep had not a small shadow cloaked by a larger one shimmered by outside. *Arre*, but this is an awfully small female shadow! The national bird jerked upright. A woman on the prowl in Khyber Pakhtunwa was no ordinary thing.

Now that he was fully alert, he began to watch. He would have recognised Ali Anwar's wife. But she was away with her children, not here. And anyway, why would she turn into a shadow of night and walk these dangerous streets?

Arre, it's them! His partridge-brain, which was small in size but brilliant as a viper's stone, lit up. Why, this is the prisoner woman! All of Khyber knew about the two outlaw women who'd come from the enemy country next door. Like a flash of lightening, this revelation burst brilliantly beyond the confines of his tiny partridge thoughts, at which he lost his balance and staggered, and would have tumbled off his perch if he hadn't braced himself. Still, in reestablishing equilibrium he let out a shriek.

For every action there is a reaction. The shriek was heard by Ali Anwar, who was seated next to his father, the comatose Anwar senior. Ali Anwar rushed to the door near the window and looked up to where the partridge sat. The partridge had not yet decided if he should he fly away or stay where he was, when a crow—*La hawla wa la quwwat illa billah! There is no power, no strength, without Allah*—appeared from nowhere and alighted on the same perch, though at a safe distance. Now the partridge looked over at the crow, wondering if this interloper had come to steal his bugs, and glared suspiciously at Ali Anwar, and thought about how he had yet to attempt to chase him away; but who could tell the state of his emotional landscape today? Ali Anwar regarded both birds with a whattobelievewhatnottobelieve look, and the crow hopped a bit further away, as if to say, how am I to know who is friend and who is foe? In other words, all three set about a game of suspicion-fuelled peekaboo.

In this entire accidental tangle, the story floated out during the coming days that the tall shadow melted into the night's stars and the small shadow sat right down where Ali Anwar (Junior) had been sitting, but whether this happened thanks to everyone being in cahoots, or it just shook out the way wild things tend to, no one is entirely sure.

But there was a mother. Who sat down beside a person who was paralysed.

★

28

Anwar, Chanda. Said Ma.

Anwar lay motionless. A soft glow emanated from the lamp by his side, a lamp with a perforated shade. His eyes were closed. Ma watched his face. Then she too closed her eyes.

Anwar, Chanda. Said Ma.

She remained silent. For how long? The birds couldn't tell. If what they say is true, then she was seeing him for the first time since forever, so what could they have to say—this is what they told their children. That's why Ma remained silent. Eyes closed. Then she began to sing. A soft voice, sharp and jagged, tuneless at times. As if she'd not practiced since forever. She stopped and laughed. Somewhat bashfully. Then began to sing again. Now she sang without stopping, without laughing.

> *Kaahe karat ho maan kaahe pe itna gumaan*
> *Why do you act so proud*

She paused and opened her eyes for a moment.

Then she recites: *More prabhu deen dayal—my lord, my prabhu, compassionate towards the helpless...araj karat Ibrahim mere maula— my lord, Ibrahim humbly requests...*

She'd grown tired perhaps, or stopped to think. Eyes closed, the lines on her forehead deepening.

This time she opened her eyes slowly and leaned over Anwar's face in order to look at his closed eyes. Raga Puriya Dhanashri, she whispered to herself or to Anwar or to both. Ma's cheeks looked red in the dim speckling of the lamp, or her blood raced from the strain on her aging lungs.

And then she sang out:

Ja re kaagaa ja re main bhejungi sandeswa
Jab se piya pardes gae sukh ki neend na aaye
Go messenger crow go I will send a message with you
Ever since my beloved went away I haven't slept in peace

Oh! she cried—no—she *looked* like, *oh!* Because as she sang, she suddenly noticed her Buddha, behind Anwar's head, on the bedside table. Then she actually did exclaim, *Oh!*

The crow let out a *caw* in the same spirit. By now, he and the partridge had relaxed in each other's company. Each had gleaned that the other was uninterested in bugs and worms, and was instead absorbed in watching a woman emerge from the darkness for a tryst with an old flame. Ali Anwar had forgotten them completely and dozed off in an armchair on the nearby veranda. Why would the voice of a classical singer, one so soft and tuneless, charm a pair of birds? But who isn't charmed when they hear their own name? Kaaga! cawed the crow. He glanced rather proudly at the partridge and his heart blossomed with the spirit of generosity. He wished to extend the wing of friendship. We two birds. You and me, we speak the same language, just the pronunciation is slightly different, and we call it by a different name, he chattered.

Just like the Hindustani and Pakistani spoken by these two humans, the partridge laughed amiably.

Shush, the crow warned, let's not get in the way of this tryst.

For sure, said the partridge, and they sat quiet and attentive, wing in wing like obedient children, so that the story's main characters could go on with the telling. Yes, they both sensed danger, but it was a love story, so even if a shot was fired, or the Apocalypse occurred, at least the romance wouldn't lose its shine.

Seeing her Buddha, Ma whispered into the ear of Anwar, lying supine: there's a heart in this stone, and in my brother with the lump on his forehead.

The birds were ignorant of classical music, but their sharp ears caught the rustling of love.

If my heart-of-stone and my brother-lump had not taken care of me I'd never have survived to come and see you today. Then she smiled slightly, waved her hand, wobbled her head flirtatiously in the manner of a romance heroine, and began to hum. The same tune, *kaaga ja re main bhejungi sandeswa jab se piya pardes gaye sukh ki neend na aaye.*

The crow started to sway, although he had no knowledge of *sa* or *re* or any other musical notes.

I went to sleep. Anwar. I slept and slept. I kept coughing. TB. I kept coughing and sleeping. Brother Lump rescued me and then disappeared. Heart-of-stone stayed with me. Like you, my consciousness was unconscious. When I awoke I learned that all the directions had changed places.

She again began singing a raga. Bade Ghulam Ali Khan. Remember? She laughed. Haveli Miyan Khan? The soirees at Mochi Gate?

Her melody and rhythm did not improve from singing, but her voice had opened up a bit. She sang and stopped and reminisced, and Anwar stayed silent.

The Takiya Mirasis—you must remember? No?

Seeing Anwar silent she became more talkative. There were those songs, you remember. We went every week, to the tomb of Asif Jah and Noor Jahan. On the other side of the Ravi. Then we'd go to the garden. Into some corner. You and me. Chewing soft grass. My bangles. They'd all break. Anwar. She bowed her head and smiled bashfully.

She placed a hand on Anwar's cheek. His head rolled towards her. His eyes half opened from the motion. Ma withdrew her hand. She leant over and turned her head sideways like a bird, to peer into Anwar's eyes.

Anwar, you…her words weren't clear in this twisty-turny pose. The crow and partridge also twisted their necks, but who was paying attention to them?

And how could I have gone to you? All the same, when I went with Doctor Sahib to look for my people in the refugee camps, I used to imagine that you must have come secretly to find me as well. I would think, I am you, I am gazing over the tent cities. Where is my Chanda among all these? Tent city. Filled with refugees like ants, every day thousands more. You must have returned. Thinking, I won't find her in this crowd—Chanda, where should I start? It seemed to me that I should wave my chunni from the top of a tent and stay buried in there until your arrival. But I had no chunni with me from our time together. I just had this statue, just like the one we'd seen together in the museum. After which we'd eaten murgh chhole and gotten upset stomachs. Remember? Do remember.

At some point, Ma's head rested lightly on Anwar's chest. She burst out laughing. But of course, how could you have come to find me? Where would you have come? She began to trace her finger over Anwar's face as she laughed, as though her finger were a pencil and she was drawing a picture. She pressed a dimple into his cheek, and when she caressed his lips gently on the side they actually broke into a sort of a smile. No one survived. Where could I have returned to? Ma tried to open his eyelids, practically poking her finger into his eye, like a child. Those were not the days of returning. We ended up staying wherever we were. She laughed.

She kept laughing, kept singing, kept tenderly drawing with her finger on his face, even speaking and falling silent as well.

There was no one sitting there to account for how much silence went on, how much speaking; about what exactly she reminded Anwar of from those days, days that were different, simpler; or who had gotten lost in the days that had changed and were no longer simple, who had since become friends and who enemies: no one was noting any of this down.

Like so many other things, the night of Chanda's and Anwar's tryst has not been recorded anywhere, neither in government records nor in a personal diary.

But that night in Khyber that lay silent beneath the diamond-studded sky belonged indeed to the two of them.

Ma would sit back and then lean over again. For a long time she hummed a raga in her rasping voice, and the two beings rested side by side, one seated, one supine, truly lost in the old times, in love beyond any border or boundary.

That's why, when Ma burst out laughing, and said, Yaar, they made you and me two separate countries, Anwar smiled too.

Ali Anwar, seated on the veranda, had become like a bird that sleeps with one eye open, on the alert for a hawk or a demon or a bullet or a cannonball. The two birds on the awning, residents of two nations, stayed alert in solidarity. After all, the man could have a slingshot or whatnot hidden inside that shawl, who can say? And then since one of us is an outsider, and the other's flesh is considered tasty, we both have good reason to fear. Keeping vigilant was in everyone's best interests.

So, everyone in their own orbit. But these two are so much so that no one else can compare. Nothing compares to two pure hearts. There's nothing so delicate as the experience of ephemeral purity. Only this can span centuries. Erase distance. Bridge chasms.

Now everything is fine, said Ma. We survived. You were fine. Life stabilised.

Ma shaking Anwar's hand. Touching Anwar's lips. Anwar's eyes white, pupils rolled back, seeming to gaze at Ma. His slightly parted lips smiling at her. Two sensibilities warm to one another. That have lived fulfilling lives and met again at last.

Such was the softness of the night, the sun was inspired to stay a while in its company. As the sun had crept softly to night's side, night wrested free its wrist, murmuring that it was quite late, it had to go. It was this romantic tussle of theirs that made Ali Anwar sit up. Pulling himself together with a clatter, he opened the door to his father's room.

His father's hand was in Ma's.

You didn't come, Ma said, I forgive you. I didn't come, do forgive me.

She stood and slowly placed Anwar's hand on his chest.

The sliver that Ali Anwar saw was this scene with the hand. An old hand, but newly warmed by love, and lying comfortably on his father's chest where it had lain cold, alone, for some years since the stroke. There was a heart in the chest that was beating, and the warmth of it made the hand rise, approximating a gesture of farewell. Anwar's hand had risen in farewell and from his lips softly emerged the word: *forgiveness*.

His son Ali Anwar heard *forgiveness*.

Nowhere is this night recorded.

★

29

People aren't willing to believe that stories can be true. They think they're exaggerations, unrealistic, mythical. Flimsy. But actually, what isn't true are the stories that are flimsy versions of reality—which is itself considered true.

The young are not prepared to believe their elders. You were not the ones who created the world, they say, you were the ones who destroyed it, and now we are busy trying to save it, and save it we shall. The elders debate them, saying we were the ones who saved nature and culture, we didn't cut corners, the destruction is all yours, the greed yours, American ways yours; the ghost of technological progress all in you. But you stayed limited, insist the young. Slaves to custom and tradition; you did what you were told. And the old scowl and say, we too fell in love, we too made jumps and crossings. You'll never understand that the tales of our deaths are the tales of our passionate living.

What neither the old nor the young say is that we together have created divisions, which is something that should never happen.

All the same, there are some great souls who don't think in terms of old and young, or of divisions, and don't go on about *in my day* and *nowadays*. But no one listens to them, because people listen to those who stand up front, in centre stage, beneath the glaring spotlight. Who has time for what lies in forgotten corners? Well, we do have Vinod Kumar Shukla in Raipur, outside of whose window resided the magic of truth within the wall, or…but who knows about that? Or in Bihar, when Nagarjun spake from behind his bushy farmer's beard: *Everyone's eyes sparkled for the first time in ever so long, the crow scratched his wings for the first time in ever so long*…but who knows about that? In the capital, there was a certain Nirmal Verma, who carved his words in crystalline prose, but even those folks in the capital don't know about him. If anyone chanced to see the sunlight he described, they would assume it came from abroad, totally unaware that all the while, those shimmering rays emanated from Shimla.

Sometimes when we read literature as literature, we realise that stories and tales and lore don't always seek to blend themselves with the world. Sometimes they march to their own blend. They don't have to be contemporary or complementary or congruent or connubial with the real world. Literature has a scent, a soupçon, a *je ne sais quoi*, all its own. And that is its style.

But this is the world, it never lets up. The world is in dire need of literature because literature is a source of hope and life. So the world finds a way to dissolve into literature via harum-scarum hidden-open paths. It quietly ends up soaked in the stuff. It tiptoes into literature. It seeks to erase its despair by revelling in unique ways of freeing itself from the world that literature employs. And succeeds when the tale of a dying woman evolves into a story about her thriving and flourishing, and Khyber causes a matchless guileless love to blossom in full. The world gets stirred up, and out of the violence and revenge of Khyber, out of the hills, out of the glimmering of precious stones and sky, it gathers sunlight. Green patches of shoots and leaves greet the world amongst the rubble of destruction.

That's why the world tiptoed happily into the love story for a time, but ultimately couldn't keep quiet for joy.

That night, the night-tryst-lady from one side of the border held a clandestine assignation with her beloved from the other side. But what happened next? Stories upon stories went *bam bam* and danced about, as though celebrating a wedding. They cried because the lovers wept. They embraced because the lovers hugged, they cursed partitions because the lovers had to ask forgiveness, *sorry*, two countries were created, promises were broken, separate homes were built. All the people in the entire world felt sorry for the distances that had been created.

And how stupid that lovers must descend into the maw of death.

For that morning had not yet quite dawned when from the home of the Ali Anwars, junior and senior, two shadows again emerged to walk along the street. But did anyone inform anyone else that permissionless, visa-less shadows were on the prowl in the early morning? What choice did the subordinates of the bureaucracy have then but to pull the trigger? Tuned in as they were, it was as if their senior gave the order in their heads and they obeyed.

At that very moment the big shadow screamed, *Run!* And it ran. The little shadow did not run. It was eighty years old, and it had been practicing flipping, not running. The bullet hit it from behind, but its back had already got skilled at flipping, there was no question of falling on one's face. And the marvellous fashion in which it soared up: some asserted that before the bullet even hit, it had executed a perfect, well-practiced leap and flown over the edge of the cliff.

At that moment, the sun changed direction. That morning the sun rose in the west and bowed before the small shadow in a salaam. As she soared up, she glittered in the sun's adoration. Like a falconess—and then lay back in the air like a queen, as though on a comfortable bed, and in that pose of repose, she jerked her cane and snapped it shut *click click click* and out popped the butterflies, and they fanned out to all the four worlds, and she herself descended to her own earth. At which point, she lay upon the ground beneath the sky, in her desired position, where no one could taint the splendour of her final moment by partitioning it between Hindustan and Pakistan.

★

30.

He was a Delhi-ite, but he was old school; the old ways, the rustic ways, die slowly. He yawned deeply, making pinching gestures as he snapped his fingers before his open mouth, as though extracting his yawns after coaxing them forth. He sat on one of the ancient leather upholstered sofas in Nehru Library, flipping through an old newspaper. As he shifted in his seat with a yawn, the leather—yes, it too was old, but it certainly wasn't rustic—gently hissed as though to imitate his snapping pinches. The researcher glanced about with embarrassment, worried such sounds might sound a bit uncouth, for in this respect he was no longer old school, nor rustic. After this, he continued to browse through the paper.

In those days the memory market was hot. At every university in the world, at every research institute, everyone was interrogating memory. Those intellectuals who bring out a book a year had of course jumped on the bandwagon. The Munna Bhais and Munna Behins were so hard at work that at many Asian educational institutions, and some African too, they'd begun to hold seminars on the subject, and were receiving tons of project proposals. The Nehru library researcher was also hard at work with a senior team of a secular inclination that was engaged in excavating memories of attacks by Vaishnavas on Jains and Buddhists, in order to compare and contrast this with other communal memories of the present. Many young scholars were showing up to search through the troves of old newspapers and journals at the Nehru Library.

So thus it happened that he was sitting on the sofa, yawning, passing wind. Now whether it was because he was bored of memory, or embarrassed about passing wind, who can say? His eyes wandered, and fell upon a column from an old newspaper, where he read a sensational bit of news: Crossing the Border: *An octogenarian lady from Delhi crosses the border on foot without a visa in search of an old lover.*

And just like that, an obsession with finding related news items began. It being the very nature of *and just like that* for things to start happening…*just like that*. These clippings had nothing whatsoever to do with memory research, but they had caught his eye, and he found himself moseying thataway as though his eyes had learned to sniff out such news.

There weren't even that many columns on the subject. If you were in it for the juice, far juicier topics got reported every day. But now and then a few items about the octogenarian-whoever-she-was did make the headlines, such as:

One More Missing Across the Border

and

Two Indian Ladies Trapped in Khyber Pashtun

And this, in English:

Additional Solicitor General submits that the Indian High Commission in Islamabad has written to the Pakistan Government, but the court could not issue any order in the matter and the court accepted this contention.

In the meantime, the eldest son of the elderly woman had made an appeal in court, but the Additional Solicitor General had submitted that the Indian High Commission in Islamabad had already written to the Pakistan Government, but the court could not issue any order in this case. The eldest son even stated that since both governments make such a commotion over each other's criminals, why wouldn't they do so for his mother, who has never committed a crime in her life? He wrote an open letter to the Prime Minister asking what they were supposed to do now. He was interviewed by the media. He submitted in writing and speech to the courts, the government, the media, that he'd knocked on everyone's doors; now what door was he to knock on? We don't know where to go now, he said in English. But we will not lose courage. She is our mother. Our battle will go on, he affirmed in a statement.

The researcher found even more headlines. In one newspaper:

Chandraprabhu a.k.a. Chanda's Claim

And in Punjabi, another:

Charhi Javani Dadi Nu

Groovy Granny: Young at Heart.

Some reports stated that the daughter had accompanied her mother to that side out of pity for the mother's old age obsession. The daughter was avoiding speaking with journalists, etc., but all the same she had told someone, who had told some publication, that she had been sleeping when Ma had disappeared, and the strange thing about that was that she was a terrible insomniac. The next day she found out that no one knew what had happened. And she was repatriated forcibly and put on an airplane by an officer. Ma's state of mind had been a bit touch-and-go during the prison days, so the family was worried where she might be, how she would be getting on, since she had got lost before.

When his girlfriend arrived, the researcher started telling her bits of the tale in the library canteen over bread pakoras.

Can't be, she said. But since it has to do with Partition, it also could be. And she put on her glasses and said, Look, I can't read these words, my prescription has changed, I guess I better get new glasses.

It could be, I believe it, said the researcher. If someone came to research it, we'd eventually find it written somewhere. I've found the Civil Marriage Act, but did anyone actually have such marriages? Where is that list?

Bhayya ji, this is not your research.

Say something, anything, but don't call me bhayya, scolded the researcher. And in a serious tone he added that this was the problem: in the absence of written facts, everything turns into Bollywood.

What would we do without Bollywood? Even birds in far-off corners have entertained themselves by making up Bollywood scripts. Coma, Partition, guns, love, death, religion, bullets flying–flowing like sand, women going out at night where men don't go, it's got everything: salt pepper coriander fenugreek mustard seed ajwain kalaunji asafoetida mint anardana, all the masala, it's all there. Someone's even added a pinch of chiraunji. Shadows in the darkness, two women perhaps, killed in flight. But most said that there was one woman who had become so small she could slip through anywhere, a jail was no big thing for her, and she showed up at the bedside of the Bade Sahib to demand her portion. Bade Sahib, our Sarkar, the Big Boss, Ali Anwar himself had chased her and she ran, stealing a statue worth lakhs that had been excavated here. Then what happened, our Officer ji shot her himself, saved both statue and stature from her evil eye, and saved his home as well. But others said, where we live, women are not shot at, he must have thought it was some murderous beast, or rather, it must in fact have been a beast that our brave one felled. It must be lying dead in the hills now, a search is underway.

But how long should anyone search? This is the era of ennui, new inventions every day, out with the old. It is indeed the bitter end of stories and tales.

In the Nehru Library, no one tells the story of the two women, one small, one big.

★

31

Death comes to all. Even to birds. The chukar, whom most people would call a partridge, and which gourmands enjoy cooking and eating, died. The crow's heart broke.

No one tells their tale, although other stories of ornithological friendships are famous the world over. Take just one example: the tale of the friendship between Garuda and the parrot. That tale is centuries old, and those in the world who are educated, and thus familiar with great ancient civilizations, are certainly familiar with that friendship, and those who are not, it is clear, wherever they may be, are absolute ignoramuses. The two were such close friends that the thought of death upset them. You are immortal, but what will happen to me, asked the parrot, which put Garuda in a melancholy frame of mind. You are close to Vishnu, ask him for a boon for me. Garuda went to Vishnu and begged, Oh Lord, please grant the gift of immortality to my beloved friend. No problem, replied Vishnu affectionately, I'll tell Brahma ji, and he approached him with Garuda's wish. O Vishnu, quoth Brahma, I am but the Creator, and that is the department of the Destroyer, Shiva. So let's go on over there together. Consider it done, Shiva assured them; I'll tell Yama right away, and he called for the God of Death. When Yama arrived, he listened to what the three gods had to say and pressed his palms together and bowed his head. Unfortunately, O Trimurti, my messenger just brought that parrot in. Surely you realise I'd already considered the fact that the parrot was Garuda ji's very best friend, and so I'd made his death a near impossibility, except for under the following circumstance: if ever, for any reason, Brahma, Vishnu, and Shiva happen to appear together at the same time, the demise of the parrot will occur. Which has come to pass. I beg your forgiveness. Et cetera.

But that story does not belong here. In this tale, the partridge and the crow forged a deep friendship because circumstances had rendered the two of them witnesses to a unique night which they watched wing in wing, eyes misty with tears.

But it's more than that. The partridge was a creature of restraint. What he saw filled him with pain, but he kept up a brave and unwavering front, like all men. Yet when the wing of the crow clasped in his own fluttered with emotion, he experienced a strange sensation. That he too might soon fall to weeping. At one point he even tried to remove his wing, but the crow wrapped his own around him more tightly. Both burst into tears.

Two things emerge from this: one, if the scene is a tear-jerker, don't get stuck with a sobber, because you too will burst into tears, and two, if by chance you experience something emotional with someone else, the seed of friendship will be planted. And finally, if you are from India and your friend is from Pakistan, no one can ever break the two of you apart.

But who cares about Indo–Pak friendships? This is the era of the gleeful promotion of competition and enmities. When hate is on the rise, talk of love seems mushy and clammy. Who connects great love stories like Laila-Majnun, Shireen-Farhad, Chanda-Anwar to Khyber? Khyber enters the headlines for murderers, Kalashnikovs, the Taliban, drone attacks, school bombings, and other such atrocities. Most likely an alien looking down from space would immediately notice Hindustan and Pakistan so clearly glutted with lights that, borders visible or no, it would observe that there's always an air of celebration about that particular spot on that particular planet. How could it know that proclaiming divisions has become a celebration for some? A jubilee of hatred. The joy of rifts.

In just the same way, how would anyone know that for many years these two birds flew all about, wing in wing, but in governmental terms they were from two sides. The partridge resided among the Pathans and the crow from needlessly separated India.

What's more, nobody even knows that this was the same crow that in the early days of his youth believed that violence was manly and was so accustomed to fighting over every little thing that when he spoke of love he'd speak in a mock-aggressive tone: You didn't come to see me today, so I'm gonna crush you; or: If you nuzzle beaks with anyone but me I'll twist your beak and hang it in mine like it's Churchill's cigar. It was he who had come up with the plan to drop a large rock or boulder onto the head of Bade and crack it open like a coconut or watermelon. The Crowess had warned him about his raucousness and aroused in him a consideration for others. Once this crowish sympathy had awakened he'd turned peacenik, and taken to knocking his head on the window to enquire after the wellbeing of Bade whenever he passed by the house, and if it was early in the morning he would peer softly through the window to see if sleeping Bade was moving at all.

His neck twitches, sometimes he himself twitches, as he flings his ebony form against this corner, that corner, to say, The sun's coming up, Babu, everyone in the world's getting up and going to work now, and as soon as something stirred within—a stretch, a yawn—he tapped impatiently on the windowpane with his beak. At his tapping, Bade would reach out a hand and pull the curtain back from the window.

At that very moment, the sun would be casting off its tangled raiment—the dark layers of night—and slipping into fresh sunshiney attire, and would sit down with the two of them. Bade and the crow would smile as though to say *Hi! Hello!* Bade would yell, Chai! He'd capture the crow with biscuits. The crow's greed would drool with love. Pleasure would flow into pain. The crow would smack his whole head against the windowpane: Thank you, be glad not sad, caw caw, he'd sing crowishly.

No one has any idea that Bade didn't stop at serving the crow biscuits and rotis, but also bared a good deal of his heart to him as well.

No one knows that if the crow didn't come for many days, Bade would start waiting for him. When he did come he'd feel overjoyed at the crow caw-cawing on the windowsill, like he was announcing the arrival of a new guest, who, surely, would be none other than Amma, hence he considered the crow's arrival auspicious.

No one knows that Bade keeps water in a small aluminium dish for the crow which he himself changes frequently, so that if the crow arrives hot and thirsty he can cool off either by drinking it or fluttering his wings about and bathing.

No one knows that when Bade had seen the crow looking chilly, he'd filled an old shoebox with cotton and had a mattress of old muslin stitched up and spread out, as though the crow wasn't a crow but a doll, and Bade wasn't an eldest son but a little boy. No one had even noticed that sometimes the crow had an overnight stay. These were the early days of winter when Amma had gone over to that side.

No one knows that when Bade was leaving no stone unturned in his search for the missing Ma, the crow, upon witnessing his suffering and growing helplessness, took on the role of eldest son and resolved that he himself would get involved in the search. He had stopped returning to his own home and slept in the place created for him in the window on the mattress, and he watched with sympathy and tenderness as Bade tossed and turned.

Nobody even knew that the crow decided only he himself could accomplish this, but he also didn't know a single thing about such items as visas, nor had he any inkling of the Partition. He'd grown up on a completely different history. But sympathy religion love run on a different track from such affairs. Yes, the crow had felt pride in his wings before, and now he boasted to Bade, you sit tight over here, I'll fly over there, find out every single thing, then come back.

How could anyone know that he said these words in the cawcaw language in order to console and calm Bade. Bade himself did not know. Because man has forgotten the languages of other beings, and if that's not a tragedy then I don't know what is. It's all a problem of arrogance. Mankind has such faith in his own knowledge that he's got all puffed up and has thereby limited his own intelligence.

But birds and such are not encumbered by egotism. Pride in one's feathers is a simple, blameless feeling—and birds look all around, learn from all sides, learn all the time, and for this reason, many have got in the habit of sleeping with one eye closed, along with half the brain, while keeping the other eye open, especially over the course of lengthy flights, and this is true for this crow as well. Meaning, simultaneous rest and education. Evading hunters and increasing knowledge all at once. Are birds any less than yogis who have attained enlightenment? But who considers them as such? No one.

No one knows how the crow flew: over Wagah, Rahat, Lahore, Karachi, the Sindhi desert. Following after Ma and Beti, hearing this, seeing that, reaching Khyber at last.

If anyone at all ever knew, it was his friend from his Khyber days, but then you'd have to go back in time and interview the chukar and hear the entire story in partridge-tongue. Which would also be interesting. Some other time, maybe.

So by the time he reached Khyber, the crow had become familiar with a great many things: visas, Partition, religious hatred. No one had any control over these Pathans: he learned that too. They express even joy with bravado, that is, by raising their guns and shooting into the air; this he'd seen as well. He was a crow; he would not make the mistake of trusting men too easily. He knew perfectly well that they did not consider his flesh tasty, which was reassuring, of course, but also a bit humiliating; I mean to say, why should we be protected because we are evil-smelling and non-tasty, yet, even so, a human might just as well turn a gun on a crow in sport, or because he's annoyed, since everyone knows getting annoyed is second nature to men, and a heartless one could easily finish him off—just like that—so he knew to keep a low profile.

But no such grave situation occurred. He peered into cells and forts, and if a Pathan lifted his eyes towards him, he crowed craftily then sidled away, glancing all about, keeping alert from the corners of his eyes, heart pounding, hoping no one would guess what he was up to, and the moment a Pathan so much as blinked, he'd fly up silently and get the hell out of there.

He had two advantages: one, he was a crow; two, he could fly. So he could peer over closed doors and high walls as he flew.

And finally, he arrived where he'd meant to. There were four gun-toting murderer guards there, watching over two women. He flew up to the minaret of the mosque, hoping to see their faces up close so he might bring Bade glad tidings.

He'd actually seen Bade's mother and sister from that very tree which Bade had climbed and where he'd got entwined in the sari dream. So for one thing, he'd never even seen them up close, and for another, people start to look weird in prison. The growing-smaller elderly woman in a loose jhabba, mud up to her elbows, and her growing-older daughter, head covered in a chunni, face lined with wrinkles of fear and pain, pacing about.

Then the crow saw that the murderers were just a bunch of kids, and perhaps the beards were fake, and they didn't need a shave so much as the daughter, whose moustache was sprouting like tiny thorns from her upper lip. And when the old lady was tending to the plants and pointed at him and laughed, he remembered how when Bade had been watching from the tree, and she had been buried in potted plants on the balcony, she'd said exactly the same thing: *Don't even think about it!* For real, that's her, for sure; he hopped a little closer.

No one knows whether Ma had any inkling that this crow, who came to sit on the wall and had now begun hopping down to her all the way up to the flower beds, had any sort of connection with her son. She said, If you dare mess up and crush my plants—eat my petals and seeds—you wait and see!

and after this warning she began to chat up a storm with the crow. Which only the crow heard, so relaying the particulars is unfeasible. But a true crownoisseur would have noticed him fluttering about, a huge grin on his face, crying out, *This is the one, truly it is, if only I could immediately inform Bade!*

Whether Amma understood the crow's cawcawing, no one knows. But the camaraderie between the two of them revealed that contact and communication are not mere products of straightforward understanding. If there's mutual affection and solidarity, then watching plants grow green together in total silence can be an activity filled with dialogue. Now neither was alone: neither Ma, nor the crow.

All the same, it was also true that whatever conclusion was to be drawn from this, it was clear that the race of crows had no difficulty understanding any mother tongue, but mankind, throughout history, has created and destroyed its own tribe, so that it understands neither mother tongues nor father tongues nor anyother tongues. All tangled up in themselves, in a state of confusion about the difference between moral and immoral, they do a bit of claw–claw at one another in anger, but the caw caw of the crow goes right over their heads. This shortsightedness of man is something people like Ma have to end up paying for.

All the same, the two of them got on. Sometimes peaceful, sometimes Ma's *coo coo* amidst the *caw caw* of the crow. Ma would set out food for him and tell him thousands of things, among which was talk of her first love, including colourful sexual details, which gives you an idea of how much she opened up to the crow. And affectionate memories of her left-behind children, and her children's children. When she spoke of Bade, she observed that he was actually more effeminate than her daughter, that he was fond of sweeping the dust from the corners and sitting cross-legged in a rather theatrical pose, one hand under the other elbow in great style, and listening to the stories she told him, and then the crow jumped up and cried, *Yah yah caw caw,* I have seen that exact pose! Ma connected his enthusiasm with her naan and meat, and gave him a bit more, but the crow did not mind the mix-up. Will you take potato, Ma asked, but he'd bitten off all he could chew and moved away so Ma would understand.

The problem was, once the crow realised the women he'd set out to find for Bade were prisoners, he got upset and wondered how he could leave them, how he could save them, and how he could fly back and deliver that information to Bade. It had taken him so long to get here. And it hadn't exactly been a direct flight, he'd flown hither and thither listening and inquiring, and although he'd generally maintained a flight speed of thirty km per hour, or even fifty if he'd gotten a good breakfast in the morning, he hadn't initially known how to sleep while flying, so sleep time had been additional to flying time, and on top of that he'd taken long circuitous routes. Perhaps it had taken him thirteen days to reach there. Or seventeen. Twenty-three?

Now if he flew straight back, even if he slept on the wing, it would still take him ten days. Even if he were an absolute supercrow, it would take him a full week. What if disaster occurred in the meantime? How would he be able to look Bade in the eye if anything happened? Then he'd never be able to sleep on his mattress. He'd drown for shame in his nice cool birdbath.

When Ma had started getting people to kick her in the back so she could fall properly, he'd worried horribly at first. Then he too began to laugh. He realised what a lark it all was. Because he'd heard the secret words spoken by Nawaz Bhai to Ma, and Ma had told him herself that Ali Anwar had agreed.

No one knew that he'd started practicing being half asleep-half awake even in non-flight mode, and he was sleeping right there, in a carved niche above the open locked door. If anyone came, he would know about it.

★

That night, Nawaz Bhai had arrived as a shadow. Ma, already a shadow, waited outside in the yard. Both shadows silently slid the door open and came out onto the road. No one awoke, not the guard and not Beti, but the two shadows didn't realise that the crow, now a shadow of shadows, was shadowing them, and that it was three, not two, beings who set out in the Khyber fog towards Bade Sahib's bungalow.

The crow didn't know why he felt a bit choked up throughout the scene that unfolded that night.

The dim flame of the lamp trembled as though moved by the Khyber wind, and their faces shimmered in a romantic haze. Two lovers. A wife and a husband.

If an amazing sight unfolds before two individuals brought together by chance, they go from strangers to intimates. All traces of suspicion and fear are erased, as though Krishna the heart-stealer himself had swept them away, and the two individuals sidle closer together under the influence of new affection, and they stick together in friendship. Even if one of them is a crow and the other a partridge.

The strains of the love raga are like that. They purify the air and whatever is around them.

Thus it has been said that if you create lovely scenes and spread art and music all around the atmosphere, hostility and friction will fall away like crumbled lime–chalk powder. In its place, love will flow everywhere, soft and sweet.

The eyes of one lover filled with tears as the other sang songs of romantic trysts. Their story mingled with the pink of the lamplight as it fell on them, and the beautiful melody stretched and wound through the night. The soothing finale of the love story of Anwar and Chanda, which is absolutely not a sad one, the way that no immortal love story ever is.

It was a unique sight. The eyes of both half-closed and the words of the song from centuries past breaking all boundaries. Something of great value slowly returned to them both. A fine, melancholic echo of whatever had happened that shouldn't have, and whatever had happened that turned out well despite the bad times, continued to reverberate softly around them. Eyes opened slightly, smiles returned somewhat, a hand rose subtly. Forgiveness. What happened was not our fault, but we must take responsibility. Forgiveness. The entirety of history and a personal experience all suffused in one word. This was what was, this is what is, this is the collapsing of the sweetest of stories in a storm of insanity. And the gathering fog of Khyber and the chill of winter and the sharp pain of its jagged mountains. Infinite. This desire, this thirst, complete.

The birds' hearts melted. The partridge learned to weep. The friendship that was born then could have become a classic.

The two of them watched as Ali Anwar started up in a panic, crept in and told Ma to get out quickly, and how she rose and went out, and when the bullet was fired, how elegantly she flew up and floated down onto her back. The two birds were sincerely inspired, and thought to themselves, we too want such an eloquent death, no matter whence the bullet.

Overcome by the Chanda-Anwar love story, this pair of friends continued to discuss it as they swooped up through the skies. The crow knew quite a bit that humans don't, and he told all to his new best friend. Oh my, laughed the partridge, so this kind of thing also happened back then, and having expressed himself thus he burst into tears. He had become so affected that he decided he too would go once across the border, go there to see the left-behind people, and the crow encouraged him, you'll see how they exist half here, half there, and their boundaries evaporate into the air when they see the same sky stretching out on both sides.

But here their friendship was defeated. Garuda was unable to save the parrot, and the crow was unable to save the partridge. The partridge was not accustomed to flying so long and so high and he was already close to six years old. So you see, they'd only just crossed the crack that appears in the moonlight at the border when something burst, like a gun or a heart, and the bird fell. The crow caught him on the way down, and as their promise was that whoever died, the other would ensure that his fall didn't end in the ignominy of face down, the crow held the chukar face up and returned him to his favourite mountain, and laid him lovingly on his back, from which perspective everything looked glorious.

Who knows whence the bullet came for each, but both the partridge and Ma reclined magnificently.

★

33.

No, we didn't kill them, the crow and Ali Anwar used to say. Mostly to themselves, occasionally to their relations and grandchildren. Who were not particularly interested in their stories. By their time, such technological advances had been made that all things were imbued with great speed. There were now all sorts of arrangements for flying, you could just grab a corner of the contraption and the air would send you up. Like on a metro or an airplane or a helicopter. Some crows had even flown on the Concorde. And videogames had been designed where you could sit in a closed room and take a trip around the galaxy, and wipe out aliens and hostiles just by pressing a button, be up in the clouds one minute and deep in the ocean the next. It used to be that to feel the wind on your face you had to work for it, by running fast, flying, panting, but now, thanks to machines, you can sit comfortably and still feel the breeze.

So the children wouldn't be listening, but when tormented by that guilty feeling, those two, now elderly grandfathers, would tell them all the same, No, truly, I didn't kill her/him. The crow would even beat his brow and ask himself why he'd forgotten that not everyone could fly like him, and that in Khyber, as he well knew, bullets were playthings.

All Ali Anwar had to say was that he hadn't shot her. He knew there was a rumour afoot that he'd helped a burglar escape from prison, and that out of fear of getting exposed for being in league with the culprits, he'd shot her when the Khyber folk woke up and a commotion arose that night. But afterwards, he had wanted to forget, and so he had. In fact, he would mutter to himself, I only shot into the air, and after the bullet that hit her had already been shot, so it would seem that I was also in pursuit, having just realised that someone was fleeing. But for other things as well, he began to feel guilty. Why had he allowed the meeting to happen, when he'd known the dangers? And why had he dozed off outside on the front veranda, for he'd meant to return that special guest to the prison half an hour earlier, and no one would ever have been the wiser. But dawn was breaking and he'd started to hear the sound of the patrol walking by and the whole game had spilled over like a dish of raita.

So both elders, the crow and Ali Anwar, regretted deeply that they had allowed the deceased to get involved in such dangers. But the whole thing was so snarled and gnarled, what to say to whom? People don't realise you should let the speaker speak; that as they speak, they're untying a knot within them, and only then does the matter grow clear. People start rolling their eyes before they even hear a thing, they begin to argue, they start lecturing; so the speakers chose their children's children for an audience, who were young and innocent, and who also believed in their grandfathers' innocence.

The crow would raise some philosophical questions, such as: True, the partridge was not so young, nor was he accustomed to flying like me, so you could say my poor intelligence was at fault; I should have known his lungs would burst, or that he was behaving childishly despite his mature years, but tell me this, in the last stage of one's life, should one allow desires to die? When someone has got it into their head to travel the world in his last days, or they suddenly want to learn a new language, or to take up gastronomy or whateveronomy, then should we ask them, what will you gain by this skill at your age? Or should we simply respect their wishes? Even if it might cause shortness of breath, and even if it does? Will they sleep peacefully or no? The moment he thought this, the crow's heart would reply, Yes, if only they had reached Bade and his friend had managed to get to the remnants of gardens left behind over there before he was finished off, there would have been no room for sighs of regret. All the same, he would say, to console himself, I did manage to fulfil his wish that he not fall on his face; he fell like a king and lay majestically beneath the sky. Exactly like Ma ji, when the bullet flew, she...

At this point, both grandpa-beings spread out their wings, and when they did, their relations and grandchildren suddenly stopped their games and gathered round. They listened with surprise to the rest of the story, and the very smallest stretched out their hands and wings spontaneously, as though they wished to become helicopters, and they leapt up, twirling into the air, then hovered downward regally, in slow motion, with contented smiles, eyes proudly upturned, arms reaching to the sky, floating gently, backs downward, and the moment they alit upon the ground, they crossed some invisible border and lay down on the other side.

Then the children would get up and return to the day's games. The crow and Ali Anwar would be left with their thoughts. The crow would think, whatever happened, I did tell

Bade, and with the passing of the years he came to wear a peaceful look. It was true. Bade truly had felt happy once he'd seen the crow, as though he'd found the support he needed in old age. Once, when no one was looking, he ever so softly stroked the crow's neck. *Caw caw*, cried the crow, in surprise but affectionately. Are you tired? Bade had asked, as though he knew the crow had come from a great distance. He brought him water in a new plastic cup and the crow drank from his hand. The friendship matured over time, and now the two of them even played with an old tennis ball. Bade pushed the ball from here to there and the crow did the same with his beak. When he got tired, he stopped and cawcawed and lectured Bade about all sorts of kicking techniques. I have but one desire left, said the crow, opening wide his beak: once, just once, I want to kick the ball, not with a wing, but with my leg. But everyone would have misunderstood.

This is the same thing Ali Anwar says. It would have been misunderstood. Once, just once, I wanted to touch her. But everyone would have misunderstood. She was so wound up, crying, what's happening! And how had she stayed asleep, and how had she had no idea, and I wanted so much to put my hand on her shoulder. But everyone would have misunderstood. I explained to her while avoiding eye contact; I said, Please gather up your luggage, and when I returned an hour later, she was alone and had vandalised all the flower beds like a savage, and was tossing the bits of crushed plants high in the air with a strained smile of victory. Why? I felt I understood. Her world had been uprooted. But I couldn't hold out my hand. I took her to the airport myself so I could deliver her safely home. The wasteland in her eyes when she turned to leave forever. How my hand ached as I felt the desire to go and place it softly on her head. But I just couldn't do it. Regrets. Regrets.

★

EPILOGUE

The door had been accustomed to the sound of bickering for centuries. It remained immobile, unperturbed. Of what significance were eleven or twelve years when there had been centuries of experience? It didn't matter if it had been twelve years or fifteen or sixteen; no need to count. But this: the door hadn't budged. When it would have to move again, clad in new attire, it would allow new nails to be driven in, and it would be pulled along, along with the walls. Now it lived here. In the postretirement flat.

The door remained open, but attempts were underway to close it. Or rather, the door started getting locked, but Bade kept unlocking it.

A theft had recently occurred in one of the neighbouring flats. It was a gated society surrounded on all sides by spiked boundary walls, with guards at the gate who made visitors enter their details in the entry book, and ensured cars of nonresident were parked outside, and there were even CCTVs installed on all four corners, and the images showed on the monitor in the guard room; if a theft could occur here, was any place left in the world that was safe? This had occurred in not one but five homes. The thieves' faces had been covered, so the cameras were no help; they wore gloves, so they left no fingerprints; and there were plenty of valuables in the homes, so the homes had been asking for trouble.

Bahu and Susheela would lock the door with a click, but Bade was set in his ways and he would go right back and unlock it. As though releasing the door from captivity. In secret. If Bahu spoke of the thefts, Bade would say they'd all occurred in homes where the doors were locked. One gentleman was in the habit of fastening a lock on the outside of the front door and entering through the rear bathroom, so if one of his friends dropped by for a drink, they'd run up against the lock. So he drank alone in peace, then went to sleep, and the thieves had snuck in, invited and reassured by the presence of the lock, and cleaned the place out. There was only one home where the thieves were defeated. It belonged to a teacher. Stacks and stacks of books in there and vegetables from who knows what century, such as potatoes, lauki, kundru, and dishes cooked some centuries ago, and a dish of sprouted mung, and black chana akhuwa sprouting all about. The moment the thief opened the fridge, a green haze billowed into the air, and behind it a jungle of green, blue, yellow, black, full of tangled roots and branches growing and trailing everywhere, working their way out, and threatening to ensnare the rest of the home as well. The thief started back. He beheld the marvel with astonishment, then called out to a comrade, and the comrade whispered that the living room too was like a mysterious jungle on an alien planet. The first thief swore a coarse oath and picked up paper and pen, of which there was a wealth there, and wrote a note: *Dude, come join us and leave your shabby job behind*. He affixed it to the fridge with one of the magnets in a prominent position so that no one would be likely to miss it.

So it was neither locked doors that caused theft, nor unlocked ones, and Bade found a new goal in life: if others locked the door, he would come to free it. When he started getting up at night and doing this, Bahu would get up too, and Sid and his wife sided with her.

Everyone is wired in their own particular way. Each member of the household was busy living in their own orbit, but some ties are thicker than blood. As for the rest, who knows how many people exist in a state of extreme separation from one another, even under one roof and within the very same walls and door. After all, not everyone needs to divorce in broad daylight. Yes, that happens too, but here there are additional family members, such as the door, the window, the crow, that give life a special warmth, and after one reaches seventy, they give life sweet meaning.

Bade was dead set on maintaining the freedom of the door. And behaving as though they'd be robbed, and misfortunes would befall them if the door stayed locked. He was also in the habit, when Susheela's grandson came to clear the AC or the cooler or undertake some miscellaneous carpentry and fix items around the house, to watch for him lifting bits of spare change or the one and ten rupees notes Sid left lying around. Bade said nothing; but it was a matter of principle, so instead he'd send him out of the house on an errand. Suddenly. So he couldn't bring his bag, and as soon as he left, Bade would take out his wallet and remove half the loot. Of course, the grandson was poor, so what if he took a little, but it was theft after all, so don't let him get away with it, all things being equal.

Bahu, Sid, and the new daughter-in-law were all sworn enemies of the open door. But Bade was its bosom buddy.

Nowadays he was often spotted with a dust cloth soaked in a bit of newly advertised cleaning solution, painstakingly polishing the door grain by grain.

It's not a door, it's a diamond-studded treasure, Sid teased, and Bahu said the treasure was on the inside, and Bade clearly wanted it all to be looted. She fretted and fumed, fumed and fretted.

But now the fretting wasn't about whether the door should stay open or closed. Now there was a family reunion going on, and Overseas Son (formerly Serious) had returned after an absence of three years, and his bride, acquired there, had come with him.

The sons didn't talk much amongst themselves, but the wives discussed over beers how Mom was diabetic, arthritic, the last few days when she'd gotten up at night she'd fallen down, and no one else could hear because of the AC, and her husband was yawning loudly or out strolling about the house at night, and he turned on the lights so one couldn't sleep near him. So far she's only had a scratch or two, touch wood, but if something went wrong, in her condition a fracture could be very problematic, and other such worries were being expressed, and there should be a night nurse to keep watch in case she falls. Susheela can't come at night. The foreign bride agreed it was a good idea. But very expensive, said Sid's wife. We can all share, said the foreign bride, at which Sid's wife, who was proud of her candour, said, But we're doing everything, can't you people take care of something? After that the reunion began to lose its shine, and someone was always signalling to someone else to keep quiet. Someone would say, Change the subject; someone else would say, Think of the expense, and finally everyone began to add up who had given what, and people think people who live abroad are the goose that laid the golden egg. The earnings there look huge when converted, but they don't realise the cost of living abroad is also huge. They don't realise things are more expensive there, but things are expensive here too. And the whole family is over here, who will take care of us over there in our old age, we also have to think of that. When we come, we bring expensive gifts, and when he had a job here, he left his account full of savings so you could use it in times of need, and you used it all up on this and that. That was for this very situation, and now where are we going to get more money?

Everyone pay out equal portions, that will be the smoothest, insisted the ones living abroad.

The ones living here were of the opinion that if they had to be equal partners, then everything we do here without your help has to be part of it. Oh, so just because we told you to do something, the idea of equality and sharing suddenly occurred to you?

Okay, hush, that's enough, said some. Why hush, why enough? others retorted. And then people started to complain about the aunt: When our aunt needs something, she suddenly belongs to the family, when it comes time for her to give, she's modern and separate from the family.

At this Bade got up. Or maybe it was because his buddy the crow was knocking on the window. He busied himself with feeding him roti and engaging in a bit of gossiping. Are you the same guy? He asked. Or his son? Your eyes are more restless and greedy; his were emotional and sensitive, and here, near the grey of the neck he had a beard. Bade even stroked below the neck. The crow said, *Cawcaw* in our homes you don't have all this *clawclaw*. Then he stared at Bade, tired, mouth open. *Cawcaw* Bade did not understand, but love and friendship are never wanting for language. You want to talk to me, said Bade affectionately, Come, bring the water and the ball. He poured the water from the old plastic cup into his hand and the crow drank from it. He rolled the new tennis ball around and the crow kicked it back.

The two began playing ball, their backs turned to the griping and sniping. The funny thing is that all the griping disappeared as everyone gathered to watch them, and now they stopped sniping and began to speak words of delight and praise, Oh, look at them! Look! What a great player the crow is, oh, look how he kicks the ball with his beak, no, with his claw, no with his beak, no with his claw...and thus the griping recommenced.

A family is a blessed thing. It never relents; never quits and never stays steady at one point. I went over as well and thought about how I was right to live alone.

Yes, me. No need to get worked up. I didn't invite myself. I was invited. We're old friends, and even though Sid and I no longer work together, I've gotten used to hanging out with his family. I've actually changed my line of work. Even I can't believe that I was once an athlete when I look at my protruding belly now. Well, as I look all around me, there are many things I can't believe; there can be so many faces, so many lives in every person's life; is it any wonder that a tennis racket–wielder could turn into an organic manure seller, and you wouldn't be able to connect the stink that wafts from our plant with my former sweaty life and character, nor would I. That truly was someone else, someone who had a girlfriend who was from Argentina, and she...

But that would be a completely different story, whereas every entry I make here is false. My turn has yet to come up in the dense population of this story; how can I take it now? But what with the griping, I came over here to where I saw the crow and Uncle with their backs turned. To the window.

The window is open. The griping is sidling over. They won't let me butt into the debate; they say, you keep quiet, you have no idea. Then why do you gripe in front of me, my friends? Come now, enough with the griping.

I end up ignoring them. I don't belong here and it isn't my story. I've entered it, but what character am I? I don't belong.

But there's no shortage of stories in life, and perhaps one day I too will be right in the middle of one. There's a moon in the sky that throws off an unearthly light. What a beautiful night it is. The gentle breeze blows, whistling softly. It's a night full of shadows and gleaming moonlight. Stories spin by; where will they cast their net?

I leap out of the window, filled with longing. As if it's no longer a window, but the corner of a canvas that has yet to be filled with colour, a place where a plethora of new stories and characters await the moment they will take shape.

THE END

Tomb of Sand is a tale woven of many threads, encompassing modern urban life, ancient history, folklore, feminism, global warming, Buddhism, and much more. It features an octogenarian heroine. It pays homage to the rich tradition of Subcontinental literature inspired by the 1947 Partition of India and Pakistan. It is an experimental tale that plays with language and form and structure, but it's also a classic page-turner, complete with cliff-hangers and plot twists.

To the translator, however, *Tomb of Sand* is above all a love letter to the Hindi language. Geetanjali Shree writes fluently in English, but chooses to write in Hindi, her mother tongue. She relishes the sound of words, and how they echo one another, frequently showcasing their dhwani—a word that she points in the course of the novel is among the hardest to translate. But let's try. Dhwani is an echo, a vibration, a resonance. It is alliteration and assonance. Dhwani could be deliberate and playful, as in double entendre and punning, an accidental mishmash of sameness, or a mystical reverberation. Geetanjali often makes word choices that prioritize dhwani over dictionary meaning. Wordplay takes on a life of its own in many passages and sometimes even drives the narrative.

What is a translator to do with a text that is focused on its own linguicity (not a real word, I know)? I have striven throughout my translation to recreate the text as an English dhwani of the Hindi, seeking out wordplays, echoes, etymologies, and coinages that feel Hindi-esque. I have also included many fragments of poetry, prayer, prose, and songs in the original language, alongside their English renderings, and even the occasional fragment of the original that was too good to leave behind. Readers who are not familiar with the South Asian linguistic landscape will find the text packed with words and phrases from Hindi, Urdu, Punjabi, and Sanskrit. What they may not realize is that the original text was similarly packed with English. In fact, a household of the kind around which the narrative revolves is a polyphonous ecosystem in which no language is likely spoken in an 'unadulterated' form. Those who speak mostly English will liberally pepper their speech with Hindi words and phrases, and those who speak mostly Hindi will do the reverse. In fact, the original novel is artificially Hindi-centric, just as the translation is artificially English-centric. The true linguistic hybridity of such a milieu is difficult to capture in writing, and has more often been conveyed in film. The readership of the translation will likewise come from a variety of linguistic backgrounds, with some feeling the book is not translated enough into English, and others feeling it has been translated too much. For those who feel overwhelmed by all the Hindi, you will find it's all there on the internet, often with accompanying images and videos. If you have no idea what *Arre, oh, Sambha, kitne aadmi the?* means, and wonder why I didn't translate it, simply enter it into a search field and you will get pulled headlong into the classic action film *Sholay*, along with its sinister villain Gabbar Singh. Conversely, for those who feel there is altogether too much English for their liking, who feel the Hindi reaching out to them through the English, but want the English out of the way, there's always the option of reading *Ret Samadhi* itself (you could even use the English version as a crib).

And finally, a note on Partition literature: the traumatic events surrounding the 1947 Partition of India and Pakistan have led to an entire literary genre, on a scale similar to that of Holocaust literature. Some Partition literature has been written in English, but much more has been written in Hindi, Urdu, Punjabi, and Bangla. Throughout *Tomb of Sand*, reference is made to many of the great Partition authors in Hindi and Urdu, especially in the chapter that introduces the third section, when many of these writers come alive at the Wagah border between India and Pakistan. In all cases, I have given the titles of their published translations. The Partition of the Subcontinent was an epochal event with far-reaching global consequences. It is an enduring shame and a major lacuna in Western publishing that virtually all of these classic works do in fact exist in excellent English translations, but almost none have ever been published outside of South Asia.

TRANSLATOR'S ACKNOWLEDGEMENTS

I am very grateful to Deborah Smith for leading me to this translation and publishing it with Tilted Axis. Many thanks are due as well to Arunava Sinha, who helped make this connection between us. Deepest gratitude to Geetanjali Shree, for giving me permission to translate her work and striving so diligently to help me understand the work and for putting up with my foolish mistakes. Any lingering errors are, of course, my own. To my fantastic agent, Kanishka Gupta for his friendship and cheerleading. Annie Montaut, the French translator, also offered valuable insights with passages from her French version, which were enormously helpful. I am also thankful for the moral support of Jason Grunebaum, François Xavier-Durandy, Mahmud Rahman, Shabnam Nadiya, Camille Guthrie, and Zirwat Chowdhry throughout this process, as well as for my community of Twitter translators. I am, as always, thankful to my beloved husband for his support and encouragement throughout, and to the unvarnished critique of my daughter, who read over my shoulder some of my feeble early attempts at rendering the wordplay in English and laughed hysterically. Is there any need to mention my debt to my cats, Jenny Linski, Madama Butterfly, and Princess Leia for their unflagging support and continued belief in my abilities? Yes, perhaps there is.

Original Hindi edition published by Rajkamal Prakashan, India, 2018

This book has been selected to receive financial assistance from English PEN's "PEN Translates" programme, supported by Arts Council England. English PEN exists to promote literature and our understanding of it, to uphold writers' freedoms around the world, to campaign against the persecution and imprisonment of writers for stating their views, and to promote the friendly co-operation of writers and the free exchange of ideas. www.englishpen.org

tiltedaxispress.com

ISBN (paperback) 9781911284611

ISBN (ebook) 9781911284703

A catalogue record for this book is available from the British Library.

Cover design by Soraya Gilanni Viljoen

Edited by Deborah Smith and Mira Mattar

Typesetting and ebook production by Abbas Jaffary

Made with Hederis

Printed and bound by Clays Ltd, Elcograf S.p.A.

Fourth Printing

ABOUT TILTED AXIS PRESS

Tilted Axis is a non-profit press publishing mainly work by Asian writers, translated into a variety of Englishes. This is an artistic project, for the benefit of readers who would not otherwise have access to the work – including ourselves. We publish what we find personally compelling.

Founded in 2015, we are based in the UK, a state whose former and current imperialism severely impacts writers in the majority world. This position, and those of our individual members, informs our practice, which is also an ongoing exploration into alternatives – to the hierarchisation of certain languages and forms, including forms of translation; to the monoculture of globalisation; to cultural, narrative, and visual stereotypes; to the commercialisation and celebrification of literature and literary translation.

We value the work of translation and translators through fair, transparent pay, public acknowledgement, and respectful communication. We are dedicated to improving access to the industry, through translator mentorships, paid publishing internships, open calls and guest curation.

Our publishing is a work in progress – we are always open to feedback, including constructive criticism, and suggestions for collaborations. We are particularly keen to connect with Black and indigenous translators of Asian languages.

tiltedaxispress.com
@TiltedAxisPress